Warnings to the Curious

D1616870

Warnings to the Curious

A Sheaf of Criticism on M. R. James

Edited by S. T. Joshi and Rosemary Pardoe

Hippocampus Press

New York

Published by Hippocampus Press
P.O. Box 641, New York, NY 10156.
http://www.hippocampuspress.com

Cover illustration by Carl Wilton, from *Ghost Stories of an Antiquary* by
M. R. James (London: Pan Books, 1953) used by permission of
Pan Macmillan, London, UK. Copyright © Carl Wilton, 2007.
Cover design by Barbara Briggs Silbert.
Hippocampus Press logo designed by Anastasia Damianakos.

First Edition
1 3 5 7 9 8 6 4 2

ISBN13: 978-0-9771734-8-8
ISBN: 0-9771734-8-8

Contents

Introduction

S. T. Joshi

At times it seems as if Montague Rhodes James (1862–1936) led not one life, but a multitude. That the same man could have described all the mediaeval manuscripts at the various colleges of Cambridge University, prepared an edition of *The Apocryphal New Testament* and other works of biblical scholarship, and, almost incidentally, produced four landmark volumes of ghost stories in the course of a fifty-year professional career that also saw him as dean and provost of King's College, Cambridge, director of the Fitzwilliam Museum, and provost of Eton—all this makes one admire anew the native talents of one whose unassuming modesty would have shrugged off these attainments as all in a day's work.

And yet, it may surprise those many devotees of James's ghost stories to recall that no single volume exclusively concerning his supernatural work has yet appeared. What we have to date are three works of biography, all splendid in their way (a memoir by S. G. Lubbock and formal biographies by Richard William Pfaff and Michael Cox), and a collection of essays—the product of a symposium held at Cambridge in 2001—devoted exclusively to his scholarly work and its long-lasting ramifications. That last volume, *The Legacy of M. R. James* (2005), seems, perhaps unwittingly, to suggest that James the author of "Casting the Runes" and "The Treasure of Abbot Thomas" simply does not exist; and while some enthusiasts of the ghost stories are perhaps guilty of the opposite prejudice that James the scholar and antiquarian does not exist, no one who has read his ghostly tales with any sensitivity can deny that scholarship and antiquarianism infuse those works in a significant way. It may be a source of regret that the "legacy" of James the scholar can be appreciated only by those few individuals learned in the ancient languages and in the history of mediaeval Europe; but perhaps readers of the ghost stories owe it to themselves to explore more diligently how his scholarship makes the ghost stories the distinctive literary monuments they are.

The fact that James evidently took his ghost stories lightly, as something to read to friends at convivial gatherings or to schoolboys over a campfire, does not mean that we need do so. Henry James dismissed *The Turn of the Screw* as a potboiler, but few readers or critics will follow him in that judgment. M. R. James's four volumes of ghostly tales—*Ghost-Stories of an Antiquary* (1904), *More Ghost Stories of an Antiquary* (1911), *A Thin Ghost and Others* (1919), and *A Warning to the Curious* (1925)—received few reviews in the British press (only the third was published simultaneously in the United States). As these reviews are not likely to be familiar to many readers, a sampling of them here may prove illuminating. One of the most revelatory was the anonymous review of *Ghost-Stories of an Antiquary* in the *Spectator*: "There can be no question about the literary merit of these eight stories, and of the ingenuity which Dr. James has shown in their construction. But we must own to an indifference as to constructed ghost stories."[1] In spite of the prodigious number of ghost stories published in the later Victorian period, critics' prejudice against the genre persisted for much of the twentieth century. The anonymous reviewer of the same volume in the *New York Times* also made some curious judgments, as indicated by the following: "Mr. James manages at times to give out a pretty well-defined creepy feeling—but his ghost stories are not quite the real thing in spite of the pains he takes to pile up detail in the setting and have the horror itself as undefined, shapeless, and elusive as may be."[2]

The *Times Literary Supplement* tended generally to be much more accommodating to James's work, reviewing favourably not only his books of ghost stories but several of his other volumes as well. The online edition of this journal has now identified many of the authors of anonymous reviews, and some interesting facts have thereby emerged. The review of *More Ghost Stories of an Antiquary* was written by one Sir Claud Schuster, later Baron Schuster of Cerne. He remarked acutely: "The mind set wandering in homely surroundings, all congruous with one another, is startled to imagination, and through imagination to horror, by the sudden inrush of the incongruous."[3] Much more significantly, the reviewer of *A Thin Ghost* proves to be none other than Walter de la Mare, who in a dense and sensitive review of this volume, along with Sir Thomas Graham Jackson's *Six Ghost Stories*, reveals an awareness of James's ghostly technique as only a fellow practitioner could. Remarking of "The Story of a Disappearance and an Appearance," de la Mare writes: ". . . though Dr. James's tales may make no pretence but to amuse, this one carries off that pretence with a singularly malevolent and in-

1. "Ghost Stories," *Spectator* No. 4017 (24 June 1905): 925.

2. "The Ghost Collection," *New York Times Saturday Review of Books* (22 July 1905): 483.

3. "Some Ghost Stories," *Times Literary Supplement* No. 560 (3 October 1912): 402.

delible grimace."[4] The extent to which James's tales had by this time become widely recognised as preeminent in their field is signalled by the anonymous review of *A Warning to the Curious* in the *New York Times Book Review*:

> . . . the ghost stories of the present Provost of Eton College have long enjoyed such distinction that they are in a class by themselves. So much so that the appearance of a new book by this author is in the nature of a literary event. No other ghost stories remotely approach the authentic James touch of actuality. No other writer of the macabre attains his horrid effects by such skillful cumulation of detail. These two qualities alone would raise him to the highest level, but would not notably differentiate his work. To these, however, he adds a third, peculiar to himself; adeption [*sic*] in the exquisite gradations of factual horror.[5]

James was, however, probably taken aback by the squeamish *Spectator's* comment about this volume: "Dr. James is, moreover, a traditionalist in the manner of loopholes. Always he cunningly leaves one for a natural explanation. Some readers may feel, though, that the details of these loopholes are a little too unpleasant. Indeed the one criticism an admirer might make is that the unpleasantness is gratuitous."[6]

Somewhat more attention was accorded to *The Collected Ghost Stories* (1931). Perhaps the most noteworthy—at any rate, the most prominent— review was by Peter Fleming in the *Spectator*, who astutely analysed the methods by which James has become "an acknowledged master of his craft":

> The first secret is tact. I say tact rather than restraint because he can and does pile on the agony when his sense of the dramatic tells him to. . . . It is tact, a guileless and deadly tact, that gauges so nicely the force of half-definitions, adjusting the balance between reticence and the explicit so that our imaginations are ever ready to meet his purpose half-way.[7]

Around this time, James's work began attracting the interest of writers and critics beyond newspaper and magazine reviewers. H. P. Lovecraft devoted some glowing pages to James in "Supernatural Horror in Literature" (1927)—a somewhat remarkable feat, in that Lovecraft only read James for

4. "Eleven Ghosts," *Times Literary Supplement* No. 938 (8 January 1920): 19.

5. "A Book of Ghost Stories and Other Works of Fiction," *New York Times Book Review* (3 January 1926): 8.

6. "A Book in Its Season," *Spectator* No. 5085 (12 December 1925): 1107.

7. Peter Fleming, "The Stuff of Nightmares," *Spectator* No. 5364 (18 April 1931): 633.

the first time in late 1925, a few weeks after receiving from his friend
W. Paul Cook the offer to write his historical treatise. Lovecraft, like James,
was both a practitioner and a theoretician of the form, although Lovecraft
appears to have been rather more receptive to work by other writers than
the fastidious James, whose several essays on ghost stories make no secret of
his distaste for certain authors of supernatural fiction who have, in his judgment, gone beyond the pale of decorum. Lovecraft would later moderate his
early enthusiasm for James, writing in 1932 to a correspondent who apparently found James wanting:

> About M. R. James—I think I can see what you mean, but can't classify him
> quite as low as you do. And if you can't see his utter, prodigious & literally
> incalculable superiority to the W[eird] T[ales] plodders I must again urge you
> to give your sense of appreciation a radical analysis & overhauling. James has
> a sense of dramatic values & an eye for hideous intrusions upon the
> commonplace that none of the pulp groundlings could even approach if they
> tried all their pitiful lives. But I'll concede he isn't really in the Machen,
> Blackwood, & Dunsany class. He is the earthiest member of the "big four."[8]

James would certainly have echoed that comment about "W. T. plodders"
and "pulp groundlings," although very likely he placed Lovecraft himself in
that class. As it is, the only significant article on James in his lifetime was
Mary Butts's piece in the London Mercury for February 1934. Butts, a well-
known novelist, wrote something of a panegyric, but makes good points on
James's "precise, detached, elegant style" and some features of his
characterization.

Upon James's death on 12 June 1936, obituaries and testimonials by
friends and colleagues were not slow in appearing. Stephen Gaselee's obituary in the Proceedings of the British Academy is rightly regarded as one of the
best, a moving account by a man who had known James for thirty-five years.
Both Gaselee and Shane Leslie, who wrote a much later memoir (disguised
as a review of several books by James) in 1966, speak of the ghost stories in
somewhat baffled tones, as if they don't quite understand why they are so
popular with a public that knows little or nothing of James's scholarly work,
which to them is the alpha and omega of James's achievement.

James, in fact, has not always been well served even by his admirers. The
Swiss scholar Peter Penzoldt, who produced a generally meritorious study,
The Supernatural in Fiction (1952), wrote a chapter on James not noted for its

---

8. H. P. Lovecraft to J. Vernon Shea (5 February 1932), Selected Letters 1932–
1934, ed. August Derleth and James Turner (Sauk City, WI: Arkham House,
1976), p. 15.

factual accuracy, and which asserted bluntly that "His stories are straightforward tales of terror and the supernatural, utterly devoid of deeper meaning."[9] It would appear that Penzoldt meant to praise James in this formulation. Even the noted American critic Austin Warren, whose studies of mainstream writers won him deserved praise, can only make this unremarkable conclusion in his descriptive essay "The Marvels of M. R. James, Antiquary" (1969): "The ghost stories of Montague James have their rightful place in the final chapter of recent books on the tradition of the Gothic Romance."[10] By far the best treatments of James in general histories of the ghost story are those by Julia Briggs (*Night Visitors: The Rise and Fall of the English Ghost Story*, 1977) and Jack Sullivan (*Elegant Nightmares: The English Ghost Story from Le Fanu to Blackwood*, 1978). And yet, one token of James's enduring fascination is an early article, L. J. Lloyd's "The Ghost Stories of Montague Rhodes James," published in 1947. Even if the article is more noted for its enthusiasm than for its critical acuity, it attests to the fact that James's ghost stories had by this time won them a consistent audience even at a period when contemporary supernatural fiction was in a bit of a lull, temporarily eclipsed by the cognate fields of fantasy and science fiction.

Scholarship on James may have benefited indirectly from the "horror boom" of the 1970s and 1980s, when the popularity of such writers as Stephen King and Peter Straub led to the reconsideration of older writers such as Lovecraft, Arthur Machen, and Algernon Blackwood. By this time a "fan" base for writers old and new had formed, so that a journal like *Ghosts & Scholars*, founded in 1979 by Rosemary Pardoe, could find a ready audience. While the avowed purpose of *Ghosts & Scholars* was to publish "stories in the tradition of M. R. James," the journal welcomed articles on James's work ranging from the exhaustive (Simon MacCulloch's four-part treatise, "The Toad in the Study") to the specialised (notes on minute particulars of James's tales exactly analogous to James's own scholarly notes on ancient and mediaeval texts). It can be stated unequivocally that *Ghosts & Scholars* has effected a revolution in the study of M. R. James, and it is no accident that a substantial proportion of the articles in this book are taken from that source.

And yet, James's tales have elicited commentary in many other venues, ranging from American scholarly journals (*Victorian Newsletter, Studies in Short Fiction, Modern Fiction Studies, Extrapolation*) to specialised British journals (*Country Life, Folklore, Hertfordshire's Past, Durham University Journal*) to

9. Peter Penzoldt, *The Supernatural in Fiction* (London: Peter Nevill, 1952), p. 191.

10. Austin Warren, "The Marvels of M. R. James, Antiquary" (1969), in Warren's *Connections* (Ann Arbor: University of Michigan Press, 1970), p. 107.

scholarly or fan magazines in the supernatural realm (*Haunted, Fantasy Commentator, Studies in Weird Fiction*). Not all this work is necessarily exemplary, and some of the academic contributions are beset by such failings as obfuscatory jargon, implausible hypotheses, and a simple ignorance of the sources and nature of James's writing. But it is an encouraging sign that an increasing number of the better articles of the last decade or so—in particular, by Helen Grant, Nicholas Connell, Jacqueline Simpson, and Martin Hughes— are successfully fusing our understanding of James the scholar with that of James the creative artist, and showing how the one facet of James melds with the other.

In a sense, the scholarship on the ghost stories of M. R. James is only beginning. Admirable work has been done by scholars and critics of the past seven decades or more, but that work must now be built upon, augmented, and perhaps surpassed by analyses that look at James as a unity of multifaceted parts rather than as a kind of schizophrenic who sealed off the various aspects of his life, work, and character into discrete compartments. There is no need to worry about James's continuing popularity and critical esteem, as annotated editions of his work by Michael Cox, S. T. Joshi, and the towering monument known as *A Pleasing Terror* (2001) attest, to say nothing of his influence on writers ranging from Robert Aickman to Ramsey Campbell to Michael Chabon. What now needs to be addressed is how James drew upon his own life, the history and topography of his native land, and the work of his predecessors in ghostly fiction to produce tales that, in contrast to Peter Penzoldt's judgment, reveal greater depths than even multiple readings will reveal.

I. Some Notes on Biography

Montague Rhodes James 1862–1936

Stephen Gaselee

The outwardly uneventful life of the late Provost of Eton can be conveniently recorded in a chronological table—

Born: 1 August 1862.
Temple Grove: 1873.
Scholar of Eton: September 1876.
Scholar of King's College, Cambridge: 1882.
Fellow of King's: 1887.
Director of the Fitzwilliam Museum: 1893–1908.
Provost of King's: 1905.
Vice-Chancellor of Cambridge: 1913–15.
Provost of Eton: 1918.
Died: 12 June 1936.

He was born at Goodnestone in Kent, the son of Herbert James, who was at Eton (both as Oppidan and Colleger) and at King's, and after Goodnestone was Rector of Livermere in Suffolk, where he died in 1909, exactly twenty-seven years before M. R. J., at the age of 86.

M. R. J.'s preparatory school was the old-established Temple Grove, where had been Archbishop Benson before him, A. C. Benson and Edward Grey with him, and E. F. Benson a little after him; the headmaster in his time was the impressive O. C. Waterfield, described in the writings of the Bensons and by M. R. J. himself in *Eton and King's*. I was there myself twenty years later, but do not remember any stories of him: but in college at Eton, where I also followed him at the same interval, there was still a legend of him as the learned boy who, having exhausted the resources of the Boys' Library, somehow extracted from Vice-Provost Dupuis the key of the College (then often called the Fellows') Library and worked at the manuscripts there, learned Ethiopic (he told me that he afterwards forgot the syllabary, but took up Coptic instead), and read the whole of Dickens. His tutor, H. E. Luxmoore, no outstanding scholar but a man of exemplary piety and the finest taste, had a great effect on his life and character, and remained one of his greatest friends until death parted them in 1926. Church music, too, he learned to know and love—not only in the College chapel but by as many visits as school hours allowed to St. George's, Windsor. He never shone at games (though Twelfth Man for "College Wall"), but was a popular and respected boy-president of the Literary Society, a member of "Pop," and editor of the *Eton College Chronicle*: he was three times in the "Select" for the Newcastle Scholarship, the great prize of Eton classics. and divinity, finally winning it in 1882.

He had, therefore, no difficulty in getting an Eton scholarship at King's, and while he was there won the Bell and Craven scholarship, the Carus Divinity and Jeremie (Septuagint) prizes; and first classes in both parts of the classical tripos were quickly followed by a Fellowship.

Let me here pause a moment to consider what line his interests were taking at that time. From talks with him I have the impression that he had at first intended to devote himself especially (never exclusively—his learning was too wide) to classical archaeology, witnessed by his publication of his excavations in Cyprus, with the expedition led by Hogarth, in the *Journal of Hellenic Studies* in 1887–8: but the subjects which may be generally comprised under the name of Apocrypha were already drawing him, and we find a steady stream of published works of that kind between 1889 and 1897, of which the most important were *The Testament of Abraham, The Gospel and Revelation of Peter*, the Latin *Fourth Ezra*, and two series of *Apocrypha Anecdota*. Such works continued to the very end of his life; but meanwhile another interest was arising, and one by which he became more known to the world at large, and has left even more substantial monuments.

Others perhaps could have done the work, or some of it, on Apocrypha: but his encyclopaedic knowledge, marvellous memory, vast industry, and curious *flair* made him uniquely fitted for his great series of books cataloguing medieval manuscripts in the greater libraries of England. Such publications began at about the time he became Director of the Fitzwilliam Museum, and a mere list of the libraries catalogued shows the enormous volume of his output: 1895, Eton, Fitzwilliam, Jesus, King's; 1898, Mr. H. Y. Thompson; 1899, Peterhouse, Trinity; 1902, Mr. H. Y. Thompson (second series); 1903, the ancient libraries of Canterbury and Dover; 1904, Emmanuel; 1905, Christ's, Clare, Pembroke, Queens'; 1907, J. P. Morgan, Mr. H. Y. Thompson (third series), Gonville and Caius, Trinity Hall; 1909, Magdalene, Corpus; 1912, McClean collection at the Fitzwilliam Museum, Mr. H. Y. Thompson (fourth series); 1913, St. John's; 1921, John Rylands Library at Manchester; 1923, Pepysian Library; 1925, St. Catharine's; 1930, Lambeth; and 1932, Aberdeen University Library.

Perhaps I can best show his method by quoting a description of a single manuscript (though I shall have to shorten it). I take an English Apocalypse in the library of my own College—a fine book, though by no means one of the great pictorial manuscripts of the world.

5. APOCALYPSE
[Class-marks and references in previous catalogues]

Vellum, $12^1/_{10}$ $7^7/_{10}$, ff. 36 + 26, two volumes (1) double column of 18 lines, the rest of the page occupied by a picture, (2) double columns of 44 lines. Cent. xiv early and xv(?).

Given by Simon Gunton. Perhaps from Croyland. On fly-leaf is:

Iste liber constat Domino [erasure] . . machus C.

At end is scribbled:

Dan Jhoon London moken of Croylande . . .

[and five more lines]

Collation: 1 fly-leaf, 1^8–5^8 (wants 8) 6^8 7^8 8^{10}.

On f. i*a* on a scroll in capitals: LIBER APOCALIPCIS.

On f, i*b*, verses in English (xiv) and a note, xvii:

Per hoc exordium iudices lector utrumne

Johannes Haintonus (de quo Pitseus pag. 612)

autor fuerit sequentis operis.

Added by Waterland(?):

Floruit Anno 1428.

There is another similar note that a manuscript of the Apocalypse without the verses is in the University Library.

The verses are headed: Beatus qui legit etc.

(*a*)   Jon blessis hom alle þat þis boke reden
Wit gode entent and hor god dreden

ll. 17, 18.   Þere to duelle euere in pees
In ioye and blis y^t neuer shall cees. Amen.

(*b*)   Who redes þis boke of ymagerie
hit wil hom comfort and make redie

ll.13, 14.   God gif vs grace þat sight to haue
To reule vs riȝt we may be saue. Amen.

Contents:

I. Text and exposition of the Apocalypse with pictures   f. 1

    Inc. prol. Apoc. Iohannis apostoli.

          Apocalipsis Iohannis tot habet sacramenta quot uerba.

    (No more of the prologue is given.)

    Inc. textus. Apocalipsis Ihesu Christi etc.

    The letters to the seven Churches are omitted.

    The exposition is that most commonly found in the illustrated Apocalypses. In this case it begins f. 2*b*.

    Et uidi in dextera sedentis etc. De dextera et sigillis quid dominus dederit in sequentibus dicemus. Liber uero scriptus etc.

    The text of Apoc. xxi ends f. 39*b* and has no exposition.

II. Comment on the Apocalypse in English.   40

    Prol. Seynt poule apostle seis. Alle Þat w^d lyue pityousely or holily in crist ihesu (Prologues of Gilbert Porrée.)

    Þis boke among*us* oÞ*er* bok*us* of Þo new lawe is clepid prophecie.

    The text is underlined in red.

    Ends f. 65*a*: graunt vs to lyue and dye in hym Þt we may regne w^t hym in his blis in body and soule w^t outen ende. Amen.

    Beatus qui legit etc.

    This is a version from the French. The latter has been edited by Delisle and P. Meyer for the Société des Anc. Textes Français. Another copy of the English is in MS. Pepys 2498.

    The first volume is illustrated with 78 half-page paintings. These are enclosed in frames of pink and blue with white lines on the colour, and squares of gold at the angles. They have no coloured grounds. Gold is employed for nimbi, crowns etc. The general scale of colour is subdued. The drawing rapid, spirited and delicate.

    There are also most beautiful ornaments in red, growing out of the text, foliage work and grotesques. It would not be easy to find better specimens.

    The pictures are as follows—

    [Here follows nearly four pages of detailed description of the illustrations. I give only the first and the last.]

i. John lies on island. He has scroll: Pathmos propter uerbum domini et testimonium. ihesu fui in spiritu in dominica die etc. *to* uocem que loquebatur mecum. Apocalipsis reuelacio interpretatur.

Above him, angel with scroll: quod uides scribe in libro et mitte septem ecclesus.

Four islands in the sea. *L*. Insula tilis, Garmosia insula; *R*. Bosforum mare, Insula Sardi.

A ship with crew on *L*. Ground in front. . . .

78. f 39b. John kneels to Christ who has cross-topped staff. Angel on R.

The book very evidently belongs to the second family of manuscripts of the Apocalypse described by MM. Delisle and Meyer in *L'Apocalypse en français au xiiie siècle* (Soc. des Anc. Textes Fr. 1901). None of this family has pictures of the miracles of Antichrist, and a few only begin and end with scenes from the life of St. John. This manuscript was not known to the editors, who mention the copy in the Pepysian Library.

This is a fair specimen of M. R. J.'s descriptive work: the accounts of some manuscripts of less interest are of course shorter, of others much longer (the above, as I have said, is much abbreviated); and I estimate that in the great series of catalogues which I have enumerated, he dealt with some fifteen to twenty thousand in all. Surely an unparalleled achievement.

I must mention also similar work which perhaps gave him even more pleasure than this summary cataloguing. On many occasions he was able to devote a whole book to the description of a manuscript of outstanding interest—sometimes a publication for general issue, sometimes a more or less private edition, as for the Roxburghe Club, of which he was a valued and enthusiastic member. Such are: 1904, Description of the Quaritch *Cantica Canticorum*; 1909, The Trinity College Apocalypse (Roxburghe); 1913, Walter de Milemete (Roxburghe); 1916, The Chaundler MSS. (Roxburghe); 1920, La Estoire de St. Aedward le Bel (Roxburghe); 1921, the Egerton Genesis (Roxburghe); 1922, the Corpus Peterborough Psalter and Genesis; 1923, the Holkham Bible picture-book (Walpole Society); 1924, the Trinity College, Dublin, Matthew Paris's Life of St. Alban; 1925, An English medieval sketch book in the Pepysian Library (Walpole Society); 1926, Drawings of Matthew Paris (Walpole Society); 1926, the Bromholm Psalter (Roxburghe); 1927, the Perrins Apocalypse; 1927, the Old Testament illustrations (xiiith century) in the book sent by Cardinal Maciejowski to Shah Abbas (Roxburghe); 1928, the Cambridge Bestiary (Roxburghe); 1929, Marvels of the East (Roxburghe); 1932, the Dublin Apocalypse (Roxburghe); 1933, the Romance of Alexander;

1935, the Canterbury Psalter (Roxburghe), and 1935, the Bohun MSS. (Roxburghe). I may also mention here his edition, for the Roxburghe Club, of Horman's *Vulgaria*, first printed by Pynson in 1519, a book of Etonian interest, for it was originally meant for the use of Eton scholars—one of his few works on printed books as opposed to manuscripts.

But it is now time that I return to his outward life. When I went to Cambridge in 1901, he had become (after being Dean) Tutor of King's. He never really enjoyed administrative positions, though he performed the functions of Tutor with care and conscience; but he gave up his time to such routine work with resignation, and was always delighted to welcome his pupils (and others) in the evenings. Conversation was general, but he was pleased above all to resolve questions on learned subjects; which he would either answer from his own great store of knowledge, or by that faculty particularly ascribed to lawyers, of knowing exactly where the required information was to be found. I think, from descriptions given me by my father, this was much in the tradition of Henry Bradshaw—who was frequented by M. R. J. as an undergraduate, for he died in 1886—and the answer would be thus—let it be remembered that it was before the days of gas (save for a ring on the staircase or in the gyp-room)—:

> Pick up one of those candles [the room was lighted by one oil lamp and a pair of candles], go into the next room and take the book case on the left. Then on the second shelf from the top, about twenty books along, there should be a book called X, and somewhere about page 150, there should be what you require. Bring it here and let me see.

I was never one of his closest intimates, but he did not mind being questioned about his opinions, and I gained some impressions. He was a devoted son of the Church of England, and would describe himself as protestant, though he liked a grave and dignified ceremonial: he had some sympathy with the tractarians, but none with "the ritualists": in politics uninterested, but faintly conservative. As a smoker—and he smoked a good deal—his tastes, at any rate in his Cambridge days, were to me extraordinary. There are many men who care neither for cigars nor cigarettes, and I know others who, even at a College Feast, would with a word of apology light a pipe when the rest started their cigars; but I do not think that I ever knew another man who only liked *new* briar pipes. Most of us regard a new pipe as something to be coaxed into friendliness after some period of discomfort, and greatly regret when old age breaks it up or makes necessary to discard it because it has become irremediably foul; but M. R. J. enjoyed a pipe only when it was new, and laid it aside in favour of a successor just at the moment when most of us would be beginning to enjoy it.

His holidays were greatly occupied in the exploration of provincial France, his immediate and expressed intent being to visit all the French Cathedrals, including of course those which were suppressed at the Revolution. He said that he did not know Notre-Dame, but he had of course been there: it was only that he had a considerable distaste for Paris. I said to him once that I believed that I had seen one French Cathedral that he had not. "Which?" "Nice." "Well, I think that you will continue to have the advantage of me there." When he could not or did not go to France, the Suffolk of his ancestry and his early years was perhaps the most frequent scene of his wanderings, often (as in France) on a bicycle, and he frequently crossed the border into Norfolk. I think he would very gladly have allowed himself to be described as a man "of the Eastern Counties."

Once or twice during the Cambridge years when I knew him well I asked him how he had come to specialise in the descriptive cataloguing of manuscripts which I have mentioned above, and I was about to try to put his answers into continuous form when it occurred to me that it would be better to give his own words, written in retrospect (*Eton and King's*, 1926, pp. 198 sqq.):

> Dr. Waldstein had offered me a post under him in '86, as Assistant Director of the Fitzwilliam Museum, where I was able not only to keep up an interest in Classical Archaeology, but also to go on describing on an extended scale the illuminated manuscripts that form part of Lord Fitzwilliam's magnificent bequest. Needless to say, one learnt a great deal from the process of describing every single picture in some 130 manuscripts. So fascinating was the employment that I determined I would extend it to other Cambridge libraries. Nor was it long before I realised that the survey, if it was to be really useful, must include *all* the medieval manuscripts, not only those that had pictures; so that before long I was making bargains with kind and long-suffering Colleges that if they would print catalogues of their manuscripts I would make those catalogues. The result has been a row of seventeen or eighteen Cambridge catalogues, besides others done for Eton, Westminster Abbey, the Rylands Library, and Messrs. H. Yates Thompson and Pierpont Morgan: and, one of the stoutest of all, that of the medieval manuscripts of Lambeth. . . .
>
> I have had to handle so many collections of miscellaneous volumes that I have been distracted from specialising on any one class or period, and though I imagine myself able to date most books correctly enough, I cannot and never could cultivate the sort of brain and eye, such as Jenkinson possessed in a marvellous degree, which carries in it the special form of the letter *g* (say) and can tell you with certainty that it does not occur after the year 850. The fact is that since I began to busy myself with these things, the department of learning called palaeography has been more and more justifying its claim to be called an exact science. The multiplication of photographic fac-

similes enables a student to have under his eye all the extant examples of writing of a given date. The methods of abbreviation and contraction of words that were in use in different *scriptoria* and different countries have been studied and classified. The scripts of Corbie, Laon, Reichenau, Lyons, and several other centres are known entities. As time goes on, we shall be able to differentiate yet more minutely. What applies to writing is true of illumination as well. The younger workers in the field can look forward to discriminating the ateliers at which miniaturists worked in France or England in a way which was not dreamt of thirty years ago. I follow their advance with interest and pleasure, but cannot emulate them. If I have had a part to play, it has been that of making known, with what fulness of description I could, the existence of a mass of material, and assigning dates and provenances which are in the main, I hope, correct. But I have had to learn my job as I went on: my catalogues were on a scale that had not been tried before, and the later ones compare (in my judgement) favourably with the earlier, which I could now improve in many respects.

He did not find his work at the Fitzwilliam Museum very arduous. "They were the great days of the University," said recently a shrewd and friendly observer, "when the University Librarian could be found pursuing flies on Coe Fen, while the Director of the Fitzwilliam studied medieval manuscripts in the University Library." In 1908 he found that his work as Provost of King's (which included the congenial work of Senior Fellow of Eton) was enough for him, and resigned the Directorship, being succeeded by the enthusiastic Sir Sydney Cockerell: and I think that from then until the War he was very happy, taking even the Vice-Chancellorship more easily than I had expected. I saw a good deal of him in those years: I remember him coming to dinner with me on my thirtieth birthday, and bringing with him as a present from his own library an eighteenth-century publication of Coptic texts: he came a good deal to Magdalene, owing to his close friendship with Arthur Benson, and with the two of them I played many a game of Jacoby, that only card-game for three, and with him alone in King's many a game of Piquet, at which he taught me all I know, always assuring me at the same time that Walter Fletcher was a much better player than he was.[1]

The War broke out towards the end of the first year of his Vice-Chancellorship, and I well remember his speech on 1 October, 1914, as he took up the second. I was Proctor at the time, and stood very near him as he spoke; these are some of his words:

---

1. It was before this time, I think, that he learned Danish and Swedish. He wanted to read folk-stories of those languages—and Hans Andersen—in the original.

The remembrance of what has been brilliant or sorrowful in the three terms has paled, for the time at least, before the events of the Long Vacation. The University meets in such circumstances as it has never known. We shall be few in number, and perpetually under the strain of a great anxiety. We may be exposed to actual peril: in any case we must look forward to straitened resources and, what is more, personal sorrows. Yet there is no doubt that we are bound to carry on our work; for by it we can render definite service to the nation. Our part, while we encourage all of our students who are capable of doing so to serve their country, and while we surrender to that service many valued teachers, is to prepare more men—especially in our medical schools—for rendering active help, and to keep alive that fire of "education, religion, learning, and research" which will in God's good time outburn the flame of war. Let us devote ourselves to making useful men of the new generation. Let us confine our own controversies within the narrowest limits, and be ready if necessary to postpone them altogether. Let our advanced work—however irrelevant it may seem to the needs of the moment—be unremittingly and faithfully pursued.

(The University did not carry out his advice wholeheartedly, for a successful agitation to remove compulsory Greek from the Little-go was begun before its younger members were back from war work: but by that time the Provost had left Cambridge.)

The present Vice-Provost of King's, Dr. J. H. Clapham, says with truth "War he took simply and vehemently." He had always been fond of all things French (except Paris) and disliked most things German (except their scholarship), and merely found his natural feelings heightened and corroborated: but I do not think that I ever heard him say anything bitter, though indignation was vehement enough. Cambridge was comparatively quiet in the early War years, before it was so successfully made into a training camp for cadets, and he worked steadily at manuscripts and various archaeological questions.

In 1918 he was offered the Provostship of Eton, and I do not think that he had any doubt about accepting. I naturally saw less of him there than in earlier years at Cambridge, though I went three times to stay with him there, once to examine for the Newcastle Scholarship, once for the Election of Scholars, and once simply on a visit: and I have the impression that until his last illness he was perfectly happy in that great and utterly congenial position. The uncovering and preservation of the wall pictures in College Chapel was a great delight to him, and he described them with loving care and fullness in 1928 and 1929 (Publications of the Walpole Society, vols. xvi and xvii): but he had many other interests, such as the adornment of Lower Chapel, reading the lessons (at which he excelled) and occasionally preaching in the College Chapel, and devising plays about St. Nicholas, to be acted on Founder's day during the Feast in Hall by the Lower Chapel Choir, and the making of "the king of Siam's Garden," which was not only a thing of beauty in itself, but opened up a new view of the Provost's Garden and of a part of the College Buildings previously hidden. I should say also that he got—and gave—as much pleasure from his contact with the boys as from any other activity of his busy life: not only from the parties of little boys at Sunday breakfasts and of big boys on Sunday evenings, but from the Shakespeare Society and casual talks in the Playing Fields: they felt—as did the Masters—that they were in touch with a great man, a man of the world in the best sense of the word, in the tradition of Provost Savile and Provost Wotton, and with one who loved them and every stone of the place, who had at last returned to the spot where his heart had always been. During the last years of his life he could not get about much—his legs were not what they had been: his health began to fail early in 1936, and the action of his heart weakened: he died peacefully on 12 June 1936, and was buried on 16 June: the funeral service took place in the College Chapel, attended by hundreds of Old Etonians and others, the boys (except for the Scholars and the "First Hundred," who were in the Chapel) lining School Yard, as the procession with the coffin passed from the Cloisters to the Chapel's north-west door. The singing of the choir of the Founder's prayer, *Domine Jhesu Christe, qui me creasti . . .* is one of the most affecting things in my memory.

I take from the memorial notice by Mr. C. H. K. Marten, Vice-Provost of Eton, in the *Eton College Chronicle* this list of his distinctions—

> From the University of Cambridge he received the M.A. in 1889, the Litt.D. in 1895, and the D.D. in 1934. He received the Hon. D.Litt. of the University of Dublin in 1907, the honorary LL.D. of the University of Saint Andrews in 1911, the honorary D.C.L. of the University of Oxford, June 1927, an honorary membership of the Royal Irish Academy 1926, and the Gold Medal of the Bibliographical Society 1929. He was a fellow of the British Academy, and of the Society of Antiquaries: and he was a member of the Royal Commissions on Public Records, and Historical Monuments, and on the Universities of Oxford and Cambridge. He received the Belgian Order of Leopold in 1918. Above all, in 1930, he received the Order of Merit from the King.

I have touched in this brief memoir on some of his personal characteristics, but I think that I must say a little more. He was a man of simple and deep religious feeling. Learned biblical scholar as he was, he did not think much of the "higher criticism," at any rate when it was destructive; and I have heard him say that the biblical documents were subjected to criticism not only unfair in itself, but of a kind that no one would ever have dreamed of applying to the secular literary remains of antiquity.

In profane literature, too, his tastes were simple. Dickens, Mrs. Henry Wood, Ballantyne, Le Fanu, Sherlock Holmes, Anstey, Pett Ridge, and P. G. Wodehouse were perhaps among his favourites, and visitors will remember the piles of "shockers" in his room: he even knew Le Queux and Oppenheim apart, and had an opinion on their comparative merits. He could also write other than learned works. I never greatly cared for his (or any other) ghost stories,[2] but experts tell me that they are among the best of their kind: their antiquarian setting is admirable, and so is the representation of the speech of common folk in them. Among writings for the general public, I should rate very highly his comprehensive work on Abbeys (1925) and his stories from some of the less known Old Testament Apocrypha (1913).

He was a good, and late, sleeper (unless Chapel called), and enjoyed good plain food and sound wine. Talking of Robertson Smith, he says, "An evening with the circle at Christ's (and the '47 port) was—well, there are a great many *clichés* that could be used—let me spare you and say it was *exceedingly pleasant.*" I remember that he occasionally produced Burgundy as an after-dinner wine: and in the Lodge at King's I first saw Hollands brought out late in the evening as an alternative to whisky. Late in life crosswords, at the solution of which he was incredibly skilful, brought him a new pleasure.

He was never an athlete (though good at games which required a straight eye, if there was not too much rapid movement about them), and I suppose that bicycling was his chief physical recreation: bicycling in the Eastern (and other) counties, but above all bicycling in France, visiting the cathedrals. He liked to go to French churches for service, and enjoyed the *Vexilla Regis* in Passion-tide, and the *O filii et filiae*, with plain-song modulated in a curious jig-like fashion, at the Easter Vespers. He had no very high opinion of the sermons preached at such services: "Too often sham miracles or shoddy saints." It was above all his company that was important to him, and I suppose that these cycling travels, at home or abroad, with congenial companions were his ideal recreation.

I do not intend to speak of those of his friends who are still alive: but as he had a genius for friendship, I shall mention one or two who died before him. I think I saw him most deeply moved at the deaths of J. W. Clark (1910), Vice-Provost Whitting (1911), Walter Headlam (1908), and Walter

---

2. Housman used to say that the couplet in one of these ("A Neighbour's Landmark")

> Than that which walks in Betton Wood
> Knows why it walks or why it cries

was good poetry.

Fletcher (1933): the loss of the last-named and of his brother Sydney (Eton Master, Headmaster of Malvern, and Archdeacon of Dudley) cast a shadow over the latter years of his life. And here I must mention again his tutor, Luxmoore, who had become linked to him by friendship as well as admiration, and died ten years before him. With younger men the form his friendship took was—I take the risk of using a rather dreadful word—help (intellectual or other) playfully extended: and he had the invaluable power of answering a silly question in such a way that you afterwards saw that it was silly, but without making you feel a fool.

It is daring, and may be considered impudent, for a person like myself to endeavour to make any general estimate of his life's literary work, but I do not think that this memoir would be complete without it, and I must try.

On Apocrypha I should think he made the greatest advance since the days of Fabricius (though Fabricius was more a collector and bibliographer than an investigator), and M. R. J.'s work is of the kind that is, so far as we can see, permanent. But I suppose that his work on medieval manuscripts is, really, even much more important than his identification, publication, and criticism of Apocrypha, and he acquired for the purpose an exceptional knowledge of medieval iconography, derived both from MSS. and from sculptures; and developed a special interest in tracing the homes and movements of the written books. Here, while we are astounded by the vast sum of his descriptions and identifications, the very amount of them makes it inevitable that there should be small imperfections: some of these were due to his handwriting, which was only good if he tried hard, and positively cruel for the compositor, and to the fact, which he admitted, that he was by no means a perfect proof-reader. "The printer," I have heard him say, "read Holy Trinity the first time I wrote Holy Family in a description of an illumination, and then put Holy Trinity each time I used the other phrase: and I fear that I removed none of these misprints from my proofs." But no true scholar would have it otherwise; there has never been before, and probably there will never be again, a single man with the same accomplishment and combination of memory, palaeography, medieval learning, and artistic knowledge, and it was better for such studies that he should extend his cataloguing over almost the whole English treasures of this kind, and get his results printed and accessible to the scholars of the present and future than that he should confine himself to a few manuscripts or collections and attain absolute accuracy and completeness in his description of them. Further, in his editions of a few illuminated manuscripts of the very first class, as in the books he edited for the Roxburghe Club, he showed that he was capable of perfect description when he had an object really worthy of his highest powers. Many of his accounts of manuscripts will have to be worked over again by specialists of the future: but to him will be due the fact that they are known and available to the specialists at all. In scholarship comparisons are even more difficult than in other qualities and attainments: he had not the lightning flashes of insight of Walter Headlam, or the deadly precision of Housman; but I consider him in *volume* of learning the greatest scholar it has been my good fortune to know.

Authorities

M. R. James. *Eton and King's*. London, 1926.

[A. F. Scholfield.] *Elenchus Scriptorum Montacutii Rhodes James* . . . Cambridge: Privately printed, 1935.

Eton College Chronicle, 13 June 1936, Memorial issue: notices by C. H. K. M[arten] and others.

Cambridge Review, 9 October 1936: notice by J. H. C[lapham].

Personal knowledge.

Montague Rhodes James

Shane Leslie

Eton and King's. By M. R. James (Williams & Norgate).
M. R. James. By S. G. Lubbock (Cambridge University Press).
Ghost Stories of an Antiquary. By M. R. James (Arnold).
The Five Jars. By M. R. James (Arnold).

These books may constitute the lighter side of Monty's life, at least what is known to the public in such as "recollections, mostly trivial"; a long fairy story written for the daughter of a lost friend and two volumes of ghost-stories, which reached a fame rare in the academical world. On the other side his serious Bibliography (collected by A. F. Scholfield of King's) amounts to twenty-six pages (apart from Inscriptions, etc.).

Dr James was unique in holding the Provostships of King's and Eton in succession. Other King's dons have justified biography such as Henry Bradshaw, Oscar Browning, Lowes Dickinson, and Maynard Keynes, but Monty, the most remarkable and certainly the most loved of all, has received little but excellent obituary notices. Can a biography be ever transcribed from the vast collection of his catalogues of mediæval MSS or from his lifetime of friendships and conversation or not? In the latter case he would need a Boswell and in the former case a learned computer.

In the legend of both colleges he has remained "the Provost" not only in achievement but venerated by all as "Monty." It was significant that his fellow-divinity amongst Cambridge heads of college, Dr Montagu Butler of Trinity, was never alluded to as "Monty" even by his two wives. Dr James preferred to be wedded to his two beloved colleges.

It was known that he possessed a famous memory which could not forget, a golden disposition to friends (few of them being of his learning's calibre), one perfect sense of academical humour, and a talent for spinning and reading aloud a personal type of ghost-story which must be reckoned part of his deepest nature. In fact his belief in ghosts marched parallel with his religion.

What wonderful lumber his memory carried. Not only the facts in storage which made him the greatest mediævalist of his times. He knew the ancient French and English cathedrals even to their heights and lengths: their glass and imagery whether it remained there or not. Most strangely by collecting mediæval press marks he had acquired a unique knowledge of the contents of ancient libraries which had ceased to exist. Missals he could at first sight refer to their date and diocese and generally suggest their probable wanderings since their dislocation by Reformation and Revolution.

Whether his life, letters, and career can be achieved in book form, he certainly made it as difficult as possible for the biographer. Frankly, he owned early in life, he did not need a career, he wrote no real autobiography and as friends and printers grieved to learn he wrote illegibly. His book on *Eton and King's* (comprising his whole life) contained far more information about others. Childhood he omitted until he reached Temple Grove, a private school famous for its headmaster, Ottiwell Waterfield, who has been humbly described by his most famous boys—Arthur Benson and Monty James. He was a great man, for he deeply influenced them both, nor did they meet a greater man at Eton where both became scholars. Monty enjoyed the happiest career possible, ending with the Newcastle Scholarship, "the Derby" so to speak of the Eton course. After his Cambridge years, like his fellow-winner of the Newcastle, Dean Inge, he made a brief failure as an Eton master. Inge was deaf to boys and James was bored by them in class, for he preferred to charm than instruct the typical Etonian of the Eighties.

At heart he was a story-teller not a pedagogue. Outside the classics he had already devoted himself at Eton to Dickens and the Apocrypha but not as others read them, as parerga to serious work. He knew much of Dickens by heart and every character in a quiet smiling way. If he had given the same immense interest to any classic, Latin or Greek, no doubt he would have found himself on every schoolboy's shelf with Jebb and Postgate. For him the Apocrypha stretched far beyond the Bible into the delightful, uncanonical and even lost Books of the Old and New Testaments. What use he may have been to the ordinary undergraduate toiling for conventional honours may be questioned. But King's had a feeling for Fellows some of whom might have qualified themselves for entry into a Dickens novel. He was allowed to follow his innocent bent, cataloguing and describing forgotten manuscripts. In the end he catalogued whatever were available in all Cambridge. He was without a competitor but on his lonely way he was noticed on the Continent. Lord Acton, on becoming Regius Professor at Cambridge, was surprised to learn that a singular, easy-going Fellow of King's was included amongst these European authorities—but on what subject? It was rather difficult to describe. He had won his Fellowship by revising or guessing the text of a lost Book of St Peter. Later discovery proved him correct! Lord Acton was puzzled and a little pained to hear that he devoted his evenings to entertaining a type of undergraduate who amused him and themselves—as a rule not top-scholars nor athletes. At any rate the two greatest Memories were at the same University in Monty and Acton for a time.

Monty lived a serene and monkish existence surrounded by chosen friends and choice books but in a state of considerable confusion. By this or aught else he was seldom worried. It might be said he was untroubled by Divines and Divas. He had no taste to engage in the academical form of matrimony which had begun to destroy the calm character of the celibate colleges. At that time the Master of Trinity had married *en secondes noces* a lady of tender years on the strength of her examination papers—but then Dr Butler enjoyed the privileges of the Patriarchs.

Monty from an early age felt a certain quiet aversion to ladies with the exception of those safely married to his friends. Very little is recorded in university periodicals about his Cambridge years but the *Granta* once recorded some details of biography. Apparently three weird sisters visited him in his rooms, probably on charitable rather than amorous intent. He excused himself by slipping into his inner room and leaving by a window. At any rate the weird ones were left sitting until they gave up hopes for whatever they hoped.

No other information was then given save that be hoped to be Cambridge Librarian and that he wore spectacles, a rare sight amongst the young. He played a useful part in quelling the feeling between old Etonians at King's and those newly admitted from other schools.

He had arrived from Eton as "an unrepentant sap" where he had began to collect his curious sheafs of learning. He thought "nothing could be more inspiriting than to discover that St Livinus had his tongue cut out or that David's mother was called Nitzeneth." What is remarkable was that he never forgot a grain or let it drop out of a sheaf. Schoolboy hobbies became erudition in the mature man. Great omniscients like Whewell of Trinity, Jowett of Balliol, or Mahaffy of Dublin allowed their knowledge to be bandied and noised abroad. It was always difficult to dislodge knowledge of Monty's immense collection. From the first he did not wish for a career or even a respectable home. He was perfectly happy with the steady passage of undergraduates whom he set himself to make equally happy. From the first he was secretive to his teachers. When Acton enquired when an erudite of such leisurely habits found time to work, King's College answered that they just did not know. It had to be accepted that he read rare and difficult books rapidly and what he read he never forgot.

At Eton in the sixth form he had allowed no time to be lost during the Thucydides lesson by taking in an armful of Ethiopic books. This was due to

Dr Hornby's lackadaisical methods. It was never known how Hornby admonished him at the request of Queen Victoria's secretary, Sir Henry Ponsonby, after Sir Henry diverted a translation of Baruch from the Ethiopic which Monty and a friend had humbly offered to the Queen by book post! Meantime he had developed his powers as a mimic. Much has been lost of old Eton life because his voice has not been preserved mechanically to echo Austen Leigh's admonishments in a high nasal drawl or Edmond Warre intoning "The Raft of Odysseus" to a startled class or Mr Mozley "Mad Moses" being guyed by his division who set themselves up as a Mozleian Club of which the first rule was to assemble a quarter of an hour later than their puzzled preceptor. This was an inimitable power he carried to Cambridge. As long as he remained at King's so long remained certain quaint echoes from the voices of the ancient race of dons.

One last gift came from his pre-Raphaelite tutor Henry Luxmoore. The two masters, Luxmoore and Henry Broadbent, who implanted him with lasting fruits of knowledge, survived to see him return as Provost. Such was the way at Victorian Eton—a quaint and ludicrous gathering of masters set with one or two inspired teachers—William Johnson, Broadbent, and Luxmoore. Boys interested in human nature or the classics took their choice.

Luxmoore opened a new country to Monty, "the sacred soil of France," which in those days was assailed by British schoolboys as a land of frog-eaters, who boxed with their feet and whose bearded youths were marshalled in walking line by masters. France in the last quarter century of the nineteenth was never mentioned at school without hisses and gentlemanly catcalls. Monty learnt otherwise, and from thirty expeditions at least learnt the beauty of French cathedrals. The late French historian J. E. C. Bodley claimed that he had visited the seventy cathedrals of France. Monty used to reckon there were 143 and that he had visited all except two, Toulon and Nice. Some were rather difficult to find. Neither Baedeker nor Augustus Hare could record Glandèves, whose apse had become a barn, or Bethléem, whose choir was the dining-room of a hotel. He could have written a complete guide, without notes or hesitation, to French cathedrals.

The Victorians were happier in their holiday progresses abroad. Railways were not plagued by tourists and roads not devoured by motors like clouds of ants and glow-worms without their harmlessness. Roads had been ever the legacy of the ages to pedestrian and tramp. Monty and his friends after "a little toying with train and tricycle" had settled on the safety bicycle by 1895. Adventurous dons had already favoured the tricycle in Europe. Oscar Browning had pedalled across the Alps in the tracks of Hannibal as part of the practical education of George Curzon. Monty carried out a continuous Continental class for his increasing friends whereby the art and architecture of all that was remote and mediæval was settled in their minds. French holidays were days of bliss unfiltered by motor fumes. They could sight "wide prospects from the tops of hills at night, the smell of vineyards in flower in early morning: the sighting of the next Cathedral Tower above the poplars." The familiar *châteaux* of Touraine he left alone but he explored every Department except the Ardennes. His personal cure for a sleepless night was to count not sheep nor widows but French Departments till he fell to Morpheus.

Monty learnt from few, preferring to be self-taught in the paths he had chosen. Henry Bradshaw as University Librarian inspired him with reverent affection to staying late in crowded rooms on the chance of getting an impossible question answered. "What curious things did he not know," was Monty's summary of his character that would often be made of Monty's own.

Often their lives read similarly, so much so that Monty can be thought of basing his ambitions on Bradshaw's. They both adopted the monastic view of college existence. Both aimed at being librarians and no more. Bradshaw was able to understand Swedish after shutting himself up in a hotel with a grammar and a dictionary. Monty learnt Danish in the train sufficiently to prepare accurate translations of Hans Andersen. Bradshaw collected unique and lost learning for the benefit of others without ever writing the book that he alone could have written on Chaucer. They were both difficult correspondents. It was Bradshaw, when sent prepaid postcards with *No* or *Yes* on them, posted both in answer to the same query. Monty might send an answer on a postcard but possibly quite illegible! Their bland and fascinating (at least to all bibliophiles) faces hang in the same line in King's Hall.

How will Monty be remembered by successive generations of Etonians or Kingsmen? In his lifetime it was by his mimicry and afterwards by the written trivialities which vastly amused us in Cambridge days. His description of the great Dr Kennedy entering the Senate House "like an apoplectic macaw" or Professor Mayor whose characteristics were derived from Lewis Carroll's White Knight. His happiest drollery befell Mr J. E. Nixon whom he had long turned into a character that only Kingsmen knew. Like Captain Kettle, Nixon was deficient of a hand but various hooks hung his wall according as he needed the artificial in taking a deck of cards or conducting a madrigal club. According to Monty "the speeches of Mrs Nickleby run admirably into Nixonese," and Monty was an admirable judge of both. Nixon was famous as a lifelong obstructionist at college meetings even to voting down his own proposals in the famous cry of rhetoric: "*Yes*, a thousand times, yes—or rather *No*, a thousand times no!"

In those golden days Monty with others built up a folklore of adventures enjoyed between Nixon and the learned Bishop Westcott (long forgotten re-viser of the Bible) not unlike the ludicrous mistakes with which Flaubert immortalized *Bouvard et Pecuchet*. Their Cambridge parallels were supposed never to meet without Nixon suffering some cruel misadventure mostly at Westcott's hands. The saga is alas long extinct, having naturally died with its kindly impersonator. Such scenes were vividly recounted in mimicked tones as causing poor Nixon to tumble off the triforium of the Abbey during the Jubilee of 1887. Quite truly Monty admitted he could have restored the *Pickwick Papers* should every copy be destroyed in a catastrophe. Possibly he could have written a Cambridge *Pickwick* by collecting his own selections from the whole University.

It was astonishing what models Dickens could have secured amongst the old Heads of College from whom Monty salved titbits—Dr Corrie of Jesus, so ancient that his uncle had served at the Battle of Culloden, Ben Latham of Trinity Hall with stories of ravens and of his widow-proof room, Dr Robin-son who voted himself into the Mastership of St Catherine's, remaining there for forty-eight years, and the later Roberts Master of Caius who pos-sessed two eyes, one of glass. It was possible to tell which was glass because it alone showed any signs of humanity.

With his immense knowledge of the Victorian novel he never wrote the final survey. With his uncanny knowledge of Scripture in the Bible he gave his overwhelming instinct to the Apocrypha, both of New and Old Testa-ment, with lingering research into lost and suspected books. Bible readers have been puzzled by reference to a Book of Japhet which no one has read. Apocrypha—the "hidden" Scriptures were the romance of his life while as for the Apocalyptic or "revelations" his devotion was such that the Oxford Orator in administering his degree referred to him as "apocalypticotatos," the single word which might have been found on his heart or been engraved on his tomb. In a childhood dream he found himself opening a shiny Folio Bible with an unknown book included with a Hebrew name.

When it was necessary to advance a thesis for a Fellowship if he were to remain at King's he restored a lost *Apocalypse of Peter* from the dead. With a half a dozen surviving clues he "wove a web of considerable size." But who was to say he was right until "a few years later a large piece of the text, found in Egypt in 1884, was printed and served to confirm my main guesses or con-clusions." In this there were accounts of Heaven and Hell which resembled an early foresight of Dante. The catalogue of torments is, however, con-cluded by comfortable words when our Lord promises St Peter that all sin-ners will be saved by the prayers of the righteous. Salvation all round may have been a little too much for the early Christians so Peter ordered this

Revelation to be hidden in a box that foolish men may not see it; Monty's impression being the author "tried to break the dangerous doctrine of the ultimate salvation of sinners gently to his readers."

In the first centuries Christians were crazy in their search for new Gospels, spurious Acts, and more and more exciting Revelations, at least more than was known to the Angels in Heaven. To Monty "as folklore and romance they are precious and to the lover of mediæval literature and art they reveal the solution of many a puzzle."

For instance St Augustine's reference to the gardener's daughter who died at St Peter's prayer! This was a mystery till an *Epistle of Titus* was found which told how a gardener begged Peter's prayers for the best the Lord could give. The girl fell dead! When Peter restored her to life it turned out it would have been the best for her after all—for she was promptly ruined by a slave in the house.

One apocryphal legend, the *Domine quo vadis*, became as well known as anything in the Gospels, thanks to a Polish novelist. Monty's translation of the original passage is worth giving in its simplicity:

> And as Peter went forth of the City he saw the Lord entering into Rome and when he saw Him he said: Lord whither thus? And the Lord said unto him: I go into Rome to be crucified. And Peter said unto Him: Yea Peter I am crucified again. And Peter came to himself.

This is the Apocrypha at its most picturesque and whether true or not carried its lesson like much of what Jerome rejected. Monty could talk freely about the Gelasian Decree which had early listed books which dropped unfortunately out of circulation. He thought their most sensational entry referred to "the Book of Og the Giant who is said by the heretics to have fought with a Dragon after the Flood"—an unnoticed mention of some Loch Ness monster? To him the most thrilling lore was the *Gospel to the Hebrews* which no doubt contained the matrix of the early Gospels. Though the famous story of the woman taken in adultery does not appear in St John's Gospel and is set aside by modern translators—Monty pointed out that Papias had found it in the *Gospel of the Hebrews*. How interesting he found the *Acts of Pilate*, so seldom read by ecclesiasts. They supply a keen touch of irony when the astounded Jews interviewed the soldiers whose watch was so unsuccessful at the tomb. On hearing what the soldiers had to say, the Jews closed down the argument by asserting: As the Lord *liveth*, we believe you not! As a way of contradicting the Resurrection it sounds like an Irish bull.

Perhaps most interesting it was to tread the by-paths of lost Scripture with Monty and to learn that when Pilate asked our Lord what was Truth? He remained not silent but offered a superb answer replying: "Truth is of

Heaven," whereat Pilate said: "Is there not Truth upon earth?" and Jesus said unto Pilate: "Thou seest how they which speak the Truth are judged upon earth."

Surely the irony of such a dialogue remains too splendid to be lost.

In the end Monty wrote a Lost Apocrypha of the Old Testament for the S.P.C.K. and an Apocrypha of the New Testament for the Clarendon Press. At any rate William Hone's once popular volume was for ever replaced by a masterpiece.

No classic in any language came under Monty's editing, not even Dickens, though George Gissing wrote a handbook which could be admired and even copied. The only writer who suddenly received Monty's homage, albeit a minor Irish story-teller, was Sheridan Le Fanu, and why? The dead editor of the *Dublin University Magazine* had written the weirdest and ghastliest romances of his day. He set the style Monty needed for his own ghost-stories if he was to release his mind's own mystical complex. Grammar, Greek, Mythology, all that would have adorned a King's don writing at the turn of the century were totally neglected. Monty would not lecture and he would not teach. He was bored by a short session of digging in the ruins of Cyprus. He was far more interested in investigating graveyards and psychical possibilities at home. Though he kept to what he pretended to imagine and invent, he drew from Le Fanu a striking form of the English ghost-story which in a series of supposed adventures of an antiquary gave him public fame through the English-speaking world. Far from being the issue of a side hobby they were his relief from a secret madness in his inner soul—the obsession that in spite of all the art and beauty of the world and the unfailing friendships which met him at every corner of the world, the malevolent and diabolical survived around him in the invisible. His friends wished he would believe in fairies instead of the curses, runes, and appalling catastrophes he distributed to the innocent victims of his tales. Monty visited Dublin not so much to vindicate the Book of Kells as to visit the scene of the *House by the Churchyard*. He set out to raise Le Fanu from the grave. He edited *Madam Crowl's Ghost and Other Tales of Mystery*. He introduced *Uncle Silas* into the World's Classics. "Green Tea" with its horrible haunting by a dead monkey and "Mr Justice Harbottle," the wicked old Judge, tried, condemned and sunk under his own imaginings, were restored to the shelf of the finest Victorian horror-grotesque. Monty found Le Fanu touched the effective detail and deliberate leisureliness which the perfect ghost-story requires in the telling and which he never missed in his own rare but intensely heard recitals. Fortunate were those who were admitted to a *première* of a newly hatched ghost-story generally at Christmastime. Even agnostics were frightened temporarily. Superb rose his voice reading aloud a great chapter of *Ecclesiastes* with King's or Eton Chapel as his sounding-board. There was no lesson read aloud in a humble village church which failed to make an awesome impression. He was well described in the West Country as though an Apostle come to preach to the lower orders of Nature. No one could imagine his slow recital of the chapter about the Witch of Endor and the ghost of Samuel, though his Cambridge audience would prefer and pray for his great version of the Trial of Mrs Bardell versus Mr Pickwick. But for sheer drawing-room dealings with ghosts he excelled Augustus Hare and the second Lord Halifax who suffered from the same complex.

Though he had aimed at the life of a happy recluse, fate pushed him into public life unexpectedly—first into the Provostship of King's in 1905 followed by Vice-Chancellorship of the University during the First War and the Provostship of Eton before the close. His correspondence became immense and far from the rare and unique subjects on which he occasionally informed *The Times* and the learned of Europe. He took over Eton affairs as no Provost before. He restored the mediæval paintings in the Chapel. He became the delight and confidant of all boys who could appreciate him. With the greatest timidity he became a particular friend of King and Queen. He was recipient of their Order of Merit. He descended in history as "the Provost" deservedly.

His most valuable correspondence was reduced to exchanges with librarians and the learned. Only after his death was his letter writing published with the widow of his favourite Kingsman Jim McBryde. It could be compared with that between Bishop Thirlwall and Miss Jones, a happiness to both and interesting to posterity. Lewis Carroll was devoted to his "Alice" whom he put aside when she passed out of girlhood. Monty was faithful to Gwen McBryde all his life. Both the college dons wrote fairy stories for very young ladies. Monty was known as a misogynist but only in the sense that he defied matrimony and the usual purposes and pleasantries of the sex. But there could be a startling but innocent exception. He had a deep delight in a feminine side of friendship and made a holiday-home to the end of his life in a remote corner of Herefordshire with Gwen McBryde and her Jane whom he adopted in every practical way. For such friends as they who had as little use for matrimony as himself the arrangement was perfect. Letters, informing and amusing on every possible subject touching life at Eton, reached Dippersmuir by the hundred. In return the Provost found his way every possible time of holiday to the old manor house where a library gathered round him, where room and chair remained at his disposal, where he enjoyed an entire peace and felt home, sweet home as seldom vouchsafed to the academical mind. There was no need of invitation. He came and went his way enjoying birds and flowers, even owls and cats, interpreting and understanding them as only his universal mind could find place for. He could not let his mighty Memory for ever weigh him down. In return he rewarded a mother and daughter with trusteeship and constant visits to Eton and Cambridge. When Mrs McBryde's "growler" reached King's the great gates were opened—which as Monty said was a royal privilege. Likewise on the Fourth of June at Eton—issued a written card from the Lodge—"Admit Mrs McBryde's car to Weston's Yard." Etonians will prize the value of such.

After reading all the letters in this correspondence, printed or unprinted, it is impossible not to believe he was as happy in life as he was successful. All that interested he enjoyed to the full simply because he made himself a master of each and all. Only loss of friends deeply scarred the equal tenor of his life. The harvest that death reaped from Eton and King's during the First War saddened even that laughing fountain of humour, albeit he lamented the dead in the spirit of the Greek Anthology. He died leaving one constant question with his friends and readers, private and public, did he really believe in ghosts? I ventured to put that query to him in his last days. Very simply he replied to this effect—"Yes, we know there are such things—but we don't know the rules." Psychical research has not reached much further.

The Strangeness Present:
M. R. James's Suffolk

Norman Scarfe

The macabre beneath the landscape is not dispelled by nearness to the sea. What Henry James knew, and described in *English Hours* (1905)—the strangeness present on a flattened seashore—M. R. James (no blood relation, and twenty years Henry's junior) expressed in two of his best-known ghost-stories: "'Oh, Whistle, and I'll Come to You, My Lad'" (scrambling over the groynes around Cobbold's Point at Felixstowe, on a bleak, seemingly wintry, evening) and "A Warning to the Curious," which leads to a remorseless killing on the beach near Aldeburgh's martello tower.

In his brief excursion to Aldeburgh in 1897, in "the glimmering of a minute," Henry James responded to "the conditions that, grimly enough, could engender masterpieces." He was remembering Crabbe's imperishable verse-stories in *The Borough*, but also, I suppose, prophesying, as the intuitive may, the music of Britten (which, sure enough, owed much to Henry James's writing as well as to the Aldeburgh neighbourhood).

MRJ was massively more a scholar than a fiction-writer, the settings of his stories were usually authentically antiquarian. But their "engendering" was perhaps as much instinctive as academic. One envies Percy Lubbock, with whom MRJ was staying in Kent in 1903 when Henry James called and took them to his home at Rye: "a very pleasant man he is," wrote MRJ of Henry J., "talking just as he writes with punctilious effort to use the words he wants: looks like a respectable butler." As with Henry James, MRJ's greatness was recognised in his own day by the award of the O.M. and in our day by one of the most admirable biographies in the language: Richard Pfaff's *Montague Rhodes James* (1980).

MRJ's use of words, effortless as it seemed, was that of a peculiarly able linguist, ranging voraciously through Latin and Greek at school (Eton), and teaching himself Ethiopic there in order to translate one of the apocryphal books (*The Rest of the Words of Baruch*) that he had begun collecting at his preparatory school. He seems early to have understood that decorators of manuscripts, and churches, were as familiar with apocryphal literature and mere legends about the saints as they were with the Bible. When he was fif-teen, he knew at once that a bench end in Dennington church, near Fram-lingham, carved with a man crouching under his own large foot, represented the Skiapodes, a legendary Libyan tribe who used their feet as parasols. His first, and perhaps most formative teacher was his father, the Rev. Herbert James, at home in Livermere Rectory, beside Livermere Park, near Bury St Edmunds. You got there by dog-cart from Ingham Station, 2½ miles through the park, after 1876: before that, it was a six-mile drive from Bury.

Livermere took its name from one of those placid lakes in western Suf-folk (and Norfolk) that look as if they have lain there unchanged since the Dark Ages. This one was spectacularly changed when two adjacent land-owners sensibly decided on a joint "landskip." Livermere's mere became Broad Water; Ampton's, a mile south, became Ampton Water, its serpen-tine shape exaggerated as it was joined to Broad Water by an impressive "canal," Long Water.

Its level gardens and croquet lawn running south to Long Water, Liver-mere Hall's garden-front had a three-storey central bow. The view to the north-east across the mere was embellished by raising Little Livermere's church tower to very teetering, unEast-Anglian, proportions. This was per-haps Baptist Lee's work of the 1750s, when he gave that church—now a ruin—its Strawberry Hill Gothick interior. The landskip was already mature, with great avenues and rides, in a 1730ish painting (*Country Life*, December 3, 1953): so the main part may have been laid out in Charles II's time

One hint is a headstone familiar to MRJ, just beside the church porch at Great Livermere: to William Sakings, 1689, "forkner to King Charles I, King Charles II and King James II." It underlines the popularity of this Euston-Bury-Newmarket country in the years when hawking and racing were dis-placing witch-finding as a sport.

Livermere Rectory stands, though unoccupied and no longer the rectory, on the eastern edge of this park (which survived as parkland till 1923, when the Hall came down). They came to it in 1865, the Rev. Herbert James and his wife and three sons and a daughter, of whom MRJ, aged three, was the youngest. It was his true home for forty-four years, the characteristically long Victorian span of his father's pastoral care of the two Livermeres, ending only with his death in 1909. In the course of MRJ's own long service with Eton and King's—"mothers to the happiness of youth," he called them—came to take precedence as his home. At sixty, he confessed he had never had the ordinary ambition for "a profession, home of one's own, and all such." Being provost of King's, 1905–18, and of Eton, 1918–36, might seem to outsiders ambition and profession enough. "Finding out all I could about various matters" was his breathtakingly modest assessment of his pioneering and monumental descriptive cataloguing of 6,000 or so scattered medieval manuscripts, to mention only one of his "finding out" programmes.

So Livermere Rectory was the original nursery and schoolroom of a great scholar's career. Here, too, the ghost stories took embryonic shape. It is a Georgian, stuccoed, sash-windowed house, the garden enclosed by trees but with glimpses from the house of the mere and the park beyond. Michael Cox, in M. R. James: An Informal Portrait, has noticed some light-hearted verses about Livermere sent home to his sister from Cyprus when MRJ was twenty-six:

> You heard a foot pass, it trailed over the grass,
>   You shivered it came so near.
> And was it the head of a man long dead
>   That raised itself out of the mere?

There, already, are the essential ingredients of some of his stories: the sound of a foot in the grass, the head of a man long dead, and so on.

The church lies only a couple of hundred yards from the Rectory. To reach it, you still cross, as you did when Percy Lubbock's brother, Gurney, came to stay in the 1890s, a grove of mature oaks, planes, limes and chestnuts, shading the cottages of this centre of the little village, and providing a wooded walk. It leads to that end of the small churchyard which lies east of the church and is filled with the headstones of the Mothersoles, including Charles who was parish clerk when MRJ was a boy.

It can hardly be simple coincidence that Mrs Mothersole was the name of the witch whose trial in 1690 in one of his most alarming stories, "The Ash-Tree," led to there being "guests at the Hall." I have little doubt that the Hall he imagined was Livermere, rather screened from the Rectory by trees—ash trees among them. The first "guest" entering the Hall, by way of the tree, seemed like a squirrel with *more than four legs*: finally, the "guests" were found to be spiders as big as a man's head, "veinous and seared," living in the skeleton of poor Mrs Mothersole. Had the parish clerk handed on to MRJ a tradition about a local witch? We scarcely need his friend Mrs McBryde's confirmation that MRJ "had a horror of spiders, especially large ones, and of the lone one which will unaccountably turn up in the bath."

Walking west, past the Stuart "forkner," we come to some Worby headstones. When that fashionably Gothicising Dean of Southminster, in "An Episode of Cathedral History," exposed the altar-tomb "in which the night-monster had its lair" we know, from Isaiah 34, who evoked the hairy brute, with two great eyes, that knocked the Dean over. But how did the verger, who actually saw the monster, come to be called Worby? There are many tenuous connections between Suffolk and these stories, but MRJ deliberately set in this county, for instance, "Rats"—"It happened in Suffolk, near the coast." "'Oh, Whistle'" and "A Warning to the Curious" MRJ's preface kindly records as being in "real places." "'Oh, Whistle'" belongs to Felixstowe, where MRJ and other Fellows of King's spent pleasant holidays after Christmas with Felix Cobbold, banker, philanthropist and bursar at King's. The golfcourse in the story had opened near the mouth of the Deben in 1880; archaeological remains, though not of a preceptory, lay conveniently between the golfcourse and "The Lodge," the comfortable house Cobbold had built for himself. The groynes over which Professor Parkins was pursued are shown in contemporary pictures and in the drawing with which McBryde illustrated the first edition. The Bath Hotel ("The Globe" in the story) had not yet been combusted by Suffragettes and had windows in a projecting bay exactly as the story requires.

As to "A Warning," MRJ knew Aldeburgh from early childhood. His paternal grandfather, retired from the West Indies, had given in 1840 a cast-iron Tuscan pump that still stands beside the Town Steps. They lived at Wyndham House, adjoining the churchyard—again that theme. Later in life, he spent a pleasant week or two in Aldeburgh at the White Lion—in April or May—almost every year from 1921 till 1935, the year before he died: his letters from Aldeburgh record the simplest pleasures except when he remembered uncongenial work still to do such as his popular book *Suffolk and Norfolk* (1930), which did not take him long. The Suffolk half was begun and finished in a month (5 February to 12 March), interrupted by a venomous cold, and Norfolk took very little longer. The notes of his favourite details, saints painted on screen panels, and so on, were assembled years before. The eye was discerning. The work still reads delightfully.

MRJ's inestimable contribution to the county of his earliest upbringing was to make sense of the poor jumbled ruins behind the proud stone gatehouses of St Edmund's great abbey church at Bury, and to reconstruct from his unrivalled knowledge of the various collections of manuscripts the contents of the monks' library: *On the Abbey of S. Edmund at Bury* (Cambridge, 1895, M. R. James's *annus mirabilis*). Starting, without warning, on page 127, he conducts a wonderful tour of the abbey as it once stood: "We approach it through the great gate of the cemetery . . ."

He had more than fulfilled the intentions he expressed in a letter home to Livermere from school when he was not yet twelve: "I desire above all things to make an Archaeological search into the antiquities of Suffolk, to get everything I can for my Museum, and last but not by any means least to get home."

M. R. James and Livermere

Michael Cox

[The following article was written for a booklet produced for the attendees at the unveiling of a commemorative plaque to M. R. James at St. Peter's Church, Great Livermere (26 September 1998).—ED.]

Of all the places associated with M. R. James, Livermere (which does not have an entry in the otherwise admirable Oxford *Literary Guide to the British Isles*) is probably the least known to the countless readers of his ghost stories. On the other hand, his lifelong connection with the sister foundations of Eton and King's College, Cambridge have become an essential part of the Jamesian image: the precocious schoolboy, the brilliant undergraduate, the scholar of international renown, and the steady rise to authority, culminating in the provostship first of King's and finally of Eton. This "life without a jolt," as Lytton Strachey cynically described it, seems rooted in these two great educational institutions and conditioned by the historical continuities that they embodied. MRJ's ties to both Eton and King's were deep indeed, as the eloquent response in the epilogue to his published recollections makes clear: "I allow myself to dwell on the thought of the real greatness, the augustness, of the ancient institutions in which I have lived: to which I have owed the means of gaining knowledge, the noble environment that can exalt the spirit, the supplying of temporal needs, and almost every single one of the friendships that give light to life." At Eton and King's one still feels something of MRJ's presence. He spent over sixty years of his life in them, and left an indelible mark on both.

But these are public places, continually evolving, with many non-Jamesian associations, populated now by people to whom the name of M. R. James probably means little or nothing. James invested Eton and King's with a kind of mythic glory: they were "centres of light," "mothers to the happiness of youth." Yet of his 'real' home and mother he spoke little, and by calling his recollections *Eton and King's* James himself reinforced the idea that his life was somehow defined and limited—even created—by the two collegiate foundations of King Henry VI. Indeed, he appears deliberately to have constructed a view of himself that excluded all antecedent influences. *Eton and King's* begins *in medias res*, with his first view of Eton as a scholarship candidate in July 1875; it ends with his return—which he described in terms of a homecoming—as Provost in 1918. He tells us nothing about his family life, or the early experiences and influences that most autobiographers would consider it essential to lay before the reader. As a result, MRJ has become so identified with the world-famous institutions in which he spent most of his life that we forget there were other places, other environments, that made him what he was. As his beloved Eton tutor, H. E. Luxmoore, acutely observed when *Eton and King's* was published: "His reticence of all about his home and his 'inner life' (so called) may make some think that it is not there."

By "home," Luxmoore meant neither Eton nor King's but Livermere, a small Suffolk village not far from Bury St Edmunds. It was not MRJ's birthplace. He was born on 1 August 1862, the youngest of four children, at Goodnestone in Kent, to which his father had been appointed Perpetual Curate soon after his marriage. But when MRJ was three years old the family moved to Suffolk when the Rev. Herbert James was offered the living of Great and Little Livermere, in the diocese of Ely, at a salary of £400 a year— approximately a pound for every one of his parishioners. The living had been presented to him by the trustees of Jane Anne Broke, later Lady de Saumerez, the stepdaughter of his wife's uncle, Captain (later Rear-Admiral) William Horton. Miss Broke ("Cousin Jane," as MRJ called her) lived at Livermere Hall, set amidst a landscaped park, on the edge of which, close to the church, stood the three-storied stuccoed Georgian rectory to which Herbert James brought his family in 1865.

If MRJ had roots as writer, they were East Anglian in general, and Suffolk in particular. When Herbert James married Mary Emily Horton at Helmingham in 1854 he consolidated the family's Suffolk connections. As well as the Brokes, their relatives by marriage, who had been landed proprietors in East Suffolk since the early sixteenth century, William James, MRJ's grandfather, had settled at Wyndham House, next to the churchyard in Aldeburgh, some time before his death in 1842. (A cast-iron Tuscan pump, donated by him in 1840, still stands beside the Town Steps.) After he died, William's second wife, Caroline, remained at Wyndham House until her death in 1870, her good works in the town earning her a memorial window in the church, which MRJ later called "the worst painted window (perhaps) in the country." He also recalled of the church that "The first organ I heard is likewise here and the first anthem performed I know not on what occasion caused me to burst into tears of apprehension and be led from the sacred edifice." Sydney James, MRJ's eldest brother, was born in Aldeburgh in May 1855, the year of the move to

Goodnestone, and when the family returned to Suffolk he was sent to a school
in Aldeburgh run by the Rev. M. H. Begbie. His other brother, Herbert
("Ber"), was also educated in Aldeburgh. MRJ himself would often visit his
grandmother at Wyndham House and in later years, from 1921 to 1935, returned regularly to Aldeburgh to stay at the White Lion.

   We read nothing of Aldeburgh in MRJ's published recollections, though it
appears—significantly, I think—as Seaburgh in "A Warning to the Curious":

> It was not very different now from what I remember it to have been when I
> was a child. Marshes intersected by dykes to the south ... flat fields to the
> north, merging into heath.... A long sea-front and a street: behind that a
> spacious church of flint, with a broad, solid western tower and a peal of six
> bells. How well I remember their sound on a hot Sunday in August, as our
> party went slowly up the white, dusty slope of road towards them ...

Similarly, Livermere—the family's home for over forty years—finds no
mention in *Eton and King's,* and very little (directly, at least) in MRJ's
unpublished correspondence. But like his memories of Aldeburgh, MRJ's life
at Livermere and the influence of the landscape of his childhood exercised a
profound effect on his imaginative life; and, again like Aldeburgh, it was to
resurface in fiction. In his last ghost story, "A Vignette," he returned to the
place that, more than any other, had shaped his literary imagination. In this
short, rather shapeless, but strangely powerful narrative, the personal tone is
unmistakable: "You are asked to think of the spacious garden of a country
rectory," it begins, "adjacent to a park of many acres ..." We are back in the
Livermere of his childhood, described at length by S. G. Lubbock in his
Memoir of MRJ published in 1939:

> The little village is on the edge of Livermere Park, scattered about a crossing
> of roads. A long grove of trees—plane, chestnut, oak and lime—shadows a
> cart track leading to the great East Anglian church with its Decorated nave
> and chancel, and squat tower with wooden belfry. Between village and
> church a short drive leads to the Rectory with grass on the right and
> shrubberies on the left as you enter. Beyond the white-waded, slate-roofed
> house is the croquet lawn with shrubberies all about it, and a winding path
> cunningly following its gentle slopes.... Screened from the house on the
> east side is the stable, leaning to against the old tithe barn and threshing
> floor, where you played a strange form of tennis on roof and paved yard, the
> only game with a moving ball Monty was ever known to play. From the
> french windows of the Rector's study three long wooden steps led down to
> the lawn; and when you crossed the lawn a path led you through the
> shrubbery to a gate opening on to Livermere Park. Five miles away is Bury St
> Edmunds, and all about is the quiet rich East Anglian landscape.

MRJ's only published reference to his connection with Livermere was in *Suffolk and Norfolk* (1930), his charming conducted tour of the architecture (mostly ecclesiastical) and antiquities of the two counties. It is brief enough: "A mile more, and we are at *Great Livermere*. The reader will forgive a little expansiveness here: from 1865 to 1909 the rectory was my home, if not my dwelling-place." He goes on to quote from the *Concise Description of Bury* (1827); then the tone changes slightly, and a brief note of nostalgic regret is struck as he contemplates the changes that have inevitably taken place: "The Livermeres and Ampton are in one hand now, Livermere Hall is gone, and many oaks in its park are cut down. . . . But village and park have some beauty left." More expressive is an undated and unpublished fragment in which the scenes MRJ knew so well as a child are drawn in affectionate, even poetic detail:

> You know where the Ampton water tracks round rather suddenly, on one side fringed by broad reed beds—a sea of whispering green under a summer breeze and of rustling gold in autumn; while the flat shore behind them is covered thickly, first with underwood of alders and currant and raspberry bushes run wild, and then, as it slopes slightly upward, with a larger growth of beech and oak and fir, while the park fence in the ditch bounds these in turn.

It is at Livermere, not at Eton or King's, that one comes close to the secret places of MRJ's inner life. It is here that one begins to sense the sources of that responsiveness to strangeness which lay beneath the reticent, controlled exterior of a man who, whilst deeply conventional in his beliefs and outlook, was also alive to metaphysical possibilities which, if true, would call into question everything he held most dear. "A Vignette" gives us a glimpse, perhaps, of some inexplicable childhood incident that took place in the garden of the rectory at Livermere and which (as the narrator puts it) "had some formidable power of clinging through many years to my imagination"— an intimation of some anarchic 'otherness' sharing, and sometimes confronting, everyday reality. If the enclosed, well regulated worlds of Eton and King's could be said to represent established order, community, and historical continuity, Livermere and the surrounding Suffolk countryside could evoke other images. In this flat, wide-skied landscape there is sometimes an almost tangible ambivalence—a tension between nature tamed and domesticated (like the artificially conjoined waters of Ampton and Livermere) and an order of things altogether more ancient, elemental, and unpredictable.

There is beauty and peace here; but also, at certain times and under certain conditions, an undercurrent of menace. From an early age MRJ was alive to these darker resonances of the Suffolk landscape; in this respect, his childhood at Livermere may be seen as contributing the imaginative foundations of his later fiction. He must also have been aware of the immemorial beliefs still current in an isolated country village like Livermere in the nine-teenth century—beliefs referred to disapprovingly by his father when he spoke of "the quasi-religious belief of some who have an esoteric confidence in witchcraft." "I can personally testify," wrote the rector, "that the progress of the XIXth Century with all its boasted advancement has failed to explode this and kindred superstition." (One thinks immediately of Mrs Mothersole, the witch in "The Ash-Tree," who took her surname from a local family whose graves can be found in the churchyard at Livermere—amongst them that of Charles Mothersole, parish clerk at Livermere when MRJ was a boy.)

Eton and King's, on the one hand, and Livermere, on the other, seem to symbolise the two sides of MRJ's personality: the scholar and the writer of ghost stories; the public maintenance of objectivity on the question of the su-pernatural, and the private susceptibility to its existence. During his childhood at Livermere MRJ's natural fascination with the uncanny and the macabre were confirmed and deepened by the ambiguities of the landscape. We should not be surprised that in one of his earliest published ghost stories, "Lost Hearts," local sights and sounds become invested with sinister potential:

> The wind had fallen, and there was a still night and a full moon. At about ten o'clock Stephen was standing at the open window of his bedroom, looking out over the country. Still as the night was, the mysterious population of the distant moonlit woods was not yet lulled to rest. From time to time strange cries as of lost and despairing wanderers sounded from across the mere. They might be the notes of owls or water-birds, yet they did not quite resemble either sound.

Forty years later, it seems somehow inevitable that, in the last ghost story he ever wrote, MRJ would return in imagination to Livermere to describe, in the first person, how a young boy confronts something extremely nasty in the rectory garden—a face staring at him through a hole in the gate that led to the Park, a face "not monstrous, not pale, fleshless, spectral. Malevolent I thought and think it was, at any rate the eyes were large and open and fixed. It was pink and, I thought, hot, and just above the eyes the border of a white linen drapery hung down from the brows."

After the death of his father in 1909, MRJ's links with Livermere gradually dissolved, even though his sister continued to live there for a time with her hus-band, J. E. Woodhouse, who succeeded Herbert James as rector. MRJ may have lived most of his life elsewhere, but Livermere remained in his heart and imagi-nation to the end. Now, at long last, there will be a permanent memorial to his association with this quiet place—appropriately, in the church he knew so well, in which his father preached, and near which both his parents lie, beneath a tall stone cross bearing the word "PAX." He would surely have been pleased.

II. General Studies

Supernatural Horror in Literature

H. P. Lovecraft

At the opposite pole of genius from Lord Dunsany, and gifted with an almost diabolic power of calling horror by gentle steps from the midst of prosaic daily life, is the scholarly Montague Rhodes James, Provost of Eton College, antiquary of note, and recognised authority on mediaeval manuscripts and cathedral history. Dr. James, long fond of telling spectral tales at Christmastide, has become by slow degrees a literary weird fictionist of the very first rank; and has developed a distinctive style and method likely to serve as models for an enduring line of disciples.

The art of Dr. James is by no means haphazard, and in the preface to one of his collections he has formulated three very sound rules for macabre composition. A ghost story, he believes, should have a familiar setting in the modern period, in order to approach closely the reader's sphere of experience. Its spectral phenomena, moreover, should be malevolent rather than beneficent; since fear is the emotion primarily to be excited. And finally, the technical patois of "occultism" or pseudo-science ought carefully to be avoided; lest the charm of casual verisimilitude be smothered in unconvincing pedantry.

Dr. James, practicing what he preaches, approaches his themes in a light and often conversational way. Creating the illusion of every-day events, he introduces his abnormal phenomena cautiously and gradually; relieved at every turn by touches of homely and prosaic detail, and sometimes spiced with a snatch or two of antiquarian scholarship. Conscious of the close relation between present weirdness and accumulated tradition, he generally provides remote historical antecedents for his incidents; thus being able to utilise very aptly his exhaustive knowledge of the past, and his ready and convincing command of archaic diction and colouring. A favourite scene for a James tale is some centuried cathedral, which the author can describe with all the familiar minuteness of a specialist in that field.

Sly humorous vignettes and bits of life-like genre portraiture and characterisation are often to be found in Dr. James's narratives, and serve in his skilled hands to augment the general effect rather than to spoil it, as the same qualities would tend to do with a lesser craftsman. In inventing a new type of ghost, he has departed considerably from the conventional Gothic tradition; for where the older stock ghosts were pale and stately, and apprehended chiefly through the sense of sight, the average James ghost is lean, dwarfish, and hairy—a sluggish, hellish night-abomination midway betwixt beast and man—and usually *touched* before it is *seen*. Sometimes the spectre is of still more eccentric composition; a roll of flannel with spidery eyes, or an invisible entity which moulds itself in bedding and shews *a face of crumpled linen*. Dr. James has, it is clear, an intelligent and scientific knowledge of human nerves and feelings; and knows just how to apportion statement, imagery, and subtle suggestions in order to secure the best results with his readers. He is an artist in incident and arrangement rather than in atmosphere, and reaches the emotions more often through the intellect than directly. This method, of course, with its occasional absences of sharp climax, has its drawbacks as well as its advantages; and many will miss the thorough atmospheric tension which writers like Machen are careful to build up with words and scenes. But only a few of the tales are open to the charge of tameness. Generally the laconic unfolding of abnormal events in adroit order is amply sufficient to produce the desired effect of cumulative horror.

The short stories of Dr. James are contained in four small collections, entitled respectively *Ghost-Stories of an Antiquary*, *More Ghost Stories of an Antiquary*, *A Thin Ghost and Others*, and *A Warning to the Curious*. There is also a delightful juvenile phantasy, *The Five Jars*, which has its spectral adumbrations. Amidst this wealth of material it is hard to select a favourite or especially typical tale, though each reader will no doubt have such preferences as his temperament may determine.

"Count Magnus" is assuredly one of the best, forming as it does a veritable Golconda of suspense and suggestion. Mr. Wraxall is an English traveller of the middle nineteenth century, sojourning in Sweden to secure material for a book. Becoming interested in the ancient family of De la Gardie, near the village of Råbäck, he studies its records; and finds particular fascination in the builder of the existing manor-house, one Count Magnus, of whom strange and terrible things are whispered. The Count, who flourished early in the seventeenth century, was a stern landlord, and famous for his severity toward poachers and delinquent tenants. His cruel punishments were bywords, and there were dark rumours of influences which even survived his interment in the great mausoleum he built near the church—as in the case of the two peasants who hunted on his preserves one night a century after his death. There were hideous screams in the woods, and near the tomb of

Count Magnus an unnatural laugh and the clang of a great door. Next morning the priest found the two men; one a maniac, and the other dead, with the flesh of his face sucked from the bones.

Mr. Wraxall hears all these tales, and stumbles on more guarded references to a *Black Pilgrimage* once taken by the Count; a pilgrimage to Chorazin in Palestine, one of the cities denounced by Our Lord in the Scriptures, and in which old priests say that Antichrist is to be born. No one dares to hint just what that Black Pilgrimage was, or what strange being or thing the Count brought back as a companion. Meanwhile Mr. Wraxall is increasingly anxious to explore the mausoleum of Count Magnus, and finally secures permission to do so, in the company of a deacon. He finds several monuments and three copper sarcophagi, one of which is the Count's. Round the edge of this latter are several bands of engraved scenes, including a singular and hideous delineation of a pursuit—the pursuit of a frantic man through a forest by a squat muffled figure with a devil-fish's tentacle, directed by a tall cloaked man on a neighbouring hillock. The sarcophagus has three massive steel padlocks, one of which is lying open on the floor, reminding the traveller of a metallic clash he heard the day before when passing the mausoleum and wishing idly that he might see Count Magnus.

His fascination augmented, and the key being accessible, Mr. Wraxall pays the mausoleum a second and solitary visit and finds another padlock unfastened. The next day, his last in Råbäck, he again goes alone to bid the long-dead Count farewell. Once more queerly impelled to utter a whimsical wish for a meeting with the buried nobleman, he now sees to his disquiet that only one of the padlocks remains on the great sarcophagus. Even as he looks, that last lock drops noisily to the floor, and there comes a sound as of creaking hinges. Then the monstrous lid appears very slowly to rise, and Mr. Wraxall flees in panic fear without refastening the door of the mausoleum.

During his return to England the traveller feels a curious uneasiness about his fellow-passengers on the canal-boat which he employs for the earlier stages. Cloaked figures make him nervous, and he has a sense of being watched and followed. Of twenty-eight persons whom he counts, only twenty-six appear at meals; and the missing two are always a tall cloaked man and a shorter muffled figure. Completing his water travel at Harwich, Mr. Wraxall takes frankly to flight in a closed carriage, but sees two cloaked figures at a crossroad. Finally he lodges at a small house in a village and spends the time making frantic notes. On the second morning he is found dead, and during the inquest seven jurors faint at sight of the body. The house where he stayed is never again inhabited, and upon its demolition half a century later his manuscript is discovered in a forgotten cupboard.

In "The Treasure of Abbot Thomas" a British antiquary unriddles a cipher on some Renaissance painted windows, and thereby discovers a centuried hoard of gold in a niche half way down a well in the courtyard of a German abbey. But the crafty depositor had set a guardian over that treasure, and something in the black well twines its arms around the searcher's neck in such a manner that the quest is abandoned, and a clergyman sent for. Each night after that the discoverer feels a stealthy presence and detects a horrible odour of mould outside the door of his hotel room, till finally the clergyman makes a daylight replacement of the stone at the mouth of the treasure-vault in the well—out of which something had come in the dark to avenge the disturbing of old Abbot Thomas's gold. As he completes his work the cleric observes a curious toad-like carving on the ancient well-head, with the Latin motto "*Depositum custodi*—keep that which is committed to thee."

Other notable James tales are "The Stalls of Barchester Cathedral," in which a grotesque carving comes curiously to life to avenge the secret and subtle murder of an old Dean by his ambitious successor; "'Oh, Whistle, and I'll Come to You, My Lad,'" which tells of the horror summoned by a strange metal whistle found in a mediaeval church ruin; and "An Episode of Cathedral History," where the dismantling of a pulpit uncovers an archaic tomb whose lurking daemon spreads panic and pestilence. Dr. James, for all his light touch, evokes fright and hideousness in their most shocking forms; and will certainly stand as one of the few really creative masters in his darksome province.

The Art of Montague James

Mary Butts

When I was a child I remember a space in the walls of an old house where there had been a door, whose handle had been taken off, and the tall square filled with shelves for books. Behind them the key-hole was still visible, and the panels painted with peacocks' feathers—home decoration in the 'eighties'—and the shelf edges were trimmed with strips of coloured leather, cut to points and fastened with brass nail-heads. Shelves— the door stood in a dark corner of the hall—filled with 'Works,' rows of bright leather. I remember Kinglake's *Crimean War; The Decline and Fall;* the *Dutch Republics;* Byron. While the bottom rows held something which to-day one does not often see, clumps of strongly-bound magazines.

Magazines are different now. But these antiquities, the *Pall Mall,* the *Cornhill, Scribners,* had matter in them one might well want to keep. Serials by Meredith and Henry James—it was among them that I found out what a short story could be. Particularly—I was too young to remember the writer's name— a story called "Lost Hearts." It was one of those discoveries that last a life-time.

I remember, too, the day I read it. I was about eight years old. One of the great south-westerly storms, the only terrible aspect of nature that I knew as yet, was just over. I read, rapt with terror and felicity; and found in the tale more than the story to excite me. For it had made me aware of nature and my own environment. What I had just heard happening, roaring through a south-country garden, straining its trees, haunting the night and bringing in the day with uproar, was what happened in the story and accompanied its ghosts. It is hard to describe. I learned about that wind as a separate event, a thing that happened, almost as a person; and that what 'the man' wrote about was something that happened at home. A home also that was like the house of the boy, Stephen.

There was something else too—though this, I suspect, was on a later reading—it filled my mind with new things. What were "the religious beliefs of the late pagans"? What were the Mysteries? The Neo-Platonists? The Orphics? If I know some of the answers now, it was here that I first asked the questions. I was utterly fascinated. Like the child in Ruth Manning-Sanders' book, who collected "words for sermons," I went about saying these to myself. Not so much trying to find out, as sure that I should know some day.

And I never heard of Doctor James again, until the publication of *Ghost-Stories of an Antiquary*.

As a matter of fact, not until ten years after, when that volume and its sequel, *More Ghost Stories*, appeared together just before the War; then *A Thin Ghost and Others*; and, lastly, *A Warning to the Curious* in 1925. Plenty of time between each publication to let the others sink in. And somewhere in the middle, with a small daughter in view, I came across *The Five Jars*, a child's classic only comparable with *Alice*, with *The Brownies*, or with some of *Rewards and Fairies*.

It is the writer's belief that if Doctor James had chosen to write stories about any other subject under the sun, he would be considered the greatest classic short story writer of our time. Yet, in his case, it is more than usually silly—so completely fused with one another are his style and his subject—to suggest such a thing. It is impossible to think of him as writing about anything else than what is rather foolishly called "The Unseen." Idiotically, in his case. "Unseen," indeed! When the essence of his art is a sudden, appalling shock of visibility. The intangible become more than tangible, unspeakably real, solid, *present*. He is not a writer—say like Mr. Algernon Blackwood—who relies on suggestion, a strengthening atmosphere in which very little ever happens; or rather one is not sure whether it has happened or not. It is what his people *see* that Doctor James is busy with; not how it affects them. After it has happened they either die, or leave home or go to bed; or, years after, tell it to him, with permission to make a story out of it. It sounds simple. It is not. It is matter-of-fact. A very different thing. Yet in its unpretentiousness, in its absence of worked-up atmosphere, its lack of hints, it carries the driest, clearest kind of conviction. If his stories were about anything else (which heaven forbid) Doctor James would be praised for something of the same qualities for which we praise Horace and Catullus and Villon, for something terse and poignant and durable, and looked at with both eyes wide open. While, in our day at least, writing on the 'Occult'—another inadequate, loosely-used word—is felt to be a bastard of the Muses; a kind of entertainment, a kind of trick. Not quite respectable. The implication being that our emotions are stirred by situations which are essentially impossible: by a lie. That, as letters are more than a game, it is not quite fair.

The attitude is not quite consistent. Poets are allowed the full use of this material. The subjects of *Sister Helen* or *Rose Mary* do not make these poems faintly disreputable. There is "The Listeners," one of our most popular anthology numbers. Think of the Ballads. Though there the attitude of 'it was all a long time ago, and we'll hope it didn't happen' and, 'poor devils, they knew no better' doubtless enters in.

It is strange: to try and separate Doctor James' precise, elegant, detached style, where never a word is wasted, from his matter; to wish, even to imagine, it employed in any other direction, is to dislocate one's imagination, one's sense of what is conceivably possible, so perfectly is the instrument adapted to its end.

His matter. It is taken from his own surroundings and experience, in the University town, the library, the cathedral, the country inn and the country house. His people are the people who live and work in such places; the country gentleman, the student, the don. They are going about their business. Then, as a man might turn a corner or the page of a book, they meet the Unspeakable. Are brought up sharp against the dead who are not dead; who are out and about on hellish business; who, if they have long remained quiescent, are stirred by some trivial accident into hideous activity.

Or these tranquil ordinary men of learning come suddenly upon creatures, tangible as men, but of a different order; intelligences 'less than that of a man, more than that of a beast'; and of the malignancy of hell. Sometimes they escape. Not always. While neither Doctor James' Dead nor his Demons appear in any of the categories or conventions which other writers, using tradition, or maybe their own experience, have accustomed us. His ghosts, demons, 'elementals' are utterly original. New minted. And owing nothing (while at the same time everything) to the vast corpus of tradition—and whatever truth lies behind it—on the existence of such things. As in "The Uncommon Prayer-Book." Who but Doctor James would have arranged for old Lady Sadleir to reappear like this?:

"Why, Mary, here's all the books open again," says old Mr. Avery, to his daughter, the keeper's wife. And Mr. Davidson, the antiquary, reflects on his return from his walk:

> What curious evil service was that which she and a few like her had been wont to celebrate year by year in that remote valley?

Then later, the commissionaire to the police:

> It had a bit of a band tied round underneath. And the eyes, well, they were dry-like, and much as if there was two big spiders' bodies in the holes. Hair? No, I don't know as there was much hair to be seen . . . I'm sure it warn't what it should have been.

Here the unspeakable is not done by statement. It comes out obliquely, through the observers. That is often his way, whose method is one of the

sharpest realism, the driest and most direct observation. With one concession only to ideal arrangement. The reader is never for an instant irritated or
held up by his characters' incredulity, pig-headed aversion to adventure, or
search for a 'natural' explanation. If they cannot explain what is happening
to them, at least they never try to explain it away. As in "No. 13":

> His back was to the door. At that moment the door opened, and an arm
> came out and clawed at his shoulder. It was clad in ragged yellowish linen,
> and the bare skin, where it could be seen, had long grey hairs upon it.

Or in "Canon Alberic's Scrap-book":

> I have never quite understood what was Dennistoun's view of the events
> I have narrated . . . On one occasion he said: "Isaiah was a very sensible
> man; doesn't he say something about night monsters living in the ruins of
> Babylon? These things are rather beyond us at present."

These two quotations show something of his method. While the impression made by "Lost Hearts" is, in one way or another, repeated in them all.
There was what happened, reinforced by his setting and his sense of nature;
and by the inclusion of what I used to call—and still do, for that matter—
Interesting Things. The reference, so necessary in that story, to Mithras and
the Orphics. As again, in "Canon Alberic," the description of the MS. treasure, the "priceless scrapbook":

> There were leaves from a copy of Genesis, illustrated with pictures, which
> could not have been later than A.D. 700 . . . and perhaps best of all there
> were twenty leaves of uncial writing in Latin . . . Could it possibly be a frag-
> ment of the copy of Papias "On the Words of Our Lord," which was known
> to have existed as late as the 12th Century at Nîmes?

Or in "An Episode of Cathedral History" and "The Stalls of Barchester
Cathedral" the description of the choirs before "the wave of Gothic revival
smote the cathedral":

> When you enter the choir of Barchester Cathedral now, you pass through
> a screen of metal and coloured marbles, designed by Sir Gilbert Scott, and
> find yourself in what I must call a very bare and odiously furnished place . . .
> Careful engravings of a hundred years ago show a very different state of
> things. The organ is on a massive classical screen. The stalls are also classical
> and very massive. There is a baldachino of wood over the altar, with urns
> upon its corners. Farther east is a solid altar screen . . . with a pediment, in
> which is a triangle surrounded by rays, enclosing certain Hebrew letters in
> gold. Cherubs contemplate these . . .

Passing tactfully by the real effect on their nerves and on their sense of truth by the matter of Doctor James, the critics often reserve their praise for his incomparable evocation of the past. "Here," they say, "is imaginative scholarship. How he uses his research to take us back three centuries, or two, or one."

They are quite right. Though there are not many such stories, seven in all; out of which two could be called "Early Victorian." While there is one only as early as James I. One in the time of James II; and the rest somewhere in the Eighteenth Century; and one in two parts, over the space of a hundred years, from the middle of the Eighteenth to the middle of the Nineteenth. These settings, each one an earlier version of the milieu he uses today, are more than a historic reconstruction, however skilfully done. There is something distilled about them. It is not as if one were in a picture gallery, a spectator, but inside. How does he do it? Doctor James has waved his wand, but what is the spell? Again, it is by a kind of simplicity, a directness of attack. People are confused about this. If the attack comes from an unexpected quarter, they will call the work obscure; not told in the right way. This is not what they mean. The point is that the essential meaning of a tale—from whatever quarter—must "come at" the reader, undeflected, at its proper pace; which, in works of Doctor James' kind, is usually swift; so that *everything,* however brilliant or diverting, must be omitted that interferes with "telling the tale."

On the other hand, anything may be put in that helps to tell it, that gets the reader there. Doctor James' means of transport to the past are simple enough. It is harder to see why they are so effective.—This from "Martin's Close":

S. "Sir, it was this. It was about nine o'clock in the evening after that Ann did not come home, and I was about my work in the house; there was no company, there only Thomas Snell, and it was foul weather. Esquire Martin came in and called for some drink, and I, by way of pleasantry, I said to him: 'Squire, have you been looking after your sweetheart?' and he flew out at me in a passion . . . I was amazed at that, because we were accustomed to joke with him about her."

L.C.J. "Who, her?"

S. "Ann Clark, my lord. And we had not heard the news of his being contracted to a young gentlewoman elsewhere, or I am sure I should have used better manners. So I said nothing, but being as I was a little put out, I begun singing, to myself as it were, the song they danced to the first time they met, for I thought it would prick him. It was the same he used to sing when he came down the street; . . . *'Madam, will you walk, will you talk with me?'* . . . And . . . I thought I heard someone answering outside the house, but I could not be sure because of the wind blowing so high. So then I stopped singing, and now I heard it plain, saying, *'Yes, sir, I will walk, I will talk with you.'* And I knew the voice for Ann Clark's voice."

This is right; and without archaic curiosities or a syllable to startle. The curious examination goes on, between the Lord Chief Justice Jeffries and the woman who kept the inn, as to the singing of Ann Clark, when she was no longer alive.

Again the Vicar, Mr. Crome, in "The Ash-Tree":

> So much is to be said of the Symptoms seen on the Corpse. As to what I am to add, it is merely my own Experiment, and to be left to Posterity to judge whether there be anything of Value therein. There was on the Table by the Beddside a Bible of the small size, . . . [and] it came into my Thoughts, . . . to make trial of that old . . . Practice of drawing the *Sortes:* . . .
>
> I made then three trials, opening the Book and placing my Finger upon certain Words: which gave me in the first these words . . . *Cut it down;* . . . *It shall never be inhabited;* and upon the third Experiment, . . . *Her young ones also suck up blood.*

The economy is the same in his display of character. His presentation owes something to Dickens, but all are observed, not without sympathy, but with complete ironic detachment. The marvel is that, when he tells us so little, without, for instance, a hint of physical description, that we know so much. It is true he has no time to make us acquainted at length. He has to get on at once to his point, to the appalling experience that is in store. Many writers would have been content with lay figures; yet, on learning what sort of an inheritance was Mr. Humphreys', one finds out what sort of a man he was. As unlike Dennistoun or Mr. Poynter, Dr. Haynes or Squire Richards in nature, as he resembles them in representing a class of our society. While in dealing with their servants, Doctor James may be said to let himself go. They are as full of 'humours' as an Eighteenth Century play; more tenderly handled, but as little sentimentalised. He has no objection to driving in the obvious nail, that the better educated you are, the more you are likely—if not to experience—to observe, to be affected, to understand, to be curious about what is happening to you. (There is a feeling about to-day that training of the mind makes no difference.) In "The Uncommon Prayer-Book," one of the most perfect of all the stories:

> "I suppose you never notice anything else odd when you are at work here, Mrs. Porter?" [says Mr. Davidson, the antiquarian, to the keeper's wife, when the books have been found, lying open again at the 109th Psalm.]
>
> "No, sir, I do not . . . and it's a funny thing to me I don't, with the feeling I have as there's someone settin' here—no, it's the other side, just within the

screen—and lookin' at me all the time I'm dustin' in the gallery and pews. But I never yet see nothin' worse than myself, as the sayin' goes, and I kindly hope I never may."

So, in "The Mezzotint"—winner of a Symposium, held in Paris, as to which was the best tale of them all—Mr. Filcher, the skip, when he has seen the figure of a man leaving the house, travelling across the picture, "erect and stepping swiftly, with long strides towards the front":

"It ain't a picture I should 'ang where my little girl could see it, sir. I recollect once she see a Door Bible, with pictures not 'arf what that is . . . and if she were to ketch a sight of this skelinton here, or whatever it is, carrying off the poor baby . . . Should you be wanting anything else this evening, sir? Thank you, sir . . ."

There is Mr. Avery, the keeper, with his "Gregory singing," old Patten, the butler, whom long service had shown what was happening, more even than the "Master Henry" he served. Old Mitchell; the sacristan at St. Bertrand de Comminges, with the book he sold Dennistoun and the circumstance she would not explain—pages of analysis would not tell essentially more about them than we gather from a few swift pages, whose motive is not primarily to shew character at all. It is one of the mysteries of classic art, that so little should be enough. As it is one of its supreme beauties that, out of what is said, there is not a word wasted.

In the same way, with the same excellence of proportion, Doctor James attends to the other part of his setting, the place and the weather. A great many pages have been written of good, bad and indifferent prose, on the south-west wind. In "Lost Hearts," he opens with it. It is his wind. It blows again through "A Neighbour's Landmark":

. . . great trees were stirring and weeping. Between them were stretches of green and yellow country . . . and blue hills, far off, veiled with rain. Up above was a very restless and hopeless movement of low clouds travelling . . .

Then, in another tale, where he wished to give the effect of departure:

In five minutes more there was nothing but the lessening lights of the boat, the long line of the Dover lamps, the night breeze and the moon.
Long and long the two sat in their room at the "Lord Warden". . . .

These are the diversions as he permits himself. They are little more than parentheses, yet so much is evoked. It reminds one of what Lytton Strachey has to say about the art of Racine, purposely avoiding the ambitious comparisons, the striking phrases of the Romantics; content with the far harder business of understatement and classic permanence of effect.

He has an affection also for some very plain, very subtle, very unambitious English landscapes it takes a long time to appreciate and understand. Scenes that have an affinity with Constable; and which are not there, like mountains and savage valleys and rainbow-filled cataracts and eternal snows to awe and stun us and take away our breath. That ask instead years of patient contemplation and silent love—and even a silent tongue.

Here one might speak of his one book for children, which is gradually becoming more known. Though it deserved the immediate success of *Alice*, it did not get it. Instead, people discover it, talk about it with delight. Hurry home to try it on their nurseries with a very interesting success. Children (they must not be too young and they must be intelligent) are rather solemn about it: "What an *extraordinary* book. I like that. Give it me to read by myself." And have a lecture ready on Roman Britain.

It is not a perfect book. The idea is 'genial' and cries aloud for a sequel; but the rather Elizabethan 'Little People,' who appear in flights, with a too rational—a wish-fulfilment—life of their own, have a slight school-mastering touch. They are too much well-bred boys, dressed-up. Created as it were out of the wrong stuff, they jar on the rest of the book, which, with its ordinariness, is steeped in the magic which belongs to Doctor James and to no one else on earth. How plain it is, how mysterious, how lovely. Even those Little People would be another writer's excellence. The Bat-Ball. The washing, blowing on the line, that was one moment an old woman. The Cat, one of the best cats in letters, telling the author what 'comfort and help to a poor weary creature the least little bit of fish can give.' The sense of summer. The Wood. The exquisite words the Stream said. The look of the silver pieces winking on the bubbling sand of the Spring. If he would only write a sequel and insure the double delight of English children for ever.

Again, in "The Uncommon Prayer-Book," there is a comparison between a winter landscape and the same place seen again in Spring:

> The way . . . lay . . . on the top of the country, and commanded wide views over a succession of ridges, plough and pasture, or covered with dark blue woods—all ending . . . in headlands that overlooked the wide valley of a great western river . . .

In Spring, the

> same field-path led them to Brockstone. But to-day they stopped more than once to pick a cowslip; the distant woods and ploughed uplands were of

another colour, and in the copse there was, as Mrs. Porter said, "a regular charm of birds; why, you couldn't collect your mind sometimes with it."

It is enough. It is all there. The phrase "the charm of birds" is almost extravagant for Doctor James. The brevity, the unpretentiousness, the crystal transparency set the scene, with incomparable ease and mastery—for what? That is, after all, the point. What is Doctor James writing about? What is a ghost story? . . . And why is it, as he has said himself, that no other subject has ever attracted him? While how is it that the ghost stories he has written are incomparable and unique; that he has found a formula for their telling more effective and like that of no other writer? In English we have a considerable literature of the occult. One wishes one knew enough to compare it with that of other countries. One imagines French to be deficient, and German to be very good. Is it partly a question of language? Yet an audience has shivered at Doctor James, put into clumsy French. (He would translate, where a more 'atmospheric' writer would not.) Anyhow, with us, it is almost a special branch of letters, and includes some masterpieces. Some more ambitious writers are concerned with the theory of such things; with reasons, scientific or mystical, how and why they happen. In Doctor James there is not a hint of this, not the faintest breath of explanation. It is all statement; all the directest narrative.

These questions are unanswerable directly. Only one thing can be said. Years ago, he found a magical receipt, and has spent his life in perfecting the use of it. With it he can raise the evil dead; summon the abominable familiars, whose place is just across the threshold of human life. As in his longest story, "Casting the Runes." One which happens over a longer period of time than is usual with him, and so allows for an ever-so-slightly-evoked, yet sufficient, atmosphere of suspense. A critic once said that it was work that left one saying: "If I am not very careful, this sort of thing will happen to me." That is certainly true here, as the events move, delicately, inevitably, from slight point to slight point.

Mr. Dunning "was returning from the British Museum," where he had been engaged on Research, to see in the tram an advertisement which struck him as unusual. "*In memory of John Harrington . . .*" A name and a date. Then: "*Three months were allowed.*" The conductor, who, at the time, cannot account for the thing—"it seems to me as if it were reg'lar *in* the glass"—tells him next day, that, when he reached the car-depôt, it had disappeared. That evening in the street he is given a leaflet, to have it a moment later snatched away. But the day following, as he is settling down to work at the Museum, his papers fall on the floor. A stranger helps him collect them; and he is offered and *accepts* a slip from his hand, one which he thinks has fallen from those he has dropped.

He is uneasy on his way home, a feeling as though he had been 'taken in charge.' On arriving finds that his two servants have been taken away, unaccountably ill. Then, in the solitary night, he hears a door open below, and on going out to listen, feels a hot draught playing round his bare feet. Back in bed, he finds the light cut off, feels under his pillow for his watch, to encounter there a 'mouth with teeth, and with hair about it; and . . . not the mouth of a human being.' He flies to a spare room, in the fear that is also misery. Nothing more happens that night.

The next evening he is prevailed upon by a friend to stay with him, and finally to tell him what is preying on his mind. It all comes out; and the two men between them discover that the man who gave him the paper in the Museum is the man whose book he has pulverised lately in a review: that the John Harrington of the In Memoriam notice is the name of a dead man, who had once done the same thing to an earlier work by the same hand. That three months later he had been found curiously and horribly dead. That Harrington had left a brother, still, after ten years, on the track of an explanation, and suspecting Karswell, the writer of both books. Each was on witchcraft. Karswell is a man of evil reputation, and a squire of wealth and property in Warwickshire. Eventually Dunning, still oppressed by a feeling of being watched, and the younger Harrington meet. Together they examine the paper he was handed at the Museum: to find on it an unknown writing, something like runic script. "Yes," says Harrington, "this might be the identical thing that was given to my brother. You'll have to look out, Dunning, this may mean something quite serious for you." The paper is so light that it flutters out of their hands. They slam down the window and secure it, just in time. It had not been so with the late Harrington's slip. The draught had drawn it up the chimney. "You can't give it back now," his brother had said. "I know I can't, but why you should go on saying it I don't know." "I didn't, not more than once." "Not more than four times, you mean." . . .

But this one is safe, and, to reverse the operation of its foul magic, must be given back to Karswell and *accepted*. And by Dunning. It will be difficult, for he is known to him by sight. Harrington, who lives near Karswell in Warwickshire, arranges to keep a look-out, and to let Dunning know. They also have three months.

The weeks pass; but with them augments the dreadful sense of never being alone. Of being the man of whom Coleridge speaks, who:

> walks on
> And turns no more his head,
> Because he knows a frightful fiend
> Doth close behind him tread.

In the last week a telegram comes: "Leaves Victoria by boat-train. Do not miss. I come to you to-night. Harrington."

Then the journey the three men take to Dover. Dunning, disguised, opposite Karswell, who, not until the train is approaching the coast, leaves the carriage, and as he does so, lets fall his Cook's ticket, in its case, on to the carriage floor. Dunning picks it up, slips the paper into the inner pocket; and as Karswell returns, manages to say the ritual words: "May I give you this, sir? I believe it is yours." And hears the longed-for response: "Yes, it is; much obliged to you, sir." Trembling, the two men sit opposite him, while the train slows down and the air in the carriage grows hot and as if something restless had come in; while Karswell fidgets with his rugs. At the quay station, Dunning leans against a wall, faint, and Harrington follows Karswell to the gangway. To hear as he goes on board the man at the barrier ask if the other gentleman has shewn his ticket. Then three days later, the notice in the paper, of the death of a Mr. Karswell, struck on the head and instantly killed, by a stone fallen from some deserted scaffolding; and how

> after a judicious interval, Harrington repeated to Dunning something of what he had heard his brother say in his sleep: but it was not long before Dunning stopped him.

Such, in outline, is the longest of these stories, the essence of its horror, conveyed in minute, bold, significant touches. It is perfectly done; one is "fascinated by the deliciousness of sheer style." Yet one believes that many of his readers ask themselves if it is not, perhaps, a waste. Anyhow, is it quite fair? Foolish questions, which mask the actual thought: 'Since they seem so real, carry more conviction than almost any other writing on the same subject, are undoubtedly works of art, does not this mean that there must be some truth in them? And, if so, God help us.' Or, from another point of view: "Why make art out of—That?" And then—"Is he telling the truth? A truth? A possible, a probable truth?" For that does matter in art. While the extreme realism of his treatment raises the question. He is not being careful, like some writers, not to commit himself too far. It is: "This is what happened to Mr. So-and-So. Take it or leave it." Doctor James has been asked if he believes in ghosts. Here he will not commit himself—at least in print. I think we are in the presence of a mystery. By sheer art, which is in itself 'a magic,' perhaps the greatest of the magics, he has given us profound aesthetic pleasure; by a subject considered to-day to have no relation to reality, and by means of a technique as realistic as de Maupassant's.

Again it is curious. If Doctor James were to get up and say that he believes every word he has written, that he has evidence for the essential truth of each one of his stories, he would be believed, in the same way that a scientist is believed. He is the sort of man whose word is taken. While he is a great scholar, and the scholar is elder brother to the scientist.

In one form or another, his subject has haunted man's imagination since the beginning. The Un-Dead Dead, and the potencies, good and evil, but more noticeably evil, which have been thought to crowd about between the threshold of his life and any other forms of life that there may be. The evidence for their existence is, from many angles, as strong as the evidence for their non-existence. But—it is harder to follow; commonsense or even learned incredulity is essentially easier and simpler. Also more *à la mode.* For such beliefs are mixed up, almost inextricably, with superstition, wish-fulfilments, exaggerations, axes to grind, scores to pay off—with every variety of human inaccuracy and imbecility. Above all, to-day, for good and bad reasons, those that do credit to humanity and those which do not, such beliefs are unfashionable. (Though less unfashionable than they were in our fathers' day, engaged as they were, by the light of Science, in a great spring-cleaning of the human mind.)

For Doctor James is pitiless. People do not easily escape from his Creatures. They fall a victim to them. More often the bad or the disagreeable person, but the amiable and charming Mr. Humphreys did not escape "concussion of the brain, shock to the system, and a long confinement in bed." (He later married Lady Wardrop's niece, so that was all right.) But Mr. Poschwitz, the Jew dealer, who stole the prayer books from Brockstone chapel, died by the most hideous death it is possible for the mind to conceive.

Nor did the piteous Mr. Wraxall in "Count Magnus" escape, nor Sir Matthew, nor Sir Richard. Fell, in their east-country manor, where the ash tree grew, filtering the light across their bedroom window. Nor Mr. Somerton, the antiquarian squire, when he went to look for Abbot Thomas' treasure. It was death to the master in "A School Story," when the boys saw something climb in at his window who "looked as if he was wet all over"; though he, presumably, had killed his man before he was pursued by him as a ghost.

We have seen how the first Harrington died, and how near death came the next person who happened to cross Mr. Karswell and his receipts. (The writer has an idea, from wholly different sources, that one part of this story is "founded on fact.") "The Stalls of Barchester Cathedral" were the death of Doctor Haynes:

> If a bloody hand he bear
> I councell him to be ware
> Lest he be fetched away . . .
> But chiefly when the wind blows high . . .

There was what happened to Lord Saul, in "The Residence at Whitminster"—"a withered heart makes an ugly thin ghost" . . . "Oh, he was a cruel child, for certain, but he had to pay for it in the end, and after" . . . While goodness knows what the Rector had been up to, to end up like that with his head in a bag. In that tale, "An Appearance and a Disappearance," there is an awful inconsequence, which marks an even further development in Doctor James' art.

In "Two Doctors," the good physician "dreams of the Chrysalis"— ("A chrysalis is an innocent thing"—"This was not") and is found dead. In "A View from a Hill" they took away old Baxter, "whether he would or no." "A Warning to the Curious" more than justifies its name. "Wailing Well," where a child is the victim, even rouses a cry of protest. It is hardly to be wondered that man, having been told that he need no longer believe even in the possibility of such things, has accepted the assurance thankfully.

"After Dark in the Playing Fields," almost a meditation, and a pendant to the lovely, fear-touched imaginations of *The Five Jars,* may have in it something of Doctor James' personal belief:

> I do sometimes go into the Playing Fields at night still, but I come in before true midnight. And I find I do not like the crowd after dark—for example, at the Fourth of June fireworks. You see—no, you do not, but I see— such curious faces; and the people to whom they belong flit about so oddly, often at your elbow when you least expect it, and looking close into your face, as if they were searching for someone—who may be thankful, I think, if they do not find him. "Where do they come from?" Why, some, I think, out of the water, and some out of the ground. They look like that. But I am sure it is best to take no notice of them, and not to touch them.

Perhaps the doubt felt about Doctor James' subject is not only shallow scepticism, but sound, self-protective sense. Better not—certainly for the majority—better not enquire too closely; ask too many questions as to the existence of such things. Everyone who has lived much out of doors *feels* something of what he tells. Not by association with tradition, but by a direct kind of awareness, an impact on the senses—and something more than the senses. It can be a recurrent, almost an overwhelming, experience. Much ancient bogey-lore was a rationalisation of it. To-day we talk of suggestion, exorcise with the magic word "unscientific." But I doubt if our ignorant scepticism is any nearer truth than our ancestors' ignorant credulity.

It is certainly safer as it is, safer to have Dr. James give us the experience at second hand. Work his magic; imprison such things safely for us inside the covers of a book, an enduring book. And remember that, thanks to him, we have undergone an adventure which might have been deadly, with more than safety, with delight.

The Ghost Stories of Montague Rhodes James

L. J. Lloyd

It is now more than eleven years since Montague Rhodes James died in his Provost's Lodge at Eton, at the age of seventy-three. By his death a circle of devoted friends lost a greatly-loved companion, Eton one of the most distinguished of her sons, the world of scholarship its first authority on Western manuscripts, and the world of literature—though as yet it perhaps hardly realizes the fact—one of the greatest masters of the tale of ghostly horror, which this country, or any other, has yet seen.

It all began in Cambridge on 28 October 1893, during the 601st meeting of the Chitchat Society: was ever a name less ominous? The minutes of the meeting record that "Mr. James read 'Two Ghost Stories.'" And so "Canon Alberic's Scrap-book" and "Lost Hearts" made their first appearance before the world. One cannot help wondering whether the other members of the club—they included Mr. E. F. Benson—hurried rather quickly afterwards through the night air to their rooms, and whether they went along as far as they could with each other. And whether oaks were sported and locks examined with more than customary care. And whether it seemed to take them rather longer than usual to get into bed.

However this may be, "the Ghost Stories," in the words of Mr. S. G. Lubbock,

> began; and they were continued at the urgent request of a small party that was used to gather at King's just before Christmas. Some pressure was needed; and on the appointed evening the party met and waited till at last, about 11 p.m. as a rule, Monty appeared with the ink still wet on the last page. All lights except one were turned out, and the story was read. Afterwards, when he was Provost, the same ritual was preserved; but by then the small party had grown . . . (38)

The first collection, *Ghost-Stories of an Antiquary*, appeared in 1904.[1] It

---

1. *More Ghost Stories of an Antiquary* followed in 1911; *A Thin Ghost and Others* in 1919, and *A Warning to the Curious* in 1925.

was a squarish book, bound in canvas, and it contained four pen drawings by James McBryde. They are admirable drawings, but we owe the artist more than admiration for his work, for as James explains in the preface:

> I wrote these stories at long intervals, and most of them were read to pa-tient friends, usually at the season of Christmas. One of these friends offered to illustrate them, and it was agreed that if he would do that, I would con-sider the question of publishing them. Four pictures he completed, which will be found in this volume, and then, very quickly and unexpectedly, he was taken away. . . . Those who knew the artist will understand how much I wished to give a permanent form even to a fragment of his work; others will appreciate the fact that here a remembrance is made of one in whom many friendships centred. . . .
>
> The stories themselves do not make any very exalted claim. If any of them succeed in causing their readers to feel pleasantly uncomfortable when walking along a solitary road at nightfall, or sitting over a dying fire in the small hours, my purpose in writing them will have been attained.

Much virtue in that "pleasantly." And for the pious wish in general there is a tale of one who refused to allow even the title of "'Oh, Whistle, and I'll Come to You, My Lad'" to be uttered in his presence. But he no doubt had two beds in his room.

There must, one supposes, have been many who picked up the innocent-looking volume in the expectation of finding within its covers the innocuous or pedantic anecdotes which an antiquary might reasonably be expected to produce of enjoying an hour's casual reading, punctuated by those occasional, indulgent smiles which academic trifles so often trail in their wake.

What in fact they got is now a matter of literary history. The shock must have been severe, for there had been no preparation for precisely this sort of approach to the ghost story. Those who enjoyed such things were no doubt familiar with Scott or Dickens, Mrs. Oliphant perhaps, Poe, and James's cherished Le Fanu, and had been suitably intimidated by these masters of their craft; but it had been on the whole a slow and leisurely process, and sometimes rhetoric and irrelevance had numbed the receptive faculties and enfeebled the effect of all but the finest tales. The smaller fry had been ac-customed to smother themselves in ludicrous paraphernalia: phantom coaches, headless horsemen, clanking chains, spectral nuns, and what not; their language had often been more Gothick than the *Castle of Otranto*. All too often the horrific had finally subsided into rats in the wainscot or bats in the belfry, and in the final denouement the ghost had laughingly thrown aside his dread cerements and disclosed the comforting lineaments of Mr. Pickwick. At which point the author had gathered up his puppets and put them safely away for the night. But Count Magnus could hardly, it appeared, be treated quite like that. There was a deadly sort of life about these creations of the scholarly and cheerful Fellow of King's. They persisted: one thought of them at odd times; in an unfamiliar hotel bedroom, in a country lane at night (as their author had predicted), in a tram; even—*horresco referens*—in a classroom, where a very odd Latin prose indeed might suddenly be shown up. ["A School Story"]

It may be interesting and not entirely without profit to inquire for a moment into the secret of this strange and compelling power. "What," one may reasonably ask, "had an academic of even James's standing to do with the summoning of spirits from the vasty deep?" If that is any one's business it is surely the poet's: and James was not a poet. He had little of the art by which Mr. de la Mare, for example, slowly creates an atmosphere of spiritual malaise, or Ambrose Bierce that carefully-wrought world where nothing is but what is not. There is indeed no place for even the most reputable of literary airs and graces in James's discursive but grimly informative style. One thing, however, is certain. It is precisely the scholar's control, the careful restraint of the born classic, which provides these stories with the larger part of their devastating effect. No one knew better than their author the deadly power of an understatement, the value of economy, the force of a hint. And no one was more keenly aware that the gulf between the terrible and the uproariously funny is nowhere narrower than here.

Yet this very informality is itself an illusion, for it serves to conceal an intense inner excitement. It is the excitement of the antiquary and bibliophile no doubt, but who shall go about to deny that particular sort of validity? It makes its appearance at once, in the story which stands first in the canon, and it is thereafter never wholly lost. In short, these ghost stories are from one point of view at least nothing more or less than vehicles for the conveyance of James's delight in all things mediaeval, and in the men and women (though there are few of these last) who are brought into contact with them. It was basically a romantic excitement, and it goes far to explain why he was in the very first rank of scholars. One may discern a different form of it in Housman. As always it adds another cubit to the stature of the merely excellent.

James had it even as a schoolboy at Eton, for as Mr. Lubbock remarks: "A boy who could, out of the pound given him as his half's pocket money, spend on his way back to Eton sixteen shillings for the four volumes of John Albert Fabricius on the Apocrypha was obviously not as other boys" (11).

Indeed he was not, and this story has a look of inevitability as we compare it with the description of the treasure which Mr Dennistoun discovered at St. Bertrand de Coulanges [*sic*]:

Before him lay a large folio, bound, perhaps, late in the seventeenth century, with the arms of Canon Alberic de Mauléon stamped in gold on the sides. There may have been a hundred and fifty leaves of paper in the book, and on almost every one of them was fastened a leaf from an illuminated manuscript. Such a collection Dennistoun had hardly dreamed of in his wildest moments. Here were the leaves from a copy of Genesis, illustrated with pictures, which could not be later than 700 A.D. Further on was a complete set of pictures from a Psalter, of English execution, of the very finest kind that the thirteenth century could produce; and, perhaps best of all, there were twenty of uncial writing in Latin, which, as a few words seen here and there told him at once, must belong to some very early unknown patristic treatise. Could it possibly be a fragment of the copy of Papias 'On the Words of Our Lord', which was known to have existed as late as the twelfth century at Nimes? In any case, his mind was made up; that book must return to Cambridge with him, even if he had to draw the whole of his balance from the bank and stay at St. Bertrand till the money came.

This is the very stuff of romance: the impossible come to pass: the actual and tangible presence of one of those "trouvailles" which have for centuries bedevilled the imagination of the bibliophile: the poems of Sappho, an un-recorded Gutenberg, Shakespeare's manuscript of *Hamlet*. And so Canon Alberic's Scrapbook is discovered, and Mr. Dennistoun is M. R. James in disguise (you can see him sitting under the lamp in McBryde's drawing), St. Bertrand is a real place: and—well, alas, it is not quite as simple as all that. Rising behind the unsuspecting Mr. Dennistoun (who even at this greatest of moments has his rapture under control) is an appalling figure, half perceived in the shadows; and in another moment Mr. Dennistoun will have seen it too:

> The shape, whose left hand rested on the table, was rising to a standing posture behind his seat, its right hand crooked above his scalp. There was black and tattered drapery about it; the coarse hair covered it as in the drawing. The lower jaw was thin—what can I call it?—shallow, like a beast's; teeth showed behind the black lips; there was no nose; the eyes, of a fiery yellow, against which the pupils showed black and intense, and the exulting hate and thirst to destroy life which shone there, were the most horrifying feature in the whole vision. There was intelligence of a kind in them—intelligence beyond that of a beast, below that of a man.

This demon is the first of what was to be a long line of such creatures. James no doubt discovered some of them in their homes in the margins of manuscripts, on the topmost edges of cathedrals, under misericords and in odd corners of chantries. They represent, if you will, the seamier side of mediaeval life, which, as he well knew, was real enough once, before it was overlaid by sentimentality over the Gothick or the roseate visions of the nineteenth century; or had perished utterly out of mind before the appearance of either. This sinister mythology was the quarry from which he disinterred many of his agents of doom, but there are some of them whose ancestry is vastly more ancient, and who may well be coeval with the beginning of the world; though they flit from one shape to another as the ages pass, and as different tasks are required of them.

What is certain is that they are all malevolent (James was always refreshingly firm on this point)[2] and that they do not appear unless their hiding-places are disturbed, or what they have to guard is taken from them. The excited scholar, hot on some trail and stumbling on a secret, removes a stone, speaks a few words, blows a whistle perhaps, and immediately there is a rustle, a stir, a movement. Something long dormant slowly comes to life—if one may dare call it that—and the grim chase begins.

> It is thus seen that nothing is safe in this imperfect world, and that antiquaries, above all men, had better be careful. Mediaeval scrapbooks, Saxon crowns, unauthorized glimpses into the past, the treasures of Abbots, and interesting whistles picked up on the sea-shore are no doubt very fine things, but the wise man will do well to approach them with caution. Better perhaps not to approach them at all; for it may be difficult; to say the least, to restore what you have found to its rightful owner should you come to feel that it would be politic to do so—whoever, or whatever, that rightful owner may be.

This dread company of guardians and avengers emerges from every kind of lair: from tombs, from sandhills, from wells, from under gardens—even from wallpaper. They appear in country lanes, in rooms long thought to be uninhabited, in hotels, in libraries, in cathedrals. And there is no keeping them out. Sometimes they are clearly seen, but not always. Some of them inhabit bodies which were once their own but are now decayed and shrunken, covered with tattered and blackened shreds of clothing through which the miserable spectator catches a white gleam of bone. Others—and some of these the most awful—have no clearly recognizable form. They have never been even remotely human and what else they may have been, or what they are now, is any one's guess—any one, that is, whose nerves are the best part of him.

> The figure was unduly short, and was for the most part muffled in a hooded garment which swept the ground. The only part of the form which projected

---

2. See his invaluable introduction to *Ghosts and Marvels: A Selection* by V. H. Collins, Oxford, 1924.

from that shelter was not shaped like any hand or arm. Mr. Wraxall compared it to the tentacle of a devil-fish. ["Count Magnus"]

From most of them there rises a faint odour of putrefaction and mould, of centuries-old dust and cobwebs: we hear of long nails and matted hair. They should have died, but did not. And it seems they cannot. They return to their dwelling-places when their duty is done, to lie there inert—though watchful—until the stone is moved once again and a sacrilegious hand reaches forward gingerly for the treasure. Then their task is renewed, and they come out, moved by implacable malice, to carry vengeance, if need be, into the uttermost parts of the earth.[3]

Paxton looked over his shoulder and beckoned to us to come nearer to him and began speaking in a low voice: we listened most intently, of course, and compared notes afterwards, and I wrote down our version, so I am confident I have what he told us almost word for word. He said: "It began when I was first prospecting, and put me off again and again. There was always somebody—a man—standing by one of the firs. This was in daylight, you know. He was never in front of me. I always saw him with the tail of my eye on the left or the right, and he was never there when I looked straight for him. I would lie down for quite a long time and take careful observations, and make sure there was no one, and then when I got up and began prospecting again, there he was. And he began to give me hints, besides; for wherever I put that prayer-book—short of locking it up, which I did at last—when I came back to my room it was always out on my table open at the fly-leaf where the names are, and one of my razors across it to keep it open. I'm sure he just can't open my bag, or something more would have happened. You see, he's light and weak, but all the same I daren't face him. Well, then, when I was making the tunnel, of course it was worse, and if I hadn't been so keen I should have dropped the whole thing and run. It was like some one scraping at my back all the time: I thought for a long time it was only soil dropping on me, but as I got nearer the—the crown, it was unmistakable. And when I actually laid it bare and got my fingers into the ring of it and pulled it out, there came a sort of cry behind me—oh, I can't tell you how desolate it was! And horribly threatening too. It spoilt all my pleasure in my

___

3. "Already when he was installed as Provost of Eton their fame was such that Rawlins, then Vice-Provost, alluded pointedly to them in his speech on Chapel steps; and at the words 'Lemures istos' a grim smile curved the lips of the new Provost." *Memoir,* p. 39. This reference is to the stories themselves, but the latter half will serve.

find—cut it off that moment. And if I hadn't been the wretched fool I am, I should have put the thing back and left it. But I didn't."

He didn't, until it was too late; and he came to a dreadful end. ["A Warning to the Curious"]

Yet James was no mere purveyor of horrors, nor are the horrors themselves all-powerful. There is justice of a kind in this world which at times seems to slip suddenly into another dimension. Inadvertence is usually spared, and honest antiquarian curiosity can be forgiven. But the laws of this realm are capricious, and by no means to be relied upon. Mr. Dennistoun took his scrapbook safely back to Cambridge—and what a day that must have been—but poor Mr. Paxton was not so lucky, though he put his find back from whence it came. Mr. Wraxall too was harmless enough but he had to pay very heavily indeed for a few words uttered with no more than a touch of raillery. On the other hand the Reverend Mr. Somerton escaped at the trifling cost of a nervous breakdown. Let every antiquary therefore think twice, and even thrice, before he speaks, or acts: that is the plain and simple warning.

Crime and malice, however, invariably meet their just reward, terrible though this is, and it is seen that those who seek to do evil fail signally to prosper. Runes, for example, are apparently not unlike a boomerang in their effect ["Casting the Runes"], and a man who attempts to rob a poor widow of her inheritance may suffocate in a way far from pleasant ["The Tractate Middoth"]. Children who lose their hearts may come back for them ["Lost Hearts"]: so may dead men whose bones are missing ["A View from a Hill"]. Nothing unreasonable, you observe; except maybe once: in "Wailing Well." Here surely is a story which has burst the bonds of its first confining (it was read to a group of Eton scouts sitting round their camp fire), and assumed an aspect rather different from what was at first intended. "Break away from your troop and run into a wood," says the Provost, wagging an admonitory finger, "and you see what will happen to you." So far so good. Stanley Judkins was a bad boy: agreed. But this was a disproportionate punishment from a man who understood, and liked, schoolboys:

With a sudden and dreadful sinking at the heart, he caught sight of someone among the trees, waiting: and again of some one—another of the hideous black figures—working slowly along the track from another side of the field, looking from side to side, as the shepherd had described it. Worst of all, he saw a fourth—unmistakably a man this time—rising out of the bushes a few yards behind the wretched Stanley, and painfully, as it seemed, crawling into the track. On all sides the miserable victim was cut off.

Mr. Lubbock tells a different story:

> Once, on an evening late in the summer half, he was found sitting alone on a bench in Agar's Plough, where a house match was being played. He was obviously pleased and amused about something; it appeared that he had been sitting with a small new boy, and they had conversed earnestly for some time when the boy said, "You must pardon my curiosity, Sir, but are you a Master?" and when Monty explained that he was a thing called the Provost the boy replied, "Oh yes, I've often seen you about and I felt sure you were something of the kind." (45)

Nothing could be more characteristic, for nothing human was ever alien to him, and the briefest acquaintance with his work serves to reveal his acute and sympathetic observation of men and manners.[4] But there is more than this. The conversation of those of his characters who are a little removed in time has a most engaging air of authenticity about it: the very form and pressure of the scene is displayed clearly before us, whether it is a seventeenth-century courtroom, where Mr. Justice Jeffreys is trying a somewhat unusual case, an eighteenth-century vicarage, or Barchester Cathedral at an interesting moment in the history of the Gothic Revival. And is there anywhere a more delightful gallery of vergers, college servants, and other confidential factotums? Trollope himself could hardly have improved on Mr. Worby:

> "So, me knowing they were just outside, it made me bolder, and I slipped out of bed across to my little window—giving on the Close—but the dog he bored right down to the bottom of the bed—and I looked out. First go off I couldn't see anything. Then right down in the shadow under a buttress I made out what I shall always say was two spots of red—a dull red it was— nothing like a lamp or a fire, but just so as you could pick 'em out of the black shadow. I hadn't but just sighted 'em when it seemed we wasn't the only people that had been disturbed, because I saw a window in a house on the left-hand side become lighted up, and the light moving. I just turned my head to make sure of it, and then looked back into the shadow for those two red things, and they were gone, and for all I peered about and stared, there was not a sign more of them. Then come my last fright that night— something come against my bare leg—but that was all right: that was my little dog had come out of bed, and prancing about making a great to-do, only holding his tongue, and me seeing that he was quite in spirits again, I took him back to bed and we slept the night out!

---

4. "Some superficial judges thought the Provost lacking in dignity because he could descend to fun with his juniors. Nothing could be farther from the truth." *The Times*, 13 June 1936.

"Next morning I made out to tell my mother I'd had the dog in my room, and I was surprised, after all she'd said about it before, how quiet she took it. 'Did you?' she says. 'Well, by good rights you ought to go without your breakfast for doing such a thing behind my back: but I don't know as there's any great harm done, only another time you ask my permission, do you hear?' A bit after that I said something to my father about having heard the cats again. 'Cats?' he says: and he looked over at my poor mother, and she coughed and he says, 'Oh! ah! yes, cats. I believe I heard 'em myself.'

"That was a funny morning altogether: nothing seemed to go right. The organist he stopped in bed, and the minor Canon he forgot it was the 19th day and waited for the *Venite*; and after a bit the deputy he set off playing the chant for evensong, which was a minor; and then the Decani boys were laughing so much they couldn't sing, and when it came to the anthem the solo boy he got took with the giggles, and made out his nose was bleeding, and shoved the book at me what hadn't practised the verse and wasn't much of a singer if I had known it. Well, things was rougher you see, fifty years ago, and I got a nip from the counter-tenor behind me that I remembered." ["An Episode of Cathedral History"]

There is artfulness here no doubt. Ordinariness and placid domesticity (whether familiar or academic) are the perfect foil to deeds of dreadful note. But these good-humoured vignettes are not excrescences, cleverly-contrived local colour. They flower naturally out of their author's abiding interest in what was about him; in the essential savour of the daily round.

Yet this is still not all, and when we have said what we may of his learning, his seeing eye, and his humanity—all, in short, that went to make up what was Montague Rhodes James, a vast imponderable remains. That Prospero's mantle of his is not to be resolved into everyday woof and warp, and the master's wand cannot be grasped by way of the analysis of technique, however painstaking. It may be that the rich vein he discovered he also worked out:[5] others perhaps should seek fresh ground. The regretful reader

---

5. He seems to have felt this himself, in a letter written to the editor of the *London Mercury* on 12 December 1935: "I am ill satisfied with what I enclose. It comes late and is short and ill-written. There have been a good many events conspiring to keep it back, besides a growing inability. So pray don't use it unless it has some quality I do not see in it." The story in question, "A Vignette," was printed in the issue of November 1936. It had been his last, and though it is not perhaps on the level of his best there is a good deal of the old fascination in it, particularly in the description of the face seen through the gate: "It was pink and, I thought, hot, and just above the eyes the border of a white linen drapery hung down from the brows." There seems no doubt as to where it properly belonged.

(who has but thirty stories to read, and read again) can but sigh, and murmur to himself an epitaph not entirely dissimilar from one which James placed over a person of a very different sort:

IBI CUBAVIT MAGUS

Works Cited

Lubbock, S. G. *A Memoir of Montague Rhodes James.* With a List of his Writings by A. F. Scholfield. Cambridge, 1939.

The Toad in the Study:
M. R. James, H. P. Lovecraft, and
Forbidden Knowledge

Simon MacCulloch

I

H. P. Lovecraft thought highly of the stories of M. R. James. He devoted four pages to them in the "Modern Masters" section of "Supernatural Horror in Literature," concluding that "Dr. James, for all his light touch, evokes fright and hideousness in their most shocking forms; and will certainly stand as one of the few really creative masters in his darksome province." Lovecraft's enthusiasm was not reciprocated. James referred to Lovecraft's essay in a letter to a friend who had asked him to come up with authors and titles for a weird fiction collection, and credited it to "one H. P. Lovecraft, whose style is of the most offensive."

Given James's fondness for vengeance from the grave, he might have been amused to see that Lovecraft is now having his revenge for that ungracious remark. At least, Lovecraft's present-day apologists have been quick to find the James oeuvre wanting, especially in comparison with Lovecraft's. S. T. Joshi dismissed James's fiction as "thin and insubstantial," suggesting that he "knowingly limited his talents to a very restricted field." Darrell Schweitzer found James "merely quaint" when set beside Lovecraft, who "is facing, without flinching, the chief philosophical problem—and fear—of the twentieth century: the revelation, through science, of a godless, meaningless cosmos, in which mankind exists by chance, in which there are no absolute moral standards and no external source of justice or comfort."

Nevertheless Schweitzer correctly observed, following a useful comparison of the two writers' views on technique, that "Aesthetically, they are not far apart." He nicely encapsulated what difference there was when he said: "Lovecraft is a more extreme writer than James, although this is a divergence of degree rather than kind. . . . Lovecraft is, to use Clive Barker's term, an inclusionist." Despite this, he argued that there was a fundamental difference between Lovecraft and James in terms of the relationship of their fiction to their life's work as a whole: "Lovecraft's fiction is a natural and integral part of the rest of his writing and thought. James's fiction is the seasonal hobby of a man whose main interests lay elsewhere."

I hope to show that James's fiction is thematically substantial, relevant to modern readers, and a natural part of his main interests. In all these respects, James and Lovecraft are no further apart than they are aesthetically. Like Schweitzer, I see no need to discuss Lovecraft in detail. I trust that the following description of some basic similarities in outlook, followed by a detailed discussion of some of James's stories, will indicate that in terms of their central theme Lovecraft simply took what James had done a step further and thus brought it to its logical conclusion.

We can begin by mentioning the relationship of James's and Lovecraft's fiction to their intellectual lives generally. Both were first and foremost scholars, although Lovecraft was an amateur while James was a professional. Both evidently had a great thirst for knowledge and love of erudition. It seems probable that James, like Lovecraft, regarded a sense of history and cultural heritage as something to be specially cherished, as a bulwark of civilisation and a foundation for the individual's sense of identity.

For each, fiction was a relatively very small part of their life's self-expression. It was a part in which they chose to direct their efforts to the excitement of a sense of fear in their audience. Both saw fiction writing as essentially a parlour trick (to use the term that Schweitzer did in relation to James) and took great pains with the development of the ideal technique. It is reasonable to assume that their selection of themes was likewise directed towards the achievement of effect, and that it was for this reason that they were drawn constantly to the one that touched their own lives most intimately.

This is the theme of forbidden knowledge. Lovecraft and James built their lives to a great extent upon the assimilation of knowledge; in their fiction, they chose to expose the destructive aspect of this process, showing how the expansion of consciousness in its compulsive quest to secure a self-enhancing sense of meaning from the universe ultimately has the opposite effect. The horror evoked is not simply the random malignancy of a godless, meaningless cosmos—it is the diminution or displacement of the individual's sense of humanity that contact with this brings. Neither James nor Lovecraft as fiction writers were concerned with the nature of the universe as much as with the nature of the human imagination and the difficulty it encounters in sustaining a sense of full human identity in the context of an inhuman cosmos.

At the risk of overgeneralising, we might say that James's and Lovecraft's protagonists tend to be intelligent, cultivated representatives of an ordered, fatally limited world view, a brittle civilisation based on rationalism and distinctive human value. Against them are pitted barbarous antagonists who represent the chaos, irrationality, and inhumanity that an unreserved embrace of the inhuman cosmos produces. The essence of forbidden knowledge is the realisation that we may more easily be the latter than the former, and that the latter are therefore the true inheritors of the world, the former the eternal outsiders.

That realisation involves the destruction of the idea of a god in human image, which placed human values such as love, justice, and wisdom at the centre of creation. Lovecraft's fiction may be viewed as the next stage from James's in depicting the degeneration of an anthropomorphic god. At the centre of Lovecraft's fictional cosmos was Azathoth, an embodiment of all-fathering primal chaos. The central deity of James's fictional cosmos, although never explicitly stated, can be discerned as something that hovers between an Old Testament-styled god of patriarchal anger and vengeance, and his predecessors, a cruel pantheon interested in mankind chiefly as a source of sacrifices. While Lovecraft's god is utterly inhuman, James's tends merely to be savage, and his lesser supernatural beings are likewise more humanoid, or at least less inclined to assert total independence of the known animal kingdom. In either case these beings symbolise what we find when we look to the universe at large for augmentation of our sense of human identity. Thus James showed us man's image of himself being supplanted by an image of a beast, and Lovecraft that image supplanted by one of primal molecular formlessness. Their lasting literary worth is due to the fact that both were equally exercised by the question of what being human meant, and well equipped by temperament and pursuits to present that question in supernatural fiction with exceptional power.

Some of that power derives from the fact that, thanks to their scholarly lives, their stories are unusually suggestive of a rich and weighty legacy of human knowledge and civilisation. When this is undermined by the revelation of how hopelessly far beyond assimilation into a human-centred philosophy the universe really is, our sense of the terrifying power of the revelation and the catastrophe it brings is magnified by the sense of completeness with which what is destroyed has been endowed. In other words, human thought and history in James and Lovecraft is a large and detailed piece of architecture; this makes its collapse satisfyingly noisy.

Ron Weighell has argued persuasively that the power of James's stories derives from tension between his private fascination with magic and public adherence to conventional Christianity. Rosemary Pardoe has slightly modified this, suggesting that James was troubled by "the dichotomy between the comfortable Christian world view of his upbringing, which he wanted to accept but couldn't, and the darkly amoral version of pantheism which, try as he might to deny it to himself, he felt truly reflected the state of the world." Certainly there is a strong element in James's stories of a Christian Church built upon and thus undermined by paganism. There is also an acute awareness of a fall from grace, manifested in specific references to the Garden of Eden myth and more generally in a pervasive theme of guilt and punishment. Where Lovecraft's universe is indifferent to the human race, James's seems more often to be angry with us.

But the dramatic appeal of the theme of forbidden knowledge goes deeper than the question of subscription to alternative philosophies. It draws ultimately on the eternal unease of the disciplined yet enquiring mind, which scholars especially must come to terms with, engaged as they are upon what amounts to a quest for omniscience in their specialism, always aware that some newly discovered anomaly may at any time demolish a viewpoint, and with it a reputation, that has taken a lifetime's work to construct—yet unable, emotionally or intellectually, to shirk the task of uncovering the next stone. Lovecraft's and James's claim to our attention rests on the skill and insight with which they not only expressed this unease, but brought out its relevance to the question of human identity in general. In so doing, they produced fiction that is by nature subversive, regardless of the predominant world view at the time it is read, because its most basic effect is to challenge the notion that human beings are capable of sustaining a meaningful world view at all.

Let's turn now to James's stories, starting with one of the earliest. "Lost Hearts" is almost unique among his tales in its use of a child protagonist without the setting having dictated the matter, as it did in "A School Story" and "Wailing Well." (The "almost" is in deference to "The Residence at Whitminster," which, as we shall see later, is in part an expansion of "Lost Hearts.") "Lost Hearts" renders the theme of the destructive aspect of the acquisition of knowledge as a child's loss of innocence, with the revelation that god is inhuman taking the form of an orphan's discovery that his new "father" is barbarously evil. Stephen Elliott, possessed of "the keenest curiosity," puts numerous questions to the housekeeper of his new home, Mrs. Bunch, who is a valuable source of information on such questions as "Who built the temple at the end of the laurel walk?" but answers less reliably to "Is Mr. Abney a good man, and will he go to heaven?"

Abney, as James makes increasingly clear, is not a good man, and he has no intention of going to heaven if he can avoid it. Described as "a man wrapped up in his books," Abney almost immediately reveals his lack of concern for human affairs: "Take him to Mrs. Bunch's room, Parkes, and let him have his tea—supper—whatever it is." His detachment extends to the ghosts of the children he has killed; he notes early intimations of their intentions in his "book" with the same clinical interest as he notes Stephen's birthday. In his association of occult knowledge with savage inhumanity, Abney sets the pattern for James's most eminent villains.

Such a villain's fall is not an event that any writer could expect to inspire fear in his audience, and it is very much secondary to the true business of "Lost Hearts." The emotional core of the story is the effect upon Stephen's view of human nature and society, and thus of himself, that Abney's inhumanity creates. James carefully charts a steady decline in Stephen's trust in the reassurances given by adults, from the bare indication that Mrs. Bunch's reply regarding her employer's beneficence is "less satisfactory" than her earlier answers, through Stephen's ready recognition that Parkes is lying when he pretends that his description of his own supernatural encounter was a joke, to a climax in the story's final paragraph, where Stephen's access to forbidden knowledge in the form of Mr. Abney's "book" is said to have "led him to a very different conclusion" from the clearly inadequate opinion of the coroner. As the Edenic delusion in which Abney's enquiries as to his victims' lack of relatives appear "all as kind as heart could wish" falls away before Stephen's "miscellaneous cross-examination," the predatory wilderness of the real world is revealed.

The ghosts of Abney's victims represent those who have already been cast out into that wilderness. The menace that they direct towards Abney is emphasised less than the "unappeasable hunger and longing" created by the theft of their hearts. Their physical appearance cleverly appropriates a gruesome aspect of death—the fact that fingernails continue to grow for a time after it—to produce an image of fear, not of death, but of becoming a monster. The power of such spectres resides in their fusion of equally strong physical and emotional properties and the intimate relevance of these to the emotional situation of the story's protagonist. Joel Lane has covered this point well, referring to "the highly personalised nature of the supernatural encounters. There is a sense of private nemesis, of the 'ghost' being linked to some dark element in the lives of the characters." Such encounters also have a more general aesthetic force. James and Lovecraft made good use of the fact that an especially disturbing way of undermining our view of ourselves is to show us our own dead "oddly bodied." This grounds the doubt about the integrity of our natures that the story sets out to create in the one surrender to chaos that we can all be relied upon to fear and regard as inevitable, that of death and the decay that follows it. Playing on this helped James to achieve his aim to "put the reader into the position of saying to himself, 'If

I'm not very careful, something of this kind may happen to me!'" in a more subtle and profound way than he could through verisimilitude alone. As with other features of the theme of dehumanisation, Lovecraft took this further than James without disturbing its essential meaning or effect.

Becoming a monster is what Stephen is really afraid of. This is made clear in the most important and disturbing scene in the story, when Stephen discovers that one of the ghosts has visited him in his sleep and tried to claw its way to his heart. It is obvious from this that the ghosts are not to be seen as Stephen's allies in some kind of Good versus Evil confrontation, or simply as avengers. They are here to show us the outcome of the process symbolised by Abney's intention to steal Stephen's heart, namely the removal of his ability to love by virtue of a loveless upbringing, externalise his growing realisation of what is being done to him, and reflect his desperation for some token of the loving kindness that he has been led to believe defines humanity. The final point that the story makes is that once lost the ability to love is unlikely to be recovered. The boy's hurdy-gurdy remains tuneless. The ghosts do not take Abney's heart. There is no restoration at the story's end, only another open wound.

In recent years horror writers have been much exercised by the theme of child abuse and its dehumanising effects. "Lost Hearts" is as eloquent a statement as any of the psychological consequences of lovelessness. It is one example of the relevance of James's fiction to modern readers by virtue of its treatment of perennial concerns.

To show the close relationship of James's fiction to his main interests, we can turn to "Canon Alberic's Scrap-book." The story does not merely draw on James's antiquarian career to provide an interesting setting for supernatural events (which would give no grounds for saying that the story was "about" antiquarianism); the supernatural events directly express a real emotional and ethical issue arising from that career. It is an issue of narrower concern and less potency than that addressed by "Lost Hearts," hence the story is less engaging; nevertheless, it is one that remains pertinent today.

This is the tendency of the desire for knowledge to degenerate into a desire for possession, and for collecting to turn into plundering, public acquisition into private hoarding. The scrapbook of the story's title is a neat symbol for this: a book, which in the hands of a true scholar would have contained descriptions of artifacts, thus widening public appreciation of them, has become instead a repository for stolen portions of the artifacts themselves, with the opposite effect. Canon Alberic has subsequently progressed—or, more properly in terms of the story's morality, regressed—to outright treasure hunting, and in so doing has raised a demon of acquisitiveness, characterised as such by its grasping, spiderlike hands and its eyes containing "intelligence beyond that of a beast, below that of a man."

As in "Lost Hearts," we are not really concerned with the character who has already sold his soul, but with the one in whom the evidence of that transaction awakens a by no means groundless fear that his own life is leading towards the same conclusion. Dennistoun is described as having a "conscience ... tenderer than a collector's," and the story is essentially an exposition of the workings of that conscience in a situation designed to arouse, compromise, and threaten to destroy it.

With customary conciseness, James adopts a setting suggestive of a past in the process of being lost: St. Bertrand de Comminges is "decayed," it "has a cathedral which is visited by a certain number of tourists." Dennistoun hopes to salvage it, he intends to "fill a notebook and to use several dozens of plates in the process of describing and photographing every corner of the wonderful church." It is typical of James's storytelling economy that what strikes us primarily as humorous leavening is a subtle development of the story's subtext: "Mingled suspicions that he was keeping the old man from his dejeuner, that he was regarded as likely to make away with St. Bertrand's ivory crozier, or with the dusty stuffed crocodile that hangs over the font, began to torment him." This jocular observation marks the start of the shift in the ethical ground on which Dennistoun finds himself. It begins to associate Dennistoun's activity, or at least his own guilty worries about it, with plundering; by virtue of the way in which Dennistoun's "torment" derives from and mirrors the sacristan's more dreadful suffering, it foreshadows the way in which Dennistoun will later undergo a lesser version of the demonic torment of both the sacristan and Alberic.

James engineers the rest of the shift in Dennistoun's outlook from altruistic scholar to self-seeking treasure hunter with typical smoothness. When the crucial subject of the scrapbook is raised, "At once all Dennistoun's cherished dreams of finding priceless manuscripts in untrodden corners of France flashed up, to die down again the next moment. . . . Where was the likelihood that a place so near Toulouse would not have been ransacked long ago by collectors?" When he sees the book, he determines that it "must return to Cambridge with him, even if he had to draw the whole of his balance from the bank and stay at St. Bertrand till the money came." Having bought the book, Dennistoun is "impatient to examine his prize by himself," and is soon "alone in his bedroom, taking stock of Canon Alberic's treasures." It is clear from his opening statement to himself on this occasion— "Bless Canon Alberic!"—that he has by now almost become morally at one with the treasure hunter. The point when he becomes fully so is symbolised by the removal of the crucifix given to him by the sacristan's daughter, and the simultaneous appearance on the same table of the demon's hand. The fact that it is the hand that appears first confirms the demon's role as an incarnation of theft. In turn, we can see that the power of the crucifix that James places in such blatant symbolic opposition to it derives not from its religious significance but from the fact that it represents the opposite of theft, a gift freely given to a stranger. Insofar as the choice of gift is significant, it is as an icon of unsolicited sacrifice.

We may pause to note that this sort of painstaking build-up to the supernatural climax is the sort of thing that James had in mind when he spoke of the desirability of "a nicely managed crescendo," rather than the "fanfare" at the climax itself that his remark led Joshi to expect. It is a method that remains crucial to the efficacy of some of the best modern supernatural horror stories—Ramsey Campbell's "The Guy" (1973) is an excellent example.

Dennistoun manages to reverse his choice, and subsequently purges the scrapbook of its taint of greed by paying for a Mass for Canon Alberic's soul—a purging represented by the burning of the drawing of the demon in it. The fact that there is no harm in keeping a photograph of the demon reflects the harmlessness of Dennistoun's church photography by comparison with Canon Alberic's plundering. James has exorcised the guilt generated by the process of acquisition by clarifying the distinction between the sort of collecting that destroys the past and the sort that preserves it.

"Canon Alberic's Scrap-book" is a working through of a question of principle relating to James's profession. It also serves generally as an expression of belated guilt about the ransacking of ancient cultures to fill foreign museums and fear about the consequent demands for payback. Its subtle presentation of the endless transferability of guilt, and the dual moral possibilities inherent in its central character and its central artifact, make it a more psychologically convincing and morally acute approach to this topic than the standard one of a curse on Egyptian tomb robbers.

James went on to intensify the cursed treasure motif in subsequent stories, as a way of amplifying the theme of possessiveness which was one aspect of his overall theme of the loss of human identity to an inhuman universe. In "Canon Alberic's Scrap-book," the posture of the demon when it is about to attack Dennistoun suggests a possessive embrace: "The shape, whose left hand rested on the table, was rising to a standing posture behind his seat, its right hand crooked above his scalp." In "The Treasure of Abbot Thomas," James brings this image and the idea behind it into sharper focus when the protagonist pulls what he supposes to be a bag of gold out of its hole: "It hung for an instant on the edge of the hole, then slipped forward on to my chest, and *put its arms round my neck.*" The point that the would-be possessor of treasure has been possessed by it is emphasised by the "several—I don't know how many—legs or arms or tentacles or something clinging to my body." Where Dennistoun was able, in a strictly limited sense, to bring his prize home, Somerton is happy simply to escape. Even that is denied Paxton, the protagonist of James's climactic statement on the subject, "A Warning to the Curious"; he "must have dashed straight into the open arms" of his treasure's guardian.

The clear progression in these three stories from man-gets-treasure to treasure-gets-man is evident not only in the confrontation with the guardian and its outcome, but in the path by which the protagonist comes to it. Dennistoun, we may infer, is the first likely recipient for the scrapbook and its demon to have come the sacristan's way, and very nearly avoids the whole affair when the latter hesitates to carry out his opportunistic plan: "Here came a strange pause of irresolution, as it seemed; then, with a sort of plunge, he went on: 'But if monsieur is *amateur des vieux livres,* I have at home something that might interest him.'" Abbot Thomas replaces the sacristan's irresolution with an intricate and deliberate trap that seems to have been specially designed to catch an antiquarian like Somerton. Finally, in "A Warning to the Curious," Paxton is fated to dig up the crown to such a degree that he seems to have virtually no choice in the matter.

The point that possessions may end up owning us rather than vice versa is commonplace, but in these three stories James made it with uncommon power, expressing a deepening fear of attachment to objects, coupled with a desire to know without possessing, to see without touching. This feeds into his central theme of the difficulty of sustaining a sense of full human identity in the context of an inhuman cosmos; the individual looks compulsively outside himself for something on which to found his sense of identity ("Shall I live an object of envy?" asks Canon Alberic) and instead of assimilating what he finds is completely displaced by it ("Paxton was so totally without connections that all enquiries that were subsequently made ended in a No Thoroughfare").

The intensification of expression and consequent increase in power of these successive treatments refutes Joshi's allegation that "James showed little development over his career; if anything, there is a decline in power and originality . . ." James was aware of the danger of repetition, a weakness he criticised in Le Fanu. His apologetic footnote to "The Haunted Dolls' House," a written-to-order piece, acknowledges that "this is no more than a variation on a former story of mine called 'The Mezzotint.'" We can infer from this that given a freer rein James would return to a motif or plot only if he felt he had not exhausted its potential. His oeuvre yields several examples of successive renditions of key elements that are more in the nature of clarifications than mere variations.

II

At the end of the first part of this essay I suggested that James's oeuvre yields several examples of successive renditions of key elements that are more in the nature of clarifications than mere variations. Another of these occurs in relation to a complementary motif to that of cursed treasure, the cursed gift, and its associated theme, transfer of guilt. The sacristan's reluctant passing on to Dennistoun of Canon Alberic's book is developed into a more premeditated and insistent transaction in "Casting the Runes"; we might say that a cursed gift has become a gifted curse. Again, James progressed from fairly routine use of an idea to a treatment that has a strong claim to being definitive, and did so not simply by devising a more telling kind of supernatural confrontation around which to build his narrative, but by redrawing the itinerary of the story so as to bring out its moral and psychological content to the full.

"Casting the Runes" is about victimisation. It deals with how being singled out as an object of punishment, however uncalled for, produces a sense of separation from everyone except fellow victims. James sets the psychological scene with a description of a magic lantern show used by Mr. Karswell to frighten local children out of trespassing, and punish them for earlier transgressions. The episode seems to contribute nothing to the story's plot; it does, however, serve to remind us how we are conditioned from early childhood by images of dreadful and disproportionate punishment. Its progress from a wolf howling in the distance, through a monster in Lufford Park, to "a great mass of snakes, centipedes and disgusting creatures with wings" which overflows the picture, presents a condensed version of the increasingly claustrophobic persecution that Mr. Dunning is to suffer.

When the story proper gets under way, it provides another classic example of the Jamesian crescendo, "the gradual removal of one safeguard after another, the victim's dim forebodings of what is to happen gradually growing clearer . . ." ("M. R. James on J. S. Le Fanu"). These forebodings also, significantly, become more personal, beginning with an advertisement on a tram window that anyone may see, followed by the passing of a leaflet that in theory is one of many (although it is clear to the reader, if not to Dunning, that in fact the distributor has been waiting for him alone), and culminating in the passing of the runes themselves, which require not only personal delivery but personal, albeit unwitting, acceptance. Thus James creates the sense of being singled out for special attention that is essential to the guilt associated

with the receipt of punishment; the events serve not only his plot, which requires Dunning to learn about Karswell's last victim, but also the mood of
the story, which derives from its psychology.

James brings out this mood to the full when he describes Dunning's feelings as Karswell's curse begins to take effect: "It seemed to him that something ill-defined and impalpable had stepped in between him and his fellow
men—had taken him in charge, as it were." Safeguards—other passengers
on the train, his servants, electric light—are swiftly removed. Then he
touches "a mouth, with teeth, and with hair about it" in "the well-known
nook under the pillow." This invasion of the innermost sanctum of Dunning's privacy climaxes the first part of the story proper by bringing the feeling of closing in that has been driving the narrative to a conclusion in what
is probably the most exquisitely intimate of all James' horrific encounters.

It is instructive to compare "Casting the Runes" with an unpublished,
unfinished draft that was evidently a prototype for it ("John Humphreys"). In
the draft, the runes take the form of some voodoo-style objects left by a mysterious stranger on the newly inherited country estate of a Mr. Humphreys.
This causes him to be pursued by a frightful fiend whose presence causes
feelings of intense loneliness, oppression, and despair. In Humphreys's case,
however, James associates these feelings explicitly with a fear of death, and
enables them to be banished by quoting from the Bible. The warnings are
given in a book read in a dream, and subsequently in one that appears unaccountably open on Humphreys's library table.

"Casting the Runes" shows a number of improvements on its prototype,
all of them designed to sharpen the story's psychological focus. The irrelevant references to death and the Bible have been dropped. The runes must
be both handed over in person to the victim and accepted, thus tricking him
into a sense of complicity with his doom and creating a consequent increase
of guilt and isolation. The distraction of the mystery of the stranger's identity
and motive is removed—we know what Karswell is up to and why from the
beginning, which strengthens the idea of a personal vendetta and provides
the story with more suspense and a feeling of relentlessness. Where several
of Mr. Humphreys's encounters with his follower, including the climactic
one, took place out of doors in the countryside, the enclosed suburban settings of "Casting the Runes" contribute to its claustrophobia. We have already noted how the sort of warnings given to Dunning complement this
effect; there was no such complementary effect in those given to Humphreys, which did not become increasingly personalised.

But the most important question from a thematic point of view is what
we find in "Casting the Runes" in place of Humphreys's "valley of the

shadow of death" and the means of escape from it, "I will fear no evil." For Dunning, the valley of shadow is the path to self-destruction on which the fear, guilt, and ultimately self-hatred produced by victimisation sets him. It is important that neither of the demon's victims are actually killed by it, only driven, in effect, to seek out fatal accidents. Consider the sense of uselessness and burgeoning self-loathing, the inability to trust either others or oneself, conveyed by the following: "He dared not go to the museum; in spite of what the assistant had said, Karswell might turn up there, and Dunning felt he could not cope with a probably hostile stranger. His own house was odious; he hated sponging on the doctor."

Dunning's remedy is to rid himself of guilt by sending it back where it belongs. It will be apparent by now that, while "Casting the Runes" is a development of the transfer of guilt theme of "Canon Alberic's Scrap-book," it has also evolved directly from the child abuse theme of "Lost Hearts." To the classic symptoms of child abuse already noted we may add Dunning's inability to talk about what has been done to him. This is, of course, characteristic of supernatural experiences as well, as James points out in "A Neighbour's Landmark"; but James gives the unmentionability of the demon's depredations a climactic position in "Casting the Runes" when he concludes the story with a brilliantly devised triple evasion, whereby the deceased Harrington only speaks of them in his sleep; his brother eventually relents from his initial refusal to tell Dunning what was said sufficiently to repeat "something of what he has heard"; but he is quickly stopped, and the narrator passes none of it on to the reader. This also reflects the way in which the mind tries to bury a trauma; the tendency for the runes to slip away in a breeze so that they cannot be returned complements this with a splendid image for the tendency of the emotional effects of trauma to become separated from their source, leaving the latter untraceable, and for guilt to take on a life of its own. This is how the remedy for it, confrontation of the perpetrator and clarification of exactly whose is the crime, is most likely to be frustrated.

The importance of the magic lantern show to the story's structure may now be appreciated. While Dunning's book review acts as the excuse for his suffering, the charge that the abuser trumps up to transfer the guilt for the act of abuse to the victim, the magic lantern show may be seen as a representation of the act of abuse itself, an act hidden from Dunning in the "prologue" to his adult life that contains the key to its otherwise not wholly graspable course.

I have already mentioned the popularity of the theme of child abuse with modern horror writers. In the context of "Casting the Runes," we can refine this observation slightly and note the popularity of the theme of adults coming to terms with childhood abuse. Stephen King's "The Library Policeman" (1990) and Robert Devereaux's *Deadweight* (1994) are examples. Of course, James did not make the theme explicit. Probably he deemed it inappropriate for a supernatural horror story to display the fuel of its emotional processes on deck; by keeping it in the engine room in "Casting the Runes" he puts his readers more firmly into Dunning's shoes, making us share his not wholly focused foreboding and not wholly directed panic as details of his predicament emerge with a combination of stark sensuous clarity and ominous hidden significance. In any case, we need not feel obliged to pin "Casting the Runes" down to a single psychosocial scenario, because it is as central to James's theme of dehumanisation as any of his stories. Like any other vengeful revenant, Dunning returns from the valley of shadow to do to his "murderer" what has been done to him; he has, if only temporarily, been made into an outcast and a reflection of the inhumanity he has suffered.

This leads us to the idea of justice in James's fiction. Albert Power has noted the prevalence of a sense of arbitrary justice, evidently inherited from Le Fanu. The form that moral authority takes in James's work is another example of a deity revealed as savage, whereby James expresses another aspect of our failure to find support for civilised human values in the universe at large. This produces a dilemma concerning the limits of rationality where once more we shall find him very much in sympathy with more recent horror fiction.

An obsession with holding what is theirs is one of the distinguishing characteristics of James's villains. As well as Karswell there is Dr. Rant in "The Tractate Middoth," whose ploy with wills enables him to avoid letting go of his property even after death, and Count Magnus, who has achieved the same thing literally. It is notable that when, as in Karswell's and the Count's case, magic is available, the punishment of trespassers takes the same form—a chase through the woods by a supernatural being. The similarity of this to the way in which the punishment of the first trespassers, Adam and Eve, is usually depicted, can scarcely have escaped James.

This emerges all the more forcefully when we consider the stories that involve the despoiling of churches, "Canon Alberic's Scrap-book," "The Stalls of Barchester Cathedral," and "The Uncommon Prayer-Book." In the first of these, we are reminded that "Some spirits there be that are created for vengeance, and in their fury lay on sore strokes." In the second, a wood carver, inspired by a dream, uses wood from a Hanging Oak to create a talisman against murderers in the cathedral. In the third, a book dealer who steals prayer books from a chapel finds that they are capable of more than mere self-defence by virtue of the fact that they have been imbued with a desire to punish an earlier and greater enemy of the Church. One might well conclude that the moral of these tales is that the Church is as well equipped and ruthless as Count Magnus in its deployment of demons to protect its property, and that it derives its authority to be so from its deity's equally jealous protection of the fruits of the trees of knowledge of good and evil and of life.

It is possible to classify this motif as a playful revenge fantasy aimed at pillagers who interfered with the antiquarian's profession. But in "The Stalls of Barchester Cathedral" the crime is not theft but murder, and we can look to one of James's other murder stories for a fuller exposition of what "divine justice" meant to him. In "Martin's Close," a murderer is brought to justice by the ghost of his victim, an action which Mr. Attorney informs us "doth afford a great instance of God's revenge against murder, and that He will require the blood of the innocent." The fact that, uniquely for James, the revenant acts merely as witness, rather than as judge, jury, and executioner, suggests that we should attach special importance to how James portrays the justice to which the murderer is delivered in "Martin's Close." The implication is that here we are being shown in more absolute form the authority that is usually delegated to avenging spectres. Unsurprisingly, therefore, Judge Jeffreys's entirely convincing mixture of impatience, savage humour, and an anger that is always on the verge of erupting (as it does at the story's conclusion) is exactly the sort of character we can imagine James's vengeful revenants possessing. Jeffreys is more daunting than any reanimated corpse, however; he really does have the power to grant life or death, and exercises it like a stern Old Testament god of wrath and revenge, on the verge of degenerating into a pagan one of tyranny, caprice, and sacrifice.

Yet the alternative that James offers is even less attractive. This is the face, "large, smooth and pink," of a system of justice that has become a corrupt game of words, the outcome ensured by "abominable questions," the answers to which are twisted or, literally, laughed out of court—a travesty beside which Jeffreys's brutal gallows humour is almost likeable. Its hairlessness and single tooth are deliberate contrasts to the savage aspect of James's avengers, while its closed eyes are an ironic parody of "blind justice," suggestive here of a hopelessly restricted viewpoint to which we may compare Jeffreys's willingness to admit evidence of the supernatural. In "The Rose Garden," James expressed doubt about the ability of a civilised version of justice, rooted insecurely in shallow rationality, to deal reliably with the chaos of reality on our behalf.

"The Story of a Disappearance and an Appearance" echoes "Martin's Close," with the Jeffreys-like Uncle Henry, who "had more than a little of the martinet in his composition," dispensing his own justice; here, though,

James has added a well-chosen symbol for his doubts about modern society's competence to administer it in the form of the Punch and Judy show. "A Neighbour's Landmark" follows up "The Rose Garden" by painting a similarly distressing picture of the effect on our sense of security and wellbeing of unremedied injustice.

In presenting us with this unpleasant choice, James was making the same point as Stephen King's *The Stand* (1978). King's moral was that civilisation based on rationalism was bound to destroy itself because it failed to admit the essential unknowability of the universe. When it collapsed, our last resort in the face of utter chaos would be "a hard God, a jealous God" who "always asks for a sacrifice. His hands are bloody with it." James gives us less wide-screen but equally dramatic collapses in "civilised" society—the cannibalistic scholar ("Lost Hearts"), the murderous schoolmaster, archdeacon, or "gentleman of good estate" ("A School Story," "The Stalls of Barchester Cathedral," "Martin's Close"), the grave-robbing antiquary ("A View from a Hill"), the fraudulent "lady of title" ("A Neighbour's Landmark")—and suggests that "an eye for an eye" may be the nearest thing to firm moral ground that we can find. In taking this ground, however, we reduce ourselves to something that is "so ugly and frightened his children so much that he burnt it."

Lovecraft was more pessimistic still. The new dark age to which he was inclined to consign us after civilisation had failed to cope with "black seas of infinity" was one of worship of the Great Old Ones, which amounted to an orgy of indiscriminate killing—the ultimate stage in the devolution of god from dispenser of justice to unheeding recipient of futile sacrifice.

James was less radical than Lovecraft in his deconstruction of the idea of absolute justice. The fact that King was no more radical than James in this respect suggests that we should dismiss our most popular contemporary on the charge of being too old-fashioned if we do so to James. When it came to codifying an unknowable cosmos in terms that might form the basis for the survival of human society in it, both James and King felt able to resort, if not to the Bible as a whole, at least to the Old Testament; only Lovecraft substituted the *Necronomicon*.

James drew specifically on the Old Testament for what we may regard as his climactic statement on the subject of justice, one cleverly designed to show how inextricably the issue is bound to that of the limitations of rationalism. "Two Doctors" retells the story of Cain and Abel (a murder motivated by professional jealousy) in the form of a scrappy collection of "materials for a case" which was never tried. James invites the reader to "see what you can make of it." In other words, we are invited to assume the role of prosecutor and/or judge and jury, and see if we can convict Dr. Abell. As Lance Arney has shown, this is a challenge that we can scarcely resist, even though the task proves "stressful and problematic." We know that Abell killed Quinn, and why, but the how narrowly eludes us, because we have not been given all the evidence—"The *dossier* is not complete." In the end, we cannot quite make the pieces we have fit, and our case against Abell fails. Like Cain, he remains at large among us, and we cannot touch him. "Two Doctors" anticipates the idea of "interactive" fiction to make us realise afresh what the mark of Cain really means—that our estrangement through civilisation from the primitive concept of divinely sanctioned retribution leaves a gap which our feeble powers of knowledge and interpretation are unable to fill satisfactorily. The final line, in which we are told that a perhaps unwitting accessory to the murder "suffered heavy penalties," is a bitter recognition that a civilised version of justice is simply beyond us.

So too is any surety in knowledge, another lack the apprehension of which James expresses in terms of bitter loss through clear references to Old Testament myth. This is the theme of "The Residence at Whitminster," which begins with a page-long description of Thomas Ashton, Doctor of Divinity, seated in his study in a state of apparently perfect order, with the prospect of his walled garden against the mellow background of "a field that was park-like in character" before him—"But all that Dr. Ashton could find to say, after contemplating this prospect for many minutes, was: 'Abominable!'"

It is not the prospect that Ashton finds abominable, but disruption of the strictly ordered and carefully tended existence that it represents by the sorcerous activities of Lord Saul. We are reminded of the similarly peaceful landscape described at the beginning of "Lost Hearts," and the remark that ". . . all who knew anything of Mr. Abney looked upon him as a somewhat austere recluse, into whose steadygoing household the advent of a small boy would import a new and, it seemed, incongruous element." In "The Residence at Whitminster" James develops the Garden of Eden subtext of "Lost Hearts" more fully and relates it to the way an untamed, childlike imagination will inevitably overstep the boundaries of an ordered but limited world view to admit the chaos of the unknowable universe beyond. Frank Sydall plays the part of Stephen Elliott; Ashton, with his "angry eye" and disciplinarian reputation ("Your arm was stout enough in the old days . . ."), is the patriarch to whom his education is entrusted; Saul, like the ghosts in "Lost Hearts," externalises Frank's realisation that his patriarch is failing him and embodies the state of loss and degradation with which that failure threatens him.

Saul's scrying glass is the forbidden fruit that opens Frank's eyes to Ashton's shortcoming. It reveals the world beyond the garden: "The same boy now turned his face towards the wall of the garden, and beckoned with both his raised hands, and as he did so I was conscious that some moving objects were becoming visible over the top of the wall—whether heads or other parts of some animal or human forms I could not tell." It is proof that the Doctor of Divinity is not omniscient, a discovery for which the ground has been prepared prior to the scrying glass's introduction: ". . . he would often put a question to the doctor about the old books in the library that required some thought to answer." In "Lost Hearts" James depicted an orphaned humanity's loss of faith in the idea of a universe centred on benevolence; in "The Residence at Whitminster," we see the same orphan's loss of faith in the idea of a universe centred on knowledge. When we are shown Saul, the outcast of a "vain man and neglectful father," "clinging desperately to the great ring of the door," we recall not merely his Biblical namesake's necromancy, but the reason for it: "God has turned away from me and answers me no more."

The thematic relationship of the second half of "The Residence at Whit-minster" to its first half is similar to that of "The Rose Garden" to "Martin's Close"; it shows the corruption and chaos that threatens to overwhelm the value with which the story is concerned (justice in "The Rose Garden," knowledge in "The Residence at Whitminster") when we can no longer believe in a deity who embodies it in absolute form. That loss of belief is represented by the treatment given to the books written by Ashton's successor, Dr. Oldys, "which occupy a place that must be honoured, since it is so rarely touched, upon the shelves of many a substantial library." James reinforces this estrangement from the old world view by satirizing the Edenic quality of his opening description of Ashton's prospect on the world by means of Mary Oldys's parodic introduction to her letter to her friend Emily. The transparent falseness of this indicates how unsustainable the illusion of a universe organised for humankind's benefit has now become; her abrupt switch to a more natural style when she begins to describe the supernatural events emphasises the fact that the new world whose inhuman chaos they condense is both exclusive of the human-centred outlook and more real than it.

For the divinely appointed order of nature suggested by that opening description James now substitutes an invasion of unidentifiable insects. He dwells on the inability of Oldys, his niece, or Spearman to classify them, to the extent of inserting a footnote on the matter which may remind us of the classifying activities of the Royal Society, to which James refers in "Two Doctors." As in that story, James is here rubbing our noses in the limitations on our powers of knowledge and understanding, making the point that the universe is quite beyond the compass of human ordering. Oldys's climactic encounter with the giant version of the species is prefaced appropriately by assaults on his candlelight and book; his insistence on clinging blindly to the latter ironically emphasises the redundancy of his writings and the futility of faith in the power of knowledge to deal with the persistent unknowability of the universe.

In the end, as with the problem of justice, James offers a difficult choice between order maintained by clinging to an old position that no longer fully meets our needs and the chaos that we risk admitting by abandoning it. We can try to preserve the order of our household by restricting our world view to what we can understand and thus control, which is the option chosen by Dr. Oldys; if we do not, the chaos of reality will impose itself upon us in the way represented by the disorderly thought processes of Mrs. Maple. As James makes clear, neither is satisfactory; to which of the two would you take your questions?

III

At the end of the second part of this essay, I suggested that Dr. Oldys's decision in "The Residence at Whitminster" to keep the mystery of Lord Saul's activities under lock and key was an attempt to preserve the order of his household by restricting its view of the universe to what he could understand and thus control. Although James made it clear that this solution was unsatisfactory, he cannot be said to disapprove wholly of Oldys's decision. Like Judge Jeffreys's version of justice, such an arbitrary assertion of order may be all that keeps the wilderness at bay. In the final paragraph of "Stories I Have Tried to Write," he tells us: "Late on Monday night a toad came into my study: and, though nothing has so far seemed to link itself with this appearance, I feel that it may not be quite prudent to brood over topics which may open the interior eye to the presence of more formidable visitants."

The remark, describing a real occurrence,[1] is lightly made, but as we have seen, the understatedness of James's final paragraphs often conceals a climactic thematic weight. We can take the toad in the study as an image for the essence of the inspiration for all James's stories. The threat of something inhuman taking up its abode with us and ultimately expelling us recurs throughout James's work, encapsulating the idea that our increasing feeling of exposure to and isolation in a non-human universe will draw us outside and ultimately exile us from our sense of human value and the civilisation that it supports. Lord Saul's "ugly thin ghost" is James's most powerful depiction of this exile; his diminished humanity ("withered heart") has left him

---

1. M. R. James, letter of 11 November 1929; *Letters to a Friend*, ed. Gwendolen McBryde (London: Edward Arnold, 1956).

Up against that same window, particular when they've had a fire of a chilly evening, with his face right on the panes, and his hands fluttering out, and his mouth open and shut, open and shut, for a minute or more, and then gone off in the dark yard. But open the window at such times, no, that they dare not do, though they could find it in their heart to pity the poor thing, that pinched up with the cold, and seemingly fading away to nothing as the years passed on.

It is upon hearing this description that Oldys, like James, decides that the time has come to declare "enough said."

The toad is not a symbol of evil, but of that which is alien, beyond assimilation into a fully cohesive, socially reinforcing philosophy. We have noted that the tension between a desire for all-encompassing order and an inability to ignore the anomalous may be especially characteristic of the scholarly temperament. By way of example of how James went about making his personal feelings capable of wider application and appreciation, we can compare "The Residence at Whitminster" to the unpublished draft that seems to have been its prototype ("The Fenstanton Witch"). In "The Fenstanton Witch," two young necromancers, ostensibly studying at Cambridge to be priests, see more than they bargained for when they try to summon the corpse of a witch and meet a demon instead. The source of the horror in "The Fenstanton Witch" is the undermining of the university as a bulwark of civilisation by their dark and unpredictable experiments. Unsurprisingly, the story is less disturbing for those of us for whom Cambridge University is less apt to function as a symbol for the home of absolute knowledge than it may have been for James, hence his transfer of the event into the more generally accessible framework of the Christian Church in "The Residence at Whitminster." At the same time, he took the opportunity to sharpen his portrayal of both the loss of innocence and the wildness of the undisciplined imagination by making his necromancers younger, which also gives their fate a poignancy entirely absent from "The Fenstanton Witch"; we might say that he gave it another turn of the screw.

James describes "The Fenstanton Witch" in "Stories I Have Tried to Write" more fully than he does the untitled draft we have discussed in relation to "Casting the Runes," which appears only as a glancing reference to "the packet you pick up in the carriage drive . . ." But his remark that "some of them had ideas which refused to blossom in the surroundings I had devised for them, but perhaps came up in other forms in stories that did get as far as print" applies to both. The scene in "The Fenstanton Witch" of a man being dragged off by vengeful ghosts turns up in another story of necromancy, "A View from a Hill" (where the idea of binoculars as scrying glass is a fine example of how to modernise a traditional motif), while the supernatural follower mistaken for a feature of the rural landscape in the untitled piece, which the interior settings of "Casting the Runes" precluded, was put to good use in "Mr. Humphreys and His Inheritance."

The latter item exemplifies James's use of landscape to emphasise the sense of disruption of order that is central to his stories. This too can be boiled down to the image of a toad unexpectedly appearing in the study. James rejected the idea that a weird and horrific landscape enhanced the effect of weird and horrific events. In his discussion of Le Fanu, he remarked of Poe's "The Fall of the House of Usher" that the "suggestion or introduction of the mad element," combined with its antiquated style, made the story no more frightening than "a bad dream." That was certainly perceptive of the effect of Poe's story, in which the nightmarish externalisation of the workings of the subconscious is paramount. James's landscapes and supernatural beings, as we have seen, do reflect mental states, but while Poe used disquieting landscape to expose the nature of an unquiet mind, James used the contrast of reassuring landscape and shocking intrusion to dramatise an interaction of internal and external, a process of changing perception and disrupted world view Similarly, James noted that "one feels that almost anything might have happened in the War. It is the wrong setting to choose for a ghost story: you cannot make it more terrifying that way" ("The Ghost Story Competition"). The unpredictable must be given a setting whose workings we feel we understand upon which to act.

Lovecraft's landscapes tend to be more weird and horrific than James's, but this is an intensification of what James was doing rather than a reversion to Poe. In Lovecraft, the intrusion of the alien has become an irreversible occupation and corruption of the familiar by the strange. Lovecraft's more relentless sense of the eternal and inescapable presence of the Great Outside was anticipated by James in "'Oh, Whistle, and I'll Come to You, My Lad.'" Similarly, Lovecraft's more exotic supernatural beings express a degree of otherworldliness that James attained in "The Residence at Whitminster" by substituting a giant insect for the more traditional batlike demon of "The Fenstanton Witch."

To appreciate further the closeness of James's and Lovecraft's fictional themes and means of expression, and the way in which Lovecraft can be said to have taken James's viewpoint and method a step further, we can compare "The Residence at Whitminster" with Lovecraft's "The Haunter of the Dark." In Lovecraft's story, a church has likewise become the habitation of a monstrous alien entity by virtue of the use of a kind of scrying glass by the knowledge-seeking occultists who formerly occupied it. The scrying glass, and the writings and mortal remains that explain the consequences of its use, have been shut away in a tower chamber, but retain their forbidden fruit fascination. Like Mary Oldys in her dream, Blake is compelled to enter "almost without conscious initiative," and flees at the stirring of what he has awakened, leaving the door unlocked. But Blake has no father figure to lock it again for him. The church has long since ceased to be used by humanity to reinforce its view of itself as central to the universe. The books of Dr. Oldys have not merely been confined to a dusty shelf, they have been replaced by the *Necronomicon* et al., and the church furnishings have undergone a similar transformation. The Church, which in its Whitminster manifestation had survived Dissolution and Reformation, and was still "intact and in working order" in 1730, although some of its offices had dwindled, has finally succumbed—not to the advance of scientific rationalism, but to "an evil older than mankind and wider than the known universe." This is the "evil" of alienation whereby humankind has exchanged the order forced on sentience by a god in its own image for a chaos in which human and animal are indistinguishable and sentience is ultimately as formless as the originating void. Blake realises the consequences of this when he notes of the winged creature as it comes towards him: "Is it not an avatar of Nyarlathotep, who in antique and shadowy Khem even took the form of man?" The recognition that the form of man is no longer a sacred preserve leads inevitably to the final surrender of identity: "I am it and it is I." We have noted that, in his presentations of the fates of Dennistoun, Somerton, and Paxton, James moved from man-gets-treasure to treasure-gets-man. Had James written "The Haunter of the Dark" we could have pointed to a similarly symmetrical presentation of the more fundamental theme underlying the cursed treasure motif: moving from Dr. Ashton through Dr. Oldys to Robert Blake, we have moved from man-gets-universe to universe-gets-man.

As it is, we must look to an earlier story for James's most extreme statement on the subject. "Count Magnus" is James's most Lovecraftian story, and the one Lovecraft liked best, to judge by his treatment of it in "Supernatural Horror in Literature." "The Haunter of the Dark" can be seen as a combination of an evolved version of the fate suffered by Mr. Wraxall with an evolved version of the fuller background to it supplied in "The Residence at Whitminster." There are strong similarities between Lovecraft's story and "Count Magnus." In both, the narrator introduces the story as told through the protagonist's diary, indicating (more precisely, in Blake's case, speculating) that the investigations recorded there were intended to contribute towards a published work—a travel book or "some stupendous hoax destined to have a literary reflection." In both, the nature of the work to be produced is closely akin to the sort that James and Lovecraft themselves produced, alerting us to an element of self-portraiture. Both protagonists are evidently "intelligent and cultivated," and the defining feature of their personalities is an overwhelming desire to seek out the strange, the unknowable. They can't wait for the toad to visit—they must track it down and bring it home. But while Lovecraft spells this out ("avid in his quest for scenes and effects of a bizarre, spectral sort"), James merely says of Wraxall that "his besetting fault was pretty clearly that of over-inquisitiveness"—after he has alerted us to the fact that this is "a superficial opinion," for deepening of which we can presumably look to the story itself. This gives us a hint that such difference as there is between Wraxall and Blake lies in the extent to which they are willing to acknowledge their motivation and accept its consequences, an in-ference confirmed by their responses to the culminations of their fates as embodied in the supernatural entities they release upon themselves.

The similarities of the processes by which Count Magnus and the Haun-ter of the Dark are set free need not be detailed. Wraxall and Blake are chased back to their lodgings, where they spend their last hours making "wild entries" in their diaries—a final and perfectly natural attempt (both being writers) to assert their identities in the face of the approaching annihi-lation. James remains reticent—the final entries are "too disjointed and ejaculatory to be given here in full"; Lovecraft gives them in all their ejacula-tory glory. But James passes on the key item: "What can he do but lock his door and cry to God?" Indeed, it is god who comes—"the verdict was visita-tion of God." Given that these statements form, respectively, the climax of the chase and the climax of the explanation of how Wraxall died (which the details of the deaths of the Count's earlier victims have led us to expect to be highly dramatic), we are entitled to regard this irony as more than decora-tive. As with the initial description of motivation, Lovecraft makes explicit what James merely implies, by having Blake call on the names of Azathoth and Yog-Sothoth in his final moments. Thus Blake goes almost willingly into the embrace of the monstrous god his love of the weird has given him, ac-knowledging by his own pen the apotheosis of his alienation, while Wraxall's appreciation of his virtually identical fate remains buried to the end in ironi-cally revealing denial.

This difference may reflect the attitude of their creators; like many be-tween them, it is one of degree rather than kind. "Count Magnus" is James's clearest expression of his own proclivity for the strange and the danger he saw in it for his faith in conventional Christianity. As such, it draws power-fully upon a fear of rootlessness, of having no cultural foundation upon which to base one's life. Both Lovecraft and James liked to travel but also cultivated a strong sentimental attachment to "home," expressed primarily in a beloved landscape. (As an interesting sidelight to this, Adrian noted that James "seems to have been keen on novels and stories set in a New England locale.") This physical attachment, important in itself, also acted as a reminder of valued cultural ties. Equally, their liking for travel seems to have been part of a more profound imaginative impulse. Lovecraft saw one as the necessary balance to the other; in *The Dream-Quest of Unknown Kadath,* a sense of home saves the self from the chaos of the exotic. In stressing Wraxall's lack of a permanent home, James is saying the same thing. Thus Count Magnus has at least two claims to be considered a literary avatar of Nyarlathotep, and a seminal incarnation of forbidden knowledge.

"Count Magnus" illustrates how an uncontrollably restless imagination in communion with the cosmos at large will take its owner so smoothly and inexorably from self-enhancement through self-transcendence to self-obliteration that he is scarcely aware of the process. Other elements of the story contribute to its powerful association of the restlessness of the imagination with loss of humanity. Count Magnus, too, is a traveller—the fact that he has undertaken the Black Pilgrimage is what makes him the most successful and dangerous of all James's sorcerers. The punishments he inflicts upon the two men who try to usurp his hunter's rights are horrific expressions of irremediable restlessness: "but he went on pushing with his hands"; "and the eyes of Anders Bjornsen were looking up, because there was nothing to close over them."

Ron Weighell has shown that James's depiction of the Count firmly relates him to Odin in his role of leader of the Wild Hunt. In "The Residence at Whitminster," the eventual reversal of the roles of householder and intruder to which Oldys's decision to allow a "Jack-in-the-box" to remain in his home points is intensified in the case of the more rootless Saul into a reversal of the roles of hunter and hunted; that is the fate of Wraxall too. The outcome is that the Count replaces Wraxall among the living. He supplants Wraxall as thoroughly as the Haunter of the Dark supplants Blake; in both cases, the chief remaining evidence of the existence of the latter is the account bearing the name of the former. "The Residence at Whitminster" refers at an early stage to the apparent permanence of the home that gives it its title; "Count Magnus" ends with the abrupt, almost casual destruction of Wraxall's last refuge: "so I had it pulled down, and the pages of which I have given you an abstract were found in a forgotten cupboard under the window in the best bedroom." Humankind's eviction from the centre of the universe is now complete, and it has been brought about in Blake's case by the substitution for the Christian god of a completely inhuman one, and in Wraxall's by the substitution for the Christian god of a pagan one whose monstrous companion is the clearest indication that James was on the brink of taking the process of anti-anthropomorphism to its final stage as seen in Lovecraft.

The question remains as to why our sense of identity is so apt to usurpation by whatever captures our imagination. James gives the reason at the outset of many of his stories; it is because we feel potentially unreal, and if the presence of our fellows fails to mitigate this feeling sufficiently, our imagination tries to compensate by engaging our sense of who we are with other things, at the risk of losing it to them.

As with several of James's thematic concerns, "Canon Alberic's Scrapbook" is seminal. Immediately before the appearance of the demon, Dennistoun is shown talking to himself, not only in a simple declarative fashion ("I think I might give it a clean up before I put it away") but in interrogative dialogue ("Half a pipe more, did you say? I think perhaps you are right"). This has the advantage of enabling the demon's appearance to be conveyed dramatically through a present-tense, restricted-viewpoint interpolation in an otherwise past-tense, third-person narrative. It is, however, a limited advantage, because the technique quickly becomes strained; "Good God! a hand like the hand in that picture!" is strikingly and unhappily similar to Lovecraft's equally absurd "God, *that hand!* The window! The window!" ("Dagon"). Likewise, the fact that Dennistoun has temporarily left his travelling companions behind, and the sacristan's remark "It is a good thing to travel thus in company—sometimes" are typical Jamesian devices for creating foreboding; but if they were no more than that, we should be entitled to become impatient with the repeated contrivance.

There is, however, more to the isolation of the protagonist in James's stories than dramatic effect. Dennistoun's talking to himself is related directly to the psychology of his story. As we have seen, the transfer of guilt from Alberic through the sacristan to Dennistoun is a central issue. In this context Dennistoun's self-catechising can be seen as a nascent version of the persecution complex suffered by the sacristan. A similar combination of the narrative demands of the supernatural horror genre and the psychological profile of a particular story can account for the emphasis on the processes and effects of isolation in "Casting the Runes."

Yet the evidence points to a more fundamental, broadly based thematic significance to the idea, one that can be said to underlie and generate the specific imaginative states that individual stories exhibit. Dennistoun's habit is described as "inveterate"; Dunning's relative isolation is underlined before Karswell's persecution begins ("all his time to himself'; "the comfortable house in a suburb where he lived alone"). Wraxall tells us that "Like many solitary men . . . I have a habit of talking to myself aloud; and, unlike some of the Greek and Latin particles, I do not expect an answer." In "The Stalls of Barchester Cathedral," Dr. Haynes begins his description of his troubles with: "I do indeed miss Letitia's company. The house is too large for a lonely man, and visitors of any kind are too rare. I get an uncomfortable impression when going to my room that there is company of some kind." In "Mr. Humphreys and His Inheritance," Mr. Humphreys is "alone in the world," and on moving into his new property is told that everything is ready for him— "Everything, that is, except company, and there I'm afraid you'll find yourself quite at a standstill." "The Uncommon Prayer-Book" begins by describing how Mr. Davidson has been forced into isolation by "a combination of circumstances." These characters suffer different fates but the starting point for them all seems identical.

We might still say simply that James felt that a statement about his protagonist's isolation and an ironic threat of unwelcome company was a prerequisite of a ghost story. But even in "The Residence at Whitminster" he suggests that the root of Ashton's troubles was that "the homes that had been meant to accommodate eight or ten people were now shared among three." The events of "The Diary of Mr. Poynter," an amusing domestic rendition of Wraxall's fatal attraction to the *outré* combined with the unwitting evocation of a past evil epitomised by "Mr. Humphreys and His Inheritance," stem from Mr. Denton's attempt to construct a "new and considerably more convenient dwelling for himself and his aunt who constituted his whole *ménage*." James's protagonists get into trouble because they have too much empty space around them for comfort.

If they are lucky, restoration of human companionship may get them out of it at the end of the story, at least temporarily. Examples of such reversals are Dennistoun and the inn serving-men in "Canon Alberic's Scrap-book," Anderson and the other occupants of the inn in "Number 13" (whose encroaching other-dimensional room is an exceptionally neat image of the infringement of the inhuman upon our living space), Parkins and Colonel Wilson in "'Oh, Whistle, and I'll Come to You, My Lad,'" Somerton and Rector Gregory in "The Treasure of Abbot Thomas," and Denton and his bachelor friend in "The Diary of Mr. Poynter." James's point is that unless we are fortunate enough both by temperament and circumstance to be able to rely always upon the companionship of our fellows to keep our sense of our own unreality at bay, our identity is likely at some time in our lives to find itself at the mercy of our imagination's interaction with the universe at large. "Count Magnus" shows the result when that interaction is wholeheartedly pursued: the boundaries of self-definition dissolve and the Great

Outside takes complete possession of us. "'Oh, Whistle, and I'll Come to You, My Lad'" shows the result when that interaction is staunchly resisted; it is no more comforting.

Professor Parkins has been sheltered from the need to come to terms with his sense of identity in the context of the universe at large. James makes this clear in the opening scene of the story, where we find Parkins "at a feast in the hospitable hall of St. James' College." James is careful to stress that Parkins has a person on either side of him, each of whom questions him; he is rightly nervous at the prospect of "having an empty bed—not to speak of two—in what I may call for the time being my study." We move to his "large double-bedded room" at the appropriately named Globe Inn, with its "commodious table . . . surrounded on three sides by windows looking out seaward"; then to "that lonely shore" on which "company, he began to think, would really be very welcome . . . if only you could choose your companion." The climax comes with the "quality of infinite distance" of the whistle's note, and its "vision of a wide, dark expanse at night, with a fresh wind blowing, and in the midst a lonely figure." The process then goes into reverse, moving through the beach (in Parkins's mental "panorama") and the room (as its new occupant becomes the focus of attention) to end with Parkins as trapped by the person opposite him as he had been at the feast. It is both amusing and significant how James balances the "conflict now raging" in Parkins's breast as to how to escape Mr. Rogers's proposed occupation of his spare bed against his "horrid perplexity" as to how to escape the companion he has "chosen" instead.

In the image of expanding space we see Parkins's sense of gradual reduction to non-being as his companions dwindle and the Great Outside becomes visible; in the reversal of this, the result of his imagination's inevitable attempt to redress the balance by projecting the self on to the Outside with the aim of making it his own. James signals the coming into play of the imaginative faculty as a means of self-extension with a typically wry, understated, scholar-specific yet universally applicable rendition of the forbidden fruit theme: "Few people can resist the temptation to try a little amateur research in a department quite outside their own, if only for the satisfaction of showing how successful they would have been had they only taken it up seriously."

Like Wraxall's, Parkins's imagination gives him an imaginary playmate. Where Wraxall's new companion reflects the fact that he has always opened himself unreservedly to the Outside and is now therefore ripe for possession by it, Parkins's reflects the fact that he has tried to resist any communion with it at all, and now therefore can scarcely make an impression upon it. Wraxall, like Lord Saul, wants to "see all that could be seen"; Parkins has tried strenuously to exclude from his awareness anything that might disturb the "apple-pie order" of his strictly rationalist, human-centred world view. Thus Wraxall meets a god, and Parkins meets a sad flapping thing with no will or substance of its own, "its one power . . . that of frightening"; Wraxall is beyond human help, while the mere entrance of Colonel Wilson prevents Parkins from being supplanted. Yet Parkins remains haunted by things that mimic human form but remain empty or diminished—"a surplice hanging on a door," "a scarecrow in a field late on a winter afternoon"—images of the failure of his too inward looking approach to self-definition to register a strong enough sense of reality against the background of the universe at large to provide him with an adequate reassurance of his own existence. Joshi was right to point to the form taken by Parkins's companion as "a parody of the old-time ghost with its sheeted figure," but this is not done solely out of playfulness; it restates the story's theme by acknowledging that supernatural fiction too may suffer from a failure to convince as a result of myopic anthropomorphism.

In presenting us with these two alternatives, James may have been clarifying a choice that he had had to make, suggesting that conventional doctrine's power to reconcile lonely humanity with the now vast inhuman universe had shrunk to a hollow sham, but that dedication to the unconventional meant renouncing too many of the civilised values that made him who he was. He may also have been expressing the eternal dilemma of the scholar, whereby a too narrow field of enquiry produces clear-cut but fragile conclusions, while a too wide one prevents us from settling upon a conclusion at all. The ultimate source of fear in his fiction is the loss of a self-enhancing sense of meaning; in Parkins's case, this takes the form of discovery that his perfectly defined meaning is too unreal to survive; in Wraxall's, of discovery that his robustly all-embracing meaning is too overwhelming to assimilate.

James is careful to leave us in no doubt as to his sympathy and respect for both Wraxall and Parkins. Wraxall's "over-inquisitiveness" is "possibly a good fault in a traveller"; Parkins, although "rather hen-like, perhaps, in his little ways," is "dauntless and sincere in his convictions." Wraxall should have heeded his landlord's advice to "not ask anything when I have done"; Parkins, as the Colonel tells him, must "live and learn." Evidently a combination of the extremes was needed. Nigel Kneale suggested that James's stories might be part of something like that, because in them we see "a profound and disciplined mind paying what it found to be necessary dues to the irrational." However, it would be an over-simplification to describe James's fiction as no more than a series of sacrifices to Count Magnus in the

course of a life ruled by Professor Parkins. In a group of stories that specifically addresses the subject of storytelling, James indicates that the process of
supernatural fiction creation itself involves integrating the viewpoints of
Wraxall and Parkins.

IV

At the end of the third part of this essay I suggested that for James the
process of supernatural fiction creation involved integrating the too
restricted, human-centred viewpoint of a Professor Parkins with the too
wide-ranging, inhumanly inclined one of a Mr. Wraxall. This becomes
clearer when we consider a group of his stories that specifically addresses the
subject of storytelling, "The Mezzotint," "A School Story," and "There Was
a Man Dwelt by a Churchyard."

Because the way these three stories are told is thematically significant, we
had better begin by clarifying an important feature of James's technique
throughout his fiction, that of narrative layering or framing. In noting James's
fondness for sub-narratives one within another, Joshi remarked that "The degree to which the narrator wishes to dissociate himself from the actual events
is frequently remarkable." This overlooks the fact that what James was trying
to achieve was a strong impression of authorial connection with the events he
was relating. A standard third-person narrative, entirely free of the authorial
interjections that Joshi also notes are an important characteristic of James's
stories, tends to be entirely dissociated from its author; even when the first
person is used, we are not generally given any grounds for assuming that the
"I" of the story is the same as the name that appears under its title. James's
stories took advantage of the added immediacy of oral authorial delivery by
emphasising the role of the real M. R. James as narrator. Of course, to take
this to its utmost would have involved James claiming to have personally experienced the events he was relating. That would have sacrificed too much
plausibility, hence the need for a degree of dissociation. Accepting that con-
straint, we can see that an opening which, like that of "A Warning to the Curious," is ummistakably the author speaking "as himself" from real experience,
actually brings us closer to the ensuing narrative than one which, like that of
"The Haunted Dolls' House," plunges us straight into the story with no pretence that it is anything other than a product of the author's imagination. In
this respect, James was in agreement with Lovecraft, who compared the construction of a story to that of a hoax. Schweitzer has noted: "The effect is
that, for all James's prose is by far leaner, he seems a more old-fashioned
writer than Lovecraft, hearkening back to the early Victorians with their
'Dear Reader' devices." That is true; it results from the fact that James did

not take a willing suspension of disbelief on the part of his audience for granted, but invoked the authorial presence in an active attempt to instil belief. This may mean that some of his stories remain best suited, as Schweitzer pointed out, to the context of personal delivery by the author for which many of them were originally designed.

In "The Mezzotint," however, James does not, as in "A Warning to the Curious," lead us so smoothly from narrative to sub-narrative to sub-sub-narrative that we are scarcely aware of the process until we stop to analyse it. Instead, he emphasises the fact that we are reading a story within a story by making the telling of the innermost story a supernatural event in itself. In so doing, he directs our attention towards the framing process whereby a supernatural encounter that is meaningless on its own is given context. The haunted picture of the title supplies a description of the encounter; its viewers, James's sub-narrators, fill in the history that gives it meaning.

"A School Story" and "There Was a Man Dwelt by a Churchyard" are built around essentially the same supernatural encounter as "The Mezzotint": a reanimated corpse is seen to approach a window with the aim of stealing away something within on which it has a claim against the living. The openings to all three discuss storytelling traditions in ever widening terms, moving from an imaginary folklore of Cambridge academics (by referring, uniquely, to a previous story and claiming to have heard the present one from the protagonist of the earlier one, James not only forges his customary link between author and narrator but evokes an equivalent of his own storytelling tradition in which the stories relate purportedly true experiences), to "The Folklore of Private Schools," to folklore in general. This culminates in James's acknowledgement that his root story is derived from the latter: "It was not going to be a new story: it was to be one which you have most likely heard, and even told. Everybody may set it in what frame he likes best."

The need to frame meaningfully the anecdotal material of folklore to make it suitable for an adult audience is discussed in the first part of "A School Story," where the examples of "the cycle of ghost stories . . . which the boys at private schools tell each other" are "highly compressed" narratives without "explanation or sequel." The story that James's narrator then produces is less compressed—an explanation may be guessed at with adult hindsight ("I am pretty sure now, of course, that there was something very curious in his past history, but I'm not going to pretend that we boys were sharp enough to guess any such thing"). But it remains only an "approach to a ghost story," until James, like the first audience for the engraving's story in "The Mezzotint," supplies the sequel. It is significant that this sequel is less elaborate than that devised for "The Mezzotint." In turn, "There Was a Man

Dwelt by a Churchyard" not only has no sequel, but breaks off abruptly at its climax. Read as a series, the three stories show a gradual increase in compression and diminution of explanatory framework whereby they move closer to a primal folklore source.

This regression is reinforced by the fact that they also move successively closer to a child's narration. In "The Mezzotint," the perspective of all involved is thoroughly adult, save for the brief appearance of Robert Filcher, who reminds us that a child's imagination is less likely to impose a restricting framework of historical interpretation upon a narrative than to apply it literally and directly to himself. In "A School Story," we have events witnessed by children recounted with adult hindsight. In "There Was a Man Dwelt by a Churchyard," we have a story told by a child. What James actually gives us is not a faithful rendition of Prince Mamilius' recital—Mamilius "would I think have made the story a good deal shorter than this"; although James does not, as in "A School Story," supply an adult running commentary, he does give enough carefully arranged detail to enable the by now very simple interpretation of events to emerge. At the climax, however, Mamilius takes over fully to supply the sudden transition from story context to real-life context that "The Mezzotint" has indicated is symptomatic of the undisciplined childhood imagination.

As the story is gradually simplified and its narrative/interpretative framework pruned, James puts us more firmly in the place of the victim of its events. We move from being safely outside the house of "The Mezzotint," to "a dormitory at right angles to the main building" where Sampson sleeps in "A School Story," to end up with John Poole in his bedroom, watching the approach of the figure whose "curious bunched head" recalls "the head of a man or woman, a good deal muffled up" of the first story—a figure which then pounces on us in the person of Mamilius. By insisting on an increasingly strong yet crude identification with the victim of the bogeyman the stories embody a regression to childhood on the part of the listener as well as the teller.

Schweitzer said of James that "Some of his tales ('There Was a Man Dwelt by a Churchyard' most explicitly of all) are merely elaborate methods of saying 'Boo!'" But James was making the point, through a series of progressively unsophisticated, unframed retellings of essentially the same event, that adult supernatural literature could and should be more than that. It becomes more than that when childhood's uninhibited and undiscriminating desire for the marvellous, the grotesque, and the startling for its own sake, whatever its provenance, a barbaric inclination which we have seen in Mr. Wraxall (who, like Mamilius, ended up "becoming" the monster), is disciplined by the civilising selective and interpretative approach of a Professor Parkins. In moving from "The Mezzotint" through "A School Story" to "There Was a Man Dwelt by a Churchyard," we see a transition from what we might call a rehabilitated Parkins viewpoint, in which the alien is no longer blindly denied, but is nonetheless framed, catalogued, carefully chosen, delivered to Cambridge University and made the subject of discussion by academics, to that of a Wraxall-in-embryo, in which the alien is not yet of truly terrifying stature, but is nonetheless at large to the extent that it almost succeeds in crossing the boundary between fiction and reality. The one position asserts a human-centred world view and the civilisation that comes with it without quite excluding everything beyond it; the other asserts the beyond, but not quite overwhelmingly.

James recognised that achieving a viable combination of the known and the unknowable involved avoiding on the one hand over-explaining the supernatural in terms of metaphysics or moral philosophy (appropriating it for civilisation), and on the other allowing its inexplicability to replace entirely any sense of meaning in the story (giving ourselves over to barbarism). "A School Story" tells us that if we make supernatural fiction no more than the servant of didacticism the result will be as barren as sentences constructed to illustrate grammar, and the subconscious is likely to subvert such utilitarian constructs, however good a disciplinarian their instigator may be, to reveal the hidden well of barbarism and mystery over which they have been built. On the other hand, if we indulge in weird for weird's sake, we are merely trading schoolboy anecdotes.

"There Was a Man Dwelt by a Churchyard" ends with Mamilius' assertion "that he knew another story quite three times as dreadful as that one, and would tell it on the first opportunity offered." Perhaps it was out of sympathy for Mamilius' untimely demise and the expectations it dashed that James gave us "Rats." "Rats" may be taken as his own attempt at delivering a primarily anecdotal, almost frameless boo-story, a fact which is acknowledged both in its author's opening remarks ("It is an ill-proportioned tale . . .") and in its title, which is not only of the sort one would expect to appeal to small boys, but is unique in the James oeuvre in being descriptive of the horrific physical effect of the supernatural event depicted. That event is James's version of "Rawhead and Bloody Bones," a strikingly gruesome and strikingly unoriginal image presented with minimum context and maximum immediacy. James's apologetic introduction ("but that is my fault, not his") suggests that he almost expects to be punished for his barbaric disregard of framework in the same way as Mamilius, or as Charles from "An Evening's Entertainment" ("you know what happened to you the last time").

Or as Mr. Wraxall. "Rats," like "Count Magnus," is a traveller's tale whose key image is one of restlessness. We have noted that Wraxall's fate encapsulated that of humankind supplanted and cast out by the inhuman. "There Was a Man Dwelt by a Churchyard" left us at the climax of the inhuman's invasion of our home that began with "The Mezzotint." (Note how James, in Poole's talk with the innkeeper and the smith, reinforced the suggestion of a home under threat contained in the line from which the story took its title.) "Rats" shows us the outcome; as in the second part of "The Residence at Whitminster," the inhuman is now a resident of long standing, but here it seems to be not only tolerated but almost respected; the innkeeper rebukes us for disturbing its sleep! The positions of reanimated corpse as burglar and the living as householder have been reversed; now we are the intruders: "and instead of letting me open the door for him, he stepped forward and threw it open himself, and then for some moments stood in the door way holding up his candle and looking narrowly into the interior." For all its humour, "Rats" offers as bleak a depiction of our status in the universe as "Count Magnus."

But in tandem with that we must read the assertion of human civilisation made by "The Mezzotint." "The Mezzotint" remodels a common form of the traditional story of haunting, in which a crime replays itself supernaturally so that it may be punished. In "The Mezzotint," the replay reveals the punishment, not the crime. Typically of James's universe, the punishment is merciless. The haunting of the picture calls for explanation rather than action, and when this is given, the effect is only marginally a feeling that justice has been done; primarily it is a feeling of pity and terror at the motivations surrounding the crime and the consequences of the punishment. The supernatural is no longer wholly the servant of civilised human ideals, yet its action serves to arouse rather than obliterate a sense of distinctive human worth. James's degenerate god ("Gawdy") has taken his due, but it is he, once Lord of the Manor, who is now the outsider, while the incorporation of his revenge into a work of art has reasserted a human viewpoint. Notably, "It was a rather indifferent mezzotint, and an indifferent mezzotint is, perhaps, the worst form of engraving known." James wanted no suggestion that he might be inclined to worship a god called Art. What matters is that the picture is a vehicle for recording human experience and thus communicating human feeling and reinforcing the reality of a common human identity. It is not coincidental that of all James's stories "The Mezzotint" is by far the most emphatic of the social life of its characters; here, if nowhere else, the isolation that we have found at the root of the identity crisis suffered by most of his protagonists does not threaten, and the alien may be admitted with little fear that it will oust us. It is perhaps the greatest expression of the value James attached to that aspect of his life at Cambridge, including the part that centred on his stories, that he felt it appropriate to conclude "The Mezzotint" on a note of reassuring completeness, orderliness and final rest of which Professor Parkins would have approved: "the picture is now in the Ashleian Museum . . . though carefully watched, it has never been known to change again."

If "Rats" verges on sardonic comedy, a cruel schoolboy joke whose punchline scorns human aspirations to belong in the world, "The Mezzotint" hints at the ennobling process that our idea of humanity undergoes through tragedy. James's stories as a whole can be seen as a tragicomic combination of these two extremes. I introduced this discussion of them by saying that they challenged the notion that human beings were capable of sustaining a meaningful world view. At the same time, they embody a response to that challenge. James's response may be summed up as sensible map making. Refusal to draw borders banishes us to wilderness; refusal to see beyond them reduces us to unreality. But by saying "Here be dragons," we create a valid context in which to set a sense of belonging—we make home real. James hoped for a world in which human meaning and forbidden knowledge could co-exist, like the scholarly books and fantastic fiction that shared his own quarters. His stories describe such a world. It is not a peaceful one, but one that most of his readers feel at home in, because he has succeeded in convincing us that we have always lived there.

I have tried to indicate what were for James some of the more important moral and psychological aspects of existence in that world. I do not propose to exhaust those aspects here, but three more demand mention.

There is the aspect of concealed knowledge as a source of selfish power, especially prominent in "Lost Hearts," "Number 13," "The Treasure of Abbot Thomas," "The Tractate Middoth," and "A View from a Hill." This is, as we have seen, closely associated with James's "jealous god"; it also reflects his recognition of the need to give due weight to the role of educator as well as scholar, so as to avoid being like Mr. Baxter ("A View from a Hill"), who might have been "a very distinguished antiquary," "but for a certain love of opposition and controversy, and, yes, a patronizing tone as of one possessing superior knowledge, which left an unpleasant taste."

There is the aspect of the interaction of the past with the present, perhaps an unavoidable topic in stories involving revenants, but central to three stories where the unnaturally prolonged survival itself, rather than the reason for it, is the focus: "Mr. Humphreys and His Inheritance," "The Diary of Mr. Poynter," and "An Episode of Cathedral History." These make it clear that the past is no safer a place to look for confirmation of a human ideal upon which to found our identity than anywhere else. "Mr. Humphreys and His Inheritance" has an equivalent image to the toad in the study: "It was a still, stuffy evening; windows had to stand open, and he had more than one grisly encounter with a bat. Once or twice it was a question whether there was—not a bat, but something more considerable—that had a mind to join him." The past is another part of the Great Outside which cannot be ignored (all three stories are about the failure of attempts to make a clean break from it) so must somehow be accommodated without being granted pre-eminence.

Finally, there is the aspect that gets its fullest rendition in "The Ash-Tree," sexuality. I shall leave readers to practise their own skills at Freudian analysis, but ask them to remember that, whether the subject is at the heart of the story (and I think that can only be said of "The Ash-Tree") or merely one feature of its development (and as Kneale said, "In an age when every man is his own psychologist, M. R. James looks like rich and promising material"), Lane's point that we should view this as part of a wider thematic agenda is crucial. I am sure Lovecraft's supporters would wish to argue no differently on behalf of his equally rich and promising oeuvre.

This essay has concentrated on thematic analysis because it was in that area that James seemed in danger of being underrated. We should bear in mind that both James and Lovecraft were more interested in making an emotional impact with their fiction than a philosophical point. Both had other more suitable channels through which to promote their views in a purely intellectual context. Yet as Weighell has pointed out, an emotional impact requires substance as well as skill, and Schweitzer is right to say that the substance must be relevant to the reader if the effect is to be achieved. The above discussion shows why I find no lack of relevant substance in James. Nevertheless, there remain some slightly more nebulous issues surrounding the question of the two writers' relative reputations that need to be addressed, if only tentatively.

The first of these is the issue of genre. Joshi is inclined to segregate James from practitioners of more ambitious supernatural fiction by classifying him as "the perfector of one popular and representative form of the weird tale," the ghost story, a form which he suggests "does not allow very much room for expansion or originality." I find such segregation unconvincing. Lovecraft saw no need for it when dealing with James in "Supernatural Horror in Literature." The fact that, as Lovecraft predicted, James has inspired imitators means it may now be useful to speak of a "Jamesian" story as we would of a "Lovecraftian" one, but there is no call to add the word "ghost." Lovecraft evolved a convincing background of invented cosmology for his stories. James, as Weighell has shown, drew widely and deeply upon folklore, myth, and occult theory as a loose frame of reference. There is insufficient difference in approach here to warrant consigning James to some cul-de-sac of supernatural literature that Lovecraft is supposed to have travelled past. James and Lovecraft wrote supernatural horror; further refinement of classification seems more likely to confuse than to clarify the matter.

What then of Lovecraft's apparently greater present-day popularity? The Cthulhu Mythos, being the aspect of his fiction that has drawn most widespread attention, seems the most likely reason for this. That is not surprising. As Tolkien above all proved, what many readers look for in fantasy fiction is a fully realised alternative reality to which they can escape. Lovecraft went further than James down the road of creating his own "universe." In addition to the obvious appeal that has in itself, it means that Lovecraft's popularity can be sustained not only by his books but by the shared-world anthologies, role playing games, and so on based on his "concepts." Schweitzer suggested that Lovecraft appealed more to "thoughtful modern readers" because he was more relevant, but I suspect the reason for much of his popularity lies in the opposite direction—it is because he satisfies more effectively the desire for temporary escape from mundanity. In presenting the world we live in as alien more thoroughly than James did, Lovecraft did more to appease the Mr. Wraxall or Robert Blake in us, who emerges when we feel that the world is not alien enough. Both writers also appealed to Professor Parkins's love of the familiar, James more than Lovecraft; but in that respect there is no substitute for contemporaneity. Stephen King et al. have occupied most of the territory where the known and the unknowable meet on an equal footing, balanced within the text, leaving James and Lovecraft to compete for the space at the edge where we seek the thrill of forbidden knowledge for its own sake, balancing the text against our lives. Lovecraft worked nearer that edge than James, so now has the stronger appeal.

Schweitzer's point that Lovecraft was an inclusionist is also important here. As Weighell has shown, James's stories too drew upon a rich and exotic "mythos," in the form of the magic tradition, the more apocryphal aspects of the Bible, and mythology at large. But he kept this all further below the surface than Lovecraft. In so doing, he succeeded in reproducing the effect he praised in Le Fanu: "The reader is never allowed to know the full theory which underlies any of his ghost stories. . . . Only you feel that he has a complete explanation to give if only he would vouchsafe it." Lovecraft achieved the same goal, but tended to explain more than James. This was in part unavoidable, because Lovecraft's Mythos was an invention which his readers had no way of accessing save through whatever he put in the stories, while James's readers could fill in some of his blanks from other sources. All the same, there is a sense that James occasionally overestimated his readers in this respect, while Lovecraft occasionally underestimated his. To some, James's fiction will seem unambitiously folksy and rather bare; to some, Lovecraft's will seem cluttered and absurdly portentous. This may be the basis on which, as Schweitzer and Weighell have noted, James is more easily accommodated by those who wish to regard supernatural fiction as "an avowedly minor, generic form." In turn, Lovecraft may have greater appeal to those who read supernatural fiction and little else. Both sets of readers underestimate James in the same way.

There is one area where Lovecraft's inclusionist approach gives him an advantage over James in literary terms. This concerns his relationship to the tradition of supernatural horror fiction in which he was working, which is central to our third and final remaining issue, the question of influence. Joshi has shown that Lovecraft's work managed to "culminate certain trends in weird writing of the previous fifty years." There is no story idea in James that one cannot envisage Lovecraft devising or using effectively. The converse is not true. And we can only partly excuse James on the grounds that Lovecraft was of a younger generation and so naturally placed to draw on James, while James could not be expected to reciprocate, because as Schweitzer and Joshi have pointed out, James's views of some of his fellow practitioners were unjustifiably dismissive. Consistently with this, his fiction embraced less of what had gone before. James refined; Lovecraft refined and synthesised.

That may mean that Lovecraft is the more influential, because James offers narrower ground for successors to build upon. But the fact that Lovecraft took a broader view of his literary form gives us no more reason for discounting James than the subsequent still broader views taken by Fritz Leiber and Ramsey Campbell give us for discounting Lovecraft. Indeed, the best proof of James's continuing relevance to the field is the degree to which Leiber's and Campbell's work shows his influence. Lane has demonstrated in relation to Campbell that this is by no means a matter of technique alone; it derives very strongly from the psychological content of James's stories. For these most ambitious and accomplished of late twentieth-century supernatural horror writers, Lovecraft may have been the greater influence. But Lovecraft himself was not without debt to James. A tracing of themes and handling from Le Fanu through James to Lovecraft, Leiber, and Campbell seems more likely than James/Lovecraft playoffs to show us what makes supernatural horror effective for twentieth-century readers. Above all, it would remind us of the truth of Lane's observation that "all supernatural themes are displaced and concentrated treatments of recurrent human concerns," and provide further evidence that neither James nor Lovecraft settled for anything less.

Works Cited

Adrian, Jack. "An M. R. James Letter." *Ghosts & Scholars* No. 8 (1986).

Arney, Lance. "An Elucidation (?) of the Plot of M. R. James' 'Two Doctors.'" *Studies in Weird Fiction* No. 8 (Fall 1990).

James, M. R. *The Collected Ghost Stories of M. R. James.* London: Edward Arnold, 1931.

————. "The Fenstanton Witch." *Ghosts & Scholars* No. 12 (1990).

————. "The Ghost Story Competition." *Ghosts & Scholars* (Crucible, 1987).

————. "John Humphreys." *Ghosts & Scholars* No. 16 (1993).

————. "M. R. James on J. S. Le Fanu." *Ghosts & Scholars* No. 7 (1985).

Joshi, S. T. "M. R. James: The Limitations of the Ghost Story." *The Weird Tale.* Austin: University of Texas Press, 1990.

Kneale, Nigel. "Introduction." *Ghost Stories of M. R. James.* London: Folio Society, 1973.

Lane, Joel. "Writers in the James Tradition, Number 15: Ramsey Campbell." *Ghosts & Scholars* No. 18 (1994).

Lovecraft, H. P. "Supernatural Horror in Literature." *Dagon and Other Macabre Tales.* Sauk City, WI: Arkham House, 1986.

Pardoe, Rosemary. "Some Thoughts on M. R. James's World View." *Ghosts & Scholars* No. 18 (1994).

Power, Albert. "Some Thoughts on the Supernatural Writings of J. S. Le Fanu and M. R. James." *Ghosts & Scholars* No. 9 (1987).

Schweitzer, Darrell. "M. R. James and H. P. Lovecraft: The Ghostly and the Cosmic." *Studies in Weird Fiction* No. 15 (Summer 1994).

Weighell, Ron. "Dark Devotions: M. R. James and the Magical Tradition." *Ghosts & Scholars* No. 6 (1984).

Thanks to S. T. Joshi, Joel Lane, and Rosemary Pardoe for advice in the preparation of this essay.

III. Some Special Topics

On Not Letting Them Lie:
Moral Significance in the Ghost Stories of
M. R. James

Michael A. Mason

In her study of stories about the uncanny, a study entitled *Night Visitors: The Rise and Fall of the English Ghost Story,* Julia Briggs has reminded us that the ghost stories of M. R. James have never fallen out of public favor (125). They have remained in print ever since he first published them. The apparent moral purpose of his doing so may be worth investigating, although the moral force of these stories is unlikely to be the main reason for their popularity.

By 1894, when James began to publish the ghost stories which were to bring him a far wider fame than all his scholarly researches, educated readers could feel perfectly safe in dismissing his apparitions as entirely without objective existence. Anyone could experience ghosts if he deliberately cultivated the state that Tennyson had got himself into by re-reading Hallam's letters to him; just as, two or three generations into the twentieth century, anyone who stares at the sky for long enough can discover flying objects, whether or not he can identify them. From time to time, the sanity of people who described their own strange experiences might be in question; but otherwise freak weather conditions or indigestion could provide a sufficient explanation for an age as far above the vulgar errors of its ancestors as electric power could raise it. However, since this new unbelief did not seem to make the world more tolerable, perhaps tales of the uncanny might, in a limited way, minister to psychological necessities inherited by modern man from his ignorant forefathers. Besides, there is a peculiar pleasure in being terrified vicariously.

Montague Rhodes James (1862–1936) wrote his ghost stories over a period of some forty years. "I never cared," he tells us in an epilogue to his *Collected Ghost Stories,* "to try any other kind" (643). Researchers into mediaeval and other documents helped to inspire in his imagination a host of demons that might irrupt into the human dimension. His difficulty, of course, is to persuade us that they could; to give them a reason, or at least an excuse, for doing so; and to make them behave interestingly when they arrive. The first of these he achieves by the use of time, tradition, and a sense of reality.

James believes in setting a discreet barrier of time between the event and the reader. "The detective story," he says with authority, for he had read a great many of these,

> cannot be too much up-to-date. . . . For the ghost story a slight haze of distance is desirable. "Thirty years ago," "Not long before the war," are very proper openings. If a really remote date be chosen, there is more than one way of bringing the reader in contact with it. The finding of documents about it can be made plausible; or you may begin with your apparition and go back over the years to tell the cause of it; or . . . you may set the scene directly in the desired epoch, which I think is hardest to do with success. On the whole . . . I think that a setting so modern that the ordinary reader can judge of its naturalness for himself is preferable to anything antique. For some degree of actuality is the charm of the best ghost stories; not a very insistent actuality, but one strong enough to allow the reader to identify himself with the patient; while it is almost inevitable that the reader of an antique story should fall into the position of the mere spectator. (Introduction to *Ghosts and Marvels* vi–vii)

By "actuality" James means sense of present time fully as much as realism. Some of his own settings are quite remote, but he counters an effect of too much distance by precision in dating. Two periods far apart, neither of them contemporary, may be exactly given, and both events clearly described: in "The Residence at Whitminster" these are 1730 and 1823–4. That the present time is the viewpoint is scarcely hinted. If there is a midway period, the latest time being the present, the remotest period may be shadowy and the origin of ghosts. "An Episode of Cathedral History" is one of the best examples of this telescopic technique. It has a very obscure foundation in the fifteenth century, when considerable trouble since lost to history must have been experienced. When, however, the satyr escaped from its tomb in the summer of 1840, a number of people were able to guess at the nature of what had happened before. That summer of 1840 is the story's narrative area, told to "a learned gentleman" by the elderly Head Verger, who remembers in 1890 that particular adventure of his boyhood. More than twenty years later, the learned gentleman hands the story to our narrator; and now, beyond his time, the modern reader adds yet another perspective to what already had so much of the mysterious haze of distance.

A true impression of historical distance can be achieved only by a writer with a real sense of historical time, including an idea of the kind of English spoken for instance in the criminal courts in which judge Jeffreys distorted justice in the 1680s. James's reading of the *State Trials* helped him here. So did the immense scholarship of his work as an antiquary and manuscript editor, for this kind of learning gave him an authentic fictional context for the discovery by some of his characters of those manuscripts and inscriptions which left them wiser and far more wary—if they survived—than they had been before. His use of Latin, usually translated at some point, is a particular feature of James's stories. If the teacher of Latin wants to ensure that his students remember the genitive case after *memini*, or the construction of a conditional sentence with a future consequence, he cannot do better than read them "A School Story." *Si tu non veneris ad me, ego veniam ad te* comes through with sinister force. A ghost of a feeling persists that Latin, the legal, political, religious, and linguistic root of so much of western history, is the proper tongue in which to conjure and dismiss apparitions, and there is about it a certain solidity and conciseness that gives authority to the stories about them.

The sense of reality resides in James's power to create the ordinary, normal rhythm of life. His adventurers are intelligent people and, for most purposes, sensible. They are not complex characters, and are therefore, in their outlined form, all the easier for the reader or listener to identify with. A number resemble James himself in being university dons with enough freedom—in terms of seventy or eighty years ago—to go on short-range expeditions out of England as far as to Southern France or Scandinavia. Within their reach are the resources of local wisdom or of level-headed friends whose advice they would have done better to follow. It is safer, at times, to be humble and ignorant.[1] Indeed, this is the happy state of all those people who pass on oral tradition about bygone people and places and comment occasionally on what is happening in the cathedral, the distant woods, or the quiet country mansion. Through the normality of these people—innkeepers and housekeepers, gardeners and butlers, cathedral vergers, retired colonels, and so forth—the reader keeps in touch with the everyday world at the same time as he follows his intrepid hero into a confrontation with the uncanny. The general public of the countryside accordingly act as guarantors of the reality of the supernatural, in which they can believe without any difficulty.

When we come to consider the reasons for the intrusion of the supernatural into ordinary life, we find that they can be summed up in one word: disturbance. Some kind of sensitive environment has been violated by an act

---

1. Advocated by William Beckford at the end of *Vathek* as the wise alternative to "blind curiosity" and "restless ambition": one of *Three Gothic Novels*, ed. E. F. Bleiler (New York: Dover, 1966), p. 194.

of thoughtlessness, often in defiance of good advice as well as good sense; and it is then that the question of provocation arises. Provocation on the part of the disturber makes him vulnerable to some act of malice roughly classifiable as revenge.

At this point we should note that, in certain professions, encounters with the supernatural are occupational hazards. The clergy are particularly vulnerable; professors and scholars may also find themselves in strange company, as may travellers, amateur archaeologists, experimenters of many kinds, and even medical men. The reasons for vulnerability often amount to the single trouble of ambition. "That last infirmity of noble mind" it may well be, but its range—in James's stories, at least—encompasses a very wide spectrum from the simplest unnecessary curiosity to overweening vanity and uncompromising arrogance. This kind of motivation will lead a man to investigate a locked room at the inn where he is staying; or to hasten into the next world some elderly relative or superior who seems to be reluctant to remove himself from the surface of this one; or to improve his own status by deliberately seeking what certain powers of the unseen world can do for him, in return—presumably—for access through him to the physical universe. Through this channel there then passes an illicit two-way traffic, which has, however, its penalties.

We therefore often find ourselves observing a living person who has awakened trouble for himself by his temerity or even by his criminal actions. In the latter event, the kind of retribution he suffers may be no more than his just, if unmerciful, punishment. More often, what occurs is a kind of wild justice visiting any offence with death, or at least with the fear of it. The predicament of the victim is naturally the one with which the reader identifies; it is, in mundane terms, an insoluble one. It cannot be avoided. It must, like a typhoon at sea, be encountered head on and, if possible, survived. As for identification with the avenger itself, this is—by its very nature—impossible.

Although the reader feels more at ease, if this expression may be allowable in such a context, with the spirits of dead people rather than with spiritual entities of which he can have no understanding, the dead have often been those who have isolated themselves so effectually in life as to have alienated the sympathy of other people even then. James bestows upon the dead the fate of haunting their old homes for some evil action committed in life. It seems as if his earthbound spirits have chosen to keep for themselves a treasure or power of some kind in their earthly existence, and have thus bound themselves, or some part of themselves, whether voluntarily or not, to the safeguarding of it. No fruitful contact with them seems to be possible. In fact, it is essential, for James's narrative purposes, that no contact of either a prolonged or an intelligent kind ever be established.[2] The ghost is to have all the disconcerting advantages of appearance and disappearance—rather like the ghost of Banquo—but without the chance of presenting its case for reprieve, if it has one. Prolonged contact would weaken the unfamiliarity and therefore the mystery of the supernatural, and—if intelligent as well—could easily bring the story down to the colloquial level of Scrooge and Marley in *A Christmas Carol*: with Marley—it will be recalled—presenting his former business partner with a whole battery of unpaid professional consultants for Scrooge's eternal benefit. James's tales are as cautionary as Marley's advice to Scrooge, but his ghosts are all inimical. His advice can therefore take only one course: leave them alone by not tempting them out. They are powerful forces rather than individual personalities, and probably cannot do anything but whatever they are programmed, robot-like, to do. One might as well try to argue with Grendel.

Unfortunately, by the time this has become evident to the victim of such an entity's attentions, and to his friends, it may be too late for any action but a final conflict. If the enemy itself is of such a nature as to have forfeited forgiveness for sins committed, it cannot be expected to forgive any offence against itself. It is also solid enough to inflict considerable damage; James seems to prefer the tangible Scandinavian entities to be met with in saga and folklore. In his preface to the collected edition he claims to "have tried to make my ghosts act in ways not inconsistent with the rules of folklore" (viii). He edited the Latin texts of "Twelve Medieval Ghost-Stories" for the *English Historical Review* in July 1922, and found these to be "redolent of Denmark." They were local to Yorkshire and included ghosts with those powers of attacking and grappling with humans that he introduces into his own stories.

The motivation of his own spirits is, however, James's personal invention. We have noted the vanity or self-seeking of some potential victims, as well as the greed or avarice which has condemned people of former times to undergo whatever eternal trouble they are now in. Still alive or long dead, such human principals in the stories have been tainted by pride and must endure the penalty for selfish independence. No satisfying exorcism, as in Kingsley Amis's *The Green Man*,[3] no outright defeat of supernatural evil by straightforward human means, will occur in James's stories; for it does not seem to be his purpose to offer remedies, but rather to point out the risks.

---

2. Contact of both kinds may be inferred from a number of James's stories, but the contact between the narrator, as distinct from the central character, and the spirits is either minimal or nonexistent. Non-human entities in particular never make verbal or other intelligent contact with the narrator.

3. Kingsley Amis's novel describes prolonged and intelligent contact between the chief character and the ghost, which is of human origin, subtle and malignant.

However, in James's mysterious world there are many variations. It may be possible to divert the intending attacker of Mr. Goodman on to another target. If so, what target more suitable than the Mr. Badman who has been directing his supernatural agent against Mr. Goodman? One of James's better-known tales is called "Casting the Runes." Mr. Badman is an authority on the occult and resents an unfavourable review that someone has written about a book of his. Authorities may, of course, be of different kinds, just as a winegrower and an alcoholic may both claim with some authority to be experts about the same product. Mr. Karswell, the Mr. Badman in this affair, has taken some kind of apprenticeship in order to become an authority. It is not scholarly authority in the usual sense that he has, but practical experience of the occult. Regrettably, Mr. Karswell also desires to be recognised as a scholar, which he is not; and he takes such great personal offence against a certain adverse critic of his scholarship as to ensure that one of his own unusual friends shall make away with the critic. To repeat this success, which he ultimately designs to do with another offender, he chooses, reasonably enough, to employ the same technique: one of its vital preliminaries being the delivery to the victim of a slip of writing which he must freely accept, though he will not be able to comprehend the writing. The slip is duly given to the second victim; but, before Mr. Badman's familiar can operate, the brother of the first victim is contacted for advice and assistance. Second victim and brother of first victim then co-operate in returning the slip of writing to Mr. Badman; and he, having freely accepted it as part of a larger package, becomes in turn the victim and is deservedly eliminated.

I have referred to the non-human entities as powerful forces rather than personalities. James's emphasis on their impact deprives their behavior of subtlety, and requires that they call attention to themselves by sheer unpleasantness. In James's first published story, "Canon Alberic's Scrap-book," written in 1894, the intrusive demon is described as having "intelligence beyond that of a beast, below that of a man" (16). This artistic precision is less admirable than a little more artistic restraint would have been, and James would not again venture a comment of this kind on a supernatural character's IQ. A concentration of evil might indeed have some such disastrous effect on a former human being, whose behavior might in consequence become interestingly bizarre. In "Number 13," written in 1899, a human being has apparently become a demon. At any rate, Mr. Anderson, a Church historian visiting Denmark to examine archives of the sixteenth century, finds that the inn at which he has Room Number 12 also has a Room Number 13, but only at night. This interesting discovery coincides with his reading of archival correspondence about the alleged activities of a certain

Magister Nicolas Francken in the time of the last Bishop to hold the see under the Church of Rome. What Magister Nicolas Francken had done had not been set down in any surviving detail, but could be summed up in the expression "secret and wicked arts" which appeared in the accusations against him. The matter was apparently never brought to trial, as the Bishop referred to the defendant's having been "suddenly removed from among us," and this ended the documentation.

Mr. Anderson abruptly found himself able to continue it, after a fashion, when the occupant of the neighbouring room began that same night to dance and sing. The dancing, though surprisingly vigorous—as revealed by the antics of his shadow against the blank street-wall opposite his room— was silent. His singing was not, besides being of such a disturbing quality as to bring to his door a reluctant deputation armed with crowbars and a desperate determination to discover what manner of thing this was. It is at this moment of truth that the test of the writer also comes. James cannot allow a meeting, so he compromises. While the weapons are being fetched, the occupants of Rooms 12 and 14 are on guard outside the door of Room 13. While the nearer man has his head turned from it in order to address his companion, "the door opened, and an arm came out and clawed at his shoulder." If James takes the event that far, he must go a little further. "It was clad in ragged, yellowish linen, and the bare skin, where it could be seen, had long grey hair upon it." This is as far as James will go. Anderson pulls Jensen out of the way, the door shuts again, "and a low laugh was heard." This incident is enough to alarm the witnesses; to demoralise the reinforcements who hear of it when they arrive soon afterwards; to impel Mr. Anderson to encourage and organise them for the attack; and, in fact, to allow a sufficiently plausible time to elapse between the incident and the eventual attack on the door: so that, as the attack is delivered, the moment of dawn arrives and Number 13 disappears. Before the next sunset, the discovery of relics under the floorboards removes the chance of its reappearance.

The living characters in the story of "Number 13" are merely witnesses of what had apparently been happening for some time: the Faustian figure of Nicolas Francken had been translated into something extremely unpleasant, and certainly much less human than he had been in life. It is, however, when we come to consider the behavior of a demon without human origin, that we appreciate all the more the wisdom of letting them lie. "An Episode of Cathedral History" describes the architectural ambitions of a reforming Dean of the Cathedral of Southminster in the summer of 1840. James takes the opportunity to show that some architectural reforms can amount to desecration. However, the demolition revealed "many interesting features of older work," as James's narrator expresses it. The most interesting feature of all was an altar-tomb of the fifteenth century, quite plain, but with a defect in the form of a slight gap between two slabs on the north side.

The cathedral renovations most unfortunately coincide with a wave of ill health among the local residents. Unpleasant dreams disturb them and sickness actually carries some of them off. The boy who, as an elderly man, tells the story to James's narrator remembers especially the nocturnal phenomenon known as "the crying"—as this was the time when he and his dog would, by mutual agreement, share his bed until it had stopped for that night, as the dog would know. The reader's identification with a boy and his dog is, of course, strong—and almost as strong with the boy and his friend who, being members of the choir, had easy access to the cathedral and to the attempts being made to plug up the hole in the altar-tomb. After listening to an argument between foreman and plasterer about a failure to do this, the boys are alone by the tomb. One of them has looked into the gap, and seen something. "I says to Evans, 'Did you really see anything in there?' 'Yes,' he says, 'I did indeed.' So then I says, 'Let's shove something in and stir it up.'" So they roll up a music sheet and shove it in, and then, when nothing happens, Worby—our informant—whistles. Inside, something moves; the roll of music, shoved in again, is held fast and has to be torn free; and the boys, having certainly stirred up something, take fright and run. A night or two later the crying is worse than ever before, and the day after that the cathedral authorities, duly armed with crowbars, assemble in force and watch while a bar is used upon the gap in the north side of the altar-tomb. The demon emerges, though only Worby's father seems to have been favored with a view of it, and it escapes by the north door, never to be seen again. At the end of such a sickly season as that had proved to be to the residents of Southminster, it is unfortunate to have to report that the reforming Dean was none the wiser for the trouble he had initiated, and none the worse either, except for having been bowled over by the emerging demon—and even that he had managed to identify as the Canon in residence.

For ghosts as gothic as these are, as normal a setting as possible is very suitable. Everyday normality does not negate the likelihood of other dimensions. The folk wisdom of those people in James's stories who are consulted on local history seems to confirm this. In "The Rose Garden" an old man is remembered who had advised a lady's father many years before against the removal of certain garden furniture, or perhaps particularly a single post: "he's fast enough in there without no one don't take and let him out." But oral tradition is not always passed on to newcomers, and the point of this advice is not understood until the removal of the post makes it clear. We may, if we wish, discover in James's stories of such phenomena forces that exist within the human heart rather than in the universe outside us, and we can believe in them easily enough when we survey the realities of terror and horror that human beings daily inflict upon one another. Of the consequences of such actions upon the evildoers themselves as well as upon their victims we also see something. If—to keep to literary examples—Banquo's trust in Macbeth as his host leads to Banquo's murder, that murder itself has its retribution in the despair and eventual killing of Macbeth, lured to his fate by the evil forces on the heath.

But the evil forces themselves as objective existences are harder for us to accept. In James's stories they may to some extent even be useful, performing upon human evildoers the work of sharks or scavengers. Persuading us to believe that there are superhuman powers of evil may be James's oblique way of convincing us also of the strength of their opposites, though these seem to rely on human agents alone to battle against the enemy. If the healing touch is less evident in these stories than is the touch that withers, let its recall that James, for many years Provost of Eton School, must have found that the cautionary tale worked very well upon creatures of wild nature such as boys.[4] If a class in school were told the story of "There Was a Man Dwelt by a Churchyard," and the chief masculine genius in obstreperousness were fixed on in good time as the target, it might be possible to position oneself in readiness for the climax, and then to drop on him with the most gratifying effect. This, however, may be found merely to illustrate how easy the temptation can be to imitate the punitive forces in James's stories rather than those of toleration and understanding.

Works Cited

Briggs, Julia. *Night Visitors: The Rise and Fall of the English Ghost Story.* London: Faber & Faber, 1977.

James, M. R. *The Collected Ghost Stories of M. R. James.* London: Edward Arnold, 1931.

————. Introduction to *Ghosts and Marvels: A Selection of Uncanny Tales from Daniel Defoe to Algernon Blackwood*, ed. V. H. Collins. London: Oxford University Press, 1927.

————. "Twelve Medieval Ghost-Stories." *English Historical Review* 37 (July 1922): 413–22.

---

4. The identification is James's own: "some boy or other creature *ferae naturae*." *The Collected Ghost Stories*, p. 127.

Dark Devotions: M. R. James and the Magical Tradition

Ron Weighell

> Persons who busy themselves about the subject of Satanism and Black Magic are rarely to be depended upon for accuracy of statement.
> —M. R. James

Of the thirty pieces included in *The Collected Ghost Stories of M. R. James,* no fewer than thirteen use ritual magic and the related practices of divination, witchcraft, pagan cults and the evocations of demons as the core of their plots. If we exclude from the total a few appended pieces which, enjoyable as they are, strike a lighter than usual note, we find that one half of his major works of fiction are devoted to these themes, a not insubstantial total.

It is curious that this aspect of MRJ's output has not attracted closer critical attention. This may be due in part to a confusion as to his own views on the subject. MRJ observed that the *technical terms* of occultism, if not carefully handled, call into play irrelevant faculties. Imagination alone, he suggests, should be sufficient. Nevertheless, the injudicious use of technical terms and the deft employment of accurate background information are two very different things, and James knew the value of the latter. He admits modestly that he sought to make his spirits behave "in a way not inconsistent with the rules of Folklore." But this tells us little of his methods or the depths of knowledge employed.

Critical treatment of MRJ's tales, in England at least, remains on a light and often superficial level. The general view is summarised by Julia Briggs, who sees the ghost stories as a literary exercise, delicate edifices of suspense to entertain young people, and as a "bagatelle for an idle hour." The biblical references are, she suggests, academic jokes, or the means of supplying "spurious authenticity" to the plots. The implications of what he wrote apparently "never disturbed him."

Doubtless such a view will commend itself to many. There is something appealing in the image of a great man turning occasionally from events of pith and moment to toss off a cultured and clever tale. It must be said, too, that James himself did little to contradict this. However, I must confess that I cannot square this view with the evidence. These "mere bagatelles" stand comparison with works by writers who devoted their lives to the study of the occult, and have continued to exert a powerful influence on generations of readers. Also it is my experience—and that I am sure of many others—that in supernatural fiction above all other genres, the superficially clever soon palls. In exploring this contradiction, of which most critics seem unaware, we may find that bagatelles can be a little deeper than they appear.

The dominant themes of MRJ's occult fiction, the continuing power and influence of ancient ritual, and the often questionable dividing line between such practices and their Christian counterparts, are evident in the earliest of the tales, "Canon Alberic's Scrap-book." The malevolent spirit is in fact a demon originally evoked by the Canon to reveal, among other secrets, the location of treasure. To this end Alberic could have turned to any one of a number of magical texts. *The Book of The Goetia of Solomon the King* alone lists among its seventy-two demons, nine who are capable of telling "Where treasures be hid," and all, the tome warns, are dangerous if not controlled. Even a distinctly 'whiter' system akin to yoga, *The Sacred Magic of Abramelin*, contains a magic square to evoke a demon for the same purpose. There are echoes of "The Treasure of Abbot Thomas" in the warning that accompanies this square. The user may find and take possession of treasure, "provided it be not magically guarded." However, it would not have been necessary for the Canon to resort to such works. The means lay within his own Church. Many priests from the fourteenth century on became specialists in discovering treasure by prayer and incantation. Magical masses were said for this purpose, some expressly Satanic, but others throwing a lurid light on the pagan hinterland *within* the Church. In the seventeenth century, when Alberic was born, seemingly innocent masses were actually said before congregations, invoking and inverting the demon-*banishing* powers of Saint Cyrian or Saint Ambrose, to reveal treasure (Rhodes 126). Another source of MRJ's inspiration might well have been an apocryphal document he had studied in the 1890s; a magical book dealing with the fifty-eight demons conjured by Solomon with the aid of a magic ring. More will be said about this book in due course.

"Lost Hearts" employs an altogether wider frame of reference. The villainous Abney is an expert in the religious beliefs of the later pagans, a major source of theory and practice for students of magic. He owns an original group of Mithras slaying the bull, and has a complete library on the Mysteries of Orpheus, Mithras and the Neo-Platonist School. The Mithraic cult statue foreshadows in great detail Abney's intentions. In the ritual it symbolised, life sprang from the spilled blood generated by the sacrificial act. The rites of Mithras were a quest for immortality and equality with the luminous gods. Devotees attained to the celestial banquet, the earthly counterpart of which was a *sacramental communion* compared by Tertullian and Justin Martyr to the Eucharist. The prevalent theme was triumph over death in nature and the soul (James).

The Abney library must have been a fascinating one. He owned all the current works pertaining to the Mysteries. Abney got his just deserts before the publication of Thomas Taylor's *Eleusinian and Bacchic Mysteries,* but his shelves would surely have hold that great scholar's *Sallust on the Gods of the World,* with its appendix devoted to five hymns to the pagan gods by the Neo-Platonist Proclus, (much used by modern magicians), and the *Arguments of the Emperor Julian Against the Christians*; such argument, in Abney's case, falling on far from deaf ears.

The purpose of his studies was, as we might have surmised on seeing his choice of statuary, "enlightenment of the spiritual faculties" and "ascendancy over those orders of spiritual beings who control the elemental forces of our Universe." Abney quotes as an example of such attainments Simon Magus, an apt choice for a student of the Mysteries, for he was, in the eyes of his Syrian disciples, the founder of Gnosticism.

Abney's method of attaining these ends is human sacrifice involving cannibalism. To the ancients this had two main purposes: identification with the sacrifice, and through him the deity petitioned; and absorption of the life-force. It does not escape James that Abney's act is the selfish annexing of what was considered a religious rite. The pagans usually set aside the heart and offered it to the God. Seeking to assume God-like powers, Abney devours it himself.

"'Oh, Whistle and I'll Come to You, My Lad'" gives us an East Anglian setting, and a whistle found in the ruins of a preceptory built by the Templars, ostensibly a Christian Order accused of worshipping idols and trampling the cross. A building of similar design, attributed to the Order in Brittany, still displays a statue of their idol Baphomet in a monstrous form, with horns and wings. While walking away from the ruin after making his discovery, Parkins finds himself imagining just such a figure outlined against the sky. That night he cleans and blows the whistle, a rash experiment that results at first in nothing more sinister than a howling wind. In conversation next day the Colonel remarks that Parkins has whistled up the wind according to a belief prevalent in Denmark, Norway and the Yorkshire coast. This reference to places connected with Norsemen is very significant. Geurber (29) tells us that in medieval times the Pied Piper was identified with the Norse god Odin, the shrill note of the pipes with the 'whistling' wind, and the rats with the summoned spirits of the dead.

Can we be sure that such links are not coincidental? Fortunately we can, for the young MRJ enthusiastically recorded the acquisition of Sabine Baring-Gould's *Curious Myths of the Middle Ages,* and among many fascinating subjects (including some material on the Anti-Christ, who will emerge again when we confront Count Magnus), we find there a chapter on the Pied Piper, in which the links with Odin's wild hunt, and the identity of names of the soul with words signifying wind are dealt with at some length. It was from this source, I am sure, that "'Oh, Whistle'" was born.

It is a worldwide belief, from New Guinea to Greenland, that the wind indicates the presence of a demonic being. In the middle and far east, to whistle is still to invite molestation by the 'storm fiend.' Whistling was considered particularly inauspicious on or near the sea, and especially at night. Until comparatively recent times in East Anglia, the setting for the story, hunters out after dark would never whistle for their dogs, for fear of calling up a local 'fiend' (Radford), and MRJ, I would suggest, utilises the traditional method of escaping such a spirit when accidentally summoned, to introduce a typically understated piece of irony. The being that manifests in Parkin's bedroom is apparently blind, and has to grope around for him. He *moves* to evade it, and lets out a *cry,* thereby giving away his position. Had Parkins been less of an 'old woman' and listened to the Colonel when he spoke of old traditions, instead of interrupting him, he might have learnt that the proper response is to throw oneself face down, *mouth to the ground,* and keep *still.* The spirit would then have passed on without finding him, and he would have been spared the worst part of his experience.

"Mr. Humphreys and His Inheritance" tells of old mischief (again pagan magic), stirred up by the opening of a maze built by his uncle's grandfather. Here MRJ is particularly adept in his employment of magical traditions, for there are three major aspects of maze symbolism (Hall 26), and he gives us resonances of them all; with a more recent fourth, Christian Theological use as a parable, thrown in for good measure.

Labyrinths or mazes were favoured places of initiation in the ancient cults of India, Persia, Egypt, Greece and the Americas, invariably associated with a deity concealed at the centre of their passages. In the case of solar cults this would take the form of a *globe,* with the passages representing the movement of the planets. Mr. Humphreys finds that the globe at the centre of 'his' maze displays not astronomical but Satanic symbolism. Following the paths of a maze was a means of ritual invocation akin to dance. (Arthur Machen in *The London Adventure* gives details of a story he never completed, in which a girl walks the paths of an ancient maze and evokes its malignant influence.) Humphreys inadvertently does much the same thing, but something worse than the resulting mental confusion yet awaits him.

Another use of maze designs was as a trap to hold demonic forces in check. Humphreys' uncle clearly thought that his grandfather's troublesome spirit was securely bound as long as he tore up the inscribed stones and closed the maze, but he reckoned without his nephew's inquisitive nature. Employing the magical rule that some direct link is necessary between the victim and the pursuing spirit, MRJ ensures that it is not actually seen until Humphreys has entered the maze, *laid his hand on the globe* and walked out again.

Maze designs were also used like Mandalas or Yantras. Concentration upon their designs, following the path to the centre with the eye, induced a trance state accompanied by psychic visions. It is while following the plan of the maze in just such a way that Mr. Humphreys experiences his terrifying vision of the dark centre, and learns what lies within the globe.

In pagan teachings, the maze also symbolised the illusions of the lower world through which man searches for his soul. MRJ echoes this with his much-praised Christian parable. And here, as we shall see, there is the possibility of an intriguing link with another tale, "A View from a Hill."

Here we have a fine example of MRJ's inventive variations on real magical practices. Mr. Fanshawe borrows a curiously heavy pair of binoculars, and sees visions of the landscape as it was many years before. Their creator, Baxter, has constructed them by a mixture of Alchemy and Necromancy, utilising the corpses of hanged men.

The belief that the body of a man killed in the full flush of his strength by strangulation was a receptacle of magical powers, was held by many people ancient and not so ancient (Boguet). Hanged men's teeth and hair were considered particularly efficacious, and even touching such a corpse could produce miraculous 'cures.' (Thomas Hardy used this tradition to powerful effect in "The Withered Arm.") Such beliefs can be traced back to the ritual hangings in groves sacred to the Norse God Odin. The major centre of this practice, Upsala, was visited by MRJ in 1901. It was here too, that he saw the compact with the Devil signed in human blood which he mentions at the end of "Number 13." Baxter's incorporation of the brew of flesh and bones into so innocuous an object as a pair of binoculars is a totally original touch, but it has a firm foundation in myth and magic.

This brings us to the possible link with Mr. Humphreys's maze. It occurs to me that James, widely read and intrigued by the quaint, may have been familiar with Komensky's "The Labyrinth of the World," through which a pilgrim quests, resisting temptations as he goes. At one point in the narrative his guide equips him with a pair of lenses, "falsifying spectacles," that show foul as fair and black as white. Only when the pilgrim turns to Christ does he rid himself of their effect, gaining in return "sacred spectacles" which reveal "surprising wonders." The link is undeniably tenuous, but having seen what MRJ made of a legend of the Pied Piper, we could well imagine the concepts of the labyrinth and the 'distorting lenses' laying like seeds in his fertile imagination, to bring forth in due season two of his most original tales.

The Norse connection is again evident in "Count Magnus"; an Alchemist and worshipper of Satan whose Scandinavian origins seem to have inspired his outward appearance, and that of his familiar. The Count first appears figured on the side of his own sarcophagus, watching a particularly unpleasant *hunt* from the brow of a hill. He travels in a cloak and wide-brimmed hat, holding a staff, and this is the form adopted by Odin, Lord of the Hunt, when wandering abroad. Odin is often referred to as Grimnir, the hooded, and in this form seems to be linked with squat, hooded beings called the *Genii Cucullati*. Magnus's familiar is squat and hooded.

The Count is an Alchemist—the works listed are a judicious mixture of real texts and titles so like extant treatises as to strike a convincing note—but this is not the sole source of his power. He has undertaken the Black Pilgrimage to the birthplace of the Anti-Christ, the city of Chorazin, where he made worship to Satan. Chorazin has no clear history. From Jerome we learn that it lies at the North end of the Sea of Galilee, and that it was, even in his day, deserted. The meaning of its name is uncertain (but I am struck by the similarity between Chorazin and Choronzon, a demonic being conjured by Dr. John Dee the Alchemist, and later by Aleister Crowley, both of whom are linked, as we shall see, with MRJ). The epithet 'Black' Pilgrimage is a particularly sinister joke at the expense of the reader. Besides the obvious inversion of its Christian counterpart (as in Black Mass), there is a secondary meaning, far from metaphorical, that would have been recognised by all who had undertaken that hazardous journey. On turning off from the caravan route that ran past the Sea of Galilee to Damascus, and following the short paved road to the ill-famed city, how must the "singularly ugly" visage of Count Magnus have twisted into a smile to see that the walls, columns, ornamentation, indeed the entire stonework of Chorazin, was carved out of black basalt (Hastings)!

Perhaps the most famous tale utilising the Western tradition of magic is "Casting the Runes," in which, I would suggest, MRJ uses a real magician as the basis for his villain Karswell. The intriguing and much-maligned Great

Beast, Aleister Crowley, has cropped up, more or less disguised, in the fiction of authors as diverse as Dion Fortune, Somerset Maugham and H. R. Wakefield (twice). One of Wakefield's two Crowleyan tales, "'He Cometh and He Passeth By,'" clearly owes a great deal to "Casting the Runes." MRJ's character is not so broadly drawn as the others, but there are clues. Karswell buys Lufford Abbey and becomes known as the Abbot of Lufford, just as Crowley bought Boleskine House and became known as the Laird of Boleskine.

If my contention is correct, how was MRJ's attention drawn to The Beast? Crowley certainly figured in a great many newspaper reports, mostly of a sensational kind, including a couple of court cases concerning his magical practices, and was the subject of a biography by Captain J. F. Q. Fuller with a title that might have attracted notice—*The Star in the West.*

But the connections between the two men were considerably closer than this. MRJ, who made a point of meeting and mixing with students, and had a reliable memory for names, might well have met Crowley! In 1895, during MRJ's time at Cambridge, Crowley came up to Trinity. His Classics tutor was Dr. A. W. Verrall, who seems to have taken to the young man and lent a sympathetic ear when he refused to attend the Political Science lectures of the Moral Science Tripos. Crowley showed some natural facility in Latin and Greek and was even then a striking figure, dressing in the flamboyant style of the 'Decadents,' and publishing poetry in the manner of Swinburne. According to Pfaff, Dr. Verrall was one of the men with whom MRJ came into close contact.

To all but the more cynical among us it may seem unlikely that the self-effacing, celibate, Christian James would find the extrovert, profligate, Pagan Crowley so interesting that he would learn about him and use him as a character in one of his best tales, but let us bear in mind that Dr. Montague Summers, who shared MRJ's fundamental religious beliefs and taste for the unusual, kept a huge dossier on Crowley and told the poet C. R. Cammell that everything concerning him should be preserved, because he was one of the few original and really interesting men of his age. Tantalisingly, MRJ's link with Crowley does not end there, for Sir Gerald Kelly, who painted MRJ's portrait, had once been Crowley's brother-in-law! It would be nice to think that MRJ gathered some tips on the Beast from his one-time friend, but alas, the meeting occurred long after "Casting the Runes" had been published.

When "poor Mr Dunning" arouses Karswell's wrath by advising against acceptance of his paper, "The Truth of Alchemy," the mode of revenge is Runic magic. In one of his books on the Runes, Michael Howard refers to "Mr James's famous story" (*Runes* 52), and while conceding that the structure of the tale is "neat," adds that death Runes would not be so easily "controlled" as James suggests, because great care was needed to "restrain" their powers. This hardly does justice to MRJ. It is precisely because the demonic power cannot be controlled or restrained that Harrington and Dunning make no attempt to do either, but *re-direct* it by returning the slip of paper to Karswell, creating the link that renders him victim of his own plot. This is sound magical sense.

The passing back and forth of runes to the unsuspecting, which creates such tension particularly at the culmination of the tale, is a definite break with tradition. Runes were cut into leather, or carved on metal, wood or stone, none of them easily handed over without exciting suspicion. Paper is an ideal medium and can be deftly slipped into a programme or a sheaf of notes. As if to compensate for this deviation from ancient practice, MRJ goes out of his way to mention an unnecessary and seemingly innocent detail, the presence of the colour red in the formation of the lettering. As the "Grettir Saga" among others informs us, the Runes were magically charged by outlining the letters with blood. Its presence, real or symbolic, provides an authentic touch, and suggests another link between Karswell and Crowley. While there is no mention among Crowley's voluminous published works of his using Runes, he did employ blood as a source of power when anointing and charging talismans. If one were to look for a method of magical attack that was at once original in a fictional sense and consistent with Karswell's Crowleyan character, Runes could hardly be improved upon.

The technique of scrying, or crystal gazing, described in "The Residence at Whitminster," is traceable in its entirety to both Egyptian and Hebrew sources. The Egyptian version is recorded in the 'Leyden Papyrus,' a magical work dating from the third century C.E., though the material contained is clearly of much earlier origin. Its Hebrew equivalent, perhaps inspired in part by a reference in the Talmud to "Princes and Rulers of all shining objects and crystals," gives more complete details of the choosing of a male child, the anointing and placing of a crystal in his hand. He would then see figures who came in answer to an invitation recited by the Querent. It is a practice which has become a staple of magic, used by both the sculptor Cellini and Count Cagliostro, and is evidently still used today in the Middle East (Ahmed 48).

Lord Saul's invocation involves the classic mode of summoning the dark powers, the slaughter of a black cock, and the resulting manifestations point to Beelzebub as the demon petitioned. Dr. Oldys's subsequent encounter with a monstrous insect constitutes the only appearance of the Lord of the Flies in supernatural fiction (up to that time), to conform completely with the accounts of the major Demonologists.

Such observations could be multiplied and extended almost indefinitely but we still have much ground to cover, so for the present the given examples must suffice.

It has been suggested that MRJ was not interested in the nature of his spirits or the mechanisms of hauntings, only in the effects he could create. But it would be nearer to the truth to say that he avoided spoiling the structure of his tales by parading his knowledge in too blatant a form. This was, I think, what he meant when he warned against the injudicious use of technical terminology. Instead, he employed his remarkably wide frame of reference subtly, spinning a web of apparently unconnected events to create a dubious half-light in which things are never quite what they seem. This is a difficult technique, relying as it does upon the working of elegant yet convincing variations on real practices. Such methods soon expose an incomplete understanding of the underlying rationale of magic, but James's style never once let him down, never did violence to the traditions he echoed.

What I have termed the dubious half-light of MRJ's tales is never more evident than in his depiction of the part played by the Church and its ministers in the continuation of pagan influences, represented by Biblical quotations with their disturbing secondary meanings, and by the Abbot or Canon revealed to be guilty of proscribed practices. Here too, MRJ was reflecting a very real state of affairs of which his studies in the history of the Church must have made him well aware. The early Christian assimilation of Pagan deities, sacred rites and festivals is too well recorded to require detailed description here, and we have already encountered the Treasure-Mass, but this is merely a dip into deep waters. From the sixth to the twelfth centuries ordinances had to be passed forbidding idolatry and witchcraft, but the punishment was only a penance and often was not enforced. One thirteenth century priest who led his parishioners in a dance before a phallic image was given no more than a reprimand! Suffice to say that for a long while Christianity and Paganism were uneasy bedfellows. Even when the gods of the old religion were made the devils of the new, an insoluble theological problem remained. Deny the existence of the Devil and one calls into question the goodness of his Divine opposite. '*Sine Diabolo Nullus Dominus.*'

I may be accused of digression at this point, but one should remember that the decade immediately preceding the publication of MRJ's first collection saw the growth of the Decadent Movement, with its call for a reappraisal of good and evil, its obsession with diabolism and the nature of the Holy. Critics have studied Machen in the light of this period, but no one to my knowledge has seen fit to consider the equally powerful works of his contemporary James, in this way. Perhaps this is due, if I may coin a phrase, to the 'bagatelle complex': On no account must James's work be taken 'seriously.' This is a great pity, as he could scarcely have remained unaware of the movement. It even penetrated his own University in the flamboyant form of Crowley among others, and in his own way MRJ reflects the primary concerns of the age as well as any supernatural writer, and more intelligently than most.

It should also be borne in mind that this period in MRJ's life saw the final decision not to take Holy Orders, an end towards which upbringing, parental influence and natural gifts alike had conspired to direct him. There is evidence that he had considered eventual ordination a likely thing, yet as the time approached he suffered uncharacteristic depressions, and even admitted that he was near to 'losing the spiritual sense' (Cox). The decision was a momentous one, and exactly why he did not see fit to enter the Church remains, as Pfaff rightly says, one of the major questions about MRJ's life. It would be presumptuous to suggest that we could answer this question, but any consideration of it ought to take into account personal tendencies revealed by certain subjects upon which he had exercised his mind during the previous decade. Despite the insistence of his tutors that his interest should not turn into 'esoteric byways' he was, between the ages of fourteen and eighteen, gathering notes on sphinxes, curious symbols appended to certain saints, and whether or not Stonehenge was intended for serpent worship (which may have led him to the Reverend John Bathurst-Deane's monumental *The Worship of the Serpent*, a study of pagan ritual and mythology). He enthuses over the ghosts, vampires and wood nymphs in Walter Map, and devotes rather more time than his tutors may have wished to three works that are central to the study of magic: *Hermes Trismegistus, The Orphic Hymns* and *The Transformations of Apuleius*. It was at this time that he delivered a paper on "The Occult Sciences" to the Eton Literary Society (Cox), using as source material De Plancy's *Dictionnaire Infernal* (which contains a drawing of Beelzebub as a gigantic fly, contributing a little, perhaps, to "The Residence at Whitminster").

Nor were these interests limited to his adolescence. As Pfaff comments, MRJ was, in his Apocryphal studies, more interested in the Apocalypses than Gospels. This is allowed to pass without comment or investigation. Let us supply a little of both. Apocalypse is a transliteration of the Greek word for revelation, and all such writings claim to reveal hidden things seen in visions. Their language is symbolic, every element—animals, parts of the body, numbers, stars, colours and garments—requiring translation in the light of initiated knowledge. These obvious affinities with the Quabalistic symbolism of magic are not entirely coincidental. There is a Gnostic origin to much Apocalyptic literature, and there are clearly elements from those Mysteries (Hall)—in this case Eleusian and Phrygian—so dear to MRJ's fictional scholars. More interesting still is the theory that they were written to reconcile the discrepancies between the early Christian and pagan philosophies (Hall).

This, I am aware, takes us a long way from the view (Briggs 125) that MRJ's ghost stories parody his investigations into Holy Writ. Apocalyptic writings may have offered themes that had always appealed to him in a 're-spectable' form, and even helped to reconcile contradictory aspects of his own nature. If the stories reflect this, they performed a more important function in his emotional life than parody. Having ventured so far, I may as well risk outraging MRJ's shade still further by adding a pertinent observation from D. H. Lawrence's *Apocalypse*, on the subject of the Christian fear of pagan knowledge. As Lawrence points out, the instinctive policy has been, and still is, either suppression, destruction, or denial. Publicly at least, MRJ favoured the last of these.

His understandably wary attitude is illustrated by the episode of the Apocryphal document, *The Testament of Solomon*, the magical book of the fifty-eight demons already mentioned in connection with "Canon Alberic's Scrap-book." MRJ appealed in a *Guardian* article for someone to edit the document properly, but was careful to forestall potential criticism by apologising profusely for "wasting" time on a "foolish, superstitious, corrupt and bad book." Yet when an American Biblical scholar took up the request, he gave "considerable help" (Pfaff) in the collation and publishing.

Dr. John Dee, whose manuscripts in the Trinity Library he catalogued, was "always of interest" to James, though Pfaff is quite emphatic that it was only as a bibliophile that Dee interested James. But by coincidence, as A. E. Waite points out, this Alchemist had about him "a cloud of necromancy and magico-Hermetic marvels" (153). Dee's greatest contribution to modern magic is "The Enochian Keys or Calls," a powerful system of evocation later used by Crowley. In later years Crowley records a quite untypical but very Jamesian act—the reading of his own horror story, "The Testament of Magdalen Blair," to friends on Christmas Eve!

In "The Ash-Tree" the source of the horror is first indicated by quotations drawn at random from the Bible, apparently a straightforward appeal for guidance from Holy Writ. But James must have been well aware that *sortilegium*, or divination by sortes, was held in the eyes of medieval theologians to be a pestilential practice, scarcely better than witchcraft itself. What appears to be the power of the church against that of magic, turns out on closer analysis to be magic against magic. We are hardly surprised when the final clue is supplied by the behaviour of a *white* cat. The most innocent things are often animistic portents, and this benign duplicity is surely something more than a tactic of confusion. It reflects contradictions that MRJ, even as an ecclesiologist, could not escape, for they find concrete expression in the pagan-inspired gargoyles and grotesques of Church architecture.

In such works as "The Mezzotint," "A School Story," "The Tractate Middoth" and many another, MRJ proved he could write superb ghost stories *without* an overtly magical theme. That he returned to it as often as he did, in such depth, both in his fiction and in his studies, suggests to me, if I might use the apposite word, *fascination*. This should not be overstated. So vast was his output that no single subject could be called a preoccupation, but his attitude to magic, whenever he came across it, resembles that of Wraxall in "Count Magnus," a mixture of attraction and repulsion in equal measure. Wraxall is attracted to the personality of Magnus, and the more 'evil' he finds him to be, the more attracted he becomes. That this does not occur completely on the conscious level is indicated by the fact that Wraxall actually finds himself chanting a spontaneous invocation of the Count's presence, which summons him from his deathless repose. Once summoned, he pursues Wraxall to the death, but it is not *initially* the Count and his familiar who seek out Wraxall. He brings about his own fate by seeking them! Again we feel an overwhelming sense of occult ritual investing objects and places with a power stronger than the will of the individual. Neither 'goodness' nor 'innocence' offers the slightest protection. There is here an inner tension to the occult tales that has surely contributed to their lasting effect.

If MRJ was, as I suggest, more interested in the occult than most people suspect, he could hardly be called an exceptional case. The study of magic by scholars and theologians amounts almost to a tradition in English literature, from Robert Burton (1576–1640), a clergyman and student of Christ Church, Oxford, who spent most of his life in esoteric studies; to Sabine Baring-Gould, author of a sixteen-volume *Lives of the Saints*, who collected ballads, was deeply versed in Norse mythology and produced a classic study of the werewolf. His *Curious Myths of the Middle Ages* contributed to at least one James tale, and his *Strange Survivals* contains enough material to inspire a whole volume of Jamesian horrors. At the extreme point of this tradition stands Dr. Montague Summers, an authority on Restoration theatre and Gothic fiction, who studied for Holy Orders, yet wrote and edited many classic works on witchcraft, demonology, vampirism, and lycanthropy, amassing over the years a huge library devoted to these subjects. (Little wonder that he was an ardent admirer of MRJ's tales. He seems to have stepped straight out of one!)

There is evidently a body of opinion (Pfaff) that sees MRJ as a kind of Magus, displaying an omniscience bordering on the supernatural. This was due in no small part to the sheer presence of the man, which led one acquaintance to remark that he gave one the feeling that he "could, if necessary, conjure a demon out of a bottle" (Pfaff). Here we must tread carefully. It would be wrong to suggest that MRJ was, in any sense, a crypto-magician.

Montague Summers was ejected from the Christian Church under a cloud, and apparently performed at least one Black Mass (Summers, *Vampire*), with result so shocking that he subsequently set his face against Necromancy with a crusading zeal, but no such aura of brimstone, however tenuous, hangs over the other 'Monty.' He remained to the end an avowed Christian, embodying the feelings of Parkins to the letter: "A man in my position cannot, I find, be too careful about appearing to sanction the current beliefs on such subjects."

What we *are* faced with here is something altogether more subtle, an undercurrent that ran deep, often obscured, its very existence publicly denied by the man himself, but always discernable in his studies and quite central to his fiction. The core of his personality will always remain, as Pfaff says, impenetrable, but we remember Dr. Oldys in "The Residence at Whitminster," who, when confronted by the awful secrets of the press and the chest of drawers, chose not to open them but to lock them away, where they waited like "a jack in the box." MRJ found his own way of raising the lid, in stories rarely if ever equaled. As lovers of macabre fiction, I feel we should be eternally grateful that there was a place in this good and gifted man's heart of hearts that was not entirely on the side of the angels.

Works Cited

Ahmed, Rollo. *The Black Art*. 1936. London: Arrow Books, 1971.

Boguet, Henry. *An Examen of Witches*. Edited by Montague Summers. 1929. London: Muller, 1971.

Briggs, Julia. *Night Visitors: The Rise and Fall of the English Ghost Story*. London: Faber & Faber, 1977.

Cox, Michael. *M. R. James: An Informal Portrait*. London: Oxford University Press, 1983.

Crowley, Aleister. *Magick*. 1911–29. London: Routledge & Kegan Paul, 1973.

Guerber, H. A. *Myths of the Norsemen*. London: George G. Harrap & Co., 1909.

Hall, Manly Palmer. *The Secret Teachings of All Ages*. 1928. Los Angeles: Philosophical Research Society, 1978.

Hastings, James. *Dictionary of the Bible*. Rev. ed. by Frederick C. Grant and H. H. Rowley. New York: Scribner, 1963.

Howard, Michael. *The Magic of the Runes.* Wellingborough: Aquarian Press, 1980.

———. *The Runes and Other Magical Alphabets.* Wellingborough: Aquarian Press, 1978.

James, E. O. *Origins of Sacrifice.* London: John Murray, 1933.

Pfaff, Richard William. *Montague Rhodes James.* London: Scolar Press, 1980.

Radford, E., and M. A. Radford. *Encyclopedia of Superstitions.* 1948. Edited and revised by Christina Hole. London: Hutchinson, 1975.

Rhodes, Henry T. F. *The Satanic Mass.* 1954. London: Arrow Books, 1973.

Summers, Montague. *The Vampire in Europe.* 1929. Wellingborough: Aquarian Press, 1980.

Waite, A. E. *Alchemists through the Ages.* Blauvelt, New York: Rudolf Steiner, 1970.

M. R. James's Women

David G. Rowlands

Some commentators have suggested that M. R. James was a misogynist, whereas others have hinted that he contemplated marriage on several specific occasions. These speculations I am happy to leave to their originators, but I do find MRJ's treatment of his fictional women characters interesting. He certainly never uses them as objects of scorn or derision, though in one or two cases (as with the men) they are vehicles for humour. Even in the case of that distaff "Barker" character, Mrs. Ann Maple, whose voluble discourse he makes so amusing, he softens any hint of ridicule by a commendation (itself a delight of pomposity) of her worth by Dr. Oldys, whose doubtless fruity tones I always mentally allot to Felix Fulton.

There are several women in the ghost stories who only have "walk-on" parts, as it were: Mrs. Chiddock and Lady Mary Hervey; Mrs. Hunt; Eliza the serving maid at the King's Head (I hope her tip was remembered in the stress of subsequent events); and Mrs. Betts. Others like Miss Letitia Haynes and Mrs. Ashton have so few meaningful words that we are dependent upon their situation in the stories to colour them in our imaginations.

It can be tempting to "build up" the minor characters. For example, it would be possible to write several lines about the sacristan's daughter in "Canon Alberic's Scrap-book," or to speculate on the degree of domestic harmony enjoyed by Mrs. Ashton . . . but this would be getting a bit PhD-ish and Lit-ish . . . and once we start down those pathways, psychology and psychiatry lurk only just behind the bushes. No, I'd rather be in Wilsthorpe Maze with Miss and Mrs. Cooper!

Of the more developed and important characters, Dr. James has particular use for the strong-minded, determined woman who has triumphed—for good or ill—over the restrictions of sex, Society, the Establishment or the Law: not least those required to manage feebler men . . . Mrs. Anstruther, Miss Denton, perhaps Lady Wardrop and possibly even the aubergiste at St. Bertrand de Comminges.

MRJ tells us simply that Mrs. Mary Anstruther is "a stately dame of some fifty summers," and she is a force to be reckoned with throughout "The Rose

Garden." Indeed, it is 4 P.M. before she is finished directing her household, and free to resume work on the sketch of the church she is making from the shrubbery of Westfield Hall. She has her husband's time mapped out to suit her ends, and confirmation of her absolute despotism comes in a comment to that gentleman by the gardener, Collins: "'Well now, it ain't for me to go against orders no more than what it is for yourself—or anyone else' (this was added somewhat hurriedly)." We note in fact that the pliable husband, George, has to report back the success of his mission in informing Collins of the lady's wishes, before he can depart to do her bidding in Maldon. One wonders if he ever got much golfing in with Williamson.

This story is, in fact, mostly concerned with Mrs. Anstruther. She is the only one of MRJ's delightfully dominant women to get an unpleasant shock. Miss Denton ("The Diary of Mr. Poynter"), for example, gets off lightly— being shrewd enough not to have any of the curtain fabric in her room! Yet, despite her domineering, Mary Anstruther is sympathetic to her husband's nightmare (though perhaps because of her own disturbed night) and, with Miss Wilkins' narrative in mind, she leaps nimbly to the conclusion of the dream's origin—as shrewdly as does Florence Gayton in "Casting the Runes"—and proposes a reasonable theory of thought transference to account for it.

However, her ingenuity of mind and logic avail her not against the appearance of Sir ——— (William Scroggs?) in the box bushes, nor against the instant recall effect of the photograph of his portrait that the Essex Archaeological Society is hawking round. Her constitution and manner succumb to the shock, and she winters abroad: the arrangements of which also fall to husband George—we are not told whether by mandate or from force of habit. It is one of my few quarrels with MRJ that we do not know if Mrs. Anstruther came to terms with Westfield Hall and the clearing where she envisaged her Rose Garden, or whether the Hall subsequently came on the market.

Lady Wardrop is a particular joy to me. In fact all the characters of "Mr. Humphreys and His Inheritance" add immeasurably to the effectiveness of this tale—one of my great favourites. MRJ unbends to tell us perhaps a little more of her than is his wont: "stout, elderly . . . very full of talk of all sorts and particularly inclined to make herself agreeable to Humphreys . . ." She is also sensitive to atmosphere, particularly that of Wilsthorpe Maze, and shrewd enough to suggest to Humphreys how to solve the riddle of the message on the stone blocks moved from the maze to the summer-house. Her maze book would undoubtedly have made fascinating reading.

More potently forceful, perhaps, are the evil genii of their stories, either in the flesh or from beyond it: Mrs. Mothersole; Mrs. Elizabeth Merryweather; the blackmailing Jane Lee (there is no humour, only grim threat, in her misspelt letter to Archdeacon Haynes); Old Mother Wilkins (not to be confused with Miss Wilkins of "The Rose Garden"); and their Ladyships Sadleir and Ivie (Theodosia Bryan). Nor must we forget those who were but lightly drafted in intent, but nonetheless potent for that: the moustachioed Madame Giraud and perhaps Caroline Purdue (see "The Unfinished Ghost Stories of M. R. James," *Ghosts & Scholars* No. 4, pp. 38–39, 40).

Malevolence and a thirst for retribution are mingled with the pathos of such hapless victims as poor Ann Clark and Phoebe Stanley, but we are given no data to account for the origins of the terrible three women who haunt "Wailing Well." Then there are those innocents who see ghosts and have to endure them despite their fears: the innkeeper Sarah Arscott who describes so vividly to the Assizes the return of Ann Clark; and poor Emma Mitchell who, despite her dread of Betton Wood and its "walker," often perforce has to use that short cut, at the risk of hearing and (once) seeing the shrieking ghost. We are told much less about the elderly widow in the Cathedral Close who dreams of the vampire's red eyes as he (or is it she?) flits about spreading pestilence and enervation; or of the wife of the FSA whose dress is torn and stained as she sits sketching on that particular tomb.

Of the more commonplace ladies who enhance the stories, we find Mrs. Mary Porter at Brockstone (a good foil for Davidson), Miss Wilkins who has sold her house to the Anstruthers (and confides to that lady her childhood "romances" about the arbour: romances which were neither quaint nor charming), Verger Worby's mother; all of whom are limned-in with very few words of description (of Miss Wilkins, for example, we are simply told that she is of mature years), yet of whom we can conjure up surprisingly vivid pictures. Then there are Mrs. and Miss Simpson (who, in "The Tractate Middoth," marries the well-intentioned, but possibly opportunistic Mr. Garrett—though one feels he has earned any future good fortune); and Mrs. and Miss Cooper, whose company I'm sure we should find pleasantly stimulating in small doses, just as the head of their house (that Barker of Barkers) was able to entertain Mr. Humphreys with his patter. Indeed, were I a young man of slight prospects, I'm sure I should not have been averse to showing Miss Cooper the Wilsthorpe Maze myself—chaperoned by her mother of course, who doubtless would have been easy enough to lose for a while at least.

Four characters stand out as particularly good creations. There is the aforementioned Mrs. Maple ("The Residence at Whitminster") of the voluble speech ("I couldn't help thinking to myself, 'If you was bats, where should we be this night?' . . . Well, there's something to be thankful for, if we could but learn by it."). Another housekeeper, Mrs. Bunch of "Lost Hearts," is somewhat more comfortable and placid, perhaps the sort of motherly woman a small boy might befriend and confide in—though, admittedly, Stephen seemingly has no trouble in confiding his dreams to his reclusive uncle, Mr. Abney. Mrs. Bunch and Stephen while away the long evenings in chatter about Aswarby Hall and its occupants, and gradually we become aware of the implication of the sequence of events that is unfolding. Mrs. Bunch's simple beliefs and interpretations represent the reassurance of normality: a bastion against that nagging certainty of what is going to happen. . . .

The Grandmother of "An Evening's Entertainment" is a wonderful mixture of the reassuring—if illogically stern—grandparent who gets a certain satisfaction out of recounting her gruesome story to a captive audience. MRJ gives us no description of the old lady: her character and wry charm appear in the quirky asides and comments she makes on her ghastly narrative ("Don't you know—but there, how should you—what was I thinking of? Well, anyway, you mind what I say."). Even a century or so later than this narrative is set, many of us have experienced grandparents with just this degree of strict illogicality! Having scared the daylights out of the little girl at least with her story, she refuses her a night-light for her room!

Miss Mary Oldys ("The Residence at Whitminster") is perhaps MRJ's most complete attempt at a female character, and an especially delightful one (though Miss Mary Cave, in the incomplete "Speaker Lenthall's Tomb," might have eclipsed her had MRJ persevered with this tale). He takes pleasure in sharing some of her thoughts with us and particularly her confidences to a friend, Emily, in a letter. Part of this letter forms a crucial and grim part of the story, but MRJ also gives us the carefully composed opening of the missive, with its rounded phrases (not devoid—as he tells us—of traces of the influence of that leader of female thought in her day, Miss Anna Seward, known to some as the Swan of Lichfield). The story is, curiously enough, told from a number of viewpoints—that of the narrator who has to span some ninety years in putting together the incidents, that of Dr. Oldys, his niece Mary, and her young man Mr. Spearman—and in the course of the events' unfolding, each of these observers gives us an insight into Mary's character. Whether MRJ had anyone in particular in mind as the original, we cannot know, but he was certainly well-acquainted with a number of lively, intelligent young ladies (the Cropper girls, for examples), who may unwittingly have assisted him to such a felicitous character. Again, you will find little definite description, though we do learn that Mary is "fair . . . with light hair and large eyes, rather a devotee of literature."

As with his horrors, MRJ suggests far, far more than he actually says of his characters, and this, of course, is the source of his power. Read again "The Residence at Whitminster" and see how subtly this is done . . . and if Mr. Spearman is not to be envied his good fortune! The interesting question is, to what extent will his Mary become another Mrs. Anstruther?

"The Rules of Folklore" in the Ghost Stories of M. R. James

Jacqueline Simpson

Presidential Address Given to the Folklore Society, 22 March 1996

When Dr. Montague Rhodes James of King's College, Cambridge, published in 1904 the first volume of the elegant but alarming tales with which his name is now always associated, he called it *Ghost-Stories of an Antiquary;* in 1911 he followed it with *More Ghost Stories of an Antiquary.* The word "antiquary" already had an old-fashioned charm about it, and was appropriate for a scholar whose work revolved round medieval manuscripts, biblical Apocrypha, library catalogues, church iconography and the like.[1] But he was something of a folklorist too (more so than his self-deprecating remarks on the topic imply), with a particular interest in the development and persistence of local legends and historical memories, a good knowledge of traditional beliefs, and an interest in oral narration.

This does not mean, however, that he was in sympathy with the dominant group among folklorists of his time, the comparative anthropologists and mythologists, with their sweeping theories and universalist explanations. They are lampooned in the person of the sinister Mr. Karswell in "Casting

---

1. Two biographies are available. That by R. W. Pfaff (1980) concentrates on James's vast output of scholarly work; that by Michael Cox (1983; reprinted 1986) is a more rounded and vivid portrait, with plenty of personal detail, to which I am much indebted. Cox has also written the prefaces and notes to two recent selections of James's stories, relating them to their biographical contexts (James 1986; 1987). The latter includes three texts omitted from the collected edition (James 1931), namely "The Experiment," "The Malice of Inanimate Objects" and "A Vignette"; also, as an appendix, James's various comments on the craft of writing ghost stories. An article by Norman Scarfe (1986) describes the Suffolk settings used in some of the tales (my thanks to Jennifer Chandler for giving me this reference); further identifications will be found in Cox's notes to James (1987).

the Runes," who is author of a *History of Witchcraft* and a paper on "The Truth of Alchemy," about whom one of the other characters in the story comments:

> There was nothing that the man didn't swallow: mixing up classical myths, and stories out of the *Golden Legend* with reports of savage customs today— all very proper, no doubt, if you know how to use them, but he didn't; he seemed to put the *Golden Legend* and the *Golden Bough* exactly on a par, and to believe both: a pitiable exhibition, in short. (James 1931, 258–59)

That is fiction, written in 1911; in 1917 James raised the same issues in all seriousness against no less a scholar than Jane Harrison, when she wrote a paper linking the dance of Salome and the beheading of John the Baptist to the dance of Agave with the head of Pentheus in the Bacchae as "the dance of the daimon of the New Year with the head of the Old Year, past and slain." After countering Harrison's arguments, James commented:

> I have often viewed with very grave suspicion the way in which compara-
> tive mythologists treat their evidence . . . I regret to see that a researcher of
> her experience can allow herself to make public crude and inconsequential
> speculations of this kind, which go far to justify those who deny to Compara-
> tive Mythology the name and dignity of a science. I believe it to be a science,
> but only in the making. I also believe that one of the worst services that any-
> one responsible for the direction of young students can do them is to encour-
> age them to make it the subject of dissertations, or to propound any theory
> concerning it. Loose thinking, exaggeration of resemblances, ignoring of dif-
> ferences, and downright falsification of evidence, are only a few of the evils
> which a premature handling of it fosters in its votaries. (James 1917; cf. Pfaff
> 1980, 255–56)

These are stern criticisms, which went against the intellectual fashions of the day but which we can now see were largely justified. If that was "the science of folklore," then James certainly had no wish to call himself a "folklorist." At the same time, he knew that a practical knowledge of folklore was useful when reading old texts. He was quite willing to explain the curious way that in Scandinavia and Germany the feast-day of St. Stephen was linked to horse-fights and racing as reminiscent of the cult of Frey (Pfaff 1980, 133). When he edited Walter Map's *De Nugis Curialium* in 1914 he regretted his lack of expertise on "romance and folk-lore" which prevented him from offering an explanatory commentary, while for his translation of the same work in 1923 he enlisted the help of the folklorist E. S. Hartland as editor and annotator. In 1922 he published some fascinating accounts of ghostly encounters which he had discovered as addenda (in Latin) in a medieval manuscript from Byland

Abbey in Yorkshire, using comparisons with nineteenth-century Danish beliefs to explain certain obscure points (James 1922). Towards the end of his life, he translated some of Hans Andersen's fairytales (James 1930). He described one of his fictional narrators (who, as usual, seems to be a self-portrait) as one who had "dabbled a good deal in works of folk-lore" (James 1931, 517). And most significantly, he declared in the Preface to the collected volume of his ghost stories that, although he was not conscious of being indebted to any specific local legend whether written or oral, yet he had "tried to make my ghosts act in ways consistent with the rules of folklore" (James 1931, viii). This is the aspect of his work which I wish to explore here.

It is not, however, the most immediately obvious aspect. A reader who sets out to analyse the flavour of an M. R. James story will surely always be first conscious of the antiquarianism to which his titles drew attention—the easy familiarity with a world of college libraries, old manuscripts, rare books, cathedrals, private chapels, and so forth. Allied to this is the skill in literary pastiche, producing such delights as the sermon on mazes in "Mr. Humphreys and His Inheritance," the transcript of a supposed trial by Judge Jeffreys in "Martin's Close," and several similar though briefer passages. Underlying this, one can glimpse personal susceptibilities to particular aspects of the horrific—spiders, thinness, hairiness, hooded figures and linen drapery are recurrent motifs. James himself gave one deliberate piece of information as to the origins of his ideas. As a child he had seen a toy Punch and Judy set with a cardboard Ghost: "It was a tall figure habited in white with an unnaturally long and narrow head, also surrounded with white, and a dismal visage. Upon this my conceptions of a ghost were based, and for years it permeated my dreams" (James 1931a). A related clue can be gleaned from a posthumously published story entitled "A Vignette," which he sent to the *London Mercury*, but with the comment that he was "ill satisfied" with it. It is a first-person narrative where the narrator himself experiences the horror (unlike most of his others) and its setting is his own childhood home, giving it, as Michael Cox points out, "an autobiographical flavour" (Cox 1983, 151). In it he speaks of a gate with a square hole cut in it, and how one afternoon, looking from the house towards that gate:

> through that hole I could see—and it struck like a blow on the diaphragm—
> something white or partly white. Now this I could not bear, and with an
> access of something like courage—only it was more like desperation, like
> determining that I must know the worst—I did steal down and, quite
> uselessly, of course, taking cover behind bushes as I went, I made progress
> until I was within range of the gate and the hole. Things were, alas!, worse
> than I had feared. Through that hole a face was looking my way. It was not

monstrous, not pale, fleshless, spectral. Malevolent I thought and think it was; at any rate the eyes were large and open and fixed. It was pink and, I thought, hot, and just above the eyes the border of a white linen drapery hung down from the brows . . . I fled, but at what I thought must be a safe distance inside my own precincts I could not but halt and look back. There was no white thing framed in the hole of the gate, but there was a draped form shambling away among the trees . . . Why I make a lame effort to [describe it] now I cannot very well explain; it undoubtedly has had some formidable power of clinging through many years to my imagination. (James 1987, 297–98)

Such experiences, and the childhood nightmare to which James alludes in "'Oh Whistle and I'll Come to You, My Lad,'" clearly left a lasting mark on his imagination. Indeed, throughout his life there are occasional signs that, in spite of his strong Christian faith, he could not shake off a lurking fear that ghosts might exist, though his public remarks on the matter were always resolutely neutral (Cox 1983, 194; James 1987, xvi–xvii).

As well as his childhood capacity to feel and recall horror, the young Monty James soon displayed the other essential gift he would be needing—the narrative and dramatic skills to convey horror to others. At Eton, aged sixteen, he found himself "rather popular" for what he called a "dark sé-ance," i.e. a telling of ghost stories, though whether these were stories he had himself devised he unfortunately does not say. At seventeen, he addressed the Literary Society on "The Occult Sciences," particularly black magic and demonology, for which he used Collin de Plancy's *Dictionnaire Infernal;* and at eighteen he wrote two essays for the *Eton Rambler* on ghost stories, includ-ing an anecdote of his own which already shows typical features of his later material, though the handling lacks subtlety. At about the same age, he wrote another paper on fabulous animals; these activities caused his Eton tutor to comment that "He dredges the deeps of literature for refuse" (Cox 1983, 38–40). Throughout his life, he enjoyed reading his own stories aloud to small groups of friends, often as Christmas entertainment; some were composed especially for this purpose, and others to entertain the choristers of King's College (ibid. 1986, 132–35).

He was fully aware that the literary ghost story, as practised by himself and his admired forerunners Dickens and Le Fanu, was only a recent off-shoot from the older custom of oral storytelling, to which he pays tribute in the framing of two of his lesser tales, "An Evening's Entertainment" and "There Was a Man Dwelt by a Churchyard." The former begins:

Nothing is more common form in old-fashioned books than the description of the winter fireside, where the aged grandam narrates to the circle of children that hangs on her lips story after story of ghosts and fairies, and inspires her audience with a pleasing terror. But we are never allowed to know what the stories were. We hear, indeed, of sheeted spectres with saucer eyes, and—still more intriguing—of "Rawhead and Bloody Bones" (an expression which the Oxford Dictionary traces back to 1550), but the context of these striking images eludes us.

Here, then, is a problem which has long obsessed me; but I see no means of solving it finally. The aged grandams are gone, and the collectors of folklore began their work in England too late to save most of the actual stories which the grandams told. Yet such things do not easily die quite out, and imagination, working on scattered hints, may be able to devise a picture of an evening's entertainment . . . in some such terms as these . . . (James 1931, 588)

The story which follows on from this preamble turns out to be a gruesome fragment of local history, told by a granny to two children, partly so that they should not wake their bad-tempered father from his after-dinner nap, but mainly to warn them against picking blackberries in a certain lane. It is an account of the horrible deaths of two men who had shown a sinister interest in prehistoric burial mounds and heathen worship, how they were refused Christian burial and laid at a crossroads, and how the ruins of their former cottage are still infested with stinging flies—flies that had first been seen thickly clustered on the "great patches of blood" where the corpses had been carried along the lane. James presents this in a convincing pastiche of oral storytelling methods; the grandmother is telling of things that happened "before I was born or thought of," but her information comes from her own father, who had witnessed them, and is bolstered up with topographical details and appeals to current rumours—"They say horses don't like the spot even now, and I've heard there was something of a mist or a light hung about for a long time after, but I don't know the truth of that" (ibid., 600). She herself had once been bitten by one of the "horrid" flies and had had to send for "the wise man over at Bascombe"—"but what it was he bound on my arm and what he said over it he wouldn't tell us" (ibid., 603–4).

The other story to which I have referred, "There Was a Man Dwelt by a Churchyard," takes its title from Shakespeare. In *The Winter's Tale* (Act 2 scene 1) the queen's young son Mamillius declares that "A sad tale's best for winter: I have one / Of sprites and goblins," and begins "There was a man dwelt by a churchyard . . ." As James says:

There is no more of the story; Mamillius died soon after without having a chance of finishing it. Now what was it going to have been? Shakespeare knew, no doubt, and I will be bold to say that I do. It was not going to be a new story; it was to be one which you have most likely heard, and even told.

Everybody may set it in what frame he likes best. Here is mine. (Ibid., 609)

It turns out to be a variation on what is indeed a well-known type of tale (AT 366)—the man who steals something from the dead (in this case, a bag of money from a grave), and how a revenant comes to seek it, and draws gradually closer, closer, until:

> The figure whipped round, stood for an instant at the side of the bed, raised its arms, and with a hoarse scream of "YOU'VE GOT IT!"—at this point H.R.H. Prince Mamillius flung himself upon the youngest of the court ladies present, who responded with an equally piercing cry. (Ibid.)

Many children have relished stories of this kind, told as gruesome jokes, and complete with the final, unexpected, blood-curdling scream. James may well have used them himself in childhood, perhaps on his sister, or on boys in his prep school.

Although James was skilled in reproducing the tone of English conversational narratives, he took for granted that the art of formal storytelling was dead in England, or very nearly so. In "Martin's Close" he shows the folk memory of a local murder as surviving for some two hundred years, but only in obscure and fragmentary form, and only in one man's recollection. However, James discovered for himself that other countries were more fortunate. In 1892 he visited Ireland, where he was told some stories about fairies (Cox 1983, 107), but more significant were the repeated cycling holidays in Denmark and Sweden with various friends—in 1899, 1900, 1901, 1906 and 1923 (Pfaff 1980, 149–50, 222 and 405; Cox 1983, 109–10, 124 and 219).

Even before the first visit he had read "Hans Andersen and the old ballads,"[2] and so was prepared to regard Denmark as "a land of romance"; in the course of that visit he and his two companions, James McBryde and Will Stone, became "much engrossed with the folklore of Jutland, which peoples its wide and lonely heaths with many strange beings." They examined standing stones and old churches, James being especially amused by a fresco at Roskilde illustrating the medieval *exemplum* of the devil noting names of those who chatter in church. During the visit to Sweden in 1901, James saw in the University Library at Uppsala "two contracts with the devil written (and signed in blood) in 1718 by Daniel Salthenius, who was condemned to death for writing them. He escaped that and died professor of divinity at Konigsberg."[3] Two stories from James's first collection are set

---

2. Probably in the original. He had a great facility in acquiring languages, and was capable of reading a six-volume history of Sweden in Swedish (Pfaff 1980, 134).

3. The document can still be seen there, and is translated in Lindow 1978, 45.

in Scandinavian places he had visited—"Number 13" at Viborg in Denmark, and "Count Magnus" at Råbäck in Sweden—while his friend McBryde created a series of cartoons, *The Story of a Troll-Hunt*, in which the three Englishmen in search of trolls are clearly intended to be himself, Monty James and Will Stone.

Tucked away in one of James's learned articles lies a crucial clue to the extent and source of his knowledge of Scandinavian folklore. As I mentioned above, in 1922 he published the Latin texts of some ghost stories inserted into a medieval manuscript, with the following brief introductory comment:

> On blank pages . . . a monk of Byland [Abbey] has written down a series of ghost-stories of which the scenes are laid in his own neighbourhood. They are strong in local colour, and though occasionally confused, incoherent and unduly compressed, evidently represent the words of the narrators with some approach to fidelity.
>
> To me they are redolent of Denmark. Any one who is lucky enough to possess E. T. Kristensen's delightful collections of *Sagn frå Jylland* will be reminded again and again of traits which occur there. Little as I can claim the quality of "folklorist" I am fairly confident that the Scandinavian element is really prominent in these tales. (James 1922, 414)

We do not know by what happy chance James came upon the works of Kristensen, who is now regarded as one of the foremost folklorists of his age, though in his lifetime he was given little financial or scholarly support. But he clearly studied him in detail. In one footnote he cites three volumes of Kristensen's Jutland legends (1883; 1886[4]; 1888) to explain an obscure point in his own text, namely that it is dangerous for someone who has seen a ghost to look at a lamp unless he has first looked at a fire; two more notes give Danish parallels on other matters (James 1922, 415, 419 and 420). Further proof of James's appreciation of Kristensen is the fact that some years later, when translating a selection of Hans Andersen's fairytales, he inserted a couple of tales on the theme of "The Grateful Dead" from Kristensen's collections alongside Andersen's version of this tale-type, "The Travelling Companion"—presumably so that readers might compare the oral tellings with the literary treatment (James 1930, 16). Whether either Andersen or Kristensen would have been pleased at the juxtaposition is another matter.

At the end of "Number 13" James says, more accurately, that Salthenius became Professor of Hebrew.

4. The article gives the reference as "*Sagn og Overtro*, 1866," but this date is a misprint for "1886."

One question which immediately arises is, when and where did James acquire these Kristensen volumes of the 1880s? It would be natural to assume that he bought them in Denmark itself, in the enthusiasm for Jutland folklore which marked his first holiday there in 1899, and possibly influenced by the publicity Sir William Craigie had recently given to Kristensen's work.[5] On the other hand, the heart-eating motif inspiring one of his earliest tales, "Lost Hearts" (written in 1893), suggests that he had read them even earlier.[6] If so, he must have encountered them in England. Dr. Benedik Benedikz has pointed out to me that James would certainly have known Eiríkur Magnusson, an Icelander who was Under Librarian at Cambridge University Library from 1871 onwards, with special responsibility for the purchase of European materials. Eiríkur's interests included Scandinavian folklore; he was tireless in introducing younger scholars to the relatively un-

---

5. A selection of eighty-six legends from Kristensen had been included in Sir William Craigie's *Scandinavian Folklore* of 1896, though only five are about ghosts. James might also have noticed an appreciation of Kristensen which Craigie had just written in *Folk-Lore*, with the comment that "The Danish ghost is not so impressive as the Icelandic, but its doings often have an uncomfortable touch of the horrible about them" (Craigie 1898, 213). By the time James visited Denmark the prolific Kristensen had published, not merely the *Jyske Folkeminder* series to which James alluded in 1922, but also most of his *Danske Sagn* series, of which volume 5 (1897) contains ghost legends.

6. In this story, the villain hopes to obtain magic powers of flight and invisibility by eating the hearts of "not less than three human beings below the age of twenty-one years," having found this recipe "in considerable detail in the works of Hermes Trismegistus." The many writings attributed to "Hermes" are treatises on alchemy, the invocation of angels, and allegedly ancient philosophical wisdom; heretical they may be, but they do not include crude cannibalism (I am grateful to Mr. R. Weighell for confirmation on this point). James had read some of them while still a schoolboy (Pfaff 1980, 36); later, as a scholar specialising in apocrypha of the early Christian centuries, he would surely have had further occasion to explore them. It seems strange that he should blacken their reputation in this way. However, there was a genuine Danish folk belief that magic powers of flight could be got by eating the hearts of seven (or twelve) foetuses cut from their mothers' bodies, and James could have learnt this in Kristensen's 1883 volume (Kristensen 1883, 108–9 no. 156 and note) and adopted it in a bowdlerised form. *Die Handwörterbuch des Deutschen Aberglaubens* (2:16) attests to the belief in Germany too, giving as reference Carl Meyer, *Der Aberglaube des Mittelalters und der nächtsfolgenden Jahrhunderte* (Basel 1884, 279). I suspect James of indulging in mystification here, misdirecting the reader to the impressive Hermes Trismegistus, but actually using folklore—probably Danish, but just possibly German.

known delights of Nordic culture, and could well have been James's initiator in this field.

The two tales to which James gave Scandinavian settings ("Number 13" and "Count Magnus") date from 1899–1900 and 1901–2 respectively (Cox 1983, 136), but I hope to show that the Danish influence continued throughout his years as a ghost-story writer.

It is instructive to consider why Evald Tang Kristensen was so exceptional among folklorists of the nineteenth and early twentieth centuries, for this helps to explain his importance to James. First, his material included a vast number of local legends (sagn) and personal-experience narratives, many of them concerned with the supernatural and firmly rooted in actual beliefs. It was to these that James went when seeking parallels for his medieval Yorkshire manuscript, and they could have supplied many of the "rules of folklore" which he wished his own ghosts to follow, confirming the authenticity of the more fragmented British material. Secondly, unlike most folklorists of his time, Kristensen insisted on publishing tales in the plain language his informants used, without embellishments; true, he smoothed out the broken sentences and false starts which surely occurred, but he kept close to the Jutland idiom, including turns of phrase which jarred on the sensibilities of the educated classes, and pleading with his readers to accept "this simple and true-hearted quality" in regional speech (Kristensen 1876, iv–v).

This must have appealed to James, who appreciated vernacular styles. One reason he relished the records of seventeenth-century State Trials was that there alone, in his view, one could find "the unadorned common speech of Englishmen" of that period (Cox 1983, 144); he would have recognised the same quality in Kristensen. "Count Magnus" includes an inset anecdote told by the Swedish innkeeper to the English hero, which is a superb imitation of Scandinavian oral narrative style (besides being, to my taste at least, one of the most impressively grim passages he ever wrote). The Jutland style is spare, bleak, understated, swift-moving, and given to a species of sinister imprecision at moments of crisis which can sound astonishingly Jamesian— "something was scrabbling at the door and fumbling with the handle"— "sometimes people would see something come running from that field and down to the farm at night" are phrases from Kristensen (1897, 471 and 419), to set alongside James's "Mr. Gregory woke once or twice during the small hours and fancied he heard a fumbling across the lower part of his locked door" ("The Treasure of Abbot Thomas," James 1931, 161) or "she thought she saw something all in tatters with the two arms held out in front of it coming on very fast, and at that she ran for the stile, and tore her gown all to flinders getting over it" ("A Neighbour's Landmark," ibid., 529).

One of the most striking features of James's style is the interplay between the leisurely, mildly pedantic phrasing of the preliminary narrative and descriptions, reflecting the persona of the donnish "antiquary," and the rapid glimpses of horrific concrete details at the climax, vividly but tersely expressed, and never overexplained. Kristensen's volumes could have supplied many models for the latter kind of effect, and the technique for achieving it, at a time when other folklore collectors almost always smothered their material in verbiage.

Kristensen's content would have been equally congenial. Jutland ghosts are not remote historic personages, nor are they vague psychic manifestations. They are very commonly revengeful or arbitrarily malevolent, or doomed to "walk" for their past sins; they often manifest themselves in physical ways, by chasing or attacking people or, at the least, by noise and commotion in the farms. No sophisticated psychic or occult explanations are offered for their existence; Kristensen's informants—and indeed Kristensen himself—accepted them without needing to theorise about them. All this fits well with James's general concept of the revenant (palpably physical, menacing, evil or vengeful, often allied to demons) and his dislike of abstract "quasi-scientific" speculations.

As regards individual motifs, there are of course a great many that are common to British and to Danish lore—that ghosts come at dusk, but that candle-light keeps them at bay; the ghost or fiend in the form of a dog; ghosts that enter only when invited; storms at the deaths of evil men; ghosts or demonic animals guarding buried treasure; the revenge of the dead on those who steal from them or maltreat their bodies; witches that turn into hares; the learned black magician, with his satanic pact and his devilish familiars. All these are ideas that James uses, and though one can unhesitatingly say that they are folkloric, they are too widespread to trace to specific sources. The ghosts that creep slowly and stealthily towards their target in "The Mezzotint" and "Mr. Humphreys and His Inheritance" recall those in certain West of England legends, and also in Danish ones, who after having been once exorcised are returning home from their place of banishment by the length of one cock's stride, or one hen's feather or one straw, every year (Brown 1979, 26, 32, 33, 36, 62 and 78; Kristensen 1886, 245 and 247; 1897, 151). In Denmark these "cockstride ghosts" are seen as malevolent, whereas the British ones are penitential, which may make Danish influence slightly more likely here.

Other elements, however, are definitely British or Irish. The songs used to such sinister effect in "'Oh Whistle . . .'" and in "Martin's Close" are well-known Scottish and English ones; Ireland is said to be the source for the belief that ash trees are sinister, which runs counter to English ideas[7] ("The Ash-Tree"). In "A Warning to the Curious" (1925) James uses the heraldic arms of East Anglia, which show three crowns, as basis for a convincingly "traditional"-looking claim that three crowns buried on the coast guard England from invasion. This is now often taken as a genuine legend, and was told as such by "several Suffolk residents" to the folklorist Enid Porter, who seems to have accepted it as authentic (Porter 1974, 131–32 and 181). One local writer says that a sexton named Eade, living at Blythburgh in the 1950s, "believed implicitly" that the last remaining crown had saved England from a Nazi invasion (Forrest 1961, 134–35). However, no source earlier than James has yet been found. I believe he simply wove his own story round the heraldic crowns according to the "rules of folklore," possibly modelled on the spurious but popular legend of Drake's Drum or on the tale about the head of Bendigeidfran in the *Mabinogion*. I also suspect that the remark embedded in his story that "it is rather surprising" that the legend "has not made its way into print before" (James 1931, 567) is a sly hint that he himself invented it.

One motif can be definitely identified as Danish, for it has no equivalent in British lore—even though James, with characteristic cleverness, has transplanted it into a wholly English setting which conceals its origins. The story in question is "The Rose Garden," in his second collection (1911), and my attention was first drawn to its Danishness some years ago by Joan Rockwell, author of a major biography of Kristensen (Rockwell 1981). In this story, a woman is planning to have an old summerhouse pulled down to make way for a rose garden; a relative of the previous owners tells her of an odd experience she had had there in childhood:

> All at once I became conscious that someone was whispering to me inside the arbour. The only words I could distinguish, or thought I could, were "Pull, pull. I'll push, you pull" . . . And—this sounds very foolish, but still it is the fact—I made sure it was strongest when I put my ear to an old post which was part of the end of the seat. (James 1931, 199)

Despite this alarming information, the new owner goes ahead with her plan; the summerhouse is demolished, the old post uprooted. There follow sinister

---

7. In England, ash trees are credited with healing, divinatory and protective powers. I have found one Scottish story and two from the Fens where ghosts are seen near ashes (Briggs 1971, 1:478–80, 482–84 and 489–91), but this hardly seems significant. Scarfe suggests that the allusion is to actual trees, including ash trees, round Livermere Hall in the village where James grew up (Scarfe 1986, 1418); the unusual surname "Mothersole," given to the witch in this tale, occurs on gravestones in Livermere churchyard.

dreams, sounds of strange calls by night and owls hooting, and eventually the woman is horrified by glimpsing what she at first takes to be a mask but is in fact "a face large, smooth and pink," with eyes closed, among the branches of her shrubbery. It turns out that an evil seventeenth-century judge had died in the house, but his ghost had troubled the parish till several parsons assembled to lay him, and "the stake is in a field adjoining to the churchyard" (ibid., 207).[8]

There are of course ghost-laying stories in British tradition, but generally the revenant is forced into a bottle which is then thrown into water, or else banished to the Red Sea. The idea that it is pinned under a stake which must never be moved is typically Danish, as are also the phrases "You pull, I'll push" or "Pull, pull!" or "Shake it! Pull it!" heard coming from the ground; these have no British parallels, but frequently occur as an "epic formula" at the core of Danish legends. Examples are plentiful in Kristensen (1876, 245 and 248; 1880, 171–72; 1883, 118; 1897, 217–19). In Danish belief, if the ghost is released by uprooting its stake, it may manifest itself as a sinister "night-raven" (a nightjar?); hence, possibly, the owl in James's story. It may be worth noting that in one of Kristensen's versions the removal of the stake is due to the foolish obstinacy of a priest's domineering wife, who wants to turn part of the orchard into her personal garden, and secretly uproots the post, which she had promised never to disturb; with a terrifying din, a fiery ghost leaps out and chases her back to the house (cf. "the shelter of the house was gained and the door shut before she collapsed," James 1931, 206). After that, she is a reformed character (Kristensen 1880,171–72). The similarity to the nagging wife in James's story may be no coincidence.

Similarly, "A Neighbour's Landmark" transplants a characteristically

---

8. In an unfinished story, recently published under the title "John Humphreys," there is "a tall post newly covered with black and glistening tar" seen by the hero in fields which were "ancient pastures"; next day it has disappeared, and a farm worker assures him that there had never been any such thing there. This incident is the first in a series of threatening events involving black magic; James may have intended to reveal that a "ghost-post" of the Danish type had indeed once stood in the pasture and had been moved, releasing an evil spectre, or (equally possibly) the post may be one of a series of manifestations of the shape-changing ghost itself (James 1993). This story is an early draft for "Mr. Humphreys and His Inheritance," and it may well be relevant that at the climax of the latter there is a hole, seeming infinitely deep, out of which a ghost comes crawling up to attack the hero (James 1931, 355–56). The preceding imagery of the story does nothing to prepare readers for this hole; possibly James was still half consciously recalling the ghost-posts of Denmark.

Danish motif, the so-called "boundary ghost" whose sin is to have wrongfully acquired a neighbour's land, either by literally shifting a boundary stone, or by a false oath, and whose doom is to walk round it forever. It is of course true that the biblical text "Cursed be he that removeth his neighbour's landmark" was familiar in England through its use in the Anglican Commination Service on Ash Wednesday; nevertheless, land-theft is not a usual theme in English ghost legends, whereas it is common in Danish collections, including the ones which James owned (Kristensen 1876, 205–10; 1883, 115–18). There, the "boundary ghosts" are often described as shouting, screaming, or wailing as they patrol their ill-gotten land; sometimes, one can hear them coming nearer and nearer (Kristensen 1897, 104–5), just as in James; in one story, a man foolishly taunts the invisible ghost to "Shout now, man!", only to have it yell right beside him (Kristensen 1886, 199). James was certainly aware of this motif, for he alludes to it in a footnote to his paper on the "Medieval Ghost-Stories," one of which concerns a spirit that yelled "Ho, hoo, hoo!" in the night (James 1922, 419). His own story must have been taking shape in his mind at about this same period (it was first published in 1924); the story and the article both allude to a line from Sir Walter Scott ("Where walks, they say, the shrieking ghost"). Since we also know that he identified the "heroine" of this tale with a real-life English villainess (Lady Ivie, tried for forging deeds to some land at Shadwell; James 1931, 532), we can appreciate how skilfully he combined elements from varied sources—and how cunningly he covered his tracks.

The two tales that do have Scandinavian settings, "Number 13" and "Count Magnus," both deal with an evil magus or black magician, a topic to which James returned again and again, perhaps because the quest for secret knowledge represented a temptation which he as a scholar could readily understand, involving "the ability of the mind to be hooked or fascinated" (Hughes 1993, 81–82 and 87; cf. Weighell 1984; MacCulloch 1995). There are many such Faustian figures in Scandinavia and of course in British traditions too; they are often said to be priests, but that is one motif James never uses, presumably finding it offensive to his Christian convictions. Many are said to have acquired their arts by studying in the "Black School," always alleged to be in some distant university town, and presided over by the devil himself. James offers us a variation which seems to be his own invention: Count Magnus had gone on a "Black Pilgrimage" to the accursed city of Chorazin to salute the Prince of the Air (i.e. Satan—Ephesians 2:2), in order "to obtain a faithful messenger and see the blood of his enemies" (James 1931, 107).[9]

---

9. Bengt af Klintberg kindly informs me that no "Black Pilgrimage" is known in

One striking detail in "Count Magnus" is the padlocked tomb. The count lies in a copper sarcophagus with sinister engravings (but no crucifix), secured by "finely worked and massive padlocks, three in number" (ibid., 113). Three times the hero, moved by some half-conscious impulse, finds himself saying aloud that he wishes he could see the Count. Each time, a padlock opens and falls off, and the third time, the lid moves. Hunted down by the Count and his monstrous hooded "messenger," the hero comes to a bad end. This is a magnificent example of a Jamesian ghost behaving in accordance with "the rules of folklore." I have not found anything so crude as a direct source of these padlocks, Bengt af Klintberg having kindly confirmed for me that there is none in Swedish legend, though the general idea that if a buried person is mockingly greeted he will emerge in a frightful shape is common there. However, as regards the padlocks, I can point to one English tale and a cluster of Danish ones which could have provided stimulating guidance for James's creative imagination.

The English legend is one James certainly knew: that of the Witch of Berkeley, as told by William of Malmesbury (on whom James once lectured). She asked that her corpse should be sewn up in the skin of a stag and laid in a stone coffin fastened with three chains, which should be left unburied for three nights; in vain—for each night devils came and snapped one chain, and on the third night Satan kicked the coffin to pieces and carried her off (Westwood 1986, 244–45). But these chains have no padlocks. In Danish tradition, on the other hand, there are indeed padlocks, but they are rarely on coffins, the only example I have found so far being the following reminiscence about a Cunning Man:

> Knud the Smith in Elsborg claimed to be a good deal cleverer than most people, and he was a bit peculiar too. For instance, while he was still alive he had a coffin made and painted red, with a padlock to it, and he declared that he wanted to be buried in that when he died, as was indeed done. (Kristensen 1880, 205)

Elsewhere, the padlocks are linked with ghost-laying; in some cases they symbolise the power which the exorcist achieves over the revertant, and in others the stages by which the latter draws closer to the house where the ex-

---

Sweden, though the "Black School" is known there as elsewhere. Michael Cox suggests a link with a curious report in 1815 (in the *Monthly Repository of Theology and General Literature* 10:110 [1815]: 121) that "the late King of Sweden" (i.e. the deposed and exiled Gustavus IV) meant to go on pilgrimage to the Holy Land with ten companions, all to be clad in black robes and calling themselves the "Black Brethren" (James 1987, 310–11).

orcist awaits him. The motif is regularly found in the legend of how a man named Bertel the Unborn (like Macduff, he had been cut from his mother's womb) laid the ghost of a landowner named Gyldenstjaerne, who had been haunting the manor-house of Stubbergaard. In one version, it is said that Bertel set three lights and one padlock on a table, and told a girl to watch the padlock carefully, "for by that she would know if he had won the mastery, for if the lock closed properly he would have succeeded, but if it couldn't or wouldn't, then Peder Gyldenstjaerne had mastered him" (Kristensen 1876, 240). James delicately hints at this symbolism when he notes that his hero tries to re-close the first two padlocks, but fails.

In another version of the same legend, the ghost has been appearing in the form of a dog and four priests have failed to lay it:

> Then Bertel takes a padlock from his pocket, which he sets down in five separate pieces on the table in front of the four priests, and he tells them that if the padlock slides together they must do nothing to hinder it—"I'll deal with the matter myself; but if any of the pieces fall to the ground, you must come at once to save me." So the five priests remained sitting there, each with his book in front of him, and so Bertel and the dog went off together and came to the boggy pit on Ellemose Heath . . . and there he began to conjure him down. When some time had passed, the padlock began sliding about on the table back at home, time after time, time after time, and finally it snaps shut with a clang. At that very moment it was all over, the ghost gave a shriek, and so he was laid. (Kristensen 1880, 166–67; cf. 1886, 244–45)

In his 1886 volume, Kristensen gives two variants. In the first, the exorcising priest (here called Jorgen the Unborn) "took a padlock and opened it and laid it on the table, saying this would be a token for the girl that he had overcome the ghost, for the padlock would close up bit by bit"; and so it does, for when the priest returns safely from his exorcism "the girl was sitting quietly, and the padlock was shut" (Kristensen 1886, 244–45). The second illustrates the other type of symbolism. Here, the exorciser (Knud the Unborn) sets seven candles and one padlock on the table, and he and the girl keep watch. "Then the padlock on the table gave a hop, and the priest said: 'Now Gyldenstjaerne has jumped up out of his grave in Viborg.' At the second hop of the padlock he was at Hagebro, and at the third, at Stubbergaard" (Kristensen 1886, 246; cf. 252–53, where the lock and its hasp draw nearer to one another at each stage of the ghost's approach). There are also variations on this idea where the exorcist sets up three wooden pegs, which fall one by one as the ghost draws nearer. I have even found one where there are three closed padlocks lying on the table, and they spring open one by one at each stage of the ghost's journey, which is the closest to James's plot—but, frustratingly, this comes from Kristensen's last collection, published in 1934, far too late for James to have used it.

Other echoes of Danish lore can be found in certain details in "The Residence at Whitminster," alongside allusions to Irish witchcraft, satanic sacrifices, scrying, and demonic dogs. The first is when one of the characters finds that a book he is carrying is struck, or rather twitched, out of his hand in the dark (James 1931, 382), for Danish ghosts commonly knock the Bible or prayer-book out of the hand of the exorcist trying to lay them (e.g. Kristensen 1883, 147–48; 1886, 247). The second is the housekeeper's comment about the young magician's familiars: "Them that was with him, why they were such as would strip the skin from a child in its grave," for the Jutlanders believed that the Devil would steal the skin from a corpse and wrap himself in it to masquerade as a ghost (Kristensen 1886, 322).[10] The collapse of a revenant into a pile of dust once its mission is accomplished ("The Tractate Middoth," "The Uncommon Prayer-Book") also has Danish parallels which James would have known (Kristensen 1876, 163–64).

On the other hand, one thing in James that looks Scandinavian probably is not—there is no precedent for the way runes are used in his story "Casting the Runes," where a strip of paper "with some very odd writing on it in red and black [which] looked more like Runic letters than anything else" carries a curse to the person unwittingly receiving it. True, Tacitus tells how ancient Germans quite literally cast slivers of wood on the ground as a form of divination, and many scholars assume these were inscribed with runes; true, there are references in medieval Icelandic texts to runes as protective magic, so one could logically deduce that they could be harmful too; true, carved runes were sometimes coloured red. But there is nothing in archaeology or in medieval texts which corresponds at all closely to the way the evil Mr. Karswell uses runes in this story; there might of course be something relevant in the later Scandinavian grimoires, which James might have happened upon, but if so I have not yet found it.

"An Episode of Cathedral History" is rich in motifs with Danish parallels. The story centres on the discovery of an old altar tomb in the choir (on the north side, significantly) which had long been concealed under the structure of the pulpit—and "on the north side of it there was what looked like an injury: a gap between two of the slabs composing the side. It might be two or three inches across" (James 1931, 422). Once this tomb is uncovered,

---

10. There is an English variant which James might have known in *Choice Notes from "Notes and Queries": Folklore* (London 1859, 170), about a man who sold his soul to the Devil on condition the Devil might strip his skin from him after death (reprinted in Briggs 1971, 1:56, as "A Cock Scares the Fiend").

trouble begins; people fall ill, horrific wails and shrieks are heard by night, occasionally something with dully glowing red eyes is glimpsed in the dark. A woman who sits on the tomb finds the hem of her dress torn away. It proves impossible to repair the gap between the slabs, for the plaster is violently blown out again. A choirboy stoops near the chink, puts two fingers in his mouth and whistles, and at that he thinks he hears something stirring; his friend sticks a rolled-up sheet of music in, and something catches it and pulls the end off, leaving the torn end wet and black (ibid., 427–29).

All these can be seen as adaptations of Danish motifs. It is very common for a Danish haunting to manifest itself as noises rather than sights, and to cause sickness of humans or animals; the red-eyed church-dwelling ghost appears in a widespread migratory legend (e.g. Kristensen 1876, 290–92; 1897, 233–35); and the crack or hole through which a ghost regularly passes is common too, as for example in this anecdote:

> Once he was dead, he haunted the place dreadfully. As for his grave, which was the type that is built of bricks and has oak palings round it, they never could keep it bricked up as it ought to be; the eastern end of it was constantly falling down, because it was through there he used to come out. I've often gone past that grave, and always seen it in that state—perfectly all right all round, except just at the east end. (Kristensen 1880, 112–13; cf. 1897, 119, 246 and 451)

Sometimes, it is said that if one tries to stop up such holes in graves, the stones will get drawn down into the grave overnight and disappear (Kristensen 1897, 241–42). Other things may get dragged in too. One rather grotesque legend concerns the ghost of a Madam Vissing who was partly but not completely laid, so that her head and shoulders remained sticking up out of the ground, "so they set an upturned barrel over her"; years later, when the barrel was beginning to rot, a child jokingly poked a whip into a hole in it, "and then she snatched the whip away from him" (Kristensen 1897, 313–14).

The damage to the music sheet and to the hem of the woman's dress has no exact parallel in either British or Danish lore, as far as I recall, but there is one Danish motif which is fairly similar—namely, that a malevolent ghost demands that a living person should clasp his hand in token of some pledge, but the latter prudently offers a kerchief or apron instead; the ghost rips the end off, and the torn edge is then seen to be blackened and scorched.

As for whistling, particularly at night, the consequences could be quite horrific, according to Jutland beliefs. It could summon up a ghost, who might then chase you; or the will-o'-the-wisp; or the Wild Hunt; or a demonic dog; or the Devil himself, especially if you had whistled through the keyhole of a church door (Kristensen 1876, 293; 1883, 288 and 289; 1886, 195 and 290).

And this of course leads us to the most famous story James wrote, which many recall with a particular shudder: "'Oh, Whistle, and I'll Come to You, My Lad.'" As ever, the elements are admirably blended. There is the East Anglian setting; the antiquarian mystery of the whistle itself, found in the ruins of a Templar chapel, with its puzzling inscription FUR-FLA-FLE-BIS; the theme of the pursuing ghost; the artful gradations of horror, conveyed in hints and brief perceptions; the touches drawn from folklore, such as the power of candlelight and the taboo on "whistling for the wind" (about which one of the characters comments that "they believe in it all over Denmark and Norway, as well as on the Yorkshire coast"). But the most memorable feature of this particular ghost is the way it invades the unfortunate hero's hotel room and takes possession of the spare bed, so that "the clothes were bundled up and twisted together in the most tortuous confusion"; from these sheets it fashions itself a body of fluttering linen draperies. A child glimpses it by daylight, "waving" at the window; by night, it rises and attacks its victim, revealing "a horrible, an intensely horrible, face *of crumpled linen*" (James 1931, 148; his emphasis).

It does not take much detective work to relate this climax to James's personal fears—to the face, draped in white, peering through the hole in the gate in "A Vignette," or the sheeted ghost of the Punch and Judy show. Indeed, making a rare personal comment within the text of "'Oh, Whistle . . .'" itself, he tells the reader, at the moment when the hero first sees the ghost sit up in an empty bed, that "I have in a dream thirty years back seen the same thing happen"; and in his Preface he confirms that this is the one case when he based a story on his own experience, since "a dream furnished the suggestion" (ibid., vii). Though James does not say so explicitly, it must have been a childhood dream; thirty years previous to the date of publication (1904), he was only twelve.

As he read through his volumes of Kristensen, James would have come upon quite a number of tales with details that would have recalled his nightmare, for one of Kristensen's regular subdivisions is "Haunted Bedrooms," and the haunting often takes the form of dragging the sleeper's quilt or sheets off him (e.g. Kristensen 1886, 227). Still more horrible, there are ghosts that actually get inside the bed—not a spare bed, but one already occupied. The human sleeper at first rolls over to make room for the newcomer (sharing beds was quite commonplace, especially for farm-workers), but then realises it is a revenant, and flees (Kristensen 1876, 187; 1886, 224).[11] Some-

---

11. In the 1886 volume, Kristensen gave titles to individual tales (a practice he later dropped), and this one he called "The Ghost in the Bed"—a title sure to catch James's eye and recall his own nightmare fear.

times a prayer will drive such ghosts away (Kristensen 1880, 113). In one case there is a tussle in the dark, won by the living man; it turns out that the ghost came to claim the sheets because they should have been put in the grave (Kristensen 1897, 486). Of haunted rooms in certain great houses it is said that they stand empty, but "the bed has to be remade every day" because a white lady haunts the room and "every night a little dog lies on that bed," or that the bed "always has signs on it in the morning that someone has slept in it all night" (ibid., 491 and 512).

Nothing in all this, of course, equals the horror of James's conception of the creature with the face of crumpled linen, let alone the skill with which this horror is conveyed. By pointing to partial parallels in folklore for this and others among his tales, I do not mean to detract from his originality, but simply to show how the driving force of his powerful imagination allied itself to plots and motifs from traditional storytelling. The literary "rules" of a ghost story, he once wrote, are merely those of any short story (James 1987, 339); maybe so, but he also knew the "rules of folklore," and obeyed them too, with superbly effective results.

Works Cited

Briggs, Julia. *Night Visitors: The Rise and Fall of the English Ghost Story.* London: Faber & Faber, 1977.

Briggs, K. M. *A Dictionary of British Folk-Tales in the English Language.* Part B, Folk Legends. London: Routledge & Kegan Paul, 1971.

Brown, Theo. *The Fate of the Dead: Folk Eschatology in the West Country After the Reformation.* Ipswich: D. S. Brewer, 1979.

Cox, Michael. *M. R. James: An Informal Portrait.* Oxford: Oxford University Press, 1983.

Craigie, W. A. "Evald Tang Kristensen: A Danish Folk-lorist." *Folk-Lore* 9 (1898): 194–224.

Forrest, A. J. *Under Three Crowns.* Ipswich: Norman Adlard & Co., 1961.

Hughes, Martin. "A Maze of Secrets in a Story by M. R. James." *Durham University Journal* 85 (1993): 81–93.

James, M. R. "Some Remarks on 'The Head of John the Baptist.'" *Classical Review* 31 (1917): 255–56.

———. "Twelve Medieval Ghost-Stories." *English Historical Review* 37 (1922): 413–22.

———. (1931). *The Collected Ghost Stories of M. R. James.* London: Edward Arnold, 1931.

————. (1931a). "Ghosts—Treat Them Gently!" *Evening News* (17 April 1931).

————. "A Vignette." *London Mercury* 35 (1936): 18–22. Reprinted in James 1987: 293–98.

————. *The Ghost Stories of M. R. James.* Introduced by Michael Cox. Oxford: Oxford University Press, 1986.

————. *Casting the Runes and Other Stories.* Introduction and Notes by Michael Cox. Oxford: Oxford University Press/The World's Classics, 1987.

————. "John Humphreys." Edited by Rosemary Pardoe. *Ghosts & Scholars* No. 16 (1993): 1–10.

————, trans. *Forty Stories by Hans Andersen.* London: Faber & Faber, 1930.

Kristensen, E. T. *Jyske Folkesagn* (= *Jyske Folkeminder III*). Copenhagen: Gyldendalske Boghandel, 1876.

————. *Sagn frå Jylland* (= *Jyske Folkeminder IV*). Copenhagen: Karl Schonbergs Forlag, 1880.

————. *Sagn og Overtro frå Jylland* (= *Jyske Folkeminder VI*). Copenhagen: Karl Schonbergs Boghandel, 1883.

————. *Sagn og Overtro frå Jylland* (= *Jyske Folkeminder VIII*). Copenhagen: Karl Schonbergs Boghandel, 1886.

————. *Sagn og Overtro frå Jylland* (= *Jyske Folkeminder IX*). Copenhagen: Karl Schonbergs Boghandel, 1888.

————. *Danske Sagn V.* Århus: Jakob Zeuners Bogtrykkeri, 1897.

————. *Danske Sagn: Ny Raekke V.* Copenhagen: C.A. Reitzels Forlag, 1934.

Lindow, John. *Swedish Legends and Folktale.* Berkeley: University of California Press, 1978.

MacCulloch, Simon. "The Toad in the Study: M. R. James, H. P. Lovecraft and Forbidden Knowledge (Part One)." *Ghosts & Scholars* No. 20 (1995): 38–44.

Pfaff, Richard William. *Montague Rhodes James.* London: Scolar Press, 1980.

Porter, Enid. *The Folklore of East Anglia.* London: Batsford, 1974.

Rockwell, Joan. *Evald Tang Kristensen: A Lifelong Adventure in Folklore.* Aalborg & Copenhagen: Aalborg University Press, 1981.

Scarfe, Norman. "The Strangeness Present: M. R. James's Suffolk." *Country Life* 230 (6 November 1986): 1416–19.

Weighell, Ron. "Dark Devotions: M. R. James and the Magical Tradition." *Ghosts & Scholars* No. 6 (1984): 20–24.

Westwood, Jennifer. *Albion: A Guide to Legendary Britain.* London: Book Club Associates, 1986.

"A Warning to the Curious":
Victorian Science and the Awful Unconscious in M. R. James's Ghost Stories

Brian Cowlishaw

M. R. James, who published four collections of ghost stories between 1904 and 1925,[1] was "the perfect embodiment of a successful post-Victorian man of letters" (Sullivan 73): he was a graduate fellow, museum director, and finally Vice Chancellor of Cambridge, as well as a respected medievalist and biblical scholar. The standard critical approach to his stories has been to focus upon the "man of letters"—to seek the sources of the historical and archaeological details that crowd his ghost stories in his academic/antiquarian occupations.[2] That this should be the *standard* approach is a bit strange, though, considering James's own assertions that the stories are definitely not "based on my own experience" (*Stories* 5), that both the settings and the legends attaching to them are mostly imaginary, and that "the fragments of ostensible erudition which are scattered about my pages" are almost completely "pure invention" (5–6). Authors' statements about their work cannot always be trusted, but statements as direct as these should be taken more seriously than they have been.

One more fruitful approach to his stories can be found in the first half of Jack Sullivan's characterization: James as "post-Victorian." James might accurately say of himself the words he gives the narrator of "A Neighbour's Landmark": "Remember, if you please . . . that I am a Victorian by birth and education, and that the Victorian tree may not unreasonably be expected to bear Victorian fruit" (*Stories* 289). James was born in 1862, only twenty-five

---

1. The contents of these four volumes, plus the story "Wailing Well," are collected in *The Penguin Complete Stories of M. R. James*, as well as in the Wordsworth Classics edition of *Collected Ghost Stories*. References in this essay are to the Penguin edition.

2. In addition to Sullivan, see Pfaff, J. Randolph Cox, and Michael Cox.

years into Victoria's sixty-four-year reign, and he graduated from Cambridge in 1886. His roots, then, are solidly Victorian, as is his "fruit," his stories.

From this point of view, the stories prove quite revealing. What they reveal is a particularly Victorian set of assumptions about history, historical records, evolution, and human civilization that closely resembles Sigmund Freud's, but that seeks to bury what Freud seeks to uncover and decode. That is: James's stories reproduce Victorian reconstructive science's[3] assumption that history and civilization are readable, though generally only with difficulty and with uncertainty as to results. James also reproduces the Victorian doctrine of evolution—that *homo sapiens* descended from simpler organisms, some of which still survive in the present in primitive, unevolved form. In James's stories, as in Victorian reconstructive science, human existence can be conceived of in levels of development or civilization, with the most "civilized" and recent level lying nearest the top (in terms of both quality and accessibility). Earlier, lower, more "savage" levels survive below; one cannot ordinarily see them, but with the right kind of "digging" one can locate, reconstruct, and read them. James's conception of human civilization, borrowed from influential Victorian scientists, thus closely resembles Freud's. In effect, then, if not in intention, when James reproduces in his stories the views of Victorian reconstructive science, he is writing about what Freud would call "the unconscious." However, James differs radically from Freud in his attitude toward the unconscious. Whereas the Victorians and Freud saw the unearthing and reading of the past "as an important practical guide to the understanding of the present and the shaping of the future" (Tylor 1:24), James's stories suggest that the reading of the past is actually dangerous—that to unearth the savage past is to summon it to the more civilized present, with frightening, destructive results. Whereas Freud sought to read the unconscious much as Victorian scientists sought to read fossils, the geological record, and human cultures, James wants to keep the unconscious buried. Freud sought to relieve repression; James encourages it.

I. Reading the Past

In M. R. James's ghost stories, the past is always readable, if with difficulty. In this belief James follows the lead of Charles Lyell and Charles Darwin. Lyell, a very influential early-Victorian geologist,[4] first published *Principles of*

---

3. The "reconstructive sciences" included primarily biology, geology, and anthropology—branches of science which construct narratives accounting for the past out of available physical evidence.

4. To give one index of Lyell's influence: Charles Dickens mentions Lyell in

Geology in 1830. In that text, Lyell writes of "reading" the geological evidence; he envisions the world as a text, its fossils and geological formations being the "handwriting." His task as geologist is to interpret this handwriting accurately. But Lyell, "a student of Nature," recognizes he can at best become "acquainted only with one-tenth part of the processes *now* going on upon or far below the surface, or in the depths of the sea" (1:462, emphasis added), let alone the processes that occurred millennia ago. This renders all attempts to read the earth's distant past in the geological record sketchy and uncertain; geologists find themselves in much the same position as readers of human language "acquainted with just one-tenth part of the words of some living language," and then "presented with several books purporting to be written in the same tongue ten centuries ago" (1:461). Provided with such a fragmented text, a geologist could easily "declare without hesitation that the ancient laws of nature have been subverted" (1:462)—and be completely wrong. Charles Darwin, too, employs Lyell's reading metaphor, in addition to echoing Lyell's warnings. In *The Origin of Species*, published in 1859, Darwin writes:

> For my part, following out Lyell's metaphor, I look at the natural geologi-
> cal record, as a history of the world imperfectly kept, and written in a chang-
> ing dialect; of this history we possess the last volume alone, relating only to
> two or three countries. Of this volume, only here and there a short chapter
> has been preserved; and of each page, only here and there a few lines. Each
> word of the slowly-changing language, in which the history is supposed to be
> written, being more or less different in the interrupted succession of chap-
> ters, may represent the apparently abruptly changed forms of life, entombed
> in our consecutive, but widely separated formations. (316)

With such fragmentary evidence to interpret, the geologist can gather a sense of the past, but can make no complete or certain readings. For Lyell and Darwin, then, the geological-historical record is readable but only with considerable difficulty and uncertainty.

James imbibes both elements of the Victorians' attitude toward the historical record: confidence in the possibility of reconstructing and reading the

---

Martin Chuzzlewit, Chapter 22. La Fayette Kettle, an American, invites Martin Chuzzlewit to speak to the Young Men's Watertoast Association "upon the Tower of London," or, if he prefers, "upon the Elements of Geology" (363). The *Elements of Geology*, published in 1838, was a simplified recasting of the third volume of the *Principles*, cited here. Apparently the *Elements* was a book an American could expect an educated Englishman to know in 1843–44, when *Martin Chuzzlewit* was published.

past, and caution that the results may not be complete or accurate. Like the narratives of Darwin and Lyell, James's ghost stories center around reconstruction of the past by means of the available evidence. The person performing this historical reconstruction generally does that sort of work habitually, being an amateur antiquary, an academic, or both. He (there are no female investigators in James's stories) sets out to reconstruct a history, usually of an old church or of another decrepit building. Often, significantly, this place of research is a site of ruins, suggestive perhaps of the Temple of Jupiter Serapis (see Lyell 1:449–59), which mysterious ruins Lyell used to illustrate his "reading" techniques. Or at any rate, ruins in James definitely indicate a long human history waiting to be read. Ruins provide a physical location for the act of reading human history, in much the same way geological formations provided a physical location for reconstructive scientists' acts of reading geological history. While investigating the history of the ruin or building, James's investigator accidentally discovers another, secret history; the piecing-together of this secret history is the focus of the story. His investigators connect evidence from physical artifacts with fragments of private letters and journals, published histories, reference books, parish records, and other official documents, to form the narrative of the secret history. Again, this method, piecing together narratives by means of physical evidence and written texts, was precisely that of Victorian scientists.[5] Sometimes, in James's stories, part of the evidence is in another language, generally Latin; or it is written in secret code. And finally, the stories are narrated in such a way that the reader must do some of the reconstructive work; James never provides a complete, confident, explicit explanation of events in the manner of, say, a Sherlock Holmes mystery. By coding some of the evidence and leaving histories more or less incomplete and implicit, James thus emphasizes the *difficulties* in reading history as much as the *possibility* of it.

An extended example should illustrate these generalizations. In "'Oh, Whistle, and I'll Come to You, My Lad,'" a "Professor of Ontography" (*Stories* 75), one Mr. Parkins, decides to find, examine, and sketch a ruined Templar church he has read about. Note Parkins's occupation, Professor of Ontography. No such position actually existed at an English university; the invented title suggests he studies what-writing-is, which indicates his investment in words, reading, writing, and investigation in general. At the site

---

5. Lyell, for example, cites copious texts dating back hundreds of years as evidence of the geological conditions of various parts of Europe at those times, in addition to his analyses of physical evidence.

of the ruins, he sees among mysterious mounds and eminences a bare patch of earth, where the turf has been "removed by some boy or other creature *ferae naturae* [of a wild nature]" (79). (That James equates a boy with a wild creature is significant, as should be apparent in the second section of this essay.) Digging below the bare spot, Parkins finds "a small cavity" containing an object "of man's making—a metal tube about four inches long, and evidently of some considerable age" (79) This turns out to be a whistle, with inscriptions on front—

FLA

FUR   BIS

FLE

and back:

QUIS EST ISTE QUI VENIT (81)

He translates the latter inscription to read, "Who is this who is coming?" It should be noted that the Latin word "iste," the word "this" in the translation, connotes disgust. Also, in Latin grammar, "quis" and "qui," "who," can refer either to a person or a creature; there is not the "who/that" distinction that exists in English. Parkins, however, never deciphers the meaning or significance of the four three-letter words. (Or are they even words?) Nor does he decipher the swastika-like symbols. (The story was written and is set a few decades before the advent of the Nazis.) Thus he is able to make only a partial reading of this artifact—just enough to gather a cryptic warning that something dreadful is coming.

In his curiosity, Parkins blows the whistle twice; that night he experiences all sorts of frights—fears he will die, nightmares, and awful sounds in the wind. In the morning he shows the whistle and its inscriptions, and relates his experiences, to a fellow lodger at his hotel, a Colonel just back from India. Putting together the written and physical evidence, the Colonel decides that Parkins's blowing the whistle has caused bad experiences, though the Colonel can't say exactly why or how that is so. He suspects the whistle's being found at a Templar ruin probably indicates some sort of evil magic: "he should himself be careful about using a thing that had belonged to a set of Papists, of whom, speaking generally, it might be affirmed that you never knew what they might not have been up to" (86). More specifically, the Templars, who some believe to be the precursory organization to the Freemasons (see Robinson and many, many others), have long figured in conspiracy theories both supernatural and secular. However, the Colonel can only suspect; he cannot reconstruct the entire history. Nor can he explain satisfactorily what happens to Parkins the next night: Parkins is attacked by "a horrible, an intensely horrible, face *of crumpled linen*" (90) that arises from his supposedly empty spare bed. The Colonel bursts in and saves Parkins, taking away the whistle, "which he cast[s] as far into the sea as a very brawny arm could send it" (90), returning the artifact back to the oblivion whence it came. The whistle seems to have summoned the mysterious creature, but no one—including the reader, who is only told as much as the Colonel—can determine exactly what the creature was, what its powers might be,[6] why the whistle summons it, what the Templars have to do with the creature and the whistle, or what might have happened had Parkins blown the whistle once more.

Such methods and understandings of reconstructing history are typical of James's stories in general. James's characters and readers, like Victorian reconstructive scientists, can always draw connections between certain significant fragments of physical and written evidence, always construct some *sense* of what happened. However, no one can progress from there on to total explanation or to absolute certainty. And teleology—*why* certain events happen—generally remains shrouded in mystery, just as the teleology of the earth's or animals' evolution remained obscure to Darwin and Lyell.

II. Evolution and Civilization

M. R. James ghost stories also reproduce Victorian science's beliefs regarding evolution and human civilization. Specifically, the stories reveal the position first advanced by Robert Chambers and furthered later by Charles Darwin, that *Homo sapiens* descended genealogically from simpler organisms. Also, one can see behind James's stories E. B. Tylor's (and, earlier, Darwin's) doctrine of survivals.

In *Vestiges of the Natural History of Creation*, first published in 1844, Chambers placed all living creatures in a hierarchy: "The vegetable and animal kingdoms are arranged upon a scale, starting from simply organized forms, and going on to the more complex, each of these forms being but slightly different from those next to it on both sides" (236). Atop the scale in the animal kingdom is "man," for humans belong to the most complex "sub-kingdom" (239), the vertebrata; and human beings are the "typical" vertebrate—that is, the "best" of that type or sub-kingdom.

Chambers argued not only that humankind is the best representative of the best sub-kingdom, but also that humankind descended genealogically from the "lower animals": "[T]he simplest and most primitive type, under a law

---

6. The Colonel is "of opinion that . . . its one power was that of frightening" (90–91), but Parkins has other ideas.

to which that of like-production is subordinate, gave birth to the type next above it . . . this again produced the next higher, and so on to the very highest" (222, emphasis in the original), from one-celled animals all the way up to human beings. As evidence Chambers observes that "every individual amongst us actually passes through the characters of the insect, the fish, and reptile, (to speak nothing of others,) before he is permitted to breathe the breath of life!" (234–35). (Note the word "characters" here, suggestive not only of bodily forms but also of written, readable language.) Furthermore, he claims, once the fetus reaches a recognizably human state, "the varieties of his race are represented in the progressive development of an individual of the highest, before we see the adult Caucasian, the highest point yet attained in the animal scale" (199). The developing Caucasian fetus passes through the form of the "lower" races in ascending to that of the "highest": "it passes through the characters in which it appears, in the Negro, Malay, American, and Mongolian nations, and finally is Caucasian" (306). (Here again appears that important word "characters.")

For Chambers, then—not surprisingly, a Caucasian himself—the Caucasian is both the most recently evolved and the best of all creatures in the animal kingdom. But its status is not assured, for regression, and other races' progression, always remain possible. Chambers cites the example of an American Indian tribe, the Mandans, who he claims "cultivated the arts of manufacture, realized comforts and luxuries, and had attained to a remarkable refinement of manners. . . . They were also more than usually elegant in their persons, and of every variety of complexion between that of their compatriots and a pure white."[7] Supposedly the more "civilized" they became, the whiter they grew, even as individuals, which suggests that white skin is a result and signifier of "civilization." It also indicates that levels of civilization need not be congenital—they can be earned. But if they can be earned, they can be lost, too; Caucasians can easily revert to barbarism and consequently grow darker. Thus, "the varieties of mankind . . . are simply the result of so many advances and retrogressions. . . . According to this view, the greater part of the human race must be considered as having lapsed or declined from the original type. In the Caucasian or Indo-European family alone has the primitive organization been improved upon" (308–9). Skin color becomes for Chambers a reliable index of civilization, at the levels of the tribe and the individual.

Here Chambers's views on human evolution coincide with Tylor's. Tylor arranges human cultures in a hierarchy according to their levels of "civiliza-

---

7. (298–99). Chambers did not do this research himself. He uncritically cites one "Mr. [George] Catlin" on the subject of the Mandans.

tion," a term he never really defines. By reading a culture as a "complex whole" (1:1), and assigning that whole a place in his hierarchy, he hopes to "draw a picture where there shall be scarce a hand's breadth difference between an English ploughman and a negro of Central Africa" (1:7)—just as Chambers sought to arrange all organisms into a virtually seamless hierarchy.

Key to understanding James's stories, too, is Tylor's concept of "survivals." Tylor writes that even within the most civilized societies, there are "processes, customs, opinions, and so forth, which have been carried on by force of habit into a new state of society different from that in which they had their original home, and they thus remain as proofs and examples of an older condition of culture out of which a new has been evolved" (1:16). These he calls "survivals." Not only discrete phenomena observable within particular cultures, but whole societies, "modern savage tribes," can be considered survivals or "remains of an early state of the human race at large," people whose culture does not change despite "the main tendency of culture . . . [to move] from savagery towards civilization" (1:21).

The concept of survivals constitutes an anthropological version of Darwin's "Tree of Life," drawn in *The Origin of Species.* Tylor himself likens his study of cultures to Darwin's work: "What this task is like, may be almost perfectly illustrated by comparing these details of culture with the species of plants and animals as studied by the naturalist" (1:8). Darwin's "Tree of Life" illustrates his conception of the genealogy of species: one species ramifies into many, some of which become extinct; some branches die out altogether; and some species do not ramify at all, but instead continue to exist unchanged, unadapted, while other originally contemporary species change and ramify greatly (*Origin* 160–61). Thus, according to Darwin and, later, to Tylor, many levels or periods of evolution—both human and animal—exist simultaneously in the present.

James reproduces in his ghost stories the theories of Chambers, Darwin, and Tylor outlined above. One way James does this is in the making physical form of his "ghosts" resemble humans at earlier stages of evolution. Unlike most other English writers' ghosts, James's have tangible bodies. As Michael A. Mason observes, the typical Jamesian ghost is "solid enough to inflict considerable damage" (256). And these solid, tangible forms resemble the human form as it might have appeared in an earlier time. For example, James describes the ghost of "Canon Alberic's Scrap-book" thus:

> At first you saw only a mass of coarse, matted black hair; presently it was seen that this covered a body of fearful thinness, almost a skeleton, but with the muscles standing out like wires. The hands were of a dusky pallor, covered, like the body, with long, coarse hairs, and hideously taloned. The eyes,

touched in with a burning yellow, had intensely black pupils. . . . Imagine one of the awful bird-catching spiders of South America translated into human form, and endowed with intelligence just less than human, and you will have some faint conception . . . (16–17)

The avenging creature in "The Haunted Dolls' House" "might be described as a frog—the size of a man—but it had scanty white hair about its head" (272). Note the explicit linking of these humanoid creatures with other, "lower" animals: the links go beyond mere comparison (humanoid creature = spider or frog) to suggest unevolved states of *homo sapiens*, human beings as they might have looked when humans still resembled, or might have resembled, frogs or spiders. Note in the first example, too, the excessive hair as a signifier of subhumanity. According to Richard Pfaff, hair is "one of MRJ's favourite motifs" (410). Many of James's creatures resemble humans but are too hairy to *be* human; see, for example, "The Diary of Mr. Poynter," "An Episode of Cathedral History," and "A View from a Hill." In all his stories James's "ghosts" occupy places below modern *homo sapiens* in a Chambersian/Darwinian evolutionary hierarchy. Some creatures are very much subhuman: for instance, the creature menacing "The Residence at Whitminster" possesses "long thin arms, or legs, or feelers" (218), while in "Count Magnus," the "unduly short" figure "muffled in a hooded garment" (71) brandishes tentacles. The creatures always prove dangerous to the antiquarians who unearth them; sometimes the investigator escapes alive, and sometimes he does not, but he is always threatened and horrified. The creatures appear to be survivals, loathsome living fossils of earlier, less evolved states of humankind, come from the past into the present to destroy.

The other important way James reproduces Victorian beliefs regarding human evolution and civilization is in making the very appearance of the supernatural a kind of regression to an earlier, less civilized stage in humanity. For James, "civilized" and "skeptical" are synonyms. His investigators are all Caucasian, well-educated, upper-class, refined in manners and speech, and disinclined to believe in ghosts and similar rubbish. For people like this—people at the very acme of Chambers's, Darwin's, and Tylor's hierarchies—to experience firsthand and be forced to attest to the reality of the supernatural is for them to return to "a world which only a few generations ago would have been our own—a world of witchcraft and black magic, fairies and goblins, when the supernatural was too much a reality to be reasoned away" (Search 20). James's urban antiquarians move backward in time to the world of servants and rural folk. It is not the polished investigators but the "lower orders"—working-class, country, and serving people—who know the local legends and superstitions, who are most closely in touch with supernatural forces. James has them relate their information to the investigator, and thereby, to the reader, in exaggeratedly illiterate accents that highlight their dearth of civilization. "Martin's Close" describes one character, a country boy, so backward that when he gives testimony in court regarding an experience with the supernatural, "my lord could not well apprehend him, and so asked if there was anyone that could interpret him" (180); the parson, apparently more civilized than the boy but less civilized than the judge, has to translate. By connecting the supernatural with the uncivilized, James implies a cause-and-effect relationship: if the uncivilized were not to tell what they know about the supernatural, or were to become more civilized and so forget it, the truly civilized would never discover it. The supernatural would disappear; humankind would evolve beyond it, Tylor writes that "most of what we call superstition is included within survival" (1:17); James suggests that these particular survivals would *not* survive if not for the cultural foot-dragging of certain low-class types.

III. The Unconscious

Thus, in writing his ghost stories, M. R. James reproduces the assumptions of Victorian geological, evolutionary, and anthropological science. To use a Lyellian geological metaphor, James's stories portray human civilization as a thin, recently developed crust riding uncertainly atop a restless mass of older formations threatening at every moment to destroy the crust and break through to the top. One can partially, tentatively reconstruct the history of the formations by digging through and examining various strata or layers, then assembling the bits of evidence.

This conception of human civilization, of course, closely resembles that of a famous contemporary of James's: Sigmund Freud. Freud, too, writes of the human mind in terms of genealogical development and survivals, and conceives of consciousness as a recently formed, relatively complex, and highly evolved formation residing uneasily atop older, simpler ones. In *Civilization and Its Discontents*, Freud writes, much in the vein of Chambers, Darwin, Tylor, and James, "In the animal kingdom we hold to the view that the most highly developed species have proceeded from the lowest; and yet we find all the simple forms still in existence to-day" (15–16). As in the animal kingdom, in the

> realm of the mind, . . . what is primitive is so commonly preserved alongside of the transformed version which has arisen from it that it is unnecessary to give instances as evidence. When this happens . . . one portion . . . of an attitude or instinctual impulse has remained unaltered, while another portion has undergone further development. . . . [I]n mental life nothing

which has once been formed can perish . . . everything is somehow preserved and . . . in suitable circumstances (when, for instance, regression goes back far enough) it can once more be brought to light. (*Civilization* 16–17)

The mind's "primitive" and "simple forms" survive along with more complex, more highly civilized forms, just as, for James and Victorian scientists, less evolved organisms survive along with their more highly evolved descendants. More highly civilized forms of the mind reside in consciousness, comprising only a small portion of the mind, the "top"; the former remain in the unconscious, constituting most of the mind, "deeper down." As Freud explains in "The Unconscious," "at any given moment consciousness includes only a small content, so that the greater part of what we call conscious knowledge must in any case be for very considerable periods of time in a state of latency, that is to say, of being psychically unconscious" (167).[8]

In psychoanalysis, the analyst's work is a work of historical reconstruction, much like that of James's antiquaries. The analyst assembles the fragments of evidence dug up from the unconscious in an effort to reconstruct the history of the mind, as Freud explains in "Constructions in Analysis":

His task is to make out what has been forgotten from the traces which it has left behind or, more correctly, to *construct* it. . . . His work of construction, or, if it is preferred, of reconstruction, resembles to a great extent an archaeologist's excavation of some dwelling-place that has been destroyed and buried or of some ancient edifice.[9] (259)

The task proves complicated, however, and the results necessarily inconclusive, for the analyst is working only with "traces," and, too, "if an object makes its appearance in some particular level, it often remains to be decided whether it belongs to that level or whether it was carried down to that level owing to some subsequent disturbance" (259). Only fragments of the record remain, and they cannot always be arranged chronologically. Still, a dogged analyst can generally reconstruct at least a sense of the patient's psychic history—much like James's determined investigators, or the Victorian reconstructive scientists they emulate, can assemble some sense of the historical narrative in their respective fields.

Clearly, then, James's conception of human civilization bears close resemblance to Freud's. Given the close similarity of their understandings of

---

8. The dwarfing of consciousness by the unconscious parallels the way that, for Chambers, the uncivilized greatly outnumber the civilized.

9. Recall that James's investigators generally do their investigating at a site or ruins or another decrepit building.

civilization and the human mind, James can be seen as, in effect, writing about the unconscious. James does not refer directly to "the unconscious," but his stories posit its existence metaphorically: the subhuman, the uncivilized, the superstitious, the supernatural—all the horrifying phenomena unearthed by his antiquarian investigators may be considered "the unconscious," for James views these phenomena in much the same light as Freud regarded the unconscious. That is, the ghastly/the unconscious is old, unevolved, uncivilized, and large; the rational/the conscious is new, evolved, civilized, and small.

While James might be understood to be writing metaphorically about the unconscious, his plans for what to *do* with the unconscious differ radically from Freud's. Freud sought actively to dig down through the layers of memory, uncover repressed memories, reconstruct the history stored in the unconscious fragments, and use that history, once brought to the patient's consciousness, to facilitate psychoanalytic cure. James, in contrast, indicates that digging into the past/the unconscious is a mistake: the results are invariably horrifying and sometimes even fatal. To dig into the past is to transport oneself back in time to a more superstitious, savage state of humanity, and to uncover terrible things better left buried. If James's antiquarians would only let sleeping ruins lie, they would remain safe. True, the unearthed horrors belong to secret histories *other* than the ones being investigated directly, but with the past/the unconscious that is precisely the point—one never knows *what* one will dig up. James suggests that our minds work more of less like Mrs. Maple's, the Oldyses' maid in "The Residence at Whitminster":

> "How will Miss Oldys manage to make [Mrs. Maple] remember about the box?" I asked.
> "Mary? Oh, she'll make her sit down and ask her about her aunt's illness, or who gave her the china dog on the mantelpiece—something quite off the point. Then, as Maple says, one thing brings up another, and the right one will come round sooner that you could suppose." (*Stories* 221)[10]

To think of one thing, all one need do is think of another. To summon a vengeful demon, all one need do is poke around a picturesque ruin. It is the *act* of delving into the past, not the precise subject, that James finds dangerous.

---

10. As I argue above, for James, servants such as Mrs. Maple are more in touch with the supernatural unconscious than more "civilized" people. For Freud and James, all minds work essentially like hers; hers is just *closer* to those hidden forces than, say, the mind of her master, Mr. Oldys, an urbane clergyman.

Sometimes James warns directly against investigativeness. For instance, of Mr. Wraxall, protagonist of "Count Magnus," he writes, "His besetting fault was pretty clearly that of over-inquisitiveness, possibly a good fault, in a traveller, certainly a fault for which this traveller paid dearly enough in the end" (65). Wraxall's "price" was to be haunted, harried, and eventually slaughtered by the Count, after inadvertently raising him from the dead. And all Wraxall originally *intended* to investigate was materials for a travel book. In "Rats," Mr. Thomson, "in a mood of quite indefensible curiosity, and feeling confident that there could be no damaging secrets in a place [the hotel room next door] so easily got at" (343), finds a dead man, or rather an undead man, and barely escapes with his life. History/the unconscious is for James a kind of Bluebeard's chamber,[11] and he warns his readers of the dangers of opening it.

Besides providing such direct warnings, he also models repression metaphorically. His stories include example after example of some secret and/or enclosed space that is opened, reveals some horror, and is hurriedly sealed back up. In "The Treasure of Abbot Thomas," for instance, Mr. Somerton interprets a secret code that leads him to a treasure buried in an abbey well. Trouble is, sealed up with the treasure is a supernatural guardian; therefore, Somerton and his servant and friend seal up the well again. The title character of "Mr. Humphreys and His Inheritance" discovers, at the center of his newly inherited hedge maze, "a face—a human face—a *burnt* human face . . . waving black arms prepared to clasp the head that was bending over them" (204). Humphreys barely escapes the humanoid creature with his life, and immediately has the maze destroyed. And in "An Episode of Cathedral History," the repressed actively tries to escape. While renovating the Cathedral at Southminster, workmen lay bare a tomb below the altar, and worse, make a small breach in the tomb's wall. Every day a mason fills the hole with a brick—and every day the brick is pushed out again by the ghost living inside. Finally the tomb is destroyed, and out of it rushes a "thing like a man, all over hair, and two great eyes to it" (247). These secret/enclosed spaces represent the unconscious mind; the horrible creatures inside, repressed memories and desires. James shows that when one has opened those spaces/the unconscious, the best and safest thing to do is to seal them up again quickly. Otherwise, the hidden horrors will have their revenge, like the creature of "Martin's Close," who, sealed in a small cupboard for many years,

---

11. James himself uses the phrase "Bluebeard's chamber" in "The Residence at Whitminster," to describe the room containing a box that holds fatal magical artifacts (*Stories* 224).

immediately commits a gruesome murder once set free. The typical ghost story by James, then, offers a "warning to the curious":[12] do not investigate the past/the unconscious, for what you find will frighten and probably harm you. James is the ultimate Enlightenment figure, warning against even *looking* into the dark.

Thus, James, imbued with the tenets of Victorian reconstructive science, constructs in his ghost stories a model of human evolution, civilization, and mind which is strikingly Freudian. In effect, he posits both the existence of the unconscious and its readability. The attitude Julia Briggs ascribes to English ghost story writers in general is particularly true in James: "as a descendant [sic] of the beasts, [man] had a bestial inheritance within him which he must learn to sublimate and restrain" (20). Better to sublimate and restrain, for James, than to dig up, piece together and work through. To repress is to progress, both as an individual and as a species.

Works Cited

Briggs, Julia. *Night Visitors: The Rise and Fall of the English Ghost Story*. London: Faber & Faber, 1977.

Chambers, Robert. *Vestiges of the Natural History of Creation and Other Evolutionary Writings*. Ed. James A. Secord. Chicago, London: University of Chicago Press, 1994.

Cox, J. Randolph. "Ghostly Antiquary: The Stories of Montague Rhodes James." *ELT* 12 (1969): 197–202.

Cox, Michael. *M. R. James: An Informal Portrait*. Oxford: Oxford University Press, 1983.

Darwin, Charles. *The Origin of Species by Means of Natural Selection*. 1859. Ed. J. W. Burrow. London: Penguin, 1985.

Dickens, Charles. *The Life and Adventures of Martin Chuzzlewit*. 1844. The Oxford Illustrated Dickens. Oxford: Oxford University Press, 1987.

Freud, Sigmund. *Civilization and Its Discontents*. Trans. and ed. James Strachey. New York: W. W. Norton, 1961.

———. "Constructions in Analysis." *The Standard Edition of the Complete Psychological Works of Sigmund Freud*. Trans. James Strachey. Eds. James Strachey and Anna Freud. 24 vols. Vol. 23. London: Hogarth Press/The Institute of Psycho-Analysis, 1964. 255–69.

---

12. This is the title of a story by James and of his fourth published collection of stories.

————. "The Unconscious." *The Standard Edition of the Complete Psychological Works of Sigmund Freud.* Trans. James Strachey. Eds. James Strachey and Anna Freud. 24 vols. Vol. 14. London: Hogarth Press/The Institute of Psycho-Analysis, 1957. 159–215.

James, M. R. *The Penguin Complete Ghost Stories of M. R. James.* Harmondsworth: Penguin, 1984.

Lyell, Charles. *Principles of Geology.* 1830. 3 vols. Chicago: University of Chicago Press, 1990.

Mason, Michael A. "On Not Letting Them Lie: Moral Significance in the Ghost Stories of M. R. James." *Studies in Short Fiction* 19 (1982): 253–60.

Pfaff, Richard William. *Montague Rhodes James.* London: Scolar Press, 1980.

Robinson, John J. *Born in Blood: The Lost Secrets of Freemasonry.* New York: M. Evans, 1989.

Search, Pamela, ed. *The Supernatural in the English Short Story.* London: Bernard Hanison, 1959.

Sullivan, Jack. *Elegant Nightmares: The English Ghost Story from Le Fanu to Blackwood.* Athens: Ohio University Press, 1978.

Tylor, E. B. *Primitive Culture: Researches into the Development of Mythology, Philosophy, Religion, Language, Art, and Custom.* 7th ed. 2 vols. New York: Brentano's, 1924.

"They've Got Him! In the Trees!"
M. R. James and Sylvan Dread

Steve Duffy

H'mm—what's that odd smell in here? Possibly, just possibly, it's the stink of Pan; the smell of fear engendered by an incautious foray into the woods. Panic fear is nowadays held to be a contagious, baseless phenomenon, but it has its origins in a quite specific, and usually solitary experience: fear of the great god Pan. It's the sensation we get when we stray from the path and end up in the forest, where there are bears and wolves, and maybe some things that are far, far worse. Thus Liddell and Scott, cited in the *Oxford English Dictionary:* "Sounds heard by night on mountains and in vallies [*sic*] were attributed to Pan, and hence he was reputed to be the cause of any sudden and groundless fear." Of course, Pan has his positive aspect (though not the rather boringly wholesome avatar invoked by Kenneth Grahame, who seemed to want to reduce the great priapic one to some sort of cross between Jesus and Smokey the Bear); maybe, then, it's not Pan's trail we're following here after all. Maybe it's something wilder still, all fangs and claws and shadows . . . something as old as the old gods, only wholly lacking in redeeming features. But let's illustrate our concept. I'll be Dorothy; link arms with me, and let's dance off down the Yellow Brick Road. Which also led into the forest.

To begin with, look in your *Collected MRJ* (never a bad injunction, that). Remember "Wailing Well"? Unjustly overlooked, this tale, by many readers; its centrepiece is a very peculiar plantation, where lurk—well, "they hadn't much to call faces, but I could seem to see as they had teeth." They live—where? In the well? Maybe, but certainly within that "clump of bent and gnarled Scotch firs" inside the red ring on the Scouts' map. The Scoutmaster, Mr. Hope Jones, certainly thinks the firs are significant. Remember, he tries to cut down every tree within the clump, only to return with a badly gashed leg and a broken axe. "On no single tree could he make the least impression."

The erstwhile tenant of Betton Hall had better luck (we've moved on now to "A Neighbour's Landmark"). He managed to stub up the scrub oaks that comprised Betton Wood, of unpleasant memory; still, if he imagined that by doing this he would stop that which walked there from either walking or crying, he seems to have been proved wrong by subsequent events. Of course, Mitchell, the woodman, might have told him as much. His mother used never to go through the wood after dark, if she could help it: "first it's a rustling-like all along in the bushes, coming very quick, either towards me or after me according to the time, and then there comes this scream as appears to pierce right through from the one ear to the other . . ." That's a taste of the true panic experience. The wood had a bad name all through the countryside: "never a bit of game in it, and never a bird's nest there."

Of course, a certain "Ash-Tree" near Castringham Hall in Suffolk contained something of almost unutterable loathsomeness: a nest of poisonous spidery things, the unearthly get of old Mrs. Mothersole the witch. That tree was burned to the ground, and very wisely too.

Then there's "A View from a Hill." Mr. Fanshawe looks out over towards Gallows Hill (though admittedly he's using Mr. Baxter's peculiar glasses at the time), and sees—what he might be expected to see on a hill with such a name. Later, of course, he makes the trip over there, into the plantation atop the hill. Here he has his moment of true terror, in amongst the trees which seem to snag and grab at him, all the way through to the heart of that "unholy evil sort of graveyard." "Not much poaching in that cover," as the Squire sagely points out—definite echoes of Betton Wood.

Poachers were also well advised to keep clear of the long wood on the hill behind Råbäck. It was Count Magnus's wood, and he was many years dead, but even after the Count was in his mausoleum, one might still "meet with persons walking who should not be walking." By the same token, one would do well to avoid a certain thicket in Ireland, that featured in "A School Story": "*memento putei inter quatuor taxos,*" remember the well among the four yews, and more particularly, what came out of it, looking for vengeance. "An Evening's Entertainment" gives us the long covert with a few big oaks; hanging from one of those, of course, was Mr. Davis's young man, and afterwards the area was haunted by that unfortunate suicide. Flies would come at you, in those woods, like no other flies you'd ever seen, and if they stung you, your arm would swell up and go black. Reason enough to stay clear. In "The Stalls of Barchester Cathedral," there's another hanging-tree—or there was, since its wood was later used to make the unnervingly lively stall-decorations which so upset Archdeacon Haynes. What's that phrase—"the living wood"?

As much as anywhere, the park at Lufford sticks in my mind. Mr.

Karswell's lantern slides showed "a horrible hopping creature in white, which you first saw dodging about among the trees." Later, John Harrington would be found dead in amongst those very trees: what he saw can only be imagined, though I for one would rather not dwell on the matter. In *Night of the Demon,* the movie version of "Casting the Runes," Brian Wilde (playing a man driven insane through his unwise association with Mr. Karswell) gets to utter the classic line later sampled by Kate Bush: "It's in the trees! It's coming!", and if Kate hadn't beaten me to it, I'd have pinched that for my title. Some of the most effective parts of that film take place in and around the woods that circle Lufford Abbey; rarely has panic been depicted so well on the silver screen.

All this is enough to establish a pattern, I think. James seems certainly to have been aware of the power of the forest, and he used it to great effect in many of his tales. (If I were to stretch a point, I might even bring in the wilderness of the disused maze in "Mr. Humphreys and His Inheritance." And even rose-gardens have box-bushes, whose contents may not always be of the most pleasant. Ask Mrs. Anstruther.) In doing so, of course, he was working within a long-established tradition. From the earliest times, the woods have been places held to be numinous (that is, worthy of respect, of awe—which is to say, of fear); or better say, certain woods, at certain times. In *The Golden Bough* there's the sacred grove at Nemi, where the King of the Wood slew his predecessor. Elsewhere in the classical tradition, olive trees are identified with the souls of dead men; and of course the Celts spun a whole mythology round their trees. There's a tradition that the trees on some of the old Viking burial mounds house the spirits of the chieftain's bodyguards, protecting their chief in death as they did in life. On the fiction front, Algernon Blackwood has several fine tales set in the endless forests of North America. Ramsey Campbell has a quite terrifying wood in his brilliant novel *Midnight Sun.* Robert Aickman's "Into the Wood" is weirdness embodied. Stephen King's *Pet Sematary* makes good use of the Maine woods and their Native American traditions. I could go on and on; surely everyone will have a favourite chiller with a sylvan setting.

We fear the forest with good reason, it seems. Thus Angela Carter, in "The Company of Wolves":

> You are always in danger in the forest, where no people are. Step between the portals of the great pines where the shaggy branches tangle about you, trapping the unwary traveller in nets as if the vegetation itself were in a plot with the wolves who live there, as if the wicked trees go fishing on behalf of their friends—step between the gateposts of the forest with the greatest trepidation and infinite precautions, for if you stray from the path for one in-

stant, the wolves will eat you.

Here we see, in Ms. Carter's usual lapidary prose, both the proximate cause of the original panic fear—the predators, the loneliness—and the weirder, more diffuse trepidation that's involved. Because after a certain point, it wasn't just the wolves that scared people, it was the woods themselves. Whether this was merely a case of bad logic and the transfer of affect (the forest has wolves, wolves are scary, ergo, forests are scary *per se*), or whether the fear has deeper roots, you're free to decide for yourselves. Still, we're left with the concept of the forest as a place reeking with danger; a great loneliness, waiting to be filled with—what? With our fears, it would seem. Perhaps even when we've stopped believing in the old tutelary deities, once we've ceased to derive any comfort from the animist certainties of more primitive times, we can still sense something vital in a forest, and respond to it.

Sometimes it's hard to separate the notions of aliveness and sentience. If a thing is alive, the suspicion that it's conscious may never be far behind. In one of the many splendidly eerie sequences in Hitchcock's *Vertigo* (1958), Kim Novak wanders through the redwoods on the Pacific coast, addressing the giant sequoias as if they were alive—they are alive, of course (largest living things on Earth, famously), but as if they're *listening to her*. . . . And in that weird forest hush, in the filtering sunlight through the thin ocean mists, who's to say they aren't? So maybe when a writer like James peoples his woods with ghosts and demons, one of the reasons they scare us is because they operate as symbols for this unnatural, somehow unlikely emptiness; an emptiness we can populate all too readily with our own misgivings. Fear need not arise solely from external stimuli; in the absence of a direct object, we can always draw upon ourselves, our own experiences and misgivings. The fear is within us, waiting to be vested in something or other.

The first European settlers on the American continent were well aware of the terrors of the forest. Of course, those forests were quite scary—there were Indians, who might not always be friendly and bring pumpkins and maize, but come instead with hatchets; there were bears, and poisonous plants, and the woods went on forever, and many died wandering far from home . . . but there were things less easily named, too. Even the sturdy Vikings were none too keen on the *skraelings*, their name for both the Inuit and the Micmac, the Native Americans of Greenland and Vinland. *Skraeling* translates roughly as "dried-up savage wretches," though Jacqueline Simpson proposes the variant reading of *Screechers*—which takes this reader back to Betton Woods, and is very Jamesian!

The woods of North America were slow to lose this minatory aspect. Here's an excerpt from William Bradford's *Of Plymouth Plantation* (book

1.IX.), the story of the first settlers on Plymouth Rock, that expresses the sheer vertiginous sense of alienation felt by those fearful castaway pilgrims, as they stood on the beach looking inland to the forests of the New World:

> . . . what could they see but a hideous and desolate wilderness, full of wild beasts and wild men—and what multitudes there might be of them they knew not. Neither could they, as it were, go up to the top of Pisgah to view from this wilderness a more goodly country to feed their hopes, for which way soever they turned their eyes (saved upward to the heavens) they could have little solace of content in respect of any outward objects. For summer being done, all things stand upon them with a weatherbeaten face, and the whole country, full of woods and thickets, represented a wild and savage hue. If they looked behind them, there was the mighty ocean which they had passed and was now as a main bar and gulf to separate them from all the civil parts of the world.

One of Nathaniel Hawthorne's greatest tales, "Young Goodman Brown," deals with this nightmare scenario well enough to be regarded as a classic of American literature, and it's instructive to contrast it with those tales of James's we cited earlier. Young Goodman Brown is a citizen of Salem, and we first encounter him on the way out of town as evening falls, on "a dreary road, darkened by all the gloomiest trees of the forest, which barely stood aside to let the narrow path creep through, and closed immediately behind. It was all as lonely as could be; and there is this peculiarity in such a solitude, that the traveller knows not who may be concealed by the innumerable trunks and the thick boughs overhead; so that, with lonely footsteps, he may still be passing through an unseen multitude."

What would a good Puritan like Brown be doing out, this night? He's on his way, we eventually learn, to a witches' Sabbat. But he's not alone, it seems. Along the way are many familiar faces; everyone he knows in Salem, the most pious townsfolk, the deacons, the goodwives, all the upholders of faith and tradition . . . they all seem to be there, beckoning him on. Panic grows on him: eventually he's running so fast that he seems almost to fly. "The whole forest was peopled with frightful sounds: the creaking of the trees, the howling of wild beasts, and the yell of Indians; while sometimes, the wind tolled like a distant church-bell, and sometimes gave a broad roar around the traveller, as if all Nature were laughing him to scorn. *But he was himself the chief horror of the scene, and shrank not from its other horrors.*" (My emphasis.)

Here's the nub of the matter. Young Goodman Brown believes himself at a Sabbat; believes all the town of Salem to be there, and damned to boot. But Brown is some way from being a wholly reliable narrator (very modern, that), and the only verifiable presence at that Sabbat, outside the fevered imaginings of Brown, is—Brown himself. The devil (or the devil in man, as we may prefer) has the power of similitude: he may cast himself as anybody; any notable of Salem. His words to Brown have a certain ambiguity: "By the sympathy of your human hearts for sin, ye shall scent out all the places—whether in church, bed-chamber, street, field or forest—where crime has been committed, and shall exult to behold the whole earth one stain of guilt, one mighty blood-spot." It's the Devil addressing his flock, in the story; but he might almost be describing the likes of Cotton Mather, feverishly eager to convince himself of the Salem witches' guilt, to conjure evil out of innocence. Once again, even though the woods may be (rationally speaking) empty, still there's something there.

The whole Salem witch-panic (in which an ancestor of Hawthorne's played a rather vacillating part) sometimes seems to me to have arisen fully-formed from those New England forests. Forests in which God was not; in which other deities were worshipped, and received sacrifice. Young Goodman Brown, the archetypal Puritan, goes out into the trees *wanting* to find something—wanting his worst fears to be justified—and, of course, that's just what happens to him. Hawthorne never quite condemns the Puritan hysteria, nor ever suggests that it was entirely unjustified; neither, of course, does he suggest that it was anything other than hysteria. More subtly, he seems to find in it an analogue for the human condition; an illustration of the very recognisable human tendency to fear the worst, and to be able to justify those fears in whatever way comes to hand. Looking through the *OED* I find the following citation under the heading of *panic*, which seems somehow appropriate: 1708 Shaftesbury *Charact.* (1711) I. i. ii. 15 "There are many Pannicks in Mankind, besides merely that of Fear. And thus is Religion also *Pannick*."

Nature, we're told, abhors a vacuum, and left to our own devices, we're all too ready to fill the empty places. If we're not at ease with the forest, perhaps it's because we're not at ease with ourselves. In the end, even the threat of emptiness will trigger its own fear. Even when the Indians are all gone, and the last wolf killed, the woods may still be a fearful place. What will we dream of then? Of the Jersey Devil, that spectral hooved beast with its leathery wings that haunts the Pine Barrens of New Jersey; of Bigfoot in the Pacific Northwest; of Cthulhu in the swampy groves of Louisiana? Witches at their Sabbat? The dark denizens of Mirkwood? The thing in Betton Woods? The skeletons round Wailing Well? Mr. Karswell's hopping thing in white? The cry of a night-bird in the plantation at Livermere? Whatever. Perhaps all these frightful things are really displacements of a more elemental fear;

the fear of emptiness, of life without sentience or purpose, life we're unable to comprehend, or propitiate, or influence. When we go to the woods, it seems it's not enough to be prepared for wolves. We must also be prepared for their absence, lest we fill it with the contents of our own dark places. . . .

Homosexual Panic and the English Ghost Story: M. R. James and Others

Mike Pincombe

Montague Rhodes James, as we all know, is the Grand Master of the English ghost story in its "classical period," which is roughly contemporaneous with James's own career as a supernatural author from the 1890s to the 1930s. He more or less invented the "antiquarian" ghost story, which is still cultivated very purposefully by many contemporary supernatural authors in this country. But the antiquarian world of James's ghostly oeuvre—one that closely, indeed, often transparently, mirrors the one in which he moved himself as an antiquary and scholar—is surprisingly violent. James meant it to be so. He did not like gentle ghosts; he wanted them to be very nasty:

> [D]on't let us be mild and drab. Malevolence and terror, the glare of evil faces, "the stony grin of unearthly malice", pursuing forms in darkness, and "long-drawn, distant screams", are all in place, and so is a modicum of blood, shed with deliberation and carefully husbanded. (*PT* 479)

James wrote this in a short essay called "Some Remarks on Ghost Stories," published in the *Bookman,* towards the end of his career as a supernatural author in 1929. The comments just quoted come immediately after a passage in which James recorded his disapproval of what he regarded as gratuitous horror in some recent and primarily American specimens of the genre: "Reticence may be an elderly doctrine to preach [James was 67 at the time], yet from the artistic point of view I am sure it is a sound one. Reticence conduces to effect, blatancy ruins it, and there is much blatancy in a lot of recent stories." He then goes on to consider sex as well as horror: "They drag in sex too, which is a fatal mistake; sex is tiresome enough in the novels; in a ghost story, or as the backbone of a ghost story, I have no patience with it."

James was only fairly reticent about horror in his own work; but he was very definitely reticent about sex. Aficionados often point to the lack of a love-interest in his tales. Typical is the following comment by Michael Cox:

"Women figure rarely in James's stories, for this is a world where sex is not" (James 1987, xxiv). However, this statement rather begs the question: Does a world without women necessarily mean a world without sex? The answer—at least to us today—is obviously: No. And this is where "homosexual panic" comes into the picture. I take the term "homosexual panic" from Eve Sedgwick's remarks on the Gothic novel in her classic 1985 study of "English Literature and Male Homosocial Desire" called *Between Men*. Here is the gist of her argument as it might be applied to the classic English ghost story. According to Sedgwick, a society governed by patriarchy can impose a kind of ideological "terror" on its male members (one thinks perhaps of the way Victorian society treated James's near-contemporary Oscar Wilde). Once homosexuality is not only outlawed but persecuted, the threat of being accused of deviancy hangs like the sword of Damocles over every man who wishes to share in the benefits of patriarchy rather than become its dispossessed victim. It is not so much a question of "exposure" but of "accusation," because it is in the nature of this kind of political terror to be arbitrary and inexplicable. One day you wake up to find you have been denounced as a deviant, and you lose everything: family, friends, position, respect. This is the melodramatic narrative of homosexual panic. Sedgwick explains: "So-called 'homosexual panic' is the most private, psychologised form in which many twentieth-century men experience their vulnerability to the social pressure of homophobic blackmail" (89). It goes back further than the last century, however; and she goes on to relate homosexual panic to a sub-group of the nineteenth-century Gothic novel: "[E]ach is about one or more males who not only is persecuted by, but considers himself transparent to and often under the compulsion of, another male" (91).[1] Clearly, we can apply this narrative of persecution and pursuit to ghost stories in which living men are chased and tormented by the ghosts of dead men—James's "pursuing forms in darkness."

Indeed, M. R. James provides an exceptionally interesting case-study in terms of the present topic because of his addiction to a very vigorous and close physical contact with other men: "ragging." This is a boisterous game somewhere in between tag and wrestling; and James loved it. He played it at school and he played it at university. Here is an account of an episode between himself and a friend called St. Clair Donaldson, later Bishop of Salisbury, which seems to date from the year 1882, when James was a twenty-year-old undergraduate at King's: "I then called on St. Clair . . . He eventu-

---

1. Sedgwick mentions "*Caleb Williams, Frankenstein, Confessions of a Justified Sinner*, probably *Melmoth*, possibly *The Italian*" (91)—an impressive list.

ally came to my rooms and I speedily originated a rag by hanging his hat on the coal scuttle. Marshall and Thomas thought my book cases were falling and came to see if they could render any assistance. We were at that moment somewhat mixed on the hearthrug" (Cox 55). What did Marshall and Thomas make of the scene that presented itself to them as they entered James's rooms? Were they amused? titillated? shocked? A clue may be gleaned from a memoir written by Cyril Alington on Lionel Ford, another of James's close friends. It concerns the lively games which would follow the meetings of an undergraduate society called the TAF, or "Twice A Fortnight," over which James exercised, says Alington, an "informal hegemony" (59). I have not been able to find a copy of this text; but here is a passage quoting it from Cox's 1983 biography of James:

> Conversation at the TAF was what Monty was pleased to call "trivial". There was a good deal of mimicry, with Monty as the leading performer; and there were rags. Cyril Alington, later Head Master of Eton and Dean of Durham, omitted from a description of the TAF "for reasons of piety" St. Clair Donaldson's recollection of writhing on the floor "with Monty James's long fingers grasping at his vitals".

What would the spies and informers of Sedgwick's patriarchal police-state have made of that final image of Monty James's long fingers grasping at Donaldson's "vitals"? One can imagine them interrogating that last word: And just what do you mean by his "vitals," Mr. Dean?[2]

Of course, according to Sedgwick's model, it should be James himself who worried about the possibility that his grappling with Donaldson might be interpreted in terms of homosexual foreplay. But apparently he did not. On the contrary, he seems to have been quite happy to be seen rolling around with other young men; nor were these playful scuffles regarded as scandalous even by his old Eton tutor, Henry Luxmoore, who was present at many of the Christmas Eve parties at King's where James and others would read out their ghost stories. Luxmoore records in his diary for Christmas 1902 that James read an unspecified tale: "after which those played animal grab who did not mind having their clothes torn to pieces and their hands nailscored" (Cox 132). Was the forty-one-year-old Monty James still ragging even then? We may suspect that he was. And we may note that watching

---

2. The *Oxford English Dictionary* tells us that the word vitals refers to "those parts or organs of the body, esp. the human body, essential to life, or upon which life depends" (s.v. *vitals* 1 a). This could mean almost anything; but I recall that, "when I were a lad," a bout of ragging at school was brought to a successful conclusion by grasping your opponent's genitals.

these exhibitions of horse-play was part of the pleasure of Christmases at King's for the pious and elderly Luxmoore. Did James feel the "homosexual panic" which his ragging—and his general closeness to young men and boys throughout his life at Eton and King's and then at Eton again—might have inspired according to the Sedgwick model? I think the answer must be: Probably not; but others of his acquaintance certainly did. His close friend Arthur Benson, who recorded the pleasures and pains of his strong attachments to several young men in the course of his five-million-word diary over the period 1897–1925, could never bring himself even to contemplate the mention of the "two thoughts, often with me, that greatly affect my life, to which I never allude here" (quoted in Newsome 6–7).

Occasionally, we catch a fleeting glimpse of what these thoughts might have been. For example, on 24 January 1905, Benson was visited for the first time by Hugh Walpole, who would later write a number of good ghost stories and edit *A Second Century of Creepy Stories* (1937). At the time, however, Walpole was a twenty-one-year-old undergraduate at Emmanuel, with, it seems, a crush on Benson, which he revealed after desultory chat about history and literature and religion:

> Then he said [writes Benson in his diary] "And there's another thing" and then came out one of the most intime confessions I have ever heard, which I must not speak of here. The boy is evidently in very deep waters. But I could not help admiring the spirit he reveals. I don't think he is giving way. He said with a shudder "I could manage it all, if it weren't for my dreams." I asked him many plain questions, and I think he is living a sensible and manly life. (Quoted in Newsome 176)[3]

We can only guess what was said; but Benson's comments on Walpole's situation reveal the sort of picture which Sedgwick outlines in her chapter on the Gothic. It is "ghastly" and a "horror" and a "dark place to have looked into." Benson sees Walpole's dilemma (and his own, of course) in terms of a cosmic struggle between Conscience and Nature, where Conscience is designated the "voice of God," and Nature is a "strong, silent force"—wordlessly dragging Walpole to the unspeakable. Benson, then, provides good evidence for the Sedgwick model; yet James seems to have been largely immune to the fears which preyed upon his friend—and almost certainly contributed to his long periods of utterly disabling clinical

---

3. Walpole's comments on dreams and shudders are no doubt heartfelt, but they are also very literary, modelled, I suspect, on Hamlet's remarks to Rosencrantz and Guildenstern that he could be happy to live in a nut-shell—"were it not that I have bad dreams" (*Hamlet* 2.2.255–56).

depression. Largely immune; but not completely unaware at some level of artistic consciousness, as a study of two of his best and best-loved ghost stories may indicate: "'Oh, Whistle, and I'll Come to You, My Lad'" (1903) and "A Warning to the Curious" (1925).[4]

"'Oh, Whistle'" might well be seen as an example of a sort of homophobic bullying (though it is much more complicated than that). The story revolves around young Professor Parkins of St. James's College, Cambridge. Term is over, and he is about to go to Burnstow, to do some studying and play a bit of golf. Unfortunately, as he announces to his colleagues over dinner, the only room he could find was one with two beds. At this point, the "bluff person opposite," identified a few lines later as "rude Mr. Rogers" (PT 80), breaks in with a suggestion: "Look here, I shall come down and occupy it for a bit; it'll be company for you." Parkins is against the idea as he and Rogers clearly do not get on. Rogers really seems set on teasing his younger—but academically senior—colleague. On compelling Parkins to admit that he would rather he did not come, Rogers crows:

> "Well done, Parkins! [. . .] No, I won't come if you don't want me; but I thought I should do so nicely to keep the ghosts off." Here he might have been seen to wink and to nudge his next neighbour. Parkins might also have been seen to become pink. "I beg pardon, Parkins," Rogers continued; "I oughtn't to have said that. I forgot you didn't like levity on these topics."

Of course, he does remember; that is why he said it: to make Parkins blush—like a girl. And this is where homophobic bullying comes into the picture. Parkins is represented throughout the story as somewhat "unmanly" in the terms of the sort of collegiate life which James cherished and nurtured during his long spell at King's as student, fellow, and provost. It is not simply a question of effeminacy; Parkins also lacks the kind of intellectual culture which James prized as "gentlemanly." Parkins is weak on the Bible, on classical antiquity; he seems never to have read Dickens (and we may safely bet that Parkins does not smoke). Indeed, Parkins is a representative of the new—he is Professor of Ontography, a science even now yet to be invented—as opposed to the old order which the self-confessed Victorian M. R. James felt was under threat all through his life. So Parkins's effeminacy should be seen primarily, I think, as a means of further distancing him from the gentlemanly collegiality which James wanted to protect. James was not at

---

4. It is perhaps worth pointing out that the poem by Burns from which James took the title of "'Oh, Whistle'" is a song sung by a lass to her lad. He is to pretend not to know her, since his family appear to disapprove of the match; but he needs only to whistle and she will come to him. A sexual invitation, then.

all worried about effeminacy or homosexuality, as far as the record shows. But he did care about college life; and I think Parkins is a sort of scapegoat: he is carefully delineated as different in order that he should be punished, if not actually expelled from the society which James considered under threat from the new.

However, this scapegoating does have a sexual aspect; and it leads to a kind of sexually bullying element in Rogers's treatment of Parkins; not only in his trying to make him blush; but also in the veiled threats which lie beneath his manly offer to protect the girlish Parkins. He will "do so nicely to keep the ghosts off." What does Rogers mean by that? The idea is that these ghosts want to get at—perhaps even "get on"—Parkins as he lies in bed. Perhaps he envisages some kind of physical contact? In any case, though Rogers claims he will drive away the ghosts, he clearly has in himself some of their presumed malevolence towards poor Parkins; and it is hard to resist a conflation of Mr. Rogers with the ghosts from whom he claims he will protect the young professor—whilst secretly, we feel, intending to take their place as an agent of terror.

Parkins goes to Burnstow, removes a whistle from the ruined altar of an old Templars' church buried in the sands nearby, blows it, twice, despite the advice inscribed in Latin on its side, thus bringing upon himself the visitation of its ghostly custodian. The ghost—which we can tell is at least residually male because of the grammatical gender used in the inscription: *Quis est iste qui venit*—comes to his room and occupies the second bed. Next morning, the chambermaid asks which bed she should make up, since Parkins seems to have slept in both; and this produces another little scene in which Parkins's effeminacy is deftly hinted. She comes into his room as he is "putting the finishing touches to his golfing costume." I take it that the kind of clothes men wore to play golf a hundred years ago excited the same scornful comment as they do now; but there is an added touch of mockery in the image of Parkins preening himself—again: like a girl or woman, one wants to say. Parkins is also easily flustered when he reveals that—contrary to the reader's expectation—he has agreed to let Rogers come down after all:

> "I expect a friend of mine soon, by the way—a gentleman from Cambridge—to come and occupy it for a night or two. That will be all right, I suppose, won't it?"
>
> "Oh yes, to be sure, sir. Thank you, sir. It's no trouble, I'm sure," said the maid, and departed to giggle with her colleagues.
>
> Parkins set forth, with a stern determination to improve his game. (*PT* 88)

One has to admire James's economy. Parkins tries to end speculation about his own nocturnal habits by mentioning his friend, then hastens to assure the maid that it is a gentleman he is expecting, rather than a lady-friend, I suppose; and throughout the conversation seems to defer to the chambermaid's opinion. And why does she giggle with her friends? Presumably she is sharing the story of her encounter with this rather strange and ineffectual young man who sleeps in two beds at once, and the so-called "friend" he is expecting. Certainly, Parkins feels embarrassed; and James signals the young professor's attempt to restore his manly dignity with that phrase: "Parkins set forth"—as if he were a mediaeval knight in search of adventure.

There is more of this character-painting, particularly in the scenes where Parkins talks and plays golf with a more positively virile older man called Colonel Wilson, who provides a contrast to the rather sinister manliness of Mr. Rogers. That night, despite the warnings of his wise and experienced companion, Parkins does not throw away the mysterious whistle, but keeps it with him when he goes to sleep. A little later he wakes. There is someone in the other bed. It suddenly sits up and then gets up, still draped in the sheet, and goes towards the bed which Parkins has speedily vacated, listening to his movements since it is apparently blind. The last moments are worth describing in detail:

> With formidable quickness it moved into the middle of the room, and, as it groped and waved, one corner of its draperies swept across Parkins's face. He could not—though he knew how perilous a sound was—he could not keep back a cry of disgust, and this gave the searcher an instant clue. It leapt towards him upon the instant, and the next moment he was half-way through the window backwards, uttering cry upon cry at the utmost pitch of his voice, and the linen face was thrust close into his own. At this, almost the last possible second, deliverance came, as you will have guessed: the Colonel burst the door open, and was just in time to see the dreadful group at the window. When he reached the figures only one was left. Parkins sank forward into the room in a faint, and before him on the floor lay a tumbled heap of bedclothes. (PT 94)

This is perhaps the most famous passage in all of M. R. James's oeuvre: it is a scene which readers seem to have remembered very vividly, and other writers often imitate or allude to it.[5] But what is the ghost trying to do?

---

5. Rosemary Pardoe has shown that this episode struck R. Thurston Hopkins so forcibly that he introduced words and phrases from it when he gave his account of the famous veridical haunting of Number 50 Berkeley Square ("and no bird sings") in his Cavalcade of Ghosts (1956). See Rosemary Pardoe, "'I've Seen It': 'A School Story' and the House in Berkeley Square," Ghosts & Scholars 29

Wilson later explains that he has seen something like it in India, and that it could do no more than frighten Parkins. But at the time it seems that it is trying to make him fall from the window, or—could it be that it is also trying to kiss Parkins?

We remember that the ghost has occupied the bed in which Rogers was to have slept "to keep the ghosts off." At some obscure level, as I have already mentioned, James seems to be punishing Parkins, not for being, as the narrator puts it, "something of an old woman" (*PT* 81), but because he does not fit in with the collegiate culture James wished to preserve. However, James does release the threat of sexual violence latent in that culture—which was one of the essential organs of patriarchal society in the late Victorian and Edwardian periods—in the ambiguous figure of the occupant of the second bed: the Angry Ghost—but also the intimidating spectre of the overbearingly virile Mr. Rogers.

The possibility of homosexual violation figures rather more saliently in "A Warning to the Curious." Mr. Paxton is pursued by the ghostly custodian of a buried crown which he has removed from its hiding-place deep in the side of an old barrow. He replaces it after a day or two of tormenting persecution; however, the ghost does not leave matters there, but continues to haunt Paxton. The poor man is tricked into pursuing the ghost, which has cast a glamour over his eyes, so that he thinks he is running to catch up two friends whom he has met the day before at his hotel, and to whom he has confided his story. The two friends then set off in pursuit of Paxton in the

---

(1999): 41–43. Perhaps the image was so memorable because it was accompanied by one of the two pictures supplied by James's friend, James McBryde. (However, we might note that McBryde's illustration to the ghost's final pounce on Parkins does not reproduce the key details of the text, since access to the window is blocked by a heavy writing-desk.)

In passing, we may note that Cox records how H. Russell Wakefield alludes to the story in "The Triumph of Death," where "'Oh, Whistle'" is described as "a tale about some bedclothes forming into a figure and frightening an old man in the other bed" (cit. Cox 312); and that the unhappily aging Dicky Umphraville in Anthony Powell's *Temporary Kings* (Heinemann, 1973), feels like "the man in the ghost story, scrambling over the breakwaters with the Horrible Thing behind him getting closer and closer" (3). (Here is the other picture supplied by McBryde, by the way.) Parkins is, of course, young; so it is interesting to see that these readers seem to think of him as an old man. It bears out A. C. Benson's comment, apparently in connection with a reading of "'Oh, Whistle'" in December 1903, that M. R. James's characters were all "like elderly dons" (cit. Cox 312).

gathering sea-mist along the shore—noting the skeletal footprints intermingled with Paxton's tracks as they go—and eventually find him at the foot of an old coastal battery:

> You don't need to be told that he was dead. His tracks showed that he had run along the side of the battery, had turned sharp round the corner of it, and, small doubt of it, must have dashed straight into the open arms of someone who was waiting there. His mouth was full of sand and stones, and his teeth and jaws were broken to bits. I only glanced once at his face. (*PT* 354)

Paxton is finally caught in the terrible embrace of the ghost who has been pursuing him; and this open-armed embrace may well involve an equally terrible kiss. It makes sense for Paxton's mouth to be full of sand and stones because the ghost wants to make sure he does not reveal the hiding-place of the crown. But this does not explain the terrible state of Paxton's mouth and jaws. What has happened, it is hinted, is that his mouth has come into rapid and fatal contact with the teeth and jaws of the skeletal custodian of the crown: a kiss of death.

An earlier scene in that story moves us even closer to the abyss of homosexual panic. Paxton is burrowing into the mound where the crown is hidden, all the time horribly aware that someone—whom we know to be the ghost of a certain William Ager—is right behind him:

> It was like someone scraping at my back all the time: I thought for a long time it was only soil dropping on me, but as I got nearer the—the crown, it was unmistakable. And when I actually laid it bare and got my fingers into the ring of it and pulled it out, there came a sort of cry behind me—oh, I can't tell you how desolate it was! And horribly threatening, too. It spoilt all my pleasure in my find—cut it off that moment. (*PT* 348)

What are we to make of this scene? Paxton is prostrate in the tunnel, with the ghost of William Ager on his back. But where we might have imagined Paxton gasping with delight when he finally gets his heart's desire—by penetrating the ring of the crown with his fingers—the cry is transferred to the ghost on his back, and it is not a cry of pleasure but despair. A curious passage: Paxton violates both the burrow and the crown by penetrating them—and this seems to call forth a sexualised revenge on the part of William Ager, announced by the orgasm of misery and malevolence expressed in the ghost's cry, finally pursued to its own climax in what I see as the kiss of death on the shore by the battery, which the ghost celebrates with "a breathless, a lungless laugh" (*PT* 354).[6] Throughout the story the ghost is

---

6. Muriel Smith of The Everlasting Club has pointed out to me that the ghost's

described in terms of lightness: its lack of substance and visible shape. Towards the end, however, it gathers mass as it comes closer to catching its victim: footprints appear on the shore-line; and in a final and as it were tumescent climax, the ghost gathers enough substance to shatter Paxton's teeth and jaws in its horrendous kiss of death.

What I am suggesting here, of course, is that the ghost's attack on Paxton can be seen as a sort of extended homosexual rape. And I take it that homosexual rape is the severest punishment meted out to victims of the patriarchal regime. However, as with Parkins, the sexual aspect is not the primary one. Paxton is primarily punished for removing the crown because this is the last of three Saxon crowns buried along the East Anglian Coast, and, as we know from the manuscript of "A Warning to the Curious," the story was originally to have dated to the year 1917 (in the printed version the year is left blank).[7] Paxton's curiosity is tantamount to treason, then, in the anxious days of the Great War. There are other hints that Paxton is some kind of defector: he is on the point of leaving England to settle in neutral Sweden; and when the inquest is held we learn that "Paxton was so totally without connections that all the inquiries that were subsequently made ended in a No Thoroughfare" (PT 355). On the other hand, we may note certain details which detract from Paxton's "manliness": he is a "rabbity anaemic subject" (PT 342);[8] and when he tells his story, he commits the cardinal sin against the stiff upper lip: "I believe he began to cry" (PT 349). But here again these details function rather cruelly as an extra justification for the harsh treatment meted out to him.[9]

A pause for reflection may be in order. I seem to have made M. R. James seem some kind of sadistic patriarchal terrorist; whereas by all accounts he was a kind and gentle man who was loved by almost all who came in contact

---

laughter is breathless and lungless because William Ager died of consumption.

7. See Rosemary Pardoe, "The Manuscript of 'A Warning to the Curious,'" *Ghosts & Scholars* 32 (2001): 47–49.

8. Is there a sardonic reference to *Alice in Wonderland* at the back of all this? Paxton tells us he penetrated the burrow quite easily because "there was a rabbit hole or so that might be developed" (PT 346).

9. What happens to Paxton is matched only by the fate arranged for Mr. Wraxall in "Count Magnus" (1904). Here it is not a question of the kiss of death, however, since James drops the hint that the flesh from Wraxall's face is sucked off by the demon's tentacular appendage. But Wraxall is clearly a prototype of Paxton: he is a rootless bachelor, with "no settled abode in England" (PT 65), whose antiquarian leanings take him to Sweden.

with him! But my point has been that although James seems to have been relatively immune to homosexual panic himself, he may be seen to use—perhaps unconsciously—the narrative strategies of homosexual panic in stories where the punishment meted out by ghostly avengers is really located in a different scheme of retribution: Parkins is really punished because he is modern and Paxton because he is unpatriotic (in my view).[10] Nor is James the only author of supernatural fiction perhaps unconsciously to use these strategies; and I want to conclude very briefly with a ghost story by an exact contemporary of James: W. W. Jacobs—author of the famous "The Monkey's Paw." Jacobs's story "The Well" (1902) treats homosexual rape (if we can call it that) in a slightly different way from what we have seen the figure used in James's work. Here is the story:

Jem Benson (no relation to A. C.!) is a rich young man who is about to be married to Olive; but his ne'er-do-well cousin, Wilfrid Carr, whom Benson has been bailing out of financial trouble for years, threatens to spoil everything. Now he is to marry, Benson refuses to support Carr any longer; but Carr needs money and has certain incriminating letters in his possession—written by Benson to an old mistress—with which he tries to blackmail his cousin. He says: "I know a man who would buy them at [fifteen hundred pounds] for the mere chance of getting Olive from you" (Jacobs 76). Here, then, is a typically Sedgwickian situation: Olive is a counter in a patriarchal economy regulating relations of power between men. But Carr is not interested in Olive; indeed, there are several hints that he may be homosexual (marriage and honeymoons are "not in my line at all" [73]).

But to continue: the story gives us to understand that Benson does away with Carr by disposing of him down a well in an overgrown park on his country estate. Unfortunately, Olive is particularly drawn to the place, which she finds agreeably creepy; and she and Benson are sitting on it shortly after the murder, when Olive seems to hear a whisper from the well behind her: "Jem, help me out" (60)—Carr's old cry to Benson, though now intended in a physical rather than financial sense. Then Olive drops her bracelet in the well; Benson tries to fish it out that night, but fails; and early the next morning he has to go down there himself on a rope—for he cannot let anyone else see what is at the bottom. The workman above, George, feels a tremendous tug on the rope; he pulls it up gradually and with great exertion, "until at last a violent splashing was heard, and at the same time a scream of unutterable horror" (87). George pulls in the heavy burden, "jerked violently by the

---

10. See my "'No Thoroughfare': The Problem of Paxton in 'A Warning to the Curious,'" *Ghosts & Scholars* 32 (2001): 42–46.

struggles of the weight at the end of it," and finally a horrible sight is presented to his eyes: "A long pull and a strong pull, and the face of a dead man with mud in the eyes and nostrils came peering over the edge. Behind it was the ghastly face of his master; but this he saw too late, for with a great cry he let go his hold of the rope and stepped back [. . .] and the rope tore through his hands" (88).

To regain a little ground for James, admittedly at Jacobs's expense, I would say that this is a botched job. Carr's face should be behind Benson's, not the other way around; because Carr is the Angry Ghost pursuing its victim: we aficionados know that he should have grasped Benson down in the well and that he must either be face to face with him or taking him from behind—for what could be more grimly ironic than a reversal of roles in which Benson, far from finally achieving sexual possession of the lovely Olive on their wedding-night, is instead sexually possessed by the corpse of Carr in the well? We recall the other Benson's shudder when he wrote of Walpole's predicament in terms of a "dark place to have looked into." Perhaps Jacobs looked there, too, and in the dark depths of the well saw the unspeakable homosexual union which Benson glimpsed in horror. It seems to have led him into a lapse of craftsmanship which has the murderer hauling his victim into the sight of the world—the very thing he was trying to avoid.

James, however, looked into the same abyss with a certain nonchalant equilibrium; and it is pleasant to conclude this paper with the suggestion that part of his greatness as a ghost-story writer lies precisely in that curious reticence about sexual matters which might so easily be perceived as a weakness, rather than what it is: a strength. "A School Story" was first published in *More Ghost Stories of an Antiquary* (1911), but Benson records how Luxmoore told "the story (by MRJ) of the ashes, *memento putei*" in December 1906—just four years after Jacobs's "Well" appeared in *The Lady of the Barge* in 1902 (see *PT* 121, endnote). Perhaps James had read "The Well" and casually imitates it in his own tale; but his ending is very different. We have noted that Jem Benson seems compelled—whether by the ancient logic of providential narrative or the modern idea of the criminal returning to the scene of the crime—to expose his own wrong-doing; and consequently little enough is left to the imagination. But what happens to Mr. Sampson (and why) is left very much in the dark in "A School Story." His end—if it is indeed his remains which were discovered in the well in Ireland—can only be guessed at by the Irish gentleman's description: "One body had the arms tight round the other" (*PT* 121).[11] This seems just the right amount of in-

---

11. The narrator does not seem to read the inscription on the gold coin very carefully when asked by his host if he can puzzle it out: "'I think I can,' said my

formation required to produce an appropriate shudder. The very idea of being embraced by a corpse—whether male or female—is sufficently unpleasant on its own; but I hope to have given some indication in the preceding pages that for James and his contemporaries the idea of one man being embraced by the corpse of another man might have been especially horrifying.

Works Cited

Alington, Cyril. *Lionel Ford.* 1934; cit. Cox.

Cox, Michael. *M. R. James: An Informal Portrait.* London: Oxford University Press, 1983.

Jacobs, W. W. "The Well" (1902). In *Selected Short Stories.* Ed. Denys Kilham Roberts. Harmondsworth: Penguin, 1959.

James, M. R. *Casting the Runes and Other Ghost Stories.* Ed. Michael Cox. London: Oxford University Press, 1987.

————. *A Pleasing Terror: The Complete Supernatural Writings.* Ed. Christopher Roden and Barbara Roden. Ashcroft, BC: Ash-Tree Press, 2001. [Abbreviated in the text as *PT.*]

Sedgwick, Eve Kosofsky. *Between Men: English Literature and Male Homosocial Desire.* 1985; New York: Columbia University Press, 1992.

Newsome, David. *On the Edge of Paradise: A. C. Benson, the Diarist.* Chicago: University of Chicago Press, 1980.

---

friend, holding it to the light (but he read it without much difficulty); 'it seems to be G.W.S., 24 July, 1865'" (*PT* 121). Does the narrator really read it at all? Or has he come to the same conclusion that we readers have also reached—without really needing to weigh the evidence. . . .

"If I'm Not Careful": Innocents and Not-So-Innocents in the Stories of M. R. James

John Alfred Taylor

Motiveless Malignancy

In his preface to *More Ghost Stories of an Antiquary* M. R. James explains that the setting of a ghost story should be "fairly familiar and the majority of the characters and their talk such as you may meet or hear any day," because a story set in the twelfth or thirteenth century "will never put the reader into the position of saying to himself: 'If I'm not careful, something of this kind may happen to me!'"

Judging from some of James's stories, a person must be careful to the point of near-paralysis. More than one commentator has pointed out that the most innocent act can unleash supernatural malignance; as Michael Cox says in his introduction to *Casting the Runes and Other Ghost Stories,* "a chance word, an unthinking action, curiosity, or simply being in the wrong place at the right time, can all spring the trap."

Mr. Anderson in "Number 13" is certainly "in the wrong place at the right time," though all he does is check into Room Number 12 in the Golden Lion in Viborg, where there is no Number 13, at least by daylight. But at night that local annex of Hell is next door.

In "'Oh, Whistle, and I'll Come to You, My Lad,'" Professor Parkins finds a whistle and blows on it twice (without understanding its cryptic inscription). Mere curiosity. But because Parkins found the whistle in the ruins of a Templar chapel, with the Templars reputed to be heretics and idolaters, the reader is persuaded to accept the terrifying consequences—especially when accompanied by the anti-Catholic rantings of Parkins's golf partner Colonel Wilson, who sees the sinister hand of the Papacy everywhere and calls him a Sadducee when he doubts the existence of ghosts. The irascible Colonel has his comic side, but events prove his instincts sound.

Curiosity brings worse consequences in "Count Magnus." In Jutland, Mr. Wraxall learns that Magnus de la Gardie went on the Black Pilgrimage and brought back a monstrous familiar, and that even after his death the Count and his familiar punished trespassers monstrously; but the habit of talking to himself aloud is what dooms Wraxall.

Passing by the Count's mausoleum, he says: "Count Magnus, there you are. I should dearly like to see you." The second time he approaches he chants "Are you awake, Count Magnus? Are you asleep, Count Magnus?" He is actually in the mausoleum when he says, "You may have been a bit of a rascal in your time, Magnus, but for all that I should like to see you . . ." At that moment the third padlock securing the Count's coffin drops off and the lid begins to rise. Wraxall flees, but his return to England is dogged by two figures the reader recognizes. In his last disjointed notes he asks, "What has he done?" and "Is there no hope?" There isn't, and all Mr. Wraxall has done to bring his fate is talk to himself without realizing who else is listening, or what he is inadvertently summoning. (And was Wraxall saying these things completely of his own volition?)

In "Canon Alberic's Scrap-book" Dennistoun does nothing more than buy the book from the sacristan of St. Bertrand's. Though filled with pages ripped from illuminated manuscripts by "the unprincipled Canon Alberic, who had doubtless plundered the Chapter library of St. Bertrand to form this priceless scrap-book," the drawing at the end is the only thing that makes the book dangerous. A sepia drawing by Alberic de Mauléon shows Solomon facing a demon which has just strangled one of the King's guards. "It was drawn from the life."

Enough hints are given for the reader to reconstruct the Canon's story: he raised the demon to help him find treasure; it haunted him for the rest of his life; he did die in bed as predicted, but probably of strangulation rather than a sudden seizure. Possession of Alberic's drawing is what brings the demon resembling "one of the awful bird-catching spiders of South America translated into human form." Witness the sacristan's relief once he has sold Dennistoun the book; and how Dennistoun is safe once he burns the actual drawing, though a photograph of the drawing remains to frighten persons like the Lecturer in Morphology of "abnormally sane and unimaginative habits of mind."

Humphreys's only mistake in "Mr. Humphreys and His Inheritance" is to explore a yew maze on his new estate and find what he thinks is a celestial globe at its center. His late uncle Wilson had kept the gate locked to all, even Lady Wardrop, a formidable amateur of mazes. One night Humphreys sees an apparent outlier of the maze that turns into a bush against the library window the next, and finally when the windows are open on the stuffy night as he is copying the plan of the maze for Lady Wardrop, he wonders if something has crawled through the window "that had a mind to join him." The subsequent apparition of a burned thing that comes up through a hole in the center of the plan is half-explained by the discovery that the globe in the center of the maze contained the cremated remains of the man who had it laid out. Judging from the engraved figures and names, "an assemblage of the patriarchs of evil," the globe is more infernal than celestial.

The tale ends in mystery: "grateful as Humphreys was to the memory of his uncle, he could not quite forgive him for having burnt the journals and letters of the James Wilson who had gifted Wilsthorpe with the maze . . ." In spite of these lacunae, judging from the images on the globe and the infinite depth of the hole from which his scorched apparition rises, James Wilson was a diabolist or heretic and damned because of it. Also, Humphreys's uncle had the stones that originally marked the path to the center of the maze removed, but when put in the proper order they spell out PENETRANS AD INTE-RIORA MORTIS, implying that anyone penetrating the maze was reenacting the fatal arc of Wilson's life. (Could there be a connection here with the famous alchemical motto V.I.T.R.I.O.L. for VISITANS INTERIORA TERRAE RECTIFICANDO INVENIES OCCULTUM LAPIDEM?)[1]

In "The Diary of Mr. Poynter" James Denton does nothing more than have the pattern on an old piece of cloth reproduced for curtains; while the couple in "The Rose Garden" merely order a post removed, unaware that it pins down a revenant. One would say the consequences of this last were only noises at night, except that Mrs. Anstruther collapses after seeing a mysterious pink face in the garden, and when she is reminded of it by a photograph of a historical portrait, is shocked enough to have to "spend the winter abroad." Dean Burscough in "An Episode of Cathedral History" may be too insistent on stripping Southminster of "lovely stuff" from the interior of the church during the Gothic revival, loosing a vampiric lamia from a hidden tomb upon the town; but despite James's negative view of restoration, the Dean is ignorant, not criminal.

What happens in "Casting the Runes" makes more sense. Though Edward Dunning is no more than honest when he reviews Mr. Karswell's *The Truth of Alchemy* unfavorably, Karswell the magus is predictably annoyed, and sets in train a series of supernatural persecutions destined to culminate in Dunning's death. But because Karswell revenged an earlier bad review by "casting the runes" on John Harrington, Harrington's brother becomes Dunning's ally, telling him what his brother suffered, so that the two of them know enough to pass the paper with the fatal runes back to Karswell just in

---

1. "Visit the interior of the earth, purify, and find the hidden stone."

time. Karswell boards the Channel boat (followed by what?) and the news of his death in Abbeville comes soon after.

Vengeance Is Mine

James's stories of supernatural vengeance are more traditional. No monstrously disproportionate consequences of minor actions here—there is a Newtonian balance, with every action bringing an equal reaction.

In "The Ash-Tree" Sir Matthew Fell gives conclusive testimony in the witchcraft trial of Mrs. Mothersole, and he and a later descendent pay for it with their lives, because after the witch's execution her lich and dreadful progeny are nearer than they know.

"The Stalls of Barchester Cathedral" shows Dr. Haynes contriving the death of his predecessor but dying of a fall on the stairs like the former Dean, this time because of a cat carved on a choir stall come alive; the carving has power for vengeance because the wood came from the Hanging Oak, named thus because of a history of pagan human sacrifice. (A small problem here for those knowledgeable about Anglo-Saxon religion: sacrifices by hanging would be to Odin, and therefore involve ash trees rather than oaks.)

The basic action of "A School Story" is easily summarized: what seems to be a dead man is seen outside the window of one of the masters, who disappears. Thirty years pass before two skeletons are found clinging together at the bottom of a well, and it becomes clear that the teacher was stalked by the man he murdered.

"The Mezzotint" and "The Haunted Dolls' House" share the theme of past supernatural vengeance replayed in the present by mysterious means. Perhaps "The Mezzotint" is more interesting, because the engraving changes over time, but the changes are timed so the viewers see the whole sequence. And no matter how mysterious, much of the sequence is documented by the camera. Photography is explicable, but not the mezzotint; in the end we are told there is no sign of "sympathetic ink," and that the picture has never changed again.

James admits in an afterword to "The Haunted Dolls' House" that it is a variation on "The Mezzotint," and hopes "that there is enough of variation in the setting to make the repetition of the *motif* tolerable." Though what may not be tolerable is that, in both cases, children pay in the end for the actions of their parents; but then these are entertainments, not stories from the evening news.

The basic action of "The Story of a Disappearance and an Appearance" is unsurprising: a ghost returns to punish his murderers; but its effectiveness comes from the macabre undertones of Punch and Judy shows.

In "Lost Hearts" young Stephen Elliott is saved from his elderly cousin's machinations at the last moment. On the night when Mr. Abney plans to extract Stephen's heart for occult purposes, the ghosts of two earlier victims of this process revenge themselves on Abney, leaving "a terrible lacerated wound, exposing the heart." What makes their return at the right time be-lievable is that Abney's plan is driven by a ritual calendar; the night he plans to murder Stephen is the anniversary of his earlier crimes.

"Lost Hearts" isn't the only story where misuse of the dead is avenged. In "A View from a Hill" Baxter finally pays for boiling men's bones to fill his magical binoculars; and in "The Residence at Whitminster" Lord Saul ends as "an ugly thin ghost" after being hunted down either by the dead or by the doglike things he brought with him from Ireland.

Keep That Which Is Committed to Thee

In other stories by James, ghosts are more possessive than vengeful, though the distinction can be uncertain.

In "The Treasure of Abbot Thomas" the Abbot's specter appears at the well-head to mock Somerton while he grapples with the grotesque guardian of the treasure below: what makes this especially grotesque is that the guard-ian and the treasure are as good as merged. Abbot Thomas's possessiveness is memorialized by the inscription *Depositum custodi* ("Keep that which is committed to thee"). At least Somerton escapes with his life.

Not so with Paxton, the treasure hunter in "A Warning to the Curious." He has found the one remaining Anglo-Saxon crown of the three that were buried to repel invaders, and knows he is doomed even after he puts it back. The emphasis on repelling invaders through the power of the buried crown, with the invaders initially identified as German, sets the story in or around 1914–1918. The reader feels for Paxton, trying to repair the damage he has done, but still pursued as relentlessly by the spirit of the crown's hereditary guardian as Mr Wraxall was by Count Magnus and friend.

"The Uncommon Prayer-Book" involves a singularly nasty revenant (though the story suggests Lady Sadleir may have been equally nasty when alive). Her ghost revenges the theft of the prayer-books from the family chapel, her shroud seen as "a long white bundle" on top of the culprit's mo-tor car when he drives away. Later she falls on Poschwitz from the safe where he's stored the stolen books, and her bite has the same instantly hemolytic effect as snake venom.

Dr. Rant, in "The Tractate Middoth," who was buried sitting at a table in an underground chamber, is a more ambivalently possessive spirit. Before his death he wrote two wills, one leaving everything to his nephew John Eldred, the other hidden in a book and favoring his niece, Mrs. Simpson. On his deathbed he taunts her that the book is "in a place where John can go and find it any day, if he only knew, and you can't." He disliked nephew and niece both, but perhaps was angrier at Mrs. Simpson because she married a poor man. Ever since Rant's death Eldred has enjoyed the estate, and now knows that the second will is in the copy of the *Tractate Middoth* his uncle donated to the university library. He is on the point of destroying the document when the dead man asphyxiates or frightens him to death. But why now, when Eldred's been in possession of the estate for years?

Plain Haunts

But some of James's ghosts are neither malignant, vengeful, or possessive. They just endure.

The ghost of the disgraced Lord Chief Justice in "The Rose Garden" has no agenda, and the disturbances it raises after the post is removed soon die out. He is supposed to have died of remorse, but could he have been a suicide?—suicides were traditionally staked down, and if the position of the post indicates his grave, it is outside the churchyard.

In "A Neighbour's Landmark" the Lady Ivy, embodied only by a shriek and probably lacking all volition, haunts the area she gained by moving the marker.

In "Martin's Close" Ann Clark, the "natural" who haunts her murderer up to the moment of his execution, may not be doing it out of revenge, but from continued affection. Witness her ghost singing the answering part of "Madam, will you walk" outside the New Inn while Martin cowers within. In the end this constant mindless fondness may be harder to endure than anger. (For a parallel see Robert Hichens's "How Love Came to Professor Guildea.") In any case George Martin is brought to justice through the testimony of living witnesses, not by anything she does.

Anomalies

Some of James's stories fall outside these categories.

He often suggests more than he says, leaving it up to the reader to follow his hints: realizing the full pattern for oneself is one of the pleasures of reading his ghost stories. Usually he plays fair, but not in "Two Doctors," which seems to be the literary equivalent of a Rorschach inkblot. Too much is left out in this tale reconstructed from documents. What seems clear is that Dr. Abell kills his rival Quinn by magic, that Abell has gained the power to move things at a distance through a Faustian bargain, and that the luxurious second-hand bedclothes which smother Dr. Quinn were stolen from a tomb.

The reader learns there is something about "the bedstaff in [Abell's] dispensing room," but the affidavit concerning it is no longer among the documents—the final implication is that the bedstaff moved on its own, like the fireplace poker in a later scene. Though Quinn dies in a locked room, Abell seems to have had the capacity to enter Quinn's house at will.

The final paragraph of the story describes the "rifling of a mausoleum . . . of a noble family. . . . The outrage was not that of an ordinary resurrection man. The object, it seemed likely, was theft. The account was blunt and terrible. I shall not quote it."

If all that was stolen was a corpse's bedding, would the account be "blunt and terrible"? Perhaps the person who was not an ordinary body-snatcher snatched a left hand as well, enough to make a Hand of Glory that would give Abell entry in spite of locks and doors. (Maybe too melodramatic for James,[2] and perhaps unnecessary considering Abell's power to move things at a distance, but one can see all sorts of things in an inkblot.)

"Wailing Well," created to be read to the Eton Boy Scouts at their campfire at Worbarrow Bay, is much more satisfying. The boys must have enjoyed the specifically Etonian jokes (at one point James writes himself in as being struck by a cricket ball) and the story's pervasive black humor appeals to boys of all ages. But the central situation is grim: the Scouts have been warned not to go near the red ring on their maps marking off the overgrown field around Wailing Well, once good pasture, though now patrolled by four skeletons dressed in rags. "Three women and a man," as a local shepherd says. "And why they goes there still is more than the children of men can tell: except I've heard they was all bad 'uns when they was alive." Bumptious Stanley Judkins thinks he knows better, and is trapped by the dead because he tries to go where he shouldn't—when found his body has been drained of blood. Judkins seems no loss, and "the present population of the Wailing Well field consists of three women, a man, and a boy." The story never explains why the dead are confined to the vicinity, but their murderousness needs no explanation, thanks to the ancient intuition that the dead envy the living, and want the living to join them. (Anthropologists suggest that cutting the hair or other self-mutilation during mourning was meant to disguise oneself from the deceased; in the Balkans, mirrors were turned to the wall while the dead man was lying in for fear one would see him looking over one's shoulder in the mirror and be the next to go.)

---

2. And tradition suggests that the raw material for a Hand of Glory should be lopped from the remains of a hanged man.

Das Unheimlich

But what makes these stories of ghosts and demons and black magic so effective and pleasantly frightening, even for skeptical readers, the kind of persons Colonel Wilson in "'Oh, Whistle'" would call Sadducees? Perhaps an essay by an arch-Sadducee gives more than a hint. Despite its barrage of psychoanalytic jargon and Germanic philology, Freud's essay on "The Uncanny" ends with a clear thesis:

> Let us take the uncanny associated with the omnipotence of thoughts, with the prompt fulfillment of wishes, with secret injurious powers and with the return of the dead. The condition under which the feeling of uncanniness arises here is unmistakable. We—or our primitive forefathers—once believed that these possibilities were realities, and were convinced that they actually happened. Nowadays we no longer believe in them, we have *surmounted* these modes of thought; but we do not feel quite sure of our new beliefs, and the old ones still exist within us ready to seize upon any confirmation. As soon as something *actually happens* in our lives which seems to confirm the old, discarded beliefs we get a feeling of the uncanny; it is as though we were making a judgment something like this: "So, after all, it is *true* that one can kill a person by the mere wish!" or, "So the dead *do* live on and appear on the scene of their former activities!" and so on.

Freud goes on to make specific literary points. He says that in fairy stories events involving the omnipotence of thoughts, etc., do not produce uncanny feelings; but "the situation is altered as soon as the writer pretends to move into the world of common reality." Compare Freud's "world of common reality" with the James quotation at the beginning of this essay emphasizing the need for an everyday setting and characters. Or see James's suggestions in the introduction to *Ghosts and Marvels*:

> Let us, then, be introduced to the actors in a placid way; let us see them going about their ordinary business, undisturbed by forebodings, pleased with their surroundings; and into this calm environment let the ominous thing put out its head, unobtrusively at first, and then more insistently, until it holds the stage.

Thus James necessarily devotes a large portion of his art to weaving an image of the quotidian. Without this sense of the ordinary there would be no fear, no shock of the uncanny when the commonsense fabric is finally torn. To put it in Freud's German, there can be no *Unheimlich* without an idea of the *Heimlich*.

"As Time Goes On I See a Shadow Coming": M. R. James's Grammar of Terror

Steven J. Mariconda

Writing in Gale's *Dictionary of Literary Biography*, critic William Atkinson makes the seemingly bizarre claim that M. R. James should be considered a literary modernist, "for the modernist movement in all the arts questioned the possibility of unequivocal representation." The vision of the sedate traditionalist James in the company of Gertrude Stein and Pablo Picasso is enough to make one pause, if not to smirk. However, a closer reading of James tends to support rather than refute Atkinson's position. His observation that the stories' "very narratability seems to be in question" hints at the proposition that it is by the adroit use of grammar that James created his horrors, horrors of past evils that persist to trouble the present.

"It is" or "It was": Narration in James and Le Fanu

The uniqueness of James's approach to narrative grammar becomes striking when one considers his tales in the context of those of Joseph Sheridan Le Fanu. James never failed to promote Le Fanu as his exemplar, so one might reasonably conclude he used similar methods. But an inventory of the words the two writers use immediately reflects a divergence.

Le Fanu's use of traditional past-tense narrative is implied when James cites "the victim's dim forebodings of what is to happen gradually growing clearer" as a strength of Le Fanu's narration. This is supported by the frequency in Le Fanu of the verb *had*. In James, though, we find that the forms *has, be, have, been,* and combinations thereof predominate. Also evident in James is his pervasive use of *much, just, very, almost, considerable, enough, hardly,* and the ubiquitous *rather, perhaps,* and *quite*.

The marked contrast in the use of verb tense is apparent in these passages, which describe strange apparitions. First from Le Fanu:

> It [the shadow of a figure] was so thrown obliquely that the hands reached to the windowsill, and the feet stretched and stretched, longer and longer as

she looked, toward the ground, and disappeared in the general darkness, and the rest, with a sudden flicker, shot downwards, as shadows will on the sudden movement of a light, and was lost in one gigantic leap down the castle wall. ["Ultor de Lacy"]

And from James:

It would stop, raise arms, bow itself towards the sand, then run stooping across the beach to the water-edge and back again; and then, rising upright, once more continue its course forward at a speed that was startling and terrifying. ("'Oh, Whistle, and I'll Come to You, My Lad'")

Even in shorter sentences the difference in the use of tense is evident; for example:

James: The account is blunt and terrible. ["Two Doctors"]
Le Fanu: The effect of it was powerful. ["The Mysterious Lodger"]

James: There is no chimney. ["Number 13"]
Le Fanu: There was no other mode of exit. ["Schalken the Painter"]

With this distinction in mind, a review of James's work shows that he was innovative in the use of tense, aspect, and modality to create horror—to convey the intrusion of the past into the present or, more generally, to convey the uncanny commingling of temporal realities. This technique was an important influence upon subsequent writers of supernatural fiction, and has been adopted and extended to great advantage by two leading modern exponents, Ramsey Campbell and Thomas Ligotti.

"Forging the Links Between Past and Present": James's Narratology

Introducing his annotated edition of James's tales, S. T. Joshi marks the signal achievement of James as follows:

Where he differed from his predecessors . . . was in suggesting the pervasiveness of the past's influence upon the present: his tales . . . establish a continuity between past and present in which the present is entirely engulfed and rendered fleeting and ineffectual . . . ("Introduction," in CM xii)

Most commentary has naturally focused on the depth of James's antiquarian knowledge as the basis of his ability to evoke terror from history. But elsewhere Joshi astutely notes that James gave great thought and energy to "the mechanics of narrating the ghost story." He necessarily gleans this from internal evidence, as James is famously coy regarding his theory of the weird tale. James at least admits that "[a]n ancient haunting can be made terrible and can be invested with actuality, but it will tax your best endeavors to forge the links between the past and the present in a satisfying way" ("Ghosts—Treat Them Gently," *HDH* 262). He remains silent as to how he himself addresses the challenge, elsewhere noting only that "[I]f a really remote date be chosen, there is more than one way of bringing the reader in contact with it" ("Introduction to *Ghosts and Marvels*," *HDH* 248).

"More Than One Way": Grammatical Strategies in James's Narratives

This leaves the interested reader to discover for himself James's methods. In fine, James uses savvy deployment of certain elements of grammar—tense, aspect, and modality—to create his atmosphere of antique horrors malignantly active in the present.

Tense and Aspect

Tense and aspect are separate grammatical systems that work together semantically. Tense has to do with *when* an event or state of being occurred, and indicates the time (as past, present, or future) and the continuance or completion of an action or state of being. Aspect, in contrast, has to do with the *duration* or completeness of an event or state of being. And this is where things get interesting, because James skillfully plays aspectual constructions against tense forms—mixing elements which indicate that (for example) an event began in the past and "bumped up against" a more recent event in the past, or that an event that began in the past continues into the present.

Modality

Modality is grammar that reflects that narrator's attitude about what he says, his degree of certainty regarding statements he makes, and the level of commitment he attaches to his utterances. Specifically, James's tales are laced with what is called epistemic modality, which encompasses the ways in which the narrator indicates his degree of commitment to the truth of propositions, and reflects his level of knowledge or belief. The most common sources of epistemic modality in English are the modal auxiliaries—constructions like *could have been, ought to, would rather, might be*. The vigilant reader will find that it is impossible to read a page of James without encountering a veritable phalanx of these constructions, often moving in contrary epistemic directions. There is also an arsenal of qualifying adverbs—epistemic adverbs (e.g., *perhaps*) expressing uncertainty or possibility; adverbs of duration (e.g., *briefly*) that constrain time periods communicated by certain aspectual constructions; adverbs of degree (e.g., *somewhat*) that qualify the sense of another word—all these James deploys to create a veritable no-man's-land of uncertainty regarding the flux of reality—what was, what is, and what should or should not be.

"Some Future Time Which Never Came": Duration in "Count Magnus"

"Count Magnus" opens with the narrator explaining that he has assembled the tale from disparate sources. It is told largely from the perspective of Mr. Wraxall, an antiquarian who takes as his study a deadly subject—the evil Count Magnus. Wraxall haplessly resurrects the undead count, and is killed for his trouble.

The deathless state of being possessed by Count Magnus is reflected in the story's grammar, particularly in the use of adverbs of duration. At the start of the tale James describes an event (a warehouse fire) completed before another event in a possible future (the narrator's prospective further research on Wraxall).

> It is probable that he entertained the idea of settling down at some future time which never came; and I think it also likely that the Pantechnicon fire in the early seventies *must have destroyed* a great deal that *would have thrown* light on his antecedents, for he refers once or twice to property of his that was warehoused at that establishment. (CM 72–73)

Here we see two future perfect constructions (a modal [*must/would*] plus *have* plus a past participle) create a sense of the past embedded in the present.

The sense of uncertainty regarding the integrity of the present as up against the past is also enhanced here as throughout James, by what we can generally call qualifiers—epistemic adverbs, adverbs of duration, and adverbs of degree:

> *Certainly*, and *perhaps* fortunately in this case, there was neither voice nor any that regarded: only the woman who, *I suppose*, was cleaning up the church, dropped *some* metallic object on the floor, whose clang startled me.

In all his stories James leans heavily—almost intrusively—on the epistemic adverbs *perhaps* (expressing uncertainty or possibility), *quite* (to a certain extent) and *rather* (to a certain or significant extent or degree).

Because the perfect communicates duration, another type of adverb is needed to focus on or bound the time dimension implied. In the climactic scene in which Wraxall releases Magnus, James uses temporal adverbials to mark how one event—what happened in the tomb—encroaches upon to another event—Wraxall writing his account in the narrative present:

"... I stooped to pick it up, and—Heaven is my witness that I am writing only the bare truth—*before* I had raised myself there was a sound of metal hinges creaking, and I distinctly saw the lid shifting upwards. I may have behaved like a coward, but I could not for my life stay *for one moment.* I was outside that dreadful building *in less time than I can write*—almost *as quickly as I could have said*—the words; and what frightens me yet more, I could not turn the key in the lock. *As I sit here* in my room noting these facts, I ask myself (it was not *twenty minutes ago*) whether that noise of creaking metal continued, and I cannot tell whether it did or not. I only know that there was something more than I have written that alarmed me, but whether it was sound or sight I am not able to remember. What is this that I have done?" (CM 78)

The perfect constructions—"I may have behaved," "I could have said" (modal plus present perfect); "I am writing" (present perfect progressive); "I have done" (present perfect) require markers to delimit the timing of the events. Note also the use of the participles *noting* (present progressive), *creaking,* and *shifting* (past progressive) to further mark time. The result is sort of temporal cohesion in which the past and present become enmeshed, in the process throttling the doomed Mr. Wraxall.

"Have You Explored It Ever?": Labyrinthine Tense and Aspect in "Mr. Humphreys and His Inheritance"

In "Mr. Humphreys and His Inheritance" the title character's ancestor has left him a house and property. "There's an old Temple, besides, and a maze," says Humphreys's new neighbor. "Really?" he replies. "Have you explored it ever?" (CM 219). The present perfect construction with the temporal adverbial "ever" awkwardly tacked on signals trouble ahead. It seems Humphreys's ancestor practiced the dark arts; the maze casts a perpetual ill influence on those who traverse it, apparently because his cremation ashes lie within the decorative globe at the center.

The maze, as critics have noted, may be seen as a metaphor for the text itself. In the narrative James uses mixed verb tenses and aspectual constructions to create a sense of nested time in which the past is environed within the present. In one of the most beautifully written and fully realized passages in James, Humphreys's experiences a kind of reverie as he looks out his study window over the property. But note how the verb tenses shift and the aspectual construction becomes tortuous:

But *now* the distant woods *were* in a deep stillness; the slopes of the lawns *were* shining with dew; the colours of some of the flowers *could almost be* guessed. The light of the moon just *caught* the cornice of the temple and the curve of its leaden dome, and Humphreys *had to own* that, so seen, these conceits of a past age *have* a real beauty. In short, the light, the perfume of the woods, and the absolute quiet *called up* such kind old associations in his mind that *he went on* ruminating them for a long, long time. As he *turned* from the window *he felt* he *had never seen* anything more complete of its sort. The one feature that *struck* him with a sense of incongruity was a small Irish yew, thin and black, which *stood* out like an outpost of the shrubbery, through which the maze *was* approached. That, he *thought*, *might as well be* away: the wonder *was* that anyone *should have thought* it *would look well* in that position. (CM 236)

Having first set the temporal reference point *now*, James zig-zags off into a winding path of modal auxiliaries (i.e., had to own, could almost be guessed, might as well be, should have thought, would look well) that disorients the reader, much as the demonic maze deranges its fictive occupants.

"I Must Be Firm": Modal Disquiet in "The Stalls of Barchester Cathedral"

"The Stalls of Barchester Cathedral" is one of James's best stories, offering an unusually rich character study of the ill-fated Dr. Haynes, Archdeacon at Barchester Cathedral. James implies at the outset that Haynes had a hand in the accidental death of his predecessor: an unsympathetic character, surely. But as the narrative recounts, from Haynes's perspective, how the Archdeacon is set upon by then demonic statues carved on the cathedral stalls, James deftly creates an emotional ambivalence that sets the story apart. Haynes's letter to a magazine asking for help in identifying the carvings offers James the opportunity to indulge himself in a more ornate style than he usually employs:

". . . One is an exquisitely modelled figure of a cat, whose crouching posture suggests with admirable spirit [its] suppleness, vigilance, and craft. . . . Opposite to this is a figure seated upon a throne . . . but it is no earthly monarch whom the carver has sought to portray. . . . [N]either the crown nor the cap which he wears suffice to hide the prick-ears and curving horns which betray his Tartarean origin; and the hand which rests upon his knee, is armed with talons of horrifying length and sharpness. Between these two figures stands a shape muffled in a long mantle. This might at first sight be mistaken for a monk or 'friar of orders gray,' . . . A slight inspection, however, will lead to a very different conclusion. The knotted cord is quickly seen to be a halter, held by a hand all but concealed within the draperies. . . . . These figures are evidently the production of no unskilled chisel; and should it chance that any of your correspondents are able to throw light upon their origin and significance, my obligations to your valuable miscellany will be largely increased." (CM 186–87)

The present tense with interspersed present participles (*crouching, curving, horrifying*), present perfect (*is seen to be*), and future perfect (*will lead to, will be increased*) constructions paint a vivid tableaux. The use of the present perfect regarding the creator of the statues—"the artist *has sought to* portray . . . the figures *are . . . the production* of no unskilled chisel"—is especially powerful in establishing the feeling the carvings are alive.

But this is exceeded by one of the most uncharacteristically empathetic—one might even say poignant—passages in James:

> After that, as time goes on, I [the narrator/James] see a shadow coming over him [Haynes]—destined to develop into utter blackness—which I cannot but think must have been reflected in his outward demeanour. He commits a good deal of his fears and troubles to his diary; there was no other outlet for them. He was unmarried and his sister was not always with him. But I am much mistaken if he has told all that he might have told. A series of extracts shall be given: . . . (CM 187–88)

In this remarkable paragraph, the oscillating tense and aspect connote a narrator ruminating regretfully with himself over what was and what might have been:

- I *see* a shadow *coming* over him.
- [It *is*] *destined to develop* into utter blackness.
- I *cannot* but *think* [it].
- [It] must *have been* reflected in his outward demeanour.
- He *commits* a good deal of his fears to his diary.
- There *was* no other outlet for them.
- He *was* unmarried.
- His sister *was* not always with him.
- I *am* much mistaken.
- He *has* told all.
- He *might have* told [all].

In the abrupt final modal phrase *shall be given*, is it as if James pulls himself up sharp by choosing the passive verb form and the modal *shall* (evoking a sense of obligation) so as to prevent his emotions from further intruding into the narration.

Subsequent passages of excellence also show James using tense and aspect to advantage. When Haynes's hand upon the cat carving feels wet fur, the past tense, past perfect, and present participle are concatenated to create an instant of real terror: "The impression of the unpleasant feeling *was* so strong that I *found* myself *rubbing* my hand upon my surplice" (CM 188). But the horror becomes most intense near the end when the Archdeacon, who has been shadowed by what hopes to be a common domestic cat, more or less breaks down syntactically:

> A nervous man, which I am not, and hope I am not becoming, would have been much annoyed, if not alarmed, by it. The cat was on the stairs to-night. I think it sits there always. There *is* no kitchen cat. (CM 191)[1]

This passage is genuinely unnerving, seeming as it does to show the splintering of a psyche from fear. The loose grammatical parallels with the prior narrative exposition cited above strengthens the uncanny effect.

I *hope*.	I *see*.
I am not *becoming*.	A shadow [is] *coming*.
I *would have been* annoyed.	[It] *must have been* reflected.
It sits there.	He *commits* a good deal of his fears to his diary.
The cat *was* on the stairs.	There *was* no other outlet for them.
There *is* no cat.	I *am* much mistaken.
I *am not* [a nervous man].	He *has told* all.
I *am not becoming* [a nervous man].	He *might have told* [all].

The nature of the ghost story—its need to consider the possible reality of the supernatural—causes epistemic modality (attitudes of knowledge and belief) to take center stage in James. There are other flavors of modality, however, one of which is deontic. Deontic modality manifests when the narrator has to order, promise, or place an obligation on someone. The modal *must* expresses necessity, and the protagonist/victim of "The Stalls of Barchester Cathedral" has an intense necessity to escape from the demonic carvings.

> These words, *I must be firm*, occur again and again on subsequent days; sometimes they are the only entry. In these cases they are in an unusually

---

1. Note the similarity of "I think it sat there always" and "Have you explored it ever?" from "Mr. Humphreys and His Inheritance." The oddly appended temporal adverbials create a sense of unnatural duration.

large hand, and dug into the paper in a way which must have broken the pen that wrote them. (CM 193)

As Dr. Haynes *must be* firm, so *must have* the pen broken. Unfortunately for the Doctor, those modals that express the strongest sense of obligation in deontic mode are the modals that also express the strongest likelihood in epistemic mode (Berk 135). So for our purposes:

I *must be* firm = Those *must not be* demonic carvings

But apparently they were. Or are.

"Strangely Unobservant He Must Have Been": Epistemic Architecture in "Number 13"

One of James's most amusing stories is also one of his slightest: "Number 13," set in a hotel in Denmark. It uses a familiar trope—a ghostly room that sometimes exists, sometimes not. The occupants of collocated rooms hear someone acting silly in the chamber that should be on the other side of their respective walls. But there is no Number 13, only a ghost space occupied by a ghost who apparently sold his soul to the devil and having a great time for it.

The story is basically a now-you-see-it-now-you-don't shell game, with James remodeling the building using mere grammar when the protagonist isn't looking. When the latter first arrives, he has to choose a room: "Either Number 12 or Number 14 would be better, for both of them looked on the street. . . . Eventually Number 12 was selected." Either Number 12 or Number 14 *would be* better, indeed, because unlike Number 13 they exist in the present perfect.

But there is something deeply suspect, too, about the occupant of the adjacent room. The narrator reveals his degree of uncertainty with a number of modal adverbs and the modal auxiliary *must be possessed* and *must be flickering*:

He *seemed* to be a tall thin man—or was it *by any chance* a woman?—at least, it was someone who covered his or her head with *some kind of* drapery before going to bed, and, he thought, must be possessed of a red lamp-shade—and the lamp must be flickering very much. There was a distinct playing up and down of a dull red light on the opposite wall. He craned out a little to see if he could make any more of the figure, but beyond a fold of some light, *perhaps* white, material on the window-sill he could see nothing. (CM 56)

The petty annoyances of the traveler escalate as the protagonist misplaces his suitcase. But it suddenly reappears: "How it *could possibly have* escaped him the night before he did not pretend to understand; at any rate, *there it was now*" (CM 57). The linking of *there it was* and the reference point *now* indicates that the traveler is in an uncanny temporal space, where past and present have an unwholesome relation. The next morning it gets worse: the future perfect has bumped up against a past-passive modal: "Another shock *awaited* him. Strangely unobservant he *must have been* last night" (CM 57).

Complaints to the landlord only incite abuse, and the use of the past progressive—"he *was becoming* quite nervous about the question of the existence of Number 13" (CM 60)—reflects the protagonist's escalating sense that the building's history is an active, present danger.

James uses the reported speech of the landlord to jumble grammar in a yet more threatening way:

> "My Number 13? Why, *don't I tell you* that *there isn't such a thing* in the house? I thought *you might have noticed* that. If *there was it would be* next door to your own room." "Well, yes; only *I happened to think*—that is, *I fancied* last night *that I had seen* a door numbered thirteen in that passage; and, really, *I am* almost certain *I must have been* right, for *I saw it* the night before as well." Of course, Herr Kristensen *laughed* this notion to scorn, as Anderson *had expected*, and emphasized with much iteration the fact that no Number 13 *existed* or *had existed* before him in that hotel. (CM 60)

As we read this we can sense time itself flickering in a manner far more sinister than the neighbor's red lamp.

Works Cited

Atkinson, William. "M. R. James." In *The Dictionary of Literary Biography, Vol. 156: British Short-Fiction Writers, 1880–1914: The Romantic Tradition*, ed. William F. Naufftus. Detroit: Gale Group, 1996, pp. 170–80.

Azar, Betty Schrampfer. *Chartbook: A Reference Grammar: Understanding and Using English Grammar*. White Plains NY: Pearson Education, 2000.

Berk, Lynn M. *English Syntax: From Word to Discourse*. New York: Oxford University Press, 1999.

Comrie, Bernard. *Aspect: An Introduction to the Study of Verbal Aspect and Related Problems*. Cambridge: Cambridge University Press, 2001.

Huddleston, Rodney. *Introduction to the Grammar of English*. Cambridge: Cambridge University Press, 1984.

Hurford, James R. *Grammar: A Student's Guide*. Cambridge: Cambridge University Press, 1994.

James M. R. *Count Magnus and Other Ghost Stories (The Complete Ghost Stories of M. R. James, Vol. 1)*. Ed. S. T. Joshi. New York: Penguin, 2005. Cited in the text as CM.

————. *The Haunted Doll's House and Other Ghost Stories (The Complete Ghost Stories of M. R. James, Vol. 2)*. Ed. S. T. Joshi. New York: Penguin, 2006. Cited in the text as *HDH*.

Joshi, S. T. "M. R. James: The Limitations of the Ghost Story." In Joshi's *The Weird Tale*. Austin: University of Texas Press, 1990.

Kärkkäinen, Elise. *Epistemic Stance in English Conversation: A Description of Its Interactional Functions*. Philadelphia: John Benjamins Publishing Co., 2003.

Langacker, Ronald W. *Foundations of Cognitive Grammar, Vol. II: Descriptive Application*. Stanford: Stanford University Press, 1991.

Le Fanu, J. S. *Best Ghost Stories of J. S. Le Fanu*. Ed. E. F. Bleiler. New York: Dover, 1964.

————. *Ghost Stories and Mysteries*. Ed. E. F. Bleiler. New York: Dover, 1975.

Phelan, James. *Living to Tell about It: A Rhetoric and Ethics of Character Narration*. Ithaca, NY: Cornell University Press, 2004.

Prince, Gerald. *A Dictionary of Narratology*. Rev. ed. Lincoln: University of Nebraska Press, 2003.

Toulmin, Stephen. *The Uses of Argument*. Cambridge: Cambridge University Press, 1964.

Wardhaugh, Ronald. *Understanding English Grammar: A Linguistic Approach*. Malden, MA: Blackwell, 2002.

"What Is This That I Have Done?" The Scapegoat Figure in the Stories of M. R. James

Scott Connors

Supernatural vengeance is a prominent theme in the ghost stories of Montague Rhodes James. In fact, some commentators have observed that it is his principal theme. But is this merely a "naive tit-for-tat vengeance motif" that burdens James's body of work with a "curious repetitiveness and one-dimensionality" (Joshi 139)? Or is there perhaps some deeper significance to this singling out of some doomed soul?

The application of Northrop Frye's critical theories to James's ghost stories is perhaps as cheeky as Mr. Wraxall's request to see the late Count Magnus (but not as perilous personally, I hope!). Frye's theories have their roots in the same sort of secular approach to religion and mythology that James condemned both explicitly in his response to Jane Harrison's "The Head of John the Baptist," and implicitly in such stories as "The Mezzotint," "'Oh, Whistle, and I'll Come to You, My Lad,'" and "Casting the Runes." However, since Frye limited his conclusions to the content and not the origins of myth, and as they applied to literature in general, perhaps Dr. James's shade will not feel compelled to express its displeasure in any dramatic manner.

Nevertheless, Frye's theories offer the critic the opportunity for a number of insights into James' stories. Terry Eagleton provides an admirable abstract of Frye's theories in his treatise *Literary Theory* that merits repeating here. Literature is "not in fact just a random collection of writings strewn throughout history." It forms a system so that

> If you examined it closely you could see that it worked by certain objective laws. . . . These laws were the various modes, archetypes, myths and genres by which all literary works were structured. At the root of literature lay four "narrative categories," the comic, romantic, tragic and ironic, which could be seen to correspond respectively to the four *mythoi* of spring, summer, autumn, and winter. A theory of literary "modes" could be outlined, whereby

in myth the hero is superior in kind to others, in romance superior in degree, in the "high mimetic" modes of tragedy and epic superior in degree to others but not to his environment, in the "low mimetic" modes of comedy and realism equal to the rest of us, and in satire and irony inferior. Tragedy and comedy can be subdivided into high mimetic, low mimetic, and ironic; tragedy is about human isolation, comedy about human integration. (79–80)

Frye was remarkably open for his time to the consideration of "popular" or "genre" literary forms such as science fiction and detective stories, and he used ghosts to illustrate the difference between his various literary modes. For instance, he argued that while there could be no "consistent distinction between ghosts and living beings" in myth, they were not permitted in ordinary low mimetic fiction because of the skepticism of the reader. He makes an exception for the "ghost story" per se, which combines elements of both the low mimetic and ironic modes. In examining James's ghostly tales we see that they may be categorized as examples of tragic irony insofar as they deal with the exclusion from society of an individual whose freedom of action is less than our own.

Irony is derived from the Greek *eiron*, which refers to someone who is self-deprecating, and in literature it refers to "a technique of saying as little and meaning as much as possible" (Frye 40). In the introductions to his various collections, James was certainly self-effacing. In *Ghost-Stories of an Antiquary*, he wrote that "the stories themselves do not make any very exalted claim" (*PT* 2). James apparently felt his stories required no further justification than that they served "to amuse some readers" and give "pleasure of a certain sort," not once but twice, in *More Ghost Stories of an Antiquary* and in his *Collected Ghost Stories* (*PT* 114, 368). Certainly some critics have taken him at his word, notably Peter Penzoldt, who asserted that "His stories are straightforward tales of terror and the supernatural utterly devoid of any deeper meaning. They are what orally-told ghost stories originally were: tales that are meant to frighten and nothing more" (191). Yet James's stories continue to be widely published and read more than seventy years after his death, while such contemporaries as J. E. Preston Muddock ("Dick Donovan") and Frederick Cowles remain the province of the literary specialist and collector.

Samuel D. Russell and others have observed that James employed irony extensively in the telling of his tales. He disliked ghost stories that were too explicit: "Reticence may be an elderly doctrine to preach," he wrote in the *Bookman*, "yet from the artistic point of view I am sure it is a sound one" (*PT* 479). His purpose was to frighten, to excite fear and pity, and the best way to do this is to drop subtle hints and half-revelations in the course of the story and allow the reader to make the connections himself. Russell provides a useful catalog of these "half-felt manifestations." We find listed therein: "the noises in the cathedral in 'Canon Alberic's Scrap-book'; the changing position of the pictured ghost in 'The Mezzotint', seen first by persons who do not understand its significance; the prophetic *sortes* taken at random from the Bible in 'The Ash-Tree'"; and many others (625).

One way in which James excites fear in his readers is by the seemingly arbitrary fates that befall the characters in his stories. As in the tales of Sheridan Le Fanu, which James admired above all others, it seems as if the most innocent action could provoke the most savage retribution. We see his characters "going about their ordinary business," which usually involves some sort of antiquarian scholarship of the sort for which James himself was justly renowned, when some unknown action brings them to the attention of some very desiccated and malevolent entities that may or may not have once been human (*PT* 486). Late in his life his friend Shane Leslie asked James if he actually believed in ghosts. James's response was: "Yes, we know there are such things—but we don't know the rules" (56).

What Simon MacCulloch observes about "Casting the Runes" applies equally to many of James's other stories: "[it] is about victimisation. It deals with how being singled out as an object of punishment, however uncalled for, produces a sense of separation from everyone except fellow victims" (7). We read in that story that once Mr. Dunning has been slipped the fatal runes it "seemed to him that something ill-defined and impalpable had stepped in between him and his fellow-men." His servants are immediately taken ill and hospitalized, leaving him alone in his house. After he goes to bed that evening "either an economical suburban company had decided that their light would not be required in the small hours, and had stopped working, or else something was wrong with the meter; the effect was in any case that the electric light was off." Finally he lies in bed awake, but when he puts "his hand into the well-known nook under the pillow," he finds something quite unexpected, not to mention disturbing (*PT* 157). The final result of this series of progressive isolation is that Mr. Dunning should suffer a fatal accident, as did another fellow scholar who fell afoul of Karswell earlier.

This is consistent with Frye's assertions regarding tragic irony. Whatever happens to the character "should be casually out of line with his character." In a tragic work of fiction the climactic disaster is one conceivable outcome of the situation, but "irony isolates from the tragic situation the sense of arbitrariness, of the victim's having been unlucky, selected at random or by lot, and no more deserving of what happens to him than anyone else would be." The term that Frye uses to distinguish this type of random victim is the *phar-*

makos, or scapegoat. "The pharmakos," we are told, "is neither innocent nor guilty. He is innocent in the sense that what happens to him is far greater than anything he has done provokes" (41). Professor Parkin's ostensible offense was only to blow an antique whistle that he found in his walks. It was not Sir Richard Fell but his grandfather who "ate of the tree," to paraphrase Michael Wigglesworth ("The Day of Doom," stanza 168). And then there is poor Mr. Wraxall, whose ill-advised words proved an unwitting invocation, leaving him to ask in despair: "What is this that I have done?" (*PT* 75). It appears as if James's characters are in the position of the spider described by Jonathan Edwards in his sermon "Sinners in the Hands of an Angry God," since

> "There is nothing that keeps wicked men at any one moment out of hell, but the mere pleasure of God."—By the **mere** pleasure of God, I mean his **sovereign** pleasure, his *arbitrary* will, restrained by no obligation, hindered by no manner of difficulty, any more than if nothing else but God's mere will had in the least degree, or in any respect whatsoever, any hand in the preservation of wicked men one moment. [Italics added for emphasis; boldface in original.]

This "sense of arbitrariness" provokes a powerful sensation of pity in the reader, which Aristotle defined as "a feeling of pain caused by the sight of some evil, destructive or painful, which befalls one who does not deserve it, and which we might expect to befall ourselves or some friend of ours, and moreover to befall us soon" (*Rhetoric*, Book II, Chapter 8). Frye characterized this sensation as pathos, the root of which is "the exclusion of an individual on our own level from the social group to which he is trying to belong" (39).

This is apparent from the very first ghost story James read to the Chitchat Society, "Canon Alberic's Scrap-book," and its depiction of the sacristan. The story's English antiquarian protagonist, Dennistoun,

> found him an unexpectedly interesting object of study [because of] a curious furtive, or rather hunted and oppressed, air which he had. He was perpetually half glancing behind him; the muscles of his back and shoulders seemed to be hunched in a continual nervous contraction, as if he were expecting every moment to find himself in the clutch of an enemy. The Englishman hardly knew whether to put him down as a man haunted by a fixed delusion, or as one oppressed by a guilty conscience, or as an unbearably henpecked husband. (*PT* 4)

Later, after Dennistoun hears "a thin metallic voice laughing high up in the tower," he notices that the sacristan is "white to the lips," and cannot understand how a picture showing "how St. Bertrand delivered a man whom the Devil long sought to strangle" should move him to tears (*PT* 5). It is true that the sacristan has a daughter who exhibits "acute anxiety" on his behalf, but this was after all James's first story.

"Count Magnus," one of James's most intriguing tales, is the account of what happens to Mr. Wraxall. He is a tourist in Denmark who visits the tomb of Count Magnus de la Gardie, a seventeenth-century nobleman who left behind a reputation for cruelty and vindictiveness, among other things, and who was popularly regarded as having satanic associations. Since he is separated from the Count's age "by nearly three centuries" (*PT* 71)—which to an antiquarian like James was just last Tuesday—Wraxall finds these traditions to be less horrifying than picturesque, and, like a tourist to Transylvania who can't separate the romantic cinematic image of Count Dracula from the genocidal psychopath that was the real Vlad Tepes, he expresses a desire not once but three times (a number whose significance any reader of fairy tales may testify) to see him: "You may have been a bit of a rascal in your time, Magnus," he muses, "but for all that I should like to see you, or, rather—" (*PT* 75). No sooner does he utter the words than the last of three padlocks falls from Magnus's sepulcher, the other two having fallen off without his noticing when he voiced similar sentiments on two other occasions. But now he realizes that something uncanny has occurred, and cries out: "What is this that I have done?" He returns to England a "broken man," scrutinizing his fellow travelers as if trying "to put himself out of the reach of some person or persons whom he never specifies." His personality becomes more fragmented once he reaches his destination and sees two figures waiting for him at a crossroads, leaving behind notes that "are too disjointed and ejaculatory to be given" in the story, until he is found dead in a state that causes "the jury that viewed the body" to faint. James concluded one of his stories, "Wailing Well," with an observation that would appear to apply equally well to Mr. Wraxall: "If it has a moral, that moral is, I trust, obvious; if it has none, I do not well know how to help it" (*PT* 395). I suspect that most readers would classify Wraxall's failure to grasp the moral as a venial and not a mortal sin. Others felt differently.

One of the most pathetic images in James's stories occurs in "The Residence at Whitminster," when the ghost of Lord Saul, who as a youth murdered a playmate and played at sorcery, appears at a window. Mrs. Maple tells us "Oh, he was a cruel child for certain, but he had to pay in the end, and after," but tempers this condemnation with how the ghost could sometimes be seen

> Up against that same window, particular when they've had a fire of a chilly evening, with his face right on the panes, and his hands fluttering out, and

his mouth open and shut, open and shut, for a minute or more, and then gone off in the dark yard. But open the window at such times, no, that they dare not do, though they could find it in their heart to pity the poor thing, that pinched up with the cold, and seemingly fading away to a nothink as the years passed on. (*PT* 239)

It is true that Lord Saul transgressed terribly and earned his fate, but because of his position as the heir to a Protestant peerage in Catholic Ireland (a situation similar to that of Le Fanu) we are told that the latter had "no boys of his age or quality to consort with," which suggests that his alienation began before he started to exhibit behavior remarkably reminiscent of the Goth subculture currently popular among some more introverted teenagers (*PT* 223).

Or consider the fate of Stanley Judkins, whose obstinate disregard for the warnings of his elders to avoid the "Wailing Well" finds himself ambushed by the undead:

With a sudden and dreadful sinking at the heart, he caught sight of someone among the trees, waiting: and again of someone—another of the hideous black figures—working slowly along the track from another side of the field, looking from side to side, as the shepherd had described it. Worst of all, he saw a fourth—unmistakably a man this time—rising out of the bushes a few yards behind the wretched Stanley, and painfully, as it seemed, crawling into the track. On all sides the miserable victim was cut off. (*PT* 394)

It is true that Judkins was a stupid and willful youth, but this still seems to be overly harsh, and James concludes his story with the observation quoted above.

Two of James's tales, "The Rose Garden" and "Martin's Close," depict the judicial condemnation of an accused person. While George Martin in the latter tale was indisputably guilty, the nameless prisoner condemned by Sir —— was certainly innocent, which places the whole system of earthly justice in doubt just as other stories question that of the divine variety.

According to Frye, any given period tends to be dominated by one mode, a sort of literary *Zeitgeist*, but as this domination is subject to the same cyclical progression as the seasons, we see irony descending "from the low mimetic: it begins in realism and dispassionate observation. But as it does so, it moves steadily towards myth, and dim outlines of sacrificial rituals and dying gods begin to reappear" (42). Some of James's characters, notably Mr. Abney in "Lost Hearts," the *faux* druids in "An Evening's Entertainment," and the heretical Mr. Wilson in "Mr. Humphreys and His Inheritance," are instances where the outlines begin to become as disturbingly distinct as the picture in "The Mezzotint." The "Punch and Judy" show in "The Story of a Disappearance and an Appearance" is claimed by some to trace its origins back to the Lord of Misrule at Saturnalia and is related to trickster figures in mythology such as the Native American Coyote. Even the ghostly re-enactments of "The Mezzotint" and "The Haunted Dolls' House" are ritualistic. And of course James claimed to "have tried to make my ghosts act in ways not inconsistent with the rules of folklore" (PT 368).

The ritual in which the pharmakos was selected is inferred in several of James's stories. The Old Testament tells how lots were cast to select the goat upon which the sins of the Israelites were laid (Lev. 16:8). In *The Golden Bough* we read how certain Scottish clans observed the first day of May by kindling great Beltane fires. A great cake was divided into pieces, and whosoever received one particular piece was subjected to a mock-sacrifice, and "afterwards, he was pelted with egg-shells, and retained the odious appellation during the whole year. And while the feast was fresh in people's memory, they affected to speak of [him] as dead" (Frazer 619). In several of the stories the protagonist is manipulated into accepting the object that invokes the unwanted visitation. MacCulloch points out that "The runes must be handed over in person to the victim and accepted, thus tricking him into a sense of complicity with his doom and creating a consequent increase of guilt and isolation" (90). It is through a similar stratagem or gambit that Karswell is enticed into accepting them back.

In both "Canon Alberic's Scrap-book" and "The Haunted Dolls' House," the protagonist is manipulated into accepting the cursed object by others who take advantage of their avarice. Dennistoun "cherished dreams of finding priceless manuscripts in untrodden corners of France," and he welcomes the opportunity to acquire the plunder of "the unprincipled Canon Alberic" (PT 6, 8). It is apparent that the sacristan and his daughter are eager to be rid of it: she "was telling her beads feverishly," while he will accept only a token sum despite Dennistoun's attempt to soothe his conscience (which James tells us "was tenderer than a collector") by offering more (PT 10). Once the transaction is completed "the sacristan seemed to become a new man," while Dennistoun becomes convinced that "there was someone behind his back" (PT 10, 11). As in Robert Louis Stevenson's "The Bottle Imp," the mere possession of the guilty artifact condemns the inheritor. We are told that Mr. Dillett in "The Haunted Dolls' House" was skilled "in ferreting out the forgotten treasures of half a dozen counties," and while Mr. Chittenden runs him a dearer bargain than the sacristan did Dennistoun, there is a smug suggestion that he is about to receive a deserved comeuppance, as when Mrs. Chittenden states "Well, I'd rather it was him than another" (PT 289, 290). Of course, the custodian of the titular dolls' house was not in danger of eternal damnation, but was instead the recipient of something along the lines of a piece of counterfeit money that could not be redeemed for what one gave for it:

> "But I put it to you, Mr. Dillet, one of two things: was I going to scrap a lovely piece like that on the one 'and, or was I going to tell customers: 'I'm selling you a regular picture-palace dramar in reel life of the olden time, billed to perform regular at one o'clock A.M.?" (PT 296)

This was plainly not the venue of the exorcist, but of the small claims' court (Judge Jeffreys, presiding). In classical times the purpose of the pharmakos or scapegoat was to relieve the rest of the population of the burden of their sin.[1] This was certainly the case in "Canon Alberic's Scrap-book," but in the other instances discussed the social benefits were more along the lines of *pour encourager les autres*. Certainly the heterodoxical religious opinions held by Mr. Abney or Mr. Humphreys's great-uncle would seem not validated by their examples. "Wailing Well" appears to be an uncharacteristically crude and didactic example, until we remember that it was written for a troop of Boy Scouts—but it is certain that none of those who experienced that episode would ever dare approach the cistern in question. The ambivalence about the arbitrary fate of so many of his characters is certainly not unique to James, and may reflect that "dichotomy between the comfortable Christian world view of his upbringing . . . and the darkly amoral version of pantheism which . . . he felt truly reflected the state of the world" that Rosemary Pardoe describes (43). As Frye informs us, ultimately "the pharmakos is in the situation of Job" (42).

Works Cited

Aristotle. *Rhetoric*. Trans. W. Rhys Roberts. 1954. <http://www.public.iastate.edu/~honeyl/Rhetoric/rhet2-8.html>

Eagleton, Terry. *Literary Theory: An Introduction*. 2nd ed. Minneapolis: University of Minnesota Press, 1996.

Edwards, Jonathan. "Sinners in the Hands of an Angry God." (1741) <http://www.ccel.org/e/edwards/sermons/sinners.html>

Frazer, James George. *The New Golden Bough*. Ed. Theodor H. Gaster. New Jersey: S. G. Phillips, 1959.

---

1. James acknowledged recycling the plot of "The Mezzotint" in this story, but the parallel with "Canon Alberic's Scrap-book" appears not to have occurred to him.

Frye, Northrop. *Anatomy of Criticism: Four Essays.* 1957. Rpt. Princeton, NJ: Princeton University Press, 1971.

James, M. R. *A Pleasing Terror: The Complete Supernatural Writings of M. R. James.* Ed. Christopher and Barbara Roden. Ashcroft, BC: Ash-Tree Press, 2001. [Abbreviated in the text as *PT.*]

Joshi, S. T. "M. R. James: The Limitations of the Ghost Story." In *The Weird Tale.* Austin: University of Texas Press, 1990. 133–42.

Leslie, Shane. "Montague Rhodes James." *Quarterly Review* 304 (January 1966): 45–56.

MacCulloch, Simon. "The Toad in the Study: M. R. James, H. P. Lovecraft, and Forbidden Knowledge: Part 1." *Studies in Weird Fiction* No. 20 (Winter 1997): 2–12.

Pardoe, Rosemary. "Some Thoughts on M. R. James's World View." *Ghosts & Scholars* No. 18 (1994): 43.

Penzoldt, Peter. "Dr. M. R. James (1862–1936)." In *The Supernatural in Fiction.* London: Peter Nevill, 1952. 191–202.

Russell, Samuel D. "Irony and Horror: The Art of M. R. James." In *A Pleasing Terror: The Complete Supernatural Writings of M. R. James.* Ed. Christopher and Barbara Roden. Ashcroft, BC: Ash-Tree Press, 2001. 609–30.

Wigglesworth, Michael. "The Day of Doom." 1662. <http://www.puritansermons.com/poetry/doom151.htm>

IV. Studies of Individual Tales

The Nature of the Beast: The Demonology of "Canon Alberic's Scrap-book"

Helen Grant

> Imagine one of the awful bird-catching spiders of South America translated into human form, and endowed with intelligence just less than human, and you will have some faint conception of the terror inspired by this appalling effigy.

The "appalling effigy" will be recognised by all familiar with M. R. James's story "Canon Alberic's Scrap-book" as the sepia drawing of a demon which subsequently appears to the hapless Dennistoun, purchaser of the picture, and is only exorcised by the burning of the drawing. The creature is one of the most vividly and distinctly described of all James's apparitions and the tale is rated as one of James's finest by many of his readers. Yet the story raises many questions which remain tantalisingly unanswered: What exactly is the creature which appears to Dennistoun? Why did Canon Alberic summon it—and why could he not then dismiss it? Why is it linked to possession of the drawing but not to the photograph of it? And why does the sacristan insist that he will take only "two hundred and fifty francs, not more" for the scrap-book, which is clearly worth much more to a collector? These are the questions I shall attempt to answer, drawing on sources which would have been available to MRJ and which will take us as far afield as mediaeval Arabia and seventeenth-century Germany.

Our starting-point must be those details which are either given in the story or can be directly inferred from it. So, what does MRJ actually tell us? We know that Canon Alberic de Mauléon holds a dialogue with someone or something on the 12th December 1694, in which he poses questions about his own future, including whether he will find something, probably treasure. On that same night, Canon Alberic sees "it" for the first time. Approximately seven years later, in the expectation of seeing "it" again, he dies in his bed of a seizure. He leaves behind him a scrap-book of manuscripts including a sepia drawing of King Solomon confronting a demon of the night and a plan of part of the cathedral of St. Bertrand de Comminges. At the time of the main action of the story, this book is in the possession of the sacristan of the church, who lives in Canon Alberic's house, now much dilapidated, and who has clearly been haunted over a long period by the creature depicted in Canon Alberic's drawing. The sacristan sells the book to Dennistoun, but will accept only two hundred and fifty francs for it, in spite of its clearly being worth considerably more. The transaction instantly transfers the association with the demon to the new owner; within a short period Dennistoun finds himself aware of a growing discomfort and compulsion to sit with his back to the wall. At the moment when he removes the crucifix from around his neck to clean it, the demon appears to him. What would have happened to him next is not clear, as the two serving men rush into the room before the demon can do more than make a move towards his victim. The drawing is subsequently photographed and then burnt. The demon is apparently exorcised by the destruction of the drawing—the narrator says that the photograph is now in his own possession, but there is no suggestion that the demon haunts him. Finally, we have Dennistoun's own words on what he has seen, comprising a quotation from Ecclesiasticus and a reference to the night monsters mentioned in Isaiah.

Let us take first these two Biblical references, since they constitute the "eyewitness's" impression of the demon's provenance. What significance can we read into Dennistoun's references to the avenging spirits of Ecclesiasticus and the night monsters of Isaiah?

Ecclesiasticus, also known as the Book of Sirach, is thought to have been written originally in Hebrew, but of the Hebrew text only some recently discovered fragments remain. We can however examine the extant Greek version and the Latin Vulgate for a better understanding of the nature of the spirits which "in their fury lay on sore strokes." The quotation comes from Ecclesiasticus 39:28. The Greek word used here for spirits is *pneumata*. The word *pneuma* can mean a spirit or spiritual being of some sort but can also mean a wind, air, or breath. Compare the Latin Vulgate version, "*sunt spiritus qui ad vindictam creati sunt . . .*" which uses *spiritus*, again meaning either a spirit or a breath. An avenging demon could be either spirit being or wind: demons in the form of deadly winds appear for example in *The Testament of Solomon*, a text with which MRJ was very familiar (of which more later). However, we should beware of reading too much into this: the English text quoted by Dennistoun does not have the ambivalent meaning of the Greek and Latin, and furthermore the demon in "Canon Alberic's Scrap-book" always assumes an anthropomorphic form.

The context of the Ecclesiasticus quotation is more useful: Ecclesiasticus 39 describes first the ways of the wise man, then goes on to describe those good things which were created for men, such as food, drink, and fuel, and adds, "All these things shall be good to the holy, so to the sinners and the ungodly they shall be turned into evil." The quotation describing the "spirits that are created for vengeance" follows, and leads into a longer curse upon the ungodly, which includes fire, hail, famine, and death, as well as "the teeth of beasts, and scorpions, and serpents, and the sword taking revenge upon the ungodly unto destruction." And indeed Canon Alberic, who seeks the good things of life for himself, ultimately meets a bad end as a result of his unholy transaction with the demon. The godless cannot escape divine vengeance. Note that the "teeth of beasts" (*bestiarum dentes* in the Vulgate) which will rend the ungodly are reminiscent of MRJ's demon with its thin lower jaw, "shallow, like a beast's." An interesting footnote to the Ecclesiasticus quotation is that the book was originally (though erroneously) ascribed to the authorship of King Solomon, a detail likely to assume greater significance when we come on to the drawing of Solomon and the demon.

Dennistoun's second Biblical reference, to night monsters living in the ruins of Babylon, is more problematical. This is certainly a reference to Isaiah 34:14, although the ruined city is in fact Edom, not Babylon. The Revised Standard Version reads: "And wild beasts shall meet with hyaenas, the satyr shall cry to his fellow; yea, there shall the night hag alight, and find for herself a resting place." The King James version keeps the satyrs but replaces night hag with screech owl, demonstrating the difficulty of interpreting this word, which does not appear anywhere else in the whole of the Bible. The original Hebrew word used for the night monster is *Lilit*. It probably refers to Lilith, "she of the night," in legend the first wife of Adam, who later became a monster who dwelt in lonely places and preyed on children. She is associated with Lamia in classical tradition, whose children were killed by Hera and who subsequently became savage with grief and turned into a child-stealing monster; the Vulgate version of Isaiah 34:14 uses the word *Lamia* for the night monster.

So why, we might ask, does Dennistoun's experience with the demon call Isaiah's reference to Lilith—the night hag—to his mind? The demon which manifests itself in Comminges is a male demon—or is it? A careful reading of the story suggests that it is not necessarily male. The descriptions of the drawing of the demon, and of the creature as it appears to Dennistoun, both use the neutral word *it* to describe the apparition. On several occasions in the story, comparisons are drawn with female persons: Dennistoun, wondering what oppresses the sacristan so, suspects it is "a more formidable persecutor even than a termagant wife." Later at the Chapeau Rouge, when the spectral laughter is heard, Dennistoun remarks, "I wish that landlady would learn to laugh in a more cheering manner; it makes one feel as if there was someone dead in the house."

Set against this is the fact that the sacristan refers to the demon throughout as him, in both English and French (otherwise he would say, "*Deux fois je l'ai vue*"). However, in French, virtually every word which could be applied to the demon, viz. *diable, démon, esprit, vampire, monstre*, is masculine. It is quite common for those whose first language uses gender cases to carry them over into English, although they are not used in English. So we cannot preclude the demon's being female on the basis of the sacristan's imperfect English.

There are, however, greater problems with attempting to identify Dennistoun's demon with Lilith. Why would Canon Alberic summon a demon whose main attribute is preying upon children? Clearly the demon in the story has the ability to foretell the future, and to advise Canon Alberic upon the success of his treasure hunt. These are not notable features of the Lilith legend, whereas they are strongly associated with some other types of demon, which I will come onto later. In addition, there is nothing in the Lilith tradition to explain the mysterious "two hundred and fifty francs, not more." Both Lilith and Lamia were monsters motivated by revenge for their own misfortunes. In all probability Dennistoun's reference to these night monsters is intended to convey vengefulness and implacability, or simply the inscrutable nature of the wreakers of divine vengeance.

Moving on to the drawing of the demon, we might ask: what is the significance of the depiction of King Solomon? The obvious influence here is *The Testament of Solomon*, a Greek text dating perhaps as far back as the first to third centuries C.E. MRJ was not only familiar with the work but actually wrote about it (see *Ghosts & Scholars* No. 28, pp. 46–57). *The Testament of Solomon* describes how King Solomon summoned a variety of demons and controlled them by means of a ring given to him by the archangel Michael. The demons performed a number of tasks for Solomon including building the temple at Jerusalem. The last section of the *Testament* describes how Solomon was finally persuaded to sacrifice to the pagan god Moloch in order to win a foreign wife, and thereby lost God's favour and was mocked by demons.

The Testament of Solomon is one of the earliest and most comprehensive accounts of Solomon and the demons (the Old Testament does not mention the story, describing the building of the temple by Solomon in purely human terms). However, there are widespread references to it in other sources, including the Koran, which says that devils dived into the sea and performed other tasks for Solomon.[1] It also describes djinns subject to Solomon, who built whatever he wanted, including shrines and statues.[2] The *Arabian Nights*

1. Koran, Al-Anbiya' (21), v. 82.

2. Koran, Sheba (34), v. 11–13.

also features Solomonic djinn in the stories of Aladdin and of the Fisherman and the Genie (of which more later). So there was a strong tradition of stories of Solomon and the demons for MRJ to draw upon. The question is, what is the significance of the Solomon stories in the history of Canon Alberic?

There are several possibilities: one is that the Solomon legend is simply used here as a suitably ecclesiastical allegory for what happens to Canon Alberic: both Solomon and Alberic have truck with demons, and enjoy wealth or power, but suffer a reversal of fortune at the end of their lives, ultimately becoming the plaything of demons. The other possibility is that the apparition in "Canon Alberic's Scrap-book" is intended to be an actual, possibly even a specific Solomonic demon, and this I believe to be the case. Solomonic motifs recur too often in the details of the story for this to be pure coincidence. As regards which of Solomon's demons haunts the owner of Canon Alberic's scrap-book, let us first consider what we know about the demon, and whether its attributes suggest a specific identification.

Let us begin by considering what we know of Canon Alberic's traffic with the demon. This is documented through the two sheets of paper at the end of the scrap-book; one is the sepia drawing with some writing on the back, and the other is a plan of part of the church with what appear to be magical symbols on it, and a list of questions and answers from the night upon which Canon Alberic first saw the demon. "A good specimen of the treasure-hunter's record," remarks Dennistoun. We can infer that the treasure-hunt was a successful one, since Canon Alberic's relics include a very imposing tomb and a mansion "rather larger than its neighbours," though this has fallen into disrepair at the time of Dennistoun's visit. It is clearly connected with the church itself, judging by the plan of the south aisle and cloisters, marked with planetary symbols, Hebrew words, and a single cross in gold paint. If the treasure was found in the precincts of the church itself, there is a direct parallel with *The Testament of Solomon,* in which a demon in the form of a three-headed dragon tells King Solomon that there is a store of hidden gold at the entrance to the Temple that he has begun to build; Solomon sends his servant to dig it up, and he finds it where the demon told him it would be.[3] Other demons within the *Testament* also possess the power to reveal the whereabouts of treasure: the demon Ornias promises the boy who captures him with Solomon's ring that he (Ornias) will give him all the gold of the earth if he sets him free; Solomon also advises the servant who cap-

---

3. *The Testament of Solomon,* v. 55. Testament references are to F. C. Conybeare's translation, in the *Jewish Quarterly Review* 2 (October 1898): 1–45. This was translated from the only Greek edition (1837) published before MRJ wrote "Canon Alberic's Scrap-book."

tures the Arabian wind demon that if the demon offers him gold or silver in exchange for freedom, he (the servant) must mark the places where the bullion is (v. 119). The association of demons with treasure hunting is not, of course, confined to *The Testament of Solomon*: in the *Arabian Nights*, for example, the magical lamp containing the djinn is found in a vast underground treasure store. There are definite Solomonic aspects to the Aladdin story: the Moor who poses as Aladdin's uncle gives him a magic ring to protect him, and the djinn or ifrit when it appears is described as being as tall as one of Solomon's djinn. It is quite congruous therefore that the demon summoned by Canon Alberic for his treasure hunt should be a Solomonic one.

And what of the treasure itself? All we know of it from MRJ's text is that Canon Alberic asked, "Shall I find it?" and received the answer "Thou shalt," and then asked, "Shall I become rich?" and received the answer "Thou wilt." The fact that Canon Alberic needs to ask whether he will become rich implies that he was not certain that finding "it" would itself enrich him. This may mean that what he sought was the means of obtaining wealth (a treasure map?), not hidden wealth itself, or it may simply mean that he does not know the extent and value of the trove he seeks. The provenance of the hidden treasure itself can only be guessed at; there is nothing in the story to say what it was or where it came from. However, what we can say is that the history of St. Bertrand de Comminges lends itself to all sorts of possibilities for hidden treasure. That area of southern France has been subject to invasions and territorial conflicts dating back to the empires of the Romans, the Visigoths, and the Franks. The Knights Templar, long associated with stories of hidden treasure, particularly in relation to the Temple Mount in Jerusalem, were also present in the Pyrenees region.[4] It was in fact a former bishop of St. Bertrand de Comminges, Bertrand de Got, later Pope Clement V, who together with King Philip IV of France led the terrible persecution of the Templars, the aim being to extinguish their influence and take possession of their extensive wealth. It is perhaps fanciful, but somehow appropriate, to imagine some stolen Templar treasure finding its hiding place in the former bishop's old stamping ground. Moreover, the Templar connection with the temple site at Jerusalem provides another link with the story of Solomon, whose great temple was the first to stand there.

If we examine next the prophetic aspect of Canon Alberic's colloquy with the demon, there are again parallels with *The Testament of Solomon*. In

---

4. The Templars make an appearance in "'Oh, Whistle, and I'll Come to You, My Lad'": the apparition-summoning whistle is found at the site of a Templar preceptory.

verse 65 a spirit prophesises that King Solomon's kingdom shall eventually fall and the temple be ruined. Later the demon Ornias foretells the death of the wayward son of one of Solomon's workmen (v. 110ff.). It is significant that the demons only foretell negative events, and indeed Ornias takes a delight in foretelling the death of the workman's son, laughing about the prospect of the youth being sentenced to death when he only has three days to live. The demon that tells Canon Alberic that he will die in his bed is similarly toying with him; it is true that he will die in his bed, but not peacefully— rather from a "seizure" no doubt caused by the demon itself. Also, of course, though Canon Alberic may "live an object of envy" he is so tortured by the demon that he cannot enjoy his good fortune. It is worth noting in passing that this sort of sinister ambiguity in prophecies dates back to pre-Christian times: Herodotus, for example, tells the story of a prophecy given to Croesus by the Delphic oracle which he took to mean good fortune for himself, but which actually foretold his downfall.[5] The Old Testament also warns against using mediums to consult the dead in order to divine the future (e.g., Deuteronomy 18:9ff.; Isaiah 8:19ff.), depicting such practices as immoral, offensive to God and likely to end in no good. And indeed in the end even King Solomon, controller and consulter of demons, falls as prophesied.

The ability to foretell the future; the ability to find hidden treasure; the relentless pursuit of vengeance against the ungodly: these aspects could belong to more than one of the demons described in *The Testament of Solomon.* What more do we know? What of the demon's method of attacking his victim? The demon in the story never actually succeeds in touching Dennistoun, as it is thwarted by the arrival of the two serving men, but we know that the unfortunate Canon Alberic succumbed to a "sudden seizure." In addition to this, the sacristan prays to St. Bertrand (also invoked by Canon Alberic in his last despairing inscription) before a painting of the saint rescuing a man whom the devil sought to strangle. This infers that the demon's modus operandi is that of strangulation or induction of fits (or a heart attack). The demons listed in *The Testament of Solomon* are each associated with a different type of misfortune or indeed a different method of attacking their victims: Beelzebub inspires holy men to evil deeds and incites murder and war (v. 27); Atrax causes dangerous fevers (v. 87); Phêth causes consumption (v. 97). The demon which reveals the location of the gold hidden in the temple causes his victims to have fits (v. 54), and thus fills the bill in terms of

---

5. Herodotus, *Histories* 1.55. The oracle foretells that Croesus' reign will not end until a mule sits on the Median throne. Croesus thinks this is impossible, whereas in fact when the oracle refers to a mule it means a person of mixed parentage.

method of attack and treasure-hunting. In addition, the demon itself says that the means of frustrating it are associated with Golgotha, where the cross was supposed to have been planted: interesting, given that the demon seen by Dennistoun appears only after Dennistoun has removed a crucifix from around his neck. However, its appearance, as a three-headed dragon, albeit with human hands, would seem to preclude its being the creature seen by Dennistoun, which was clearly man-shaped. Similarly, we may discount Rabdos, who was a learned but ungodly man before he became a demon, tells Solomon where to find an enormous precious stone, and kills by seizing his victim by the larynx—his appearance is that of an enormous dog (v. 47ff.).

The demon Ornias is a more likely candidate: he is able to offer gold to the boy who captures him with Solomon's ring, and he can see the future. He also strangles his victims, apparently men born under the sign of Aquarius. He can take several forms—might the "talking voices" (plural) of the demon in the cathedral in "Canon Alberic's Scrap-book" perhaps be the voices of these different forms? They include a female one (we recall here the reference to Lilith discussed earlier in this article) and a beastly one: a lion. In *The Testament of Solomon* Ornias comes like a burning fire (v. 7), but since he is supposed to have sucked the thumb of the child, we must assume that he took on some more solid form to do this. It is also notable that Ornias has not made an outright assault on the boy; rather he has haunted the boy over a period of time, until his soul is oppressed and he becomes thinner by the day. The demon in "Canon Alberic's Scrap-book" haunts the Canon for seven years until the final "seizure" occurs; it has clearly haunted the sacristan for years too, since the old man has seen it twice but felt it "a thousand times" and he too appears oppressed; its movement towards Dennistoun is interrupted by the arrival of Pierre and Bertrand, but we may infer that it intended to torture him with terror rather than making an immediate attack on him. It allows Dennistoun to see its hand upon the table by him, and as he turns in horror it rises to its feet behind his chair, allowing him moments of heart-stopping terror. It makes a movement towards Dennistoun, but does not leave a mark upon him, although its presence is physical enough for the serving men to feel themselves thrust aside by it as it leaves the room: instead it leaves him with an oppressing terror. Is this, then, Ornias? There are other demons in the *Testament* whose attributes may also have influenced MRJ's depiction of the semi-bestial demon; however the demon Ornias, whose character is much more developed than that of the other demons in the *Testament*, is surely a major contributor.[6]

---

6. The possible identification of Canon Alberic's demon with Ornias was first made by Rosemary Pardoe in *Ghosts & Scholars* 15 (pp. 36–37), but my conclu-

So, if the demon in "Canon Alberic's Scrap-book" is indeed inspired by *The Testament of Solomon*, we might draw some inferences from the *Testament* about why the demon appears to be associated with possession of the drawing. Why the drawing, and not the photograph, is the question. Despite their antiquarian flavour, there is no stylistic reason why M. R. James's stories cannot include some modern aspects—the demon in "Casting the Runes" literally advertises its previous victim's fate inside a tram, for example. So it is a little facile to think that the use of modern technology has simply scared the demon off! It is more likely that the sepia drawing itself has some magical significance which cannot be transferred. Here we may refer to *The Testament of Solomon* once more, for the control or exorcism of demons through inscribed papers. In a long section of the *Testament*, Solomon summons a series of thirty-six demons related to the zodiac (v. 72ff.). These all have humanoid forms but the faces of animals and birds—perhaps an inspiration for the semi-bestial nature of Canon Alberic's demon. Each of them announces its name and the means by which it attacks human beings, and then the means by which it may be made to retreat. Some of them are exorcised by spoken words, but others are banished by the use of papers with specific inscriptions: Saphathoraél, for example, is frustrated by his victim's wearing around his neck a folded paper with the names of angels written on it (v. 83). Agchoniôn, bizarrely, is banished by writing the name Lycurgos several times, removing one letter each time (v. 103). It is not therefore too great a leap of imagination to have Dennistoun's demon exorcised by the burning of the drawing of it. The photograph, not part of the original magic, does not have the same ritual importance.[7]

Let us turn now to the curious detail of the "two hundred and fifty francs, not more," which the sacristan asks for the scrap-book. Unholy transactions are the normal fare of supernatural tales, but it is unusual to find a monetary price, and such a low one at that, quoted in the story. The precedent which immediately springs to mind is Robert Louis Stevenson's short story, "The Bottle Imp." Stevenson's tale describes how a young Hawaiian called Keawe buys a magic bottle containing an imp which can grant the owner's every wish. There are, however, two catches: whoever dies whilst in possession of the bottle must go straight to Hell, and the bottle can only ever be sold for a lower price than was paid for it. Otherwise it magically returns to the seller. The bot-

---

sions were reached independently.

7. This is not the only example of a demon controlled by the written word in MRJ's work. See "Casting the Runes"; though in that case the destruction of the paper renders the monster implacable.

tle was originally sold to Prester John for millions of dollars, but by the end of the story it is changing hands for centimes in spite of its value. The familiar theme of diabolical transactions leading to no good soon recurs: Keawe buys the bottle, but discovers that although the imp does indeed grant his wishes, there is always a price: for example, he gains the beautiful house he has always wanted by the death of some dear relatives. "The Bottle Imp" first appeared in an American paper in 1891 and was subsequently published in Stevenson's *Island Nights Entertainments* in 1893, probably the same year in which "Canon Alberic's Scrap-book" was written. It is possible therefore that the motif of the ever-lower price featured in Stevenson's story could have inspired the "two hundred and fifty francs, not more" of MRJ's tale. The sacristan is thus forced to sell the book for no more than that amount in order to be rid of it, having come into possession of it through a transaction of a slightly higher value (perhaps as part of the contents of Canon Alberic's house, which he now inhabits. He seems an unlikely collector).

But whether or not MRJ read Stevenson's story before he wrote "Canon Alberic's Scrap-book," there is actually a considerably older tradition of bottle imp stories with which he may also have been familiar. Grimmelshausen's *Trutz Simplex*, published in 1670, which recounts the adventures of Courasche (Courage), describes how the heroine buys a magic bottle from an old soldier, who tells her that it must be sold on for less than she paid for it, but neglects to tell her what will happen if she keeps it. Courasche describes the bottle imp as "something in a sealed glass bottle, which didn't look exactly like a spider but also not exactly like a scorpion."[8] The spider comparison, absent from Stevenson's story, recalls MRJ's comparison of Canon Alberic's demon with a bird-eating spider. Later, Courasche is told of the damnation which awaits the person who dies in possession of the magic bottle, by her "Bohemian mother," whom she describes as her best friend and "Sabud Salomonis," a reference to Zabud, son of Nathan, who was a royal adviser to King Solomon (1 Kings 4:5). This may imply that the bottle imp is one of the demons imprisoned by King Solomon, a not unreasonable assumption given that other stories dating considerably further back than *Trutz Simplex* feature demons imprisoned by Solomon in flasks or bottles. *The Testament of Solomon* has the demon Kunopaston imprisoned in a phial sealed with Solomon's ring and deposited in the temple (v. 68–69). The *Arabian Nights*, in addition to the Aladdin story, includes the tale of the Fisherman and the Genie, in which a poor fisherman finds a yellow copper bottle sealed with

---

8. "so etwas in einem verschlossenen Gläslein, welches nicht recht einer Spinnen und auch nicht recht einem Scorpion gleich sah." (*Trutz Simplex*, ch. 18.)

lead and bearing the seal of King Solomon; when he opens it, a djinn or ge-nie bursts forth. This is not a congenial creature in the Disney mould but an utterly terrifying monster with jagged teeth and eyes which blaze like torches. This genie is one of a group of rebel djinn who mutinied against Solomon, and was imprisoned by him in the bottle; during the first two cen-turies of his imprisonment he swore to enrich whoever set him free with the buried treasures of the earth (again the treasure-seeking motif recurs). With the passing of time he became so furious that he swore to kill his liberator instead. The genie shares this unreasonable and implacable pursuit of the innocent with the demon summoned by Canon Alberic, who after the Canon's death continues to terrorise those who possess the book.

There is one last detail of MRJ's story which I would like to examine, and that is the chronology of Canon Alberic's meetings with the demon. In the inscription on the back of the drawing of the demon, Canon Alberic tells us that he first saw the creature on the night of December 12th, 1694. The inscription is dated December 29th, 1701. The Canon's death occurs two nights later, on December 31st, 1701. Perhaps the story is simply set in De-cember to provide a suitably dark and chilling backdrop to the Canon's sor-cery, with his death occurring as the old year dies. Or perhaps the selection of the dates is purely random. Certainly an examination of the church cal-endar does not suggest that they carry any significance to the story: 12th December is the day of Our Lady of Guadalupe, 29th December the day of St. Thomas Beckett, and 31st December the day of St. Sylvester, a hetero-geneous selection of saints. Nor do these three dates follow any pattern from the pagan calendar, missing entirely the solstice on 21st. However, if we ex-amine the Jewish calendar, we find that December 12th, 1694, was 24th Kislev and the two dates in 1701 were 28th and 30th Kislev. The Old Tes-tament tells us that 24th Kislev was the date upon which the foundation stone of the new temple in Jerusalem was laid (Haggai 2:18), Solomon's temple having been destroyed by the Babylonians. 24th Kislev is also the eve of the festival of Hanukkah, which also covers the 28th and 30th Kislev. Hanukkah celebrates the rededication of the temple in Jerusalem after dese-cration by foreign troops. Once again the trail leads us back to the Temple Mount, site of Solomon's temple, in legend built by the demons. Was this intentional on the part of MRJ, an attention to the most obscure detail in the story, or is it a very spooky coincidence indeed? You decide . . .

With thanks to Dr. David G. K. Taylor, University Lecturer in Aramaic and Syriac; Fellow of Wolfson College, Oxford, for his advice on Jewish demonology.

A Haunting Presence

C. E. *Ward*

I have been haunted by the writings of Montague Rhodes James since childhood. It has not been a persistent haunting, I hasten to add, nor has it been unwelcome or in any way unpleasant; rather it has been a self-induced pleasure, returned to over and again through the years, whenever I have tired of other reading matter, ghostly or otherwise, and have once more perused one of M. R. James's other-worldly tales. Nostalgia is a much over-used word in this day and age, but I can find no better way of expressing my feelings when I reach for my *Collected Ghost Stories* in its faded blue binding, and remember the excitement of its discovery so many years before, and choose one of the tales within to read once more on a winter's evening.

It is hard to write something about M. R. James or his stories that hasn't been said before, by people far more learned and eloquent than myself. That he is the greatest writer of the genre in the English language, surpassing even his own mentor, Sheridan Le Fanu, may be questioned by some but supported fervently by countless others. Many writers can chill the spine very effectively, but James could get under the skin while doing this. There has been much discussion over the years about his writing technique. Restraint, understatement and a telling phrase, all laced with fine antiquarian knowledge have been variously dissected and analysed with an almost scientific precision, but (like ghosts themselves) the raw elements have eluded any final analysis, and Dr. James's box of tricks remains inviolate and curious as ever. Like some ingenious stage illusionist, the good Doctor shows us his magic again and again, before our very eyes, but putting a finger on "how it's done" remains as difficult as ever. Writers have imitated the style and attempted the legerdemain, and while many have come close none have ever quite reached M. R. James's pinnacle of excellence. No matter! Many of the attempts have proved more than worthwhile.

I have sometimes been asked what my favourite tale is; this is a question I've never fully been able to answer. To satisfy my inquirer I have usually mentioned "Lost Hearts," an early tale which apparently James didn't much care for, and which only appeared in *Ghost-Stories of an Antiquary* to fill up the volume at Messrs. Arnold's request.

I have always been surprised at MRJ's seeming negative attitude to this particular story, and that of the readers who have been less than enthusiastic, not to say disparaging, about it. If not actually my firm favourite, "Lost Hearts" retains a special corner in my affections, and certainly part of the reason is that it nurtured my further interest in the writings of the author. This was my first introduction to M. R. James, through the medium of television, in the memorable rendition that featured in ABC's *Mystery and Imagination* series of the mid-sixties. Indeed, it has been produced for television not once but twice, and both times quite successfully. The more cynical might attribute this to its reasonably simple storyline and easy adaptability to the medium, but it remains one of the classic short chillers in whatever guise it has assumed.

The plot is well known. An elderly scholar, reclusive and of independent means, invites his young cousin, recently orphaned, to live with him. His secret intention is to kill the boy in order to obtain his heart, which he believes will give him magical powers and, possibly, immortality. Two murders have already been committed for this purpose, and the young victims' corpses carefully concealed, but their whereabouts are frighteningly disclosed to the intended next victim, and their intrusion back into the world of the living occurs in a series of disturbing events and incidents.

The setting of Aswarby Hall, a few miles south of Sleaford in Lincolnshire, was a real place, though the house was long since demolished; according to Arthur Mee in *The King's England* it was inhabited at various times by members of the Carre and Whichcote families rather than the austere Mr. Abney. These facts notwithstanding, it is on record that one resident of the locality of Aswarby was prompted to write to M. R. James, asking the truth of the story. Further evidence of the veridical nature of his writing is unnecessary! It is one of MRJ's shorter tales, but all that we have come to recognise as "Jamesian" qualities are there. The subject matter of child-murder, an unsavoury topic which can so easily offend, is handled with a deft touch and a certain detachment by James, a detachment crucial to the story. Mrs. Bunch, Abney's kindly and unsuspecting housekeeper, when telling Stephen Elliott of the two former guests, recollects little about the girl, Phoebe Stanley, and dismisses her disappearance as possible abduction by wandering gipsies. "That pore boy," as she describes Giovanni Paoli, is "off one fine morning just the same as the girl." At no point is the reader allowed any depth of feeling or particular sympathy for the fate of the two young children so cruelly done to death. A clumsier writer than M. R. James would have failed in a few sentences where he succeeded, for this is where the real power of the story lies. Having emotionally detached the reader from the victims, James now sets his pen to turning them into instruments of fear and menace.

There is something inherently horrible about the idea of children as predators. William Golding used this theme to good effect in *The Lord of the Flies*, and, in more fantastic settings in films such as *Children of the Damned*, *The Innocents*, and *The Omen*, this lurking fear has been more fully explored—not to say exploited. Perhaps because of a deep-rooted view of children as innocent and unsullied, with a need to be cared for and protected by parental instinct, just the sound of a child's laughter tinged with evil is totally unexpected and exposes our innermost fears. The bodies of the dead children, hidden in the remotest corners of the vast and rambling Aswarby Hall, make their dreadful presence felt soon after Stephen's arrival, the girl appearing horribly to him in a disused bathroom, scratches materializing on his bedroom door and his night-gown, and conspiratorial whispers being overheard by Parkes the butler in the shadows of the wine cellar.

I have never subscribed to the idea, portrayed in the 1973 BBC production, that the dead children's main purpose was to save the intended third victim from sharing their fate. Stephen Elliott, to my mind, becomes almost as much their prey as his guilty cousin, directly terrorized by the revenants on two occasions, and surely greatly disturbed by incidents at other times. Standing at his window shortly before his planned late-night meeting with Mr. Abney, Stephen becomes aware of two figures gazing up at him from the terrace. "Something in the form of the girl recalled irresistibly his dream of the figure in the bath. The boy inspired him with more acute fear." There is an "appearance of menace and unappeasable hunger and longing," and the boy, following the fashion of the girl in Stephen's earlier encounter with her, raises his arms to reveal the torn and empty hole in his breast.

Stephen, "inexpressibly frightened" but not quite at the end of his dreadful ordeal, which must surely have reduced most children of his age to a complete wreck of humanity, goes down to Mr. Abney's study to keep his appointment. The final outcome of his cousin's death and horrific mutilation could hardly have helped to calm his feelings on that evening, or for a considerable time afterwards. A truly great story, introducing *formidable visitants* of the very worst kind.

Such is just one story of the thirty or so that M. R. James penned for an eager market. All of us wish that he had written more, but quality has at least made up for lack of quantity. Admirers of his work, myself included, still read his stories, discuss the man, and try to emulate his tales—a tradition which began before his death some sixty-three years ago and continues as strong as ever today. Monty James's torch is kept burning brightly, not least by Rosemary Pardoe, who has been indefatigable in her efforts to keep his work in the public eye through her Haunted Library publications since the very first *Ghosts & Scholars* in 1979. I am something of a latecomer to the hard-core MRJ following, despite a lifetime of admiration, but my tardiness in making Rosemary's acquaintance hasn't prevented my acquiring a full set of *Ghosts & Scholars*. Some of the early ones were purchased at something above their original cover price, but it's a collection of which I'm inordinately proud.

"A Wonderful Book":
George MacDonald and "The Ash-Tree"

Rosemary Pardoe

In his Introduction to *Meddling with Ghosts*, Ramsey Campbell suggests that "one possible source of [M. R. James's] method" might have been George MacDonald's children's novel, *The Princess and the Goblin* (1872), which "James might conceivably have read" (ix). Campbell supports his theory by quoting such lines from MacDonald as these: "But at that instant the something in the middle of the way, which had looked like a great lump of earth brought down by the rain, began to move. One after another it shot out four long things, like two arms and two legs, but it was now too dark to tell what they were . . ."

Was George MacDonald (1824–1905) a precursor of MRJ? Can we add our Jamesian Cambridge ghost story tradition to that of the Oxford fantasists like J. R. R. Tolkien and C. S. Lewis, on the list of those who were influenced by MacDonald? There is no definite proof that MRJ read *The Princess and the Goblin*, but I think we can say he probably did, as he is known to have read and appreciated other books by the same author. *At the Back of the North Wind* (1871) is mentioned in *Eton & King's* as a boyhood favourite (8), and Gwendolen McBryde recalled that he "liked MacDonald's books, particularly *Phantastes*, and was interested when I showed him a much worn and tattered copy of *Donal Grant* [1883] . . . It is a very eerie story" (*Letters to a Friend* 19). In 1915, MRJ sent a copy of *Phantastes* to a depressed and battle-traumatised Gordon Carey, with the words: "[it] has the property of taking me out of this world of unpleasantness into another and more desirable, and I hope it may do so for you" (Cox 190). On 1 October 1919, in a letter to Gwendolen McBryde, he enthused about it again: "I suppose I have already recommended George Macdonald's *Phantastes*—a wonderful book" (*Letters to a Friend* 93).

Phantastes (1858) was one of MacDonald's two successful attempts to write a book-length fairy tale not intended for children (the other being *Lilith*, 1895). We do not know exactly when MRJ first read it, but there seems to be no indication in the 1915 Gordon Carey letter that he had come upon it recently—I suspect the discovery was made during his schooldays rather than later. It is very possible to see parallels between the early sections of *Phantastes* and MRJ's children's fantasy novel, *The Five Jars* (1922), as well as the connected story, "After Dark in the Playing Fields." For instance, the narrators of both books begin their respective adventures by following a stream, and there are encounters with mischievous fairy folk who have a similar line in animal-teasing:

> Half of them were on the cat's back, and half held on by her fur and tail . . . the furious cat was held fast; and they proceeded to pick the sparks out of her with thorns and pins. . . . One little fellow who held on hard by the tip of the tail, with his feet planted on the ground at an angle of forty-five degrees, helping to keep her fast, administered a continuous flow of admonitions to Pussy.
>
> "Now, Pussy, be patient. You know quite well it is all for your good. You cannot be comfortable with all those sparks in you; and, indeed, I am charitably disposed to believe" (here he became very pompous) "that they are the cause of all your bad temper. . . ."
>
> But with a perfect hurricane of feline curses, the poor animal broke loose, and dashed across the garden and through the hedge . . . (*Phantastes* 22)

> Suddenly [the owl] broke into a loud scream, flapped its wings furiously, bent forward, and clutched its perch tightly, continuing to scream. Plainly something was pulling hard at it from behind. The strain relaxed abruptly, the owl nearly fell over, and then whipped round, ruffling up all over, and made a vicious dab at something unseen by me. "Oh, I *am* sorry," said a small clear voice in a solicitous tone. "I made sure it was loose. I do hope I didn't hurt you." "Didn't 'urt me?" said the owl bitterly. "Of course you 'urt me, and well you know it, you young infidel. That feather was no more loose than— oh, if I could git at you!" ("After Dark in the Playing Fields," *PT* 381)

Compare, also, the everyday speech of the wild animals, which the narrators acquire the ability to overhear:

> I found myself listening attentively, and as if it were no unusual thing with me, to a conversation between two squirrels. . . . The subjects were not very interesting, except as associated with the individual life and necessities of the little creatures: where the best nuts were to be found in the neighbourhood, and who could crack them best, or who had most laid up for the winter, and such like; only they never said where the store was. (*Phantastes* 34)

What I remember best is a family of young rabbits huddled round their parents in a burrow, and the mother telling a story: "And so then he went a little farther and found a dandelion, and stopped and sat up and began to eat it. And when he had eaten two large leaves and one little one, he saw a fly on it—no, two flies; and then he thought he had had enough of that dandelion, and he went a little farther and found another dandelion. . . ." And so it went on interminably . . . (*The Five Jars; PT* 558)

This is not to imply that, in *The Five Jars* (or "After Dark"), MRJ stole any ideas wholesale from *Phantastes:* on the contrary, as the books develop they become very different. MRJ's autobiographical narrator, "M (or N)," finds himself caught up in a battle, waged with the aid of the powers for good in the animal and fairy worlds, to save the five jars of magic ointment from acquisition by the vividly evoked evil fairies and their allied creatures. Mac-Donald's hero, "Anodos," on the other hand, travels the land of fairy, encountering on the way so many archetypal figures (including an almost endless supply of *animae*) that *Phantastes* might almost be a pre-Jungian sourcebook for Jungian psychology!

Nevertheless, I think MacDonald *can* fairly be considered as having had an influence on MRJ's work, and the influence may have reached at least once into his ghost stories proper (i.e. other than "After Dark").

No one has yet offered an adequate explanation of why, in "The Ash-Tree" (c. 1904), MRJ associated the eponymous tree with evil and witchcraft. Not only is the witch, Mrs. Mothersole, supposedly seen "at the full of the moon, gathering sprigs" from it, "cutting off small twigs with a peculiarly curved knife"; but later her arachnid familiars come out of the tree, and their nest is found there, along with her skeletal remains. Yet, as I pointed out in my annotations to the story,[1] although the ash-tree has strong pagan associations (Yggdrasill, the World Tree in Norse mythology, for instance), it is generally considered in folklore and custom to be a force for good and a charm *against* witches. "Perhaps," I added, "MRJ is giving us a hint that Sir Matthew Fell's evidence was trumped up. If so, Fell certainly bit off more than he could chew." The initial evidence connecting Mrs. Mothersole to the ash-tree may have been trumped up, but, by anyone's definition, she was a malevolent being—not just a *white* witch (despite the possible pagan implications of the "curved knife")—and it is not credible to see her as an innocent old soul swept up in events. Admittedly, if she had been nothing worse than the local "wise woman" and village healer, there *are* uses to which she might have been putting ash-tree leaves and bark (but not specifically "twigs," and not necessarily gathered at the full moon)—as a laxative, diuretic and astringent (and there is a cure for warts involving the sticking of

---

1. *Ghosts & Scholars* 11 (1989): 32–33; reprinted in *PT* 40.

pins into an ash-tree!). But why would she have chosen a tree so dangerously close to habitation when doubtless there were plenty of others in the vicinity? And why does MRJ give no indication at all that Mrs. Mothersole practised any sort of helpful folk medicine? The inference of his previous paragraph is that her magics and knowledge were used for far more wicked purposes: her prosperity and the influence she had over "several reputable farmers of the parish," who "did their best to testify to her character, and showed considerable anxiety as to the verdict of the jury," hints at blackmail at the very least.

Whether or not the original link between Mrs. Mothersole and the ash was real, it soon became so; and the tree's malign occupants, with their combined kitten/spider imagery, are among the most personal creations of the ailurophile and arachnophobe MRJ (incidentally, the implications of the *sortes* from Job 39—"her young ones also suck up blood"—if taken literally, are almost too horrendous to contemplate).

Jacqueline Simpson notes, in her comments on the story, that "Ireland is said to be the source for the belief that ash trees are sinister, which runs counter to English ideas" (13), but she gives no reference for the Irish connection, and it seems doubtful, as one Irish custom was to burn ash branches to keep the Devil away.[2] She adds, in a footnote (17): "In England, ash trees are credited with healing, divinatory and protective powers . . . Scarfe suggests that the allusion is to actual trees, including ash trees, round Livermere Hall in the village where James grew up" (unquestionably Livermere was an inspiration for Castringham Hall in the story). In fact, Norman Scarfe only remarks that Livermere Hall was "screened from the Rectory by trees—ash trees among them" (1418), which doesn't really seem sufficient reason for the selection of an ash in the story. Frank Adey[3] gives a nice account, from an 1857 nonfiction volume, of a haunted ash-tree in Lincolnshire; but the haunting, although disturbingly eerie ("[a] hollow voice . . . sighing and groaning"), is not noticeably evil—and there is no evidence that MRJ had read the book in question.

---

2. *Man, Myth and Magic* 5 (1970), p. 134 (entry for "Ash"). An Internet search has come up with a handful of pagan sites which claim that, in Ireland especially, as well as the ash's usual witch-repellent properties, it was/is used for the handles of witches' broomsticks (wouldn't these two activities be seriously incompatible?). I'd welcome any evidence that this latter custom predates the Wiccan revival.

3. Frank Adey, letter to *Ghosts & Scholars* 31 (2000): 57; and quoted in a footnote in *PT* 49–50. Jacqueline Simpson, op. cit., p. 17, also mentions "one Scottish story and two from the Fens where ghosts are seen near ashes . . . but this hardly seems significant."

However, there *is* an evil ash-tree in *Phantastes,* and it plays a major part in the first section of the book, where it stalks Anodos in a highly sinister, near-Jamesian manner:

> Soon a vague sense of discomfort possessed me. With variations of relief, this gradually increased; as if some evil thing were wandering about in my neighbourhood, sometimes nearer and sometimes further off, but still approaching. The feeling continued and deepened, until all my pleasure in the shows of various kinds that everywhere betokened the presence of the merry fairies vanished by degrees, and left me full of anxiety and fear, which I was unable to associate with any definite object whatever. At length the thought crossed my mind with horror: "Can it be possible that the Ash is looking for me? or that, in his nightly wanderings, his path is gradually verging towards mine?" (26)

Shortly thereafter he discovers that his worst fears are justified: "I saw plainly on the path before me . . . the shadow of a large hand, with knotty joints and protuberances here and there . . . and once I saw the fingers close, and grind themselves close, like the claws of a wild animal, as if in uncontrollable longing for some anticipated prey" (26–27). Placing himself in a position to discover what has caused the shadow, Anodos is appalled at what he sees:

> . . . the strangest figure; vague, shadowy, almost transparent, in the central parts, and gradually deepening in substance towards the outside, until it ended in extremities capable of casting such a shadow as fell from the hand, through the awful fingers of which I now saw the moon. . . . But the face . . . it was horrible. I do not know how to describe it . . . I can only try to describe something that is not it, but seems somewhat parallel to it; or at least is suggested by it. It reminded me of what I had heard of vampires; for the face resembled that of a corpse more than anything else I can think of; especially when I can conceive such a face in motion, but not suggesting any life as the source of the motion. The features were rather handsome than otherwise, except the mouth, which had scarcely a curve in it. The lips were of equal thickness; but the thickness was not at all remarkable, even although they looked slightly swollen. They seemed fixedly open, but were not wide apart. . . . But the most awful of the features were the eyes. These were alive, yet not with life. They seemed lighted up with an infinite greed. A gnawing voracity, which devoured the devourer, seemed to be the indwelling and propelling power of the whole ghastly apparition . . . (27–28)

Such a memorable image as this (described quite fully despite Mac-Donald's very *un*-Jamesian denial of his ability to describe it!) must surely have stayed with MRJ, and it might well have come to mind when he was looking for a suitably evil tree in "The Ash-Tree."

Works Cited

Campbell, Ramsey, ed. *Meddling with Ghosts.* London: British Library, 2001.

Cox, Michael. *M. R. James: An Informal Portrait.* London: Oxford University Press, 1983.

James, M. R. *Eton and King's.* London: Williams & Norgate, 1926.

———. *Letters to a Friend.* Ed. Gwendolen McBryde. London: Edward Arnold, 1956.

———. *A Pleasing Terror: The Complete Supernatural Writings of M. R. James.* Ed. Barbara and Christopher Roden. Ashcroft, BC: Ash-Tree Press, 2001. [Abbreviated in the text as *PT.*]

MacDonald, George. *Phantastes.* 1858. Grand Rapids, MI: William B. Eerdmans, 2000.

Scarfe, Norman. "The Strangeness Present: M. R. James's Suffolk." *Country Life* (6 November 1986): 1416–19.

Simpson, Jacqueline. "'The Rules of Folklore' in the Ghost Stories of M. R. James." *Folklore* 108 (1997): 9–18.

Who Was Count Magnus?
Notes towards an Identification

Rosemary Pardoe

In his *Casting the Runes* annotations for "Count Magnus," Michael Cox correctly says of the title character: "the De la Gardie family played a prominent part in Swedish history. There was a Magnus De la Gardie, a contemporary of Queen Christina and a patron of the arts, but he had nothing in common with MRJ's creation." Another of Cox's notes records the one definite link between the historical Magnus de la Gardie and Count Magnus: the former's tomb is in the De la Gardie mausoleum at the Cistercian abbey of Varnhem. Varnhem is close to Skovde, near Skara in the Västergötland (Vestergothland) area of southern Sweden, which is exactly where Count Magnus's tomb is located in the story ("[the landlord] was called away to Skara, and should not be back till evening"). MRJ visited Varnhem in 1901, and wrote "Count Magnus" sometime during the following couple of years (James 310).

Count Magnus Gabriel de la Gardie (1622–86) could scarcely have been a more different character to M. R. James's Count Magnus. A portrait of the latter shows him to have been, according to MRJ, "an almost phenomenally ugly man," whereas Magnus Gabriel de la Gardie was almost equally handsome, as evidenced by contemporary portraits and busts. He became a favourite of Queen Christina (1626–89), and with her support received many important appointments. He was sent as envoy extraordinary to France when only in his early twenties; while still in his twenties, he was "one of the chief army commanders in the Thirty Years War. . . . In 1651 he became master of the Queeres household and marshal of the realm. . . . In 1652 he was appointed president of the College Chamber and senatorial president in Västergötland and Dalsland. These posts and feudal offices made him one of the richest men in the whole country." That Queen Christina had passionate feelings towards Magnus de la Gardie seems certain but they were not reciprocated, although there were rumours that they were lovers and even that she had given birth to a child (or two!) fathered by him. In 1653, Magnus fell from grace when new foreign favourites arose in Court. Insults and accusations of treason and disloyalty flew in all directions, and Christina wrote Magnus a truly vicious letter in which she called him "unprincipled," and told him that "in future I shall be incapable of feeling anything but pity for you." His feudal properties were taken away from him and he was removed from the office of government treasurer. Later, however, he regained power and became chancellor (Stolpe 70, 77; Akerman, *Christina of Sweden* 40, 314).

Unlike MRJ's Count Magnus, there is no evidence that Magnus Gabriel de la Gardie had any interest in alchemy or the black arts, although Queen Christina, especially in later life, was actively involved with the former subject: she corresponded with other alchemists; had her own working laboratory; and possessed a large collection of alchemical and magical works, both printed and in manuscript (including John Dee's *Monas Hieroglyphica* and parts of the infamous *Picatrix*) (Akerman, "Christina of Sweden"). Magnus Gabriel de Ja Gardie, on the other hand, is noted as the person responsible, in the 1660s, for returning to Sweden one of the country's literary treasures, the sixth-century *Codex Argenteus* or Silver Bible, which he purchased and donated to Uppsala University Library, where it is on display today. (MRJ may well have seen the *Codex* when his travels took him to Uppsala in August 1901, on the occasion when he "laughed over" the contracts with the Devil signed by the teenaged Daniel Salthenius there, as mentioned at the end of "Number 13" [James 309].)

Readers of "Count Magnus" who are aware of the historicity of Magnus de la Gardie tend to assume one of two things: either that the former is definitely based on the latter, or conversely that MRJ picked the name from Swedish history pretty much at random. While the first class of reader is undoubtedly wrong, could the second be jumping to conclusions? Could Count Magnus be inspired by a historical character, and if so, might MRJ's selection of the Magnus de la Gardie name be a clue to his identity? If we look at one particular aspect of the background of MRJ's Count Magnus—his manor-house called Råbäck—we find that the answer is a possible yes![1]

There *is* an estate named Råbäck in Västergötland (on the Kinnekulle

---

1. Despite the obfuscating acknowledgement to "Count Olof de la Gardie, both for his hospitality at Rabäck [sic], and for allowing me to inspect family papers relating to his ancestor Count Magnus," we can assume that the information about a second Magnus de la Gardie given in Colin Wilson's *The Space Vampires* (1976) is as solidly based on fact as his assertion that Chorazin is in Hungary! All evidence in "Count Magnus" to the contrary, Wilson insists on placing "Rabäck" on an island in Lake Storavan in northern Sweden.

mountain) and, according to Michael Cox's *Casting the Runes* annotations, MRJ visited it and wrote a letter to his parents from there on 10 August 1901. However, he states quite specifically in "Count Magnus" that while the house in the story "is to be called Råbäck . . . that is not its name." Having chosen to place the fictional house close to Magnus Gabriel de la Gardie's real tomb, his selection of an appropriately local name for it might not even have been a conscious decision. At any rate, I think we must take him at his word when he says that Count Magnus's house is not really Råbäck. Some aspects of the fictional manor-house may have been inspired by Magnus de la Gardie's own estates in the area (surely not, however, his most famous residence, Läckö Castle on Lake Vänern, which is just that—a picture-book castle—and was only renovated, not built, by him),[2] but others seem to point elsewhere. We are told by MRJ that there is a picture in "Dahlenberg's *Suecia antiqua et moderna*," that "it is one of the best buildings of its kind in all the country," and that there was a "correspondence between Sophia Albertina in Stockholm and her married cousin Ulrica Leonora at Råbäck in the years 1705–1710." The house with which Ulrika Eleonora (1688–1741), sister of King Charles XII and briefly Queen of Sweden in 1719–20, is most closely associated is Ulriksdal, just outside Stockholm. The current exterior dates from the time when she lived there. It is still a royal palace today, and is part of a huge eco-park, very popular with tourists and day-trippers from Stockholm. "Dahlenberg's *Suecia antiqua et moderna*" is actually the *Suecia Antiqua et Hodierna* of Erik Dahlberg (1625–1703), where an extremely fine engraving of Ulriksdal appears. There is a connection between Ulriksdal and Magnus de la Gardie, for he owned the palace in the middle of the seventeenth century, but he was not the builder. Since, in the story, Count Magnus built Råbäck "soon after 1600," should we look to the founder of Ulriksdal—or Jacobsdal as it was originally called—as a possible candidate for MRJ's inspiration? I think so.

Jacobsdal was completed around 1644 and was built by one Count Jacob Pontusson de la Gardie, who was none other than the father of Magnus de la Gardie. Jacob (1583–1652) was a great Swedish statesman and soldier. He commanded the Swedish forces in Russia which captured Moscow in 1610;

---

2. As far as its appearance is concerned, Mariedal (which Magnus de la Gardie built in the 1660s for his wife, Maria Euphrosyne) is a better—but far from perfect—candidate. However, if MRJ had had this in mind, he would scarcely have resisted recounting a well-known legend associated with its location: that Magnus moved the building materials from the place where his wife wanted the house to the position that he had selected, and blamed it on trolls!

in 1626–28 he was commander in chief of the army which fought against the Polish in Livonia; and later he served as one of the regents during the minority of Queen Christina (1632–44).[3] More to the point, an engraving could serve uncannily perfectly to illustrate MRJ's description of Count Magnus's portrait: "the face impressed him rather by its power than by its beauty or goodness; in fact . . . Count Magnus was an almost phenomenally ugly man." Jacob de la Gardie also seems to have had closer links with matters esoteric than his son. There is a suggestion that he was involved in alchemy, although this has proved aggravatingly hard to pin down, but he was certainly a dedicatee of Johannes Bureus' mystical work on runes, *Adulruna rediviva*, and is known to have used runes in secret instructions to his generals.[4]

This is in no way sufficient evidence to convict Jacob de la Gardie of being MRJ's Count Magnus, but I would suggest that he was a much greater source of inspiration for MRJ than Magnus de la Gardie. Perhaps MRJ created Count Magnus as a sort of portmanteau figure based on several members of the family. There is one final piece to add to the jigsaw, implying just that.

MRJ describes several ornamented panels on the tomb of Count Magnus. "One was a battle, with cannon belching out smoke, and walled towns, and troops of pikemen." In Tallinn Cathedral in Estonia, over the Baltic from Stockholm, there is a tomb with a fine panel depicting a battle scene (even if MRJ never visited this cathedral in person, he may well have seen photographs). Here too are cannons belching puffs of smoke in the foreground, three walled towns, and armies of pikemen. It depicts the siege of Narva in 1581, which was a highlight in the career of the celebrated Swedish soldier whose body lies within. The tomb belongs to Pontus de la Gardie (1520–85), the father of Jacob and grandfather of Magnus.

Whereas, in "Count Magnus," MRJ says that Råbäck is not the real name of the manor-house, he uses an entirely different turn of phrase when first introducing the family who built it: "De la Gardie is the name by which I will designate them when mention becomes necessary." Although occasionally careless with his facts, MRJ was not prone to lack of care with his phraseology. By not ruling them out of the "Count Magnus" equation, was he hoping the reader would take the hint and do likewise?

---

3. Entry for Jacob de la Gardie in the online *Encyclopaedia Britannica*.

4. The connection between alchemy and Jacob de la Gardie was made by a poster to the Message Board of the Alchemy web site in July 1999, without any awareness of a possible link with MRJ's "Count Magnus."

Works Cited

Akerman, Susanna. *Queen Christina of Sweden and Her Circle: The Transformation of a Seventeenth-Century Philosophical Libertine.* Leiden: E. J. Brill, 1991.

Susanna Akerman, "Christina of Sweden (1626–1689), the Porta Magica and the Italian poets of the Golden and Rosy Cross." On the Alchemy web site at <http://www.levity.con)/alchemy/home.html>.

James, M. R. *Casting the Runes and Other Ghost Stories.* Ed. Michael Cox. Oxford: Oxford University Press, 1987.

Stolpe, Sven. *Christina of Sweden.* Ed. and tr. Sir Alec Randall and Ruth Mary Bethell. London: Burns & Oates, 1966.

A Haunting Vision: M. R. James and the Ashridge Stained Glass

Nicholas Connell

Dr. Montague Rhodes James (1862–1936) was an eminent academic, biblical scholar, antiquary, and palaeographer. He had been a student at Eton and King's College, Cambridge, and went on to become provost at both of those institutions. James was also the director of the Fitzwilliam Museum in Cambridge. Today he is perhaps better remembered as an author of ghost stories. One of these stories was inspired by the stained glass windows that were once part of the chapel of Ashridge House in Little Gaddesden, near Berkhamsted.

Ashridge House was built on the site of a thirteenth-century monastery, the College of Bonhommes, where a Parliament had been held in 1291.[1] The College had possessed a document entitled "Johannes de Rupesscissa," the contents of which would not have been out of place in one of Dr. James's stories. The document contained "many receipts; among others to free a house haunted with evil spirits; by fumes: Mr March had it and did cure houses so haunted by it."[2]

At the beginning of the nineteenth century Ashridge House was in possession of the Duke of Bridgewater who planned to pull down the old college and build a new mansion, but he died before the project could be carried out. His successor, the eighth Earl of Bridgewater, saw through the completion of the new house.[3] The new house was built in the gothic style by the famous architect James Wyatt, assisted by his nephew, Jeffry [sic] Wyatville. The gothic chapel was completed by Wyatville in 1814[4] after the death of

1. Edward Page, ed., *Victoria County History of Hertfordshire* (London, 1908), Volume 2, p. 209.
2. Hertfordshire Archives and Local Studies (HALS), Gerish Collection, box 30, Little Gaddesden.
3. Page, p. 210.
4. HALS, D/ECo/F26, Miscellaneous papers regarding stained glass in Ash-

his uncle in a coach crash the previous year.[5] Great quantities of stained glass were being imported into England from the Continent at this period, and this included the glass for the eleven perpendicular gothic windows of Ashridge Chapel.[6] The precise source of the glass was the Abbey at Steinfeld in the Eifel district of Germany. Steinfeld Abbey had been founded in 920 by the Benedictines but had been taken over by the Premonstratensians in 1099. However, the Ashridge glass was of a much later period. It was all sixteenth-century in origin, the earliest piece being dated 1519 and the latest 1572.[7] The glass contained scenes from both the Old and New Testaments including incidents in the life and passion of Christ.[8] The glass was removed from the windows in 1785 before being sold at a low price and sent to England when the Abbey closed in 1802.[9]

The glass was installed in Ashridge Chapel between 1811 and 1831. On one of the panes of glass depicting Amos, a glazier had etched with diamond, "An humble individual of the same name as the Prophet Amos, the Top Figure in the Head of this Window, first commenced fixing these Windows in the year 1811 & finished the Windows in the year 1831."[10] The glass was not fitted in any sequence. One commentator described it as "a shamble . . . only a brilliant ruin has remained."[11]

Dr. James may have seen the Ashridge stained glass as early as 1882 when he camped at Ashridge with the Eton Rifle Corps.[12] He returned to Ashridge

---

ridge Chapel, n.d.

5. "Short Memoirs of the Life of James Wyatt, Esq.," *Gentleman's Magazine* (September 1813): 296.

6. Bernard Rackham, "The Ashridge Stained Glass," *Old Furniture* (September 1928): 33.

7. HALS, D/ECo/F26; Montague Rhodes James, *Notes of Glass in Ashridge Chapel* (1906), Grantham.

8. Bernard Rackham, "The Mariawald-Ashridge Glass," *Burlington Magazine* 85 (1944): 269. Rackham argues that some of the Ashridge glass originated from the Abbey at Mariawald, also in the Eifel district of Germany as well as from Steinfeld. He repeats this argument in his other articles quoted in this piece.

9. Ibid., p. 266.

10. Rackham, "The Ashridge Stained Glass," p. 33.

11. HALS, D/ECo/F26; "Die alten Glasgemalde aus dem Kreuzgang der Abtei Steinfeld," *Eifelkalendar Herausgegeben vom Eifelverein*, 1930.

12. Michael Cox, ed., *Casting the Runes and Other Ghost Stories* by M. R. James (Oxford, 1987), p. 315.

Chapel in the summer of 1904 to make an examination of the glass,[13] the results of which were privately published in 1906.[14] It was not the first time that Dr. James had published an account of Hertfordshire stained glass. Many years earlier he had written about the windows in the library at St. Albans Abbey.[15] James quickly created a story built around the Ashridge stained glass to fill up his book *Ghost-Stories of an Antiquary*, which was published in November 1904. He called it "The Treasure of Abbot Thomas."[16]

Set in 1859, "The Treasure of Abbot Thomas" relates the adventure of Mr. Somerton, an antiquarian, and his search for the whereabouts of the stained glass windows that were once at Steinfeld Abbey. He discovers them in a private chapel and also learns of a rumour that Abbot Thomas von Eschenhausen of Steinfeld concealed a large quantity of gold somewhere in the monastery before his death in 1529. Somerton ingeniously deciphers a riddle written on three scrolls held by three figures depicted on the glass. He also uncovers a hidden inscription on the glass which reveals that Abbot Thomas's gold is hidden in the well of the Abbot's house at Steinfeld, but warns of a guardian of the treasure.

Somerton travels to Steinfeld and descends the well at night, where he finds a concealed hole in the well's wall. He reaches in for what he thinks are bags of gold, but when he pulls a bag out it "put its arms around my neck." The laughing ghost of Abbot Thomas appears at the head of the well and revels in Somerton's encounter with the guardian of his treasure. Somerton survives the ordeal and summons his parish vicar who seals the hole in the well during daylight hours.

In the story Ashridge Chapel was described as "a private chapel—no matter where," which belonged to a "Lord D——." The owner of Ashridge at the time the story was set was Earl Brownlow.[17] Abbot Thomas was also a fictional character holding a factual position. The story stated that Abbot Thomas had the windows put up around 1520. The Abbot of Steinfeld in that period was Johan von Ahrweiler.[18]

---

13. Ibid.

14. See n. 7.

15. M. R. James, "On the Glass in the Windows of the Library at St. Albans Abbey," *Camb. Antiq. Society* 8 (1891–94): 213–20.

16. Cox, p. xix.

17. *Kelly's Directory of Hertfordshire*, 1860, p. 345.

18. Bernard Rackham, "The Ashridge Stained Glass," *British Archaeological Association Journal*, 3rd series, 10 (1945–47): 3.

However, there were several clear similarities between incidents in "The Treasure of Abbot Thomas" and the Ashridge stained glass. Somerton found clues to the whereabouts of the treasure from inscriptions in three scrolls held by three figures: Job Patriarcha, Johannes Evangelista, and Zacharias Propheta. The Ashridge stained glass included three panels featuring the story of Job.[19] There were also two panels featuring John the Evangelist with a scroll, and a further two panels showing an unidentified prophet with a scroll.

As the narrator of "The Treasure of Abbot Thomas," James confessed that it was to his "grave disadvantage" that he had never visited Steinfeld. He also admitted to never having been there two years later when his notes on the glass were published.[20]

By coincidence another similarity emerged over twenty years after Dr. James's examination of the glass. Mr. Somerton had found Abbot Thomas's hidden inscription by chance when a black pigment border around a window came away as he cleaned the dust off the window. The Ashridge glass had its own hidden inscription—that of Amos the glazier—which was revealed when the windows were removed from the chapel in the 1920s.[21]

The Steinfeld glass remained at Ashridge Chapel until the house and estate were sold in 1928. Its owner, the third Earl Brownlow, had died in 1921, and his will instructed his trustees to sell the estate. The house along with eighty acres of land was bought and given to the Conservative Party as an educational and political training centre.[22] In 1959 it became the Ashridge Management College.[23]

The glass from the chapel was sold at auction at Sotheby's on 12 July 1928.[24] Sotheby's announced that "nobody can put the value of these windows too high; these are rare pearls in quality; it is impossible to find a similar series of glass paintings of the same characteristics, range and vintage to be bought from private sources."[25] There was a three-way bidding contest for the glass between the Fine Art Society, the Saville Gallery, and Mr. Fox of

---

19. In Dr. James's original manuscript Job was changed from "Salomon."

20. HALS, D/Eco/F26, James, op. cit.

21. "Sale of Sixteenth-Century Glass from the Chapel of Ashridge Park, Herts," *British Society of Master Glass-Painters Journal* 2 (October 1928): 210.

22. Douglas Coult, *A Prospect of Ashridge* (Sussex, 1980), p. 215.

23. Ibid., p. 14.

24. "Sale of Sixteenth-Century Glass from the Chapel of Ashridge Park, Herts," p. 210.

25. "Die alten Glasgemalde aus dem Kreuzgang der Abtei Steinfeld."

Messrs Gooden & Fox, who was representing a client. An opening bid of £5,000 was invited but this dropped to £2,000 before the bids began rising by £500 until Mr. Fox secured the windows for his client for £27,000.[26]

The buyer chose to remain anonymous but intimated that the glass would not be leaving England. Shortly after the auction the glass was donated to the Victoria and Albert Museum.[27] It emerged after his death in 1955 that the donor was Ernest Edward Cook, grandson of the travel agent Thomas Cook.[28] The majority of the Ashridge stained glass is still on public display at the Victorian and Albert Museum.

---

26. "Sale of Sixteenth-Century Glass from the Chapel of Ashridge Park, Herts," p. 211.

27. Victoria and Albert Museum, *Review of Principal Acquisitions During the Year 1928*, p. 25.

28. Letter from Victoria and Albert Museum, 19 January 2000.

A Maze of Secrets in a Story by M. R. James

Martin Hughes

In M. R. James's story "Mr. Humphreys and His Inheritance" Mr. Humphreys, the central character, arrives to take over an eighteenth-century estate, whose most prominent feature is a maze. The maze was designed to protect the religious secrets of the man who created it. The painful revelation to Humphreys of these secrets is the theme of the story. The reader encounters another kind of maze, created by the allusions and symbols which James uses: the aim of this paper is to show that, if explored, this maze too contains a message: an interesting one and one written from a philosophically interesting position.

The Interpretation of M. R. James's Stories and of "Mr. Humphreys" in Particular: Some Recent Opinions

How should James's ghost stories be approached? R. W. Pfaff, a recent biographer of James, tells us that "writers on ghost stories . . . fall not so much in praising MRJ's stories too little . . . but in paying little or no attention to the really remarkable thing about them, the brilliance of the antiquarian background" (415). He quotes a colleague of James who remarks that the material of the ghost stories is "suggested by some line of learned research and worked out with minute accuracy of detail, and at the same time with an ease and lightness of touch which can communicate . . . to the . . . reader guiltless of commerce with manuscripts."[1] The antiquarian references in "Mr. Humphreys" bear out the correctness of this comment; they are certainly worked out with minute accuracy of detail. Even without examining these references we can still find a good story, written indeed with a light touch. But by examining them we find not only a good story but also James's reflections on certain esoteric and unorthodox spiritual and theological movements—their roots, their persistence and the dangers inherent in them.

---

1. A. Hamilton Thompson in his biographical note on M. R. James, *Leicestershire Archaeological Society Transactions* 19 (1936–37): 113–17. See Pfaff 323.

Another recent biographer, Michael Cox, warns us against treating the stories as if they were on the highest literary plane and against trying to make them bear an undue weight of speculation. In particular he warns us against "dwelling on them as vehicles of unconscious psychological revelation" (149n). These are wise warnings. The antiquarian style, which gives the stories their special character, also sets firm limits to their scope. It is a style which normally places records and relics, things whose existence the modern world may not notice and whose meaning it cannot easily see, in the foreground of the story: so the things which everyone notices, such as sexual passion and political commitment, are absent from the foreground; and this absence limits the scope of the stories severely and so keeps them from attaining to the highest literary plane. But this is not to say that the stories take a narrow view of human life or are merely escapist. On the contrary, the premiss of antiquarian stories is that records and relics are very important: when properly studied they are extremely revealing of all aspects of life in the past; moreover what they reveal is still important now. Accordingly, antiquarian stories—at least those stories which contain, as "Mr. Humphreys" does, detailed and copious references to people and ideas of the past—are, in a way, puzzles: not puzzles which we solve by finding out what the author thought unconsciously but puzzles which we solve by finding out, through study of the antiquarian clues, what the author consciously intended to convey.

"Mr. Humphreys" conveys some of its author's knowledge not only of esoteric thought but of the ability of the mind to be hooked or fascinated. The idea of finding abandoned traces of the past, relics of strange or dangerous forms of thought, has a certain power to hook the mind. Humphreys is linked to his ancestor because both of them experience this power. James himself had experienced one adolescent episode of unbalanced fascination (Cox 32). This episode did not arise out of his antiquarian interests but from the popular press: he became absurdly fascinated with the events surrounding a royal wedding and with the person of the Queen. This episode does not suggest that James suffered from abnormality of mind, quite the contrary: he was like the millions who respond to the publicity machines of today, finding that the royal family provides a pleasant and (on the whole) harmless focus for sexual feeling. But the experience was no doubt a lesson to James about fascination; he would have understood that the attendant feelings might, in other circumstances, be morbid.

If James learnt something about fascination from his experience, he learnt about esoteric religion from his studies. There is no doubt that James regarded esoteric religion, at least in most of its forms, as unpleasant and dangerous. His stories more than once portray people who make the transition from antiquarian studies to the practice of magic: that is, they use what they learn in an attempt to gain supernatural power for themselves. We should notice that all these portraits are strongly negative,[2] just as we might expect from James's dislike of ghost stories which seemed to give credence to occultism.[3]

Here I refer to Jack Sullivan's comments on the ghost story tradition. His view is that the general effect of ghost stories is to create in the reader's mind the sense that we are not free of menace even when the story is over: "the deadly apparition is still at large" (10). He adds that ghost stories are enigmatic stories, suggesting the presence of a dominant enigma in the whole universe. These are stories, he says, which "relate to an inexplicable, irrational whole" (134). To my mind, James's stories are for the most part designed to have an effect somewhat different from the one Sullivan describes: they aim to make us "pleasantly uncomfortable"[4] rather than seriously alarmed; they are indeed enigmatic, but not quite in Sullivan's sense. The facts that James's deadly apparitions usually influence the world through a fixed point of contact and that the point of contact can sometimes be sealed off negates the idea that the deadly apparition is always still at large. The enigma lies in the problem of understanding the apparition so that we can be careful not to admit it to the world all over again. The antiquarian information plays an ambivalent part: on the one hand, the source of the dangers in which the characters in the stories find themselves; on the other hand, the only available means of understanding those dangers.

James writes disturbing stories but, because his characters sometimes escape the traps he sets for them, he balances fear and hope. I agree with Sullivan, whose analysis of James's style I find very valuable, that the presence of both fear and hope, horror and the avoidance of horror, creates a "unique chill and tension" (71). Tension is conveyed by the fact that, though James's characters sometimes escape from horror by a fortunate turn of events, their good fortune gives us no comforting sense of a watchful providence. Humphreys's stroke of luck is his concussion when the demonic apparition approaches: the idea of divine providence, if we think of it here, turns sour. The suggestion of being saved by concussion is, after all, close to a sarcastic parody of the belief that God sustains and enlightens us. But, for all the hints of pes-

---

2. Cf. "Lost Hearts" and "Casting the Runes." The clerical ghost in "The Tractate Middoth" may not be entirely malevolent but is certainly unpleasant enough to support my point: he has the horrifying face characteristic of James's magicians.

3. Cox 148, referring to the Introduction to *More Ghost Stories*.

4. According to James's stated purpose in the Preface to *Ghost-Stories of an Antiquary*.

simism, the stories are not without hope. The existence of an enigma in Sullivan's sense, "an irrational whole," is hinted at by James but not conceded.

In "Mr. Humphreys" the hint is conveyed by Cooper, Humphreys's bailiff, a vividly realised character with a distinctive way of talking. He is entirely supportive but has no understanding of the problems Humphreys has to face. His final suggestion to Humphreys is placed so as to constitute a kind of concluding observation within the whole series of *More Ghost Stories*: "All these many solemn events have a meaning for us, if our limited intelligence permitted of our disintegrating it." James has Cooper use the word "disintegrate" when you would expect "comprehend" or "understand" and thereby suggests that the rational universe has been shattered, leaving only an enigma which defies understanding. But the suggestion is made in a gentle way by a comic character, indicating that James is not committed to it.

The same suggestion is made more forcibly and grimly in some other stories, such as "Count Magnus" and "The Stalls of Barchester Cathedral,"[5] which I have no space to discuss here. But the fact that these stories are untypically bleak again indicates that the suggestion was not fully accepted in James's mind. The bleaker stories are certainly enough to show that James understood that the Church and the tradition for which it stands sometimes inspire very little confidence. But the general tenor of his stories reflects a mind whose confidence in the Christian tradition was under pressure but had not quite broken. It is philosophically interesting to see how the imagination develops in a mind which has reached this position.[6]

The warning, not merely frightening, quality of James's stories illustrates where he stands. The stories follow those of Le Fanu, James's principal exemplar, by offering vivid glimpses of horrors extremely hard to reconcile with the orthodox idea of a benign God bestowing a rational order on the world. In Le Fanu, these horrors may befall anyone; in James they befall those who invoke them (Sullivan 70, 75): the rest of us are thereby warned.[7] Warning is worth

---

5. In "Count Magnus" the central character is persecuted for reasons which remain enigmatic; he tries to "cry to God" but in vain. "The Stalls of Barchester Cathedral," the story of a murderous Archdeacon, prompts certain cynical reflections on the Church.

6. James's public commitment to the Church of England never wavered (Sullivan 73). Cox records James's pleasure in what was "pedestrian and Anglican and Victorian" (134) and Lytton Strachey's view of James's autobiography as suggesting a vapid, childlike character (220). But it is inconceivable that the real truth about such a lively mind was that it had never grown up or that it was really content with pedestrian forms of thought. His deeper thoughts are in the ghost stories.

7. *A Warning to the Curious* is the title of another of James's collections of ghost

while only if precautions are possible, so only in a world where some signs of rational order are found. But James's warnings contain tensions of their own, helping to keep the stories tense. He uses his antiquarian research to warn us of dangers but these often turn out to be the dangers of antiquarian research: the warning and the danger fuse. Sometimes the only way to prevent the release of demons into the present world is to destroy the very relics of the past on which antiquarian science and its power to warn depend.[8] It may seem surprising that antiquarian stories should sometimes celebrate the obliteration of the relics of the past: but obliteration is only an extreme, dramatic form of the censorship which James himself sometimes applied to aspects of the past which he found unpleasant. The most interesting example of censorship by him comes from his work on Walter Map's *De Nugis Curialium*.[9]

But from the same evidence we see that his attitude to what he found unpleasant was certainly not one of bitter intolerance. Some of *De Nugis* was, he thought, "too odious to translate": hence he resorted to omission and disguise of meaning, itself a way of misrepresenting the facts of the past. But James saw that this practice needed some justification, which he offered in moderate terms: "Map was not a great offender for his age but his public were amused at things which do not amuse us." Cox comments that we should not think of this as showing that James was affected by "'Victorian' prudery": certainly post-Victorian editors share some of James's reticence (Cox 222).[10] Indeed,

---

stories. One story in *More Ghost Stories*, "The Rose Garden," ends on a warning motto: *"Quieta non movere."*

8. Cf. "Canon Alberic's Scrap-book" and "'Oh, Whistle, and I'll Come to You, My Lad'"; also "The Stalls of Barchester Cathedral."

9. Walter Map was a twelfth-century Archdeacon of Welsh origin. James first edited the Latin text of *De Nugis Curialium* (Oxford, 1914) and later produced an English translation (Volume 9 of the Record Series of the Honourable Society of Cymmrodorion, 1923). A new and revised edition, with Latin and English in parallel, was prepared by C. N. L. Brooke and R. A. B. Mynors for the Clarendon Press (Oxford, 1983).

10. It is clear that James treated as "odious" many passages of Map which are explicitly, but only mildly, erotic. But this fact does not show that he was prudish to any special degree. If we look at Map's words in some detail we see, firstly, where James drew the line and, secondly, how Brooke and Mynors, scholars of a later generation, tend in their revised edition to draw the same line in the same place. The methods used by James are disguised translation, complete omission and reproduction in the English text of untranslated Latin. Cox briefly notes these methods and refers us to *De Nugis Curialium* III 2, a story about Galo, a knight who diverts his scheming Queen from her plan to seduce him by planting a story

the tone of James's explanation of his treatment of Map suggests rational thought rather than prudery: thought with two aspects. In the first place he tries to use his antiquarian knowledge, in this case his knowledge of the medieval attitude to obscenity, to excuse Map. To do this he must have studied other examples of medieval obscenity, moved by the enquiring antiquarian spirit which the ghost stories repeatedly ceicbrate (cf. Sullivan 90), for all that it sometimes has bad consequences. In the second place he removes the genuine record of the past because that is the only way to remove something offensive from the world. The same two aspects of James's thought are developed in "Mr. Humphreys," to whose text I now turn.

---

that he has a serious sexual problem: "*cum omnia possit a mulieribus evincere, vacuum se penitus fatetur ab opere.*" James (p. 121) puts this into reticent English—"He could extort every favour from women [but] confesses . . . that he cannot." This is deliberately to make the translation imperfect: something of the tone of the story is lost unless a phrase like "for the job, he is deeply lacking" is used; all the same, James's censored words reappear in the revised edition (p. 215). James now resorts to total omission. The Queen sends one of her servants to check the rumour about Galo: "*docet aditum, quo possit in Galonis amplexus illabi, nudamque se nudo iungere.*" James substitutes dots for this instruction; his revisers are prepared only to advance from omission to disguised translation: they have the woman "insinuate herself into Galo's good graces, with no holds barred," instead of "slip into his embraces, naked woman with naked man." Only once, as far as I can see, does James put untranslated Latin into his English text: this is a joke made by a scurrilous nun in II 17 (p. 91): "*Domnus Cunnanus nihil est nisi cunnus et anus,*" which the revisers also (p. 169) quote but do no translate. It means "Lord Cunnanus is nothing but cunt and anus" and is a play on the Celtic name Conan (see the Introduction to the revised edition, p. xl). This joke is incidental to the story and could easily be omitted by a prudish editor but James did not omit it. Indeed in his Latin edition he accepts the suggestion of the previous editor (Thomas Wright, 1850) that "est" should be introduced editorially, making the phrase into a line of verse. It would be fair to say that, because Map is not really odious or pornographic, James is oversensitive; also fair to say that he shows a dislike of vulgarity which other scholars manifestly share. Moreover, a translator commissioned by the Honourable Society of Cymmrodorion would bear in mind that an important section of his intended readership would be people of a strict nonconformist background, shocked by the least bad language. Hence it would be unfair to say that the attitudes revealed by James's work on Map amount to prudery on James's part. The question of "Victorian prudery" is important because, if we attribute that quality to James, we would feel more justified in regarding him as repressed and accordingly in searching his work for meanings of which he was unconscious: a search for which I have little sympathy.

The First Inscriptions: An Altered Prophecy

On first arrival at the estate designed by his ancestor, Humphreys notices the unfinished appearance of the house. His ancestor had unfinished business, whose nature the story reveals.

On first arrival at the maze, Humphreys finds an inscription written over the gates: "*Secretum meum mihi et filiis domus meae.*" He wonders for a moment what the origin of the words is but the story does not say whether he discovered that it is adapted from the Vulgate version of Isaiah.[11] In all versions of this passage Isaiah hears cries of triumph but, despite the fact that these cries are echoed everywhere, finds that his personal feelings are, for some reason, discordant with the feelings of the majority (Isa. 24:16). In the Vulgate the reason for his trouble is his possession of a secret: "*Secretum meum niihi, secretum meum mihi, uae mihi*"—"My secret is for me, my secret is for me, alas for me!" There is nothing in English translations from the Hebrew (and nothing in the Septuagint) to echo the reference to a secret, so Humphreys was unlikely to think readily of the real origin of these words. Wilson, Humphreys's ancestor who developed the estate, had, in any case, changed his original, so that it now reads, "My secret for myself and the children of my house." Wilson has put new words in place of the lament "*uae mihi*"; the amendment appears to give the prophecy a new and benign form, suggesting that the pain of secrecy can be avoided if the secret is shared within a family or a small group. But if this suggestion turns out to be wrong then the true meaning of the prophecy in its new form must be "My secret for myself and the children of my house—alas for me and for them." If this is the new form of the prophecy it is not benign but more distressing than its original.

The inscription also suggests a theological idea: Isaiah must have kept his secret to himself because he believed it was his duty to God to keep it; so it may be right to keep theological secrets, that is those pertaining to God or to the next world. So the secrets of the maze, which Humphreys is urged to keep, must be of this kind. The idea of secrets which it is God's will we should keep, a foundational idea for those who hold an esoteric religious belief, may develop into the more disturbing idea that God wishes us to keep our own true nature a secret between us and Him. According to this idea we can express our true relationship with God only in secret forms of worship and devotion—these forms others might find repugnant. So the words of the inscription, because they raise this idea, are a warning: the person who en-

---

11. Study of the Latin Bible is much assisted by the remarkably clear *Novae Concordantiae* of B. Fischer (Stuttgart: Fromann-Holboog, 1977).

ters runs a very serious risk, the risk of losing contact with the ordinary understanding of right and wrong.

The warning is apt because the whole idea of secret devotion contrasts
strongly with other ideas which are more popular, for instance with the basic
ideas of the Delphic Oracle, "Know yourself" and "Nothing too much":
these two precepts are linked in a fashion which presupposes that self-
knowledge is linked to self-control, so that we can make our real selves, our
real faces, as acceptable to others in public as they are to ourselves in private. Wilson's other construction, apart from the house and the maze, is a
classical temple,[12] something which suggests sympathy with the Delphic ideal
and whose pleasant appearance, at one or two points of the story, duly gives
Humphreys a false sense of reassurance. The suggestion of sympathy with reassuring forms of paganism must, considering the contents of the maze, be
merely a blind. The blind must mask his rejection of the Delphic idea that
we must make our real face into an acceptable face. Hence the repulsiveness
of his face when it appears.

The idea that God may allow us freely and unashamedly to express in
our secret devotions aspects of our nature which our fellow human beings
would condemn morally if they were expressed in public is even more suspect from an orthodox Christian than from a Delphic point of view. After
all, orthodox Christianity believes that God has publicly decreed a moral law
which we should observe in all aspects of our life. The unpleasant resonance
which surrounded the word "heresy" in former times and surrounds the
words "sect" and "cult" in modern days indicates how strong within Christian ways of thought moral suspicion of unorthodox groups is. If this suspicion is at all justified—and James suggests that it is—we might argue that
those who try to express their true nature under cover of secrecy are in constant moral danger. From this point we might argue, much more intolerantly
and dangerously, that the true nature of such people does not deserve any
expression at all: instead it deserves to be detested and shunned.

But if this line of thought, which is firmly hostile to religious and moral
esotericism, is strongly held by the majority it leads to stern demands for conformity and puts those whose real thoughts make conformity impossible into a
very painful position. Because they cannot conform with real commitment
they have in their minds something like a complex sealed maze, cut off from
the public gaze. Their self-examination becomes painful: if they look into the

---

12. Actually modelled on the Temple of the Sybil at Tivoli. The Sybil did have
connections with the underworld but, even so, was fully acceptable to mainstream paganism, as the Sixth Book of the *Aeneid* shows.

complex maze concealed in their own minds the isolation of their position, cherishing a secret which they cannot discuss, may strike them hard: Isaiah's *"uae mihi"* applies. To relieve their isolation and to hedge themselves against the hostility of the majority they may strive, discreetly but vigorously, to draw a few others into their way of thinking. Thus plain hostility towards sects helps to perpetuate sects: the more people are frightened of speaking openly the more desperately they will try to influence a few others and to do so in secret. In the story, Wilson tries desperately to influence the children of his house.

So the inscription is a warning to the child of the house that, when he enters the maze, he risks the hostility of the rest of the human race: at the same time it is an invitation to enter and therefore the promise of something desirable to be found within, a *secretum* which no longer causes its possessor to cry *"uae mihi."* But Humphreys does not recognise the origin of the inscription and therefore neither recalls the warning implied by *"uae mihi"* nor appreciates that the changed words make him a promise. So he neither thinks how to protect himself nor considers whether the promise is really attractive.

But the reader is in a position to see, even at this stage, one root of esoteric religion: the idea of a secret worth having which, though it might shock the majority, may be kept by its initiates without pain or guilt. This idea implies that the secrecy exists not because the initiates have something to be ashamed of but because the majority is unworthy to know the secret: conventional morality, symbolised by the temple, is inferior to the secret morality symbolised by the maze.

The Second Inscription: An Altered Proverb, Defaced and Restored

Humphreys, the child of the house, never finds any difficulty in getting to the centre of the maze, where he finds the inscribed and engraved copper globe which is part of Wilson's message to him. But the inscriptions on the copper globe were not meant by Wilson to be the next written message received by Humphreys after he had read the first, the altered oracle of Isaiah. He should have read, letter by letter, a message on a series of stones.

The message on the stones has been defaced by an intermediate heir. This was the younger Wilson, the older Wilson's grandson. Cooper tells Humphreys that the younger Wilson was a man of shattered health and spirits—"a valetudinarian"—and that he cherished a deep dislike of his grandfather. He expressed this dislike by destroying his grandfather's papers and by removing the stones, part of the record of his grandfather's unpleasant religion, to another building and keeping them out of order. But he did not destroy the maze. By his time, evidently, mazes were coming to be seen as attractive curiosities and destruction might have led to unwanted local publicity and protest. In recent years the protests would have been led by Lady Wardrop, a forceful personality who intends to serve local conservationist sentiment by writing a guidebook to mazes. Her surprise and regret at the destruction of mazes are exactly the sentiments expressed by a real guidebook, *The Earthworks of England*,[13] published in 1908: "It is marvellous that the memory of such things, once prominent features of rural life can die out so rapidly as it does."

It is Wardrop who eventually explains to Humphreys how to restore the series of stones and so recover the message carved on them. She initially becomes friendly with Humphreys because he gives her access to the maze, something which the younger Wilson had always refused: he kept the maze intact but unexplored. Accordingly, he found himself obeying his hated grandfather's command to keep the *secretum domus meae:* being forced into this position must have contributed to his depressive state. This fact points to the power of secrets, which James would have us notice, to entangle those who would never have wished to create them. The secret destroyed the younger Wilson: this fact shows that events have already given the revised form of Isaiah's words the more ominous of their two possible meanings— "Alas for the children of the house!"

On this showing the older Wilson was an evil man who left a corrupt legacy. Most other details of the story support this negative view of him. His deviousness is manifest in the confusing nature of the maze, which makes it impossible for Humphreys to show ordinary visitors around. His contact with internal powers is shown by the unnatural heat which repels Cooper when he touches the copper globe. The insidious nature of his presence is so borne in on Lady Wardrop that her wish to preserve the maze is quickly and remarkably changed. She soon makes it clear that she would consent to its destruction.

"Wardrop" is an older form of "wardrobe": we are perhaps to imagine her as sturdily built and with a sound, well-stocked mind. But an upper-class Englishwoman's wardrobe is, perhaps, not very receptive to anything which shocks and surprises: neither is Lady Wardrop's mind. She fulfills the role, known elsewhere in James's work, of helper and adviser to the central character. It is often a feature of these secondary characters that they are more robust or resourceful than the central character himself,[14] and this feature

---

13. The author, A. H Allcroft, is cited in W. H. Matthews, *Mazes and Labyrinths* (London: Longmans, 1922), p. 213.

14. Compare the military man in "'Oh, Whistle, and I'll Come to You, My Lad'" and the brother of the former victim who supports Dunning against Karswell in

suggests that the central character, by contrast, has weaknesses which dark forces can exploit. The dark forces find Humphreys's weak point because he becomes fascinated with the secrets of the past incautiously, before he understands their true nature. This must have been the weakness which originally snared the older Wilson when he first investigated the half-forgotten religions of the ancient world. Something of Wilson survives in Humphreys: perhaps his eventual marriage to the niece of the solid and sound Lady Wardrop is a useful correction.

When the inscription on the stones is restored on Wardrop's instructions it does indeed turn out to be rather shocking: it reads "*penetrans ad interiora mortis*"—"pressing on into the inner places of death." Here again the phrase is a slightly amended Biblical quotation, this time from the Book of Proverbs (Prov. 7:27). It is worth looking at the context of this phrase. The author of Proverbs, purportedly King Solomon, warns his young hearer against someone who is called in the King James version "the strange woman" and in the Vulgate "mulier extranea et aliena"—"the foreign, alien woman"—and his warning ends with the words, "*Viae inferi domus eius, penetrantes ad interiora mortis*"—"Her dwellings are paths to hell, leading to the inner places of death." I suggest "pressing on" for Wilson's amended motto partly because it expresses the lonely quality of his determination, a loneliness signified by his use of the singular "*penetrans*" for the plural "*penetrantes*"; he is determined, however much he is alienated from the rest of humanity, to survive even in the inner places of death. Moreover, "pressing on" recalls the sexual meaning of "*penetrans*," a meaning abundantly suggested by its Biblical context. Whether the emphasis of the Hebrew original falls on the woman's sexuality and prostitute trickery or else on her foreignness and pagan sexual freedom (the foreignness seems to be emphasised by the Vulgate's use of two adjectives, "*extranea et aliena*," where the English version uses one, "strange") is disputed among the commentators (cf. McKane 139). Whatever the truth of that dispute we shall see that both an

---

"Casting the Runes." Wilson and Karswell are very similar characters, both having a secret religion and, in due accord with the Le Fanu tradition, a dreadful face. James seems to think that there had been a decline in the standards of esoterics since the eighteenth century in that Wilson was clearly very well educated and Karswell is semi-literate—moreover Karswell, living as the story reminds us in the age of mass advertisement, sometimes ventures out of his secrecy and seclusion in the attempt to give his powerful magic a degree of publicity, both academic and commercial. The presence of effective and helpful secondary characters in James departs from the Le Fanu tradition, where, as Sullivan points out, the victims get no more help from human than from divine sources (43).

interest in forbidden pleasure, born of reaction against puritan preaching, and an interest in ideas alien to his native culture are important aspects of Wilson's personality.

At any rate, reference to the seventh chapter of Proverbs is reference to the kind of sexual freedom which that chapter condemns on behalf of orthodox religion. Wilson must have considered that condemnation from his unorthodox point of view. Just as "Solomon" imputes extreme sexual irresponsibility to those who reject his religion, Wilson would impute extreme sexual repressiveness to those who accept it. So we can note that hope of liberation from irksome sexual restrictions is another root from which esoteric religion can grow. But how could the contrary advice and urgent warnings of orthodox religion be answered? How can the esoterics' claim to moral superiority be sustained? Something of an answer to these questions is conveyed by the inscriptions on the copper globe.

The Globe

The copper globe adds substantially to the message delivered by Wilson to Humphreys. The globe turns out both to be a map of another world and to contain Wilson's ashes. By locating his ashes in a map Wilson indicates the place where he is determined that his spirit will survive. The globe is a parody of a celestial globe. The parody begins by putting Draco, the Serpent, who would be in the northern hemisphere of a celestial globe, around the equator; the pole is occupied by *Princeps Tenebrarum*, the Prince of Darkness. Where Humphreys might have expected Hercules he finds Cain; where he might have expected Ophiuchus, the Serpent-Holder, he finds Chore, plunged into the earth. Chore is presumably Korah (Num. 16),[15] who was swallowed up by the earth for attempting to usurp Aaron's priesthood. The absence of Ophiuchus suggests that there is no one in the world represented by this globe who can restrain the Serpent: and it is a "snaky" tree which is shown holding Absalom by his hair. The globe depicts the underworld not only as a place of dangerous serpents but as a place where there is sometimes darkness—*"umbra mortis"* ("shadow of death") and sometimes fire—*"Vallis Filiorum Hinnom"* ("Gehenna"), the place of unquenched burning. But, despite all their hideous surroundings, Cain and other characters are not extinguished but alive in the world depicted by the globe. Before looking further at the clue provided by Cain, Korah and Absalom we should notice

---

15. The name in the Vulgate is "Core"; there seems to be a pun on the Greek "chora," "earth," perhaps unintentional. James sometimes misspelt names with which he was familiar, for instance that of Judge Jeffreys—cf. Cox 144.

the final character depicted on the globe, the Magus Hostanes, whom Humphreys does not recognise. He is a figure of authority, robed and conversing with demons: in fact, the only figure on the globe whose existence is attested by sources outside the Bible and Christian tradition.

Ancient and medieval references to Hostanes, running with commentary to eighty-nine pages, are collected by Bidez and Cumont (2.266f.), beginning with the notice in the Elder Pliny's *Natural History*, where we read that Hostanes accompanied Xerxes, King of Persia, on his invasion of Greece in 480 B.C. The magus had more success than his king, because, according to Pliny, leading Greek thinkers flocked to talk with him: "he sowed the seeds of his pestilential art, leaving on his way an infected world everywhere he wandered'" (30.8). The second or third century Christian apologist Minucius Felix recognised as Hostanes "the foremost of the Magi both in word and deed," and accepted his belief in "wandering and malevolent demons"[16]—his companions in Wilson's engraving. Wilson evidently knew the byways of ancient literature well enough to encounter the record of Hostanes; but to Humphreys, though he was an educated man and though the record is extensive, the name of Hostanes meant nothing. By his time, education concentrated on the central, most rational exponents of ancient culture: the eccentrics and outsiders of the ancient world were being forgotten and thus the rank growths started by Hostanes were at last enfeebled.

James presents the dank, overgrown maze as the place where Hostanes' name is preserved: in doing this he was surely thinking of Pliny's testimony and of his reference to the evil seed and the infected ground—also of the bad reputation in the Roman world of the yew trees of which the maze is formed.[17] The dense, obstructive vegetation of the maze—which Humphreys tries in vain to clear for the benefit of visitors—represents the power of some unpleasant ideas to detain and entangle our minds. Humphreys's more modern education is one of the causes which frustrate Wilson's effort to create "a

---

16. Minucius Felix, *Octavius* 26. This work, all that survives of its author, is translated in the *Ante-Nicene Christian Library* (Edinburgh, 1869), Vol. 13. M. Sage in *Cyprian* (Philadelphia, 1975), pp. 47f., argues that *Octavius* was written between C.E. 197 and C.E. 250.

17. Virgil (*Georgics* 2.257) refers to yews as noxious—"*taxi nocentes.*" That to the Romans the yew was "*ein dämonischer, den Todesgöttern geweihter Baum*" is confirmed in F. Bömer's comments on Ovid's *Metamorphoses* 4.432 (Heidelberg: Carl Winter, 1976). Wilson would have been familiar with the Italian term "*albero della morte*" for yew. But we can see from Matthews (115 and 140) that there are both practical and aesthetic reasons for the use of yew (*taxus baccata*) in mazes.

secret for the children of my house": after a few generations, the secret could hardly be understood. But the evil seed has, for all that, much power. This power is marked by the fact that when Humphreys becomes aware of something malevolent advancing to meet him he sees it as the offspring of evil seed, that is as trees and bushes which contain a hostile presence.[18]

The combination of figures on the globe goes a long way towards explaining Wilson's theology. Cain was the hero of a minute Gnostic sect, the Cainites, denounced by Irenaeus.[19] It seems to have been the theory of the Cainites that the Old Testament was an arcane text, revealing between the lines that the world was temporarily not in the hands of the true God but of a witch (called Hystera—"the Womb") who pretended to be God and whose demand for blood sacrifices was, presumably, the undeserved downfall of Cain, who had at first, unlike his brother Abel, attempted to advance civilisation by tilling the land and by offering a sacrifice which contained no blood. Other losers in the struggles recorded by the Old Testament, such as Korah and Absalom, were regarded by the Cainites as heroes or victims, not as evildoers justly punished. Anyone who wished to take the Cainites' part could argue that Absalom was the victim of treachery and that Korah's claim that "all the people are holy" (Num. 16:3) is morally superior to the exclusivism of Aaron—that is to say, could argue that a morally sensitive reading exposes the arcane message.

The Magi, whom Hostanes represents, were not so interested in interpreting the Old Testament but their ideas bore comparison to those of the Cainites at two points. First, the idea of pretended Gods, that is malevolent demons who would appear to *nescii*, those not skilled in magic, and offer them false guidance, was an idea stressed by the Magi to reveal their own usefulness to the human race. James writes with some irony here. The Magi claimed to be helpful to the *nescii*: after all they knew about demons. But James shows their foremost representative, Hostanes, as a netherworld figure and companion of demons: this suggests that the science of the Magi was not a help but a threat. Can the same suggestion be made about his own antiquarian science which often, in the stories, plays a dangerous part? The point is gently made at the end of the story, where we discover that the evil magician and the author who imagined him have a common name: he is James Wilson.

---

18. Sinister Irish yew trees appear both in "Mr. Humphreys" and in "A School Story," where the murderer, a teacher of classics, sees fit to dispose of his victim among the yews, the trees of death, only to find that the victim is less dead than he would have liked. Other oppressive foliage appears in "The Rose Garden."

19. Irenaeus, *Adversus Haereses*, Book 1, chapter 31, to be found in the *Ante-Nicene Christian Library* (Edinburgh, 1868), Vol. 5, p. 113.

We also find within the religion of the Magi the idea that God does not demand blood sacrifice and that demons do demand it:[20] an idea which might be used both to unmask the deceitful demons and to confirm the Cainites' view of the Old Testament God.

Wilson's choice of figures for the globe which contained his ashes demonstrates that his theology was formed by the intersection of Cainism and Magianism. Hence he would have believed that he was morally superior to the bloodthirsty witch who pretends to be God and that he had wisdom and strength enough both to expose her deceptions and to survive her revenge. What is the way to that wisdom? The answer to this question must be part of the secret left to the children of his house. Since it is a secret it must be revealed discreetly, and since it is for the children of the house it is fitting that the key to the secret be within the house.

Before turning to the house and its library, note how a third root of esoteric religion has been suggested by the inscriptions on the infernal globe: that root is fascination, clearly felt by Wilson, with the hidden face of the past, the face which modern education may increasingly obscure. This fascination—certainly shared by James, the great student of apocrypha—cannot be wholly wrong: in so far as it expresses the rational desire not to let the prejudices of the present distort the past it is laudable. But it becomes wrong if it encourages us to revive and take seriously the illusions and moral excesses of previous generations.

At the same time the theology implied by the inscriptions on the globe shows how esoteric religion tries to overcome the problem mentioned above in connection with its second root. Faced with the urgent moral advice of orthodox religion, it replies with claims to moral superiority in spite of appearances. Orthodoxy, it says, is a systematic misunderstanding of God; moreover, if we read the sacred texts in a morally sensitive way, we will see through the misunderstanding. Faced with the threats of orthodox religion, even with the threat of death, it replies that these threats come not from the true ruler of the universe but from usurping powers and therefore can be endured: Wilson grimly claims that he can endure even the inner places of death. These replies show us how esoteric religion is an act of personal will: a determination not to accept objections which everyone else finds insurmountable. We may find this grossly irrational but we should note that, in comparison with orthodox ways of thought, esoteric religion expresses per-

---

20. The attribution of this idea to the Magi is not beyond question but is convincingly supported by F. Cumont, *The Oriental Religions in Roman Paganism* (Chicago, 1911), p. 268.

sonal autonomy. We may think that the word "ingenious," if applied to those who read the Bible as an arcane text, is too flattering: but at any rate they show a certain agility and resourcefulness of mind beside which orthodox minds may seem ponderous.

The Sermon on Pleasure and Death

The setting of the story alternates between the garden and the house, especially Wilson's library. Humphreys begins his survey of the library by reflecting on how unreadable many old books now are. The only named book which he thinks might be readable is Picart's *Religious Ceremonies*, a book whose possession hints discreetly at the owner's unorthodoxy, more plainly at his interest in religious ideas which belong outside his native culture.[21] But looking at the books and pamphlets he initially thinks unreadable,[22] he comes upon one, an old sermon called *A Parable of this Unhappy Condition*, which he finds himself reading with interest.[23]

A Parable is the centrepiece of "Mr. Humphreys" because it is a story in itself, beautifully elaborated—"one of Monty's best parodies, his pseudo-seventeenth-century meditation on mazes" (Cox 143). Note that it reflects the spiritual climate of the seventeenth century, even though it is found in an eighteenth-century library. Literary reflections on mazes were not uncommon: Matthews collected examples, some puritanically gloomy, going

---

21. Information about Bernard Picart (1673–1733) may be found in several works of reference. The *Biographie Universelle* (inspired by L.-G. Michaud and completed in Paris in 1854) takes a rather dim view of Picart; a more favourable view is found in E. and E. Haag, *La France Protestante* (Geneva, 1966) and in Roth and Wigoder's *Encyclopaedia Judaica* (Jerusalem, 1972). Picart was a great engraver and his principal work was entitled *Cérémonies et coûtumes religieuses de tous les peuples du monde*, whose six-volume English edition appeared in 1733. His work was continued by others after his death; these others wrote about religion in a more and more sceptical and scathing manner.

22. The two supposedly unreadable authors mentioned are the fifteenth century Bishop Tostado of Avila and the sixteenth century Jesuit Pineda. Tostado was at one stage forced to retract heretical opinions and Pineda, represented in the Library by his commentary on Job, also wrote *De rebus Salamonis*—"*curieux et savant*" according to the *Biographie Universelle*: Solomon has, of course, an important place in the occult tradition. Tostado and Pineda are mentioned in the *New Catholic Encyclopaedia*.

23. The sequence is: discovery of the globe, reading of the sermon, examination of the globe.

274   WARNINGS TO THE CURIOUS

back to 1496 (193–99). A *Parable* is a reflection on what we might call the logic of mazes. Mazes are structures which are inviting but also threatening: the threat is that we may get lost (with unforeseeable consequences) but the maze is none the less inviting because it will (for some reason—we may not clearly see what the reason is) be satisfying to get to the structure's heart. The sermon represents the view, quite contrary to Wilson's, that the inescapable threat far outweighs the uncertain promise. Its author correctly perceives that the maze is a model for the world as puritans see it, full of dangers. So the emotion with which he surrounds his story is fear of unknown hazards and the title states his overriding conviction, which is that this life is an unhappy condition.

The sermon refuses to be part of Humphreys's plan for a catalogue of the library:[24] when he has read it once, he can never find it again. The preacher's parable—James captures an antique style in an astonishingly convincing way—concerns a man who enters a maze and there finds a jewel of great price, just as Humphreys had found the copper globe. The man in the parable escapes with the jewel but is subject, after nightfall, to certain terrors, especially to the sense of pursuers who never quite face or catch up with him but always stop when he stops, always move when he moves. The biblical reference to the night as the time "when all the beasts of the forest do move" (Ps. 104 [Vulgate]:20) is used to remarkable effect, creating a compelling picture of fear. The preacher claims that the jewel corresponds to the pleasures of this world and the terrors to the price which we must pay for seeking those pleasures.

The fact that the sermon vanishes when the relics of Wilson's strange religion are destroyed indicates that it has a connection with him, though it is wholly orthodox and therefore survived the younger Wilson's censorship. Old Wilson, the eighteenth-century heretic, cannot have agreed with seventeenth-century Puritanism, though it must have influenced his upbringing: so his connection with the sermon must lie in the fact that the puritan spirit was the genesis of his unorthodoxy. He attempted to escape from it and this attempt was understandable because it was a religion dominated by intense fear of the pleasures of life: not that this justifies his choice of an escape route which has the opposite fault, spiritual recklessness marked by the readiness to venture *ad interiora mortis*.

---

24. Humphreys is like Wilson in many ways: both can be fascinated with strange relics of the past. But Wilson unreservedly guards his secrets: Humphreys, at least initially, wants not only to examine the contents of the house but to publish what he finds and also to collaborate with Lady Wardrop's plans for a guidebook, describing the maze to the general public.

But a chink of sympathy for Wilson is opened up and can be closed only if we agree with the sermon that life here on earth is, inescapably and by the set providence of God, an unhappy condition. James would not have expected such agreement from twentieth-century readers; nor do his stories, which suggest that demonic dangers can often be overcome, urge his readers to abandon their comparatively confident view in favour of the old puritan fears. To James personally the evangelical religion, which is the descendant of Puritanism, had become somewhat alien (Cox 72).

The preacher, who speaks for orthodox Christianity, would have it that the precious object found in the maze is mere transitory pleasure, bought at a terrible price, and that the maze should, accordingly, be shunned. But precious, hidden objects may symbolise arcane knowledge;[25] and what Humphreys found in the maze was not in itself sensuously pleasant but rather a reminder of Wilson's religious beliefs and ethics. The foundation of Wilson's ethics must be the rejection of the preacher's doctrine that total commitment to pleasure brings only death and is therefore to be shunned. This doctrine is powerful and may be salutary, instilling a prudent fear. But it is also dangerous: it may actually lead us to embrace what we fear.

The power inherent in this doctrine is manifest whenever the human race faces certain moral predicaments: the association between pleasure and death seems to lie in the human mind waiting to be invoked. The predicament faced by "Solomon" was created by the departure of young people from traditional morality, something which he pictured as seduction by a strange woman. This problem for ever takes new forms. We find one contemporary form if we consider the warnings produced by the British Government when it undertook to inform us about AIDS. The first series of television warnings used pictures of bleak gravestones and the sound of the *Dies Irae*. A later series showed a seductive woman and the message was that, though she was outwardly beautiful, she carried death in the inner places of her body. This modern television icon, whom we might call the casual partner, corresponds remarkably to the word-painted icon whom the Book of Proverbs calls "the strange woman." If television advertisements used Latin mottos then *"penetrans ad interiora mortis"* would have been highly apt, with the puritan meaning that in the search of sexual pleasure we find only death. The sermon left by Wilson for Humphreys could reasonably be taken as a commentary on Solomon's warning phrase.

---

25. An ancient example of this imagery is provided by the Gnostic Acts of Thomas, which contains a long passage named by modern scholars "the Hymn of the Pearl": cf. B. Layton, *The Gnostic Scriptures* (London: SPCK, 1987), pp. 366–75.

But the danger inherent in the doctrine and in all the dramatic warnings which the doctrine inspires is that the warnings may increase our fascination with the dangerous thing. This is what happens to Humphreys: the reading of the sermon seems only to increase the interest he feels in the maze and in the secrets associated with it. Therefore he is drawn towards Wilson, who stands for a secret ethic in which the preacher's doctrines and warnings are all discarded. The result, of course, is fascination in Humphreys's mind which leads to the climactic scene and to the encounter with Wilson: though whether Humphreys meets Wilson in reality or in his overwrought imagination we cannot be quite sure. Wilson struggles "like a wasp from a rotten apple" out of a black hole which appears in Humphreys's plan of the maze, a hole which both repels and fascinates Humphreys and which turns out to be a gateway to hell. When Wilson, with his face repulsively burnt in the unquenched fire, tries to seize him, Humphreys falls back and is concussed. When he returns to consciousness he acts drastically to break his link with Wilson. He destroys the globe and grubs up the maze.

In the encounter scene, the sexual symbolism of forbidden depths is vigorously used. Wilson's attempted contact with Humphreys is a kind of embrace and arouses Humphreys's strongest spasm of disgust. But it is obvious from the narrative of the encounter that fascination as well as repulsion is present in Humphreys's mind. The existence of fascination is all the more emphasised if we read the encounter not as a real event but as the product of Humphreys's imagination, unable until the last minute to tear itself away from Wilson and the mysterious theology for which Wilson stands.

The story encourages us to share Humphreys's disgust because of the loathsome nature of Wilson's appearance. Does it encourage us to approve his decision to destroy the maze? The acceptance of the decision by Lady Wardrop shows that it reflects orthodox thinking. But orthodox thinking may be too ready to overlook the more unpleasant aspects of human history and to substitute a bland fiction for the truth. Moreover, if something unpleasant and hitherto secret is, like the maze, obliterated from the record by conscious decision, then those who take the decision find they still have a secret: they know something which the record does not show. Humphreys's entanglement in secrecy is not entirely ended, though the secret has taken a new form.

Still, the lightening of the atmosphere at the end of the story makes it clear that Humphreys did the right thing: he had, in all the circumstances, to take drastic action against the inheritance he received from Wilson. I mentioned above that other ghost stories, as well as the translation of Walter Map, show that the decision to rewrite or censor the record of history was, in James's opinion, sometimes inevitable; but also that this option has another and more positive aspect. It is not an opinion which springs from any bitter form of intolerance or disgust: these would be alien to the antiquarian temper, whose purpose is to discover the past in a spirit which is objective and free of distorting emotion. And if we are not to be bitter towards what we condemn we have to seek some understanding of it. This dual view is developed through the warning aspect of James's stories, including "Mr. Humphreys."

New Dangers

Wilson's claim to our understanding lies in the fact that his strange and reckless form of religion was a reaction against the fear-laden and oppressive religion of the puritans. Humphreys can claim that he was rightly afraid of the dangerous, demon-releasing relics which he inherited from Wilson. But the danger is that an excessively fear-laden reaction to strange ways of thought merely turns the cycle again, causing yet another reaction against an orthodoxy which has become cautious and joyless. Did Humphreys do the right thing but under the spur of an excessive fear?

The story suggests that Humphreys's specific fears of Wilson and Wilson's influence, the fears which led him to grub up the maze, were indeed exaggerated; but there is a sting in the tail of this suggestion. We need not really be afraid of those forms of esoteric religion which cannot survive except in conditions which were possible only in the past; Wilson's religion was one of those forms. The car which brings Lady Wardrop (and brings her from a residence named Bentley!) is not just a sign of her modernity but also a sign that the reclusiveness and isolation of the Wilson demesne is less and less possible; that spiritual experiments cannot be conducted in the twentieth century behind screens made in the eighteenth. This point is reemphasised by Wardrop's observation that very few mazes are left. Moreover, Wilson's arrogant attempt to rewrite Isaiah's prophecy has led only to the fulfilment of the prophecy in the bleakest possible way: not only the founder of the secret but also the children of his house have been severely troubled. The words of scripture stand; the esoteric variant vanishes.

The sting in the tail arises because these considerations are not wholly comforting: therefore there was at least some justification for Humphreys's fears. Specific forms of esoteric thought do indeed come and go. But desire for secrecy, impatience with sexual restriction and fascination with what is strange, the roots from which these changing forms grow, still survive. The story, if I have interpreted it correctly, reminds us that these roots spread wide and deep in human nature; that the esoterics appeal to our natural desire for a truly personal, autonomously chosen belief or way of life; that the agility of mind which supports strange beliefs will always find admirers. So the fact that the words of scripture concerning secrecy and secret beliefs have not been discredited and that efforts to modify them have been in vain is not a fact which provides reassurance to the modern world. As ever, the words convey a warning. That this warning still matters is the message at the centre of James's maze of allusions.

Warnings have a dual nature: in the first place they cause fear, in this case fear of secret experiments which go too far; in the second place they call for understanding of what we fear. Someone in James's philosophical position is able, for all that he has not abandoned orthodoxy, to see the side of orthodoxy which inspires least confidence: accordingly he is well-placed to understand the perennial, therefore modern, attractiveness of rival, heretical ways of thought. Warning stories are the natural imaginative product of a mind which is aware of an attraction which it does not, in the end, follow. "Mr. Humphreys" is a warning story springing from this understanding. The story is written in the antiquarian manner and so makes no specific predictions of how twentieth-century technology, which it glimpses, will deliver its impact on moral and spiritual life. The story does not foresee the specific spiritual climate of our time, the age of contraception—hence of freer experiment in sexual relationships—and of mind-bending drugs, whereby people experiment on themselves. But it does, through its contrast between the heretic Wilson and the orthodox preacher, help us to see why some people are driven to secretive spiritual experiment, into which others are then drawn by fascination: alas for them and for us.

Works Cited

Bidez, J., and F. Cumont. *Les Mages Hellénisés*. Paris, 1938.

Cox, Michael. *M. R. James: An Informal Portrait*. London: Oxford University Press, 1983.

James, M. R. "Mr. Humphreys and His Inheritance." *More Ghost Stories of an Antiquary*. London: Edward Arnold, 1911.

McKane, W. *Proverbs*. London: SPCK, 1970.

Pfaff, Richard William. *Montague Rhodes James*. London: Scolar Press, 1980.

Sullivan, Jack. *Elegant Nightmares: The English Ghost Story from Le Fanu to Blackwood*. Athens: Ohio University Press, 1978.

I am indebted to my colleague Dr. P. J. Fitzpatrick for the benefit of his extensive antiquarian knowledge and for advice on many other aspects of this paper.

Thin Ghosts: Notes toward a Jamesian Rhetoric

Jim Rockhill

Although considerable attention has been devoted to exploring the use of history, folklore, and the arts in M. R. James's ghost stories, the skill with which the author has crafted his tales to deliver a shiver to their reader rather than dry acceptance of scholarship masquerading as fiction has been taken for granted by a majority of those analyzing his work. Among the few critical studies which have yielded insights into James's fiction by calling attention to techniques employed by its author in arriving at his effects, the most illuminating have been the chapter on James in Peter Penzoldt's *The Supernatural in Fiction* (Penzoldt's careful delineation of how James's method produces subtler and more powerful effects than demonstrated by most of the practitioners of "The Pure Tale of Terror" having appeared in an earlier chapter of the same book), and Jack Sullivan's "The Antiquarian Ghost Story: Montague Rhodes James" in *Elegant Nightmares*. To these should be added a recent book devoted not to James but his literary mentor, Joseph Sheridan Le Fanu; because many of the rhetorical devices identified by Victor Sage in *Le Fanu's Gothic: The Rhetoric of Darkness* are equally apparent in the work of Le Fanu's disciple. All these studies are valuable as a foundation for further examination of James's work, but they have not brought to light the full range of Jamesian rhetoric or the richness lent to his fiction by its author's artful deployment of these resources. The purpose of this study, therefore, is to demonstrate how these devices and others operate to propel the narrative, heighten atmosphere, and enhance tension within a single tale.

Since many of James's detractors and supporters alike would have it that there is little of substance behind these cunningly wrought fictions beyond the simple desire to elicit a pleasurable shudder from an attentive audience, it is perhaps best to deal with that objection before proceeding with an analysis, which may otherwise be deemed an expense of spirit in a waste of time. The author, in the donnish self-deprecatory mode he assumed whenever called upon to discuss the merits of his own fiction, would be the last person to claim that his work plumbs either spiritual or psychological depths. By all accounts, he was reasonably comfortable with his faith, the society in which he lived and his position in it. The depth in James's fiction lies not in the characters or their relationship with this world, but in the structure and interaction of the supernatural events themselves. One always gets the sense in James's tales that another world lies just out of sight, long existent, impinging upon our own through ties of history and folklore, patiently waiting for someone careless enough to trip the catch or neglect the latch hitherto responsible for preventing the intrusion of an earlier, under-civilized, under-educated, irrational, and often bestial mode of existence long-since buried and forgotten under the urbane veneer of contemporary society. James's oases are simply larger and easier to escape to than either Le Fanu's or Lovecraft's, in which that other world not only impinges upon but frequently saturates our own. Unlike the run of ghost stories in which one's willing suspension of disbelief begins to unravel once one examines the manifestations or what brought them into existence, the more one studies the phenomena behind James's tales (as proven amply by Rosemary Pardoe, Michael Cox, Jacqueline Simpson, and sundry others), the more interesting they become: the supernatural world at which the tales hint is vast, elaborate, and inscrutable even to those who, like James's scholars, are best equipped to understand it.

To dismiss these works as shallow, dispensable trifles with no more to recommend them than their author's "preoccupation—bordering upon obsession—with technique" (Joshi 142), not only reflects an inaccurate assessment of the world James depicts, it also underestimates the role rhetoric has played throughout history in transmuting even the most familiar themes into literature. Not unlike the scores of poets who wrote on the *carpe diem* theme throughout the past several centuries, James is as intent on the sound, shape, texture, and tread of his stories as he is on their substance. Even though his subject matter only rarely deviates from "what oft was thought" (as Alexander Pope has so memorably phrased it), James's artistry ensures that the details are consistently fresh, the pace carefully gauged, and the structure so ingeniously varied that he repeatedly delivers what had been "ne'er so well expressed" within supernatural literature. If, according to Robert Aickman's assertion, "The true ghost story is akin to poetry" (Aickman 65), James's ability to craft enduringly entertaining fiction from the hoariest of themes, while making intricate use of a variety of rhetorical devices earns him a place among the supreme poet-craftsmen of the genre.

*　　*　　*　　*　　*

"The Residence at Whitminster" has been little discussed or appreciated since its first appearance as one of three new tales added to make up the contents of James's third collection, *A Thin Ghost and Others* (1919). Its elaborate plot involving multiple linked supernatural phenomena lacks not only the fascination of that cryptic exercise in compression, "Two Doctors," but also the directness of its other companions in the volume—"The Diary of Mr. Poynter," "An Episode of Cathedral History," or "The Story of a Disappearance and an Appearance," Nonetheless, the story has long been a favorite of mine and repays close reading. It is virtually a novel in miniature, encapsulating the importation of witchcraft and necromancy from Ireland, two tragedies occurring in one century that have repercussions in the next, a haunting attended by multiple phenomena, a variety of narrators each given an individual voice, and even imbedded oral ghost story. It may not be as perfectly constructed as the earlier tales, because toward the end of the story, James's love of mimicry leads him to expand upon one narrator's penchant for strict and unimaginative accuracy to the point of dryness, then inserts a comic episode involving a garrulous and befuddled rustic housekeeper, which threatens to burst the tale at its seams. Otherwise, James has constructed this story with great care, using a variety of devices and shifting viewpoints to drive his narrative.

The tale's opening paragraphs establish a mode of viewing the action from the outside in and the inside out, which the author will repeat with varying emphases and levels of intensity throughout the story. In the first paragraph, James offers the reader, or "superficial observer" as he calls him, a silent view into the room of Dr. Thomas Ashton, Doctor of Divinity, in the year 1730, the month of December, past three in the afternoon. This is an oddly impersonal view full of incidental detail, yet so precariously balanced between the distant era and the voyeuristic viewpoint that it results in a curious sensation of being simultaneously drawn in and held back. This sensation is modified only slightly in the less objective second paragraph, in which the reader now shares Doctor Ashton's view out of the room. Here James establishes distancing devices based on time, place, inside and outside, only to soften them and draw the reader into the world of his characters, just as later in the tale, similar instances of dumb-show will not only draw the viewer into another world or another time, but also draw presences from the viewed, supernatural world into the viewer's own.

After these initial paragraphs of precisely the same length, James banishes this preliminary dumb-show with the introduction of sound in the short third paragraph, followed by the first of several paragraphs in this tale, which convey tension through the incorporation of dialogue. Although the recently

282 WARNINGS TO THE CURIOUS

introduced element of sound establishes itself not only through this dialogue and a recurrent reference to bells, this fourth paragraph also bears elements of the tale's exposition. Someone in the house is extremely ill, and bells must be quieted so as not to disturb him and hasten his death.

At this point, James inserts another short paragraph informing the reader that he had opened the tale *in medias res*, and leading the reader even further back in time.

The sixth paragraph quickly establishes the background and other details about the building in which most of the tale's events will take place, and James follows this with a paragraph offering a brief history of the building's occupants. The person said to be mortally ill in the fourth paragraph turns out to be Dr. Ashton's young adopted son, and his companion is the teenaged son of a selfish Irish lord. James spares no time making it clear that Dr. Ashton had accepted the guardianship of this teenager, Lord Saul, in hopes of preferment and the disposal of the young man's considerable annual allowance, despite early rumors that the young lord was "possess'd," spent too much time "moping about raths and graveyards," and was in the habit of frightening the "servants out of their wits."

Confirmation of some of these early suspicions concerning the young man's uncanniness occurs when by touching a horse, Lord Saul nearly upsets the chaise in which he arrived, throwing the postilion and injuring the foot of a servant. In this eighth paragraph, as in nearly every other scene in which he appears, Lord Saul responds to any "accident and commotion calmly enough," which does not occasion harm or inconvenience to himself, and maintains a "smooth and pleasant" voice. This smooth and pleasant voice translates into a ready charm in the next paragraph, where the servants are "almost falling over each other in their efforts to oblige him," despite the resumption of his rambles in the graveyard and a brief hint that no young woman will remain in the house with him. Jack Sullivan has written of such reticence:

> The narrators seem determined to maintain good manners, even when presenting material they know to be in irredeemably bad taste. Alternating between casualness and stiffness, chattiness and pedantry, James's narrators maintain an almost pathological distance from the horrors they recount. This contradiction between scholarly reticence and fiendish perversity becomes the authenticating mark of the antiquarian ghost story. (Sullivan 82)

In this case, however, this reticence has already been grounded not only by what one can assume to be the expected behavior of an eighteenth-century churchman, but by the self-interest James had already imputed to Dr. Ashton: the good doctor is hardly in a position where thinking the worst of a young man whose presence brings 200 guineas into the household annually, and whose father's gratitude might lead to an Irish bishopric, would benefit him or the rest of his family. As in the story's several scenes in dumb-show, Dr. Ashton may be assumed to view and even record Lord Saul's behavior without the ability, or inclination, of fully understanding what he has seen.

That the narrative is based on Dr. Ashton's own account, James makes clear in the tenth paragraph, a particularly fussy specimen of attestation, which specifies the sources used, apologizes for them not being "sharper and more detailed" until crises attendant upon "the final incident" in the doctor's household, and yet insists that "there is no need to doubt that the writer could remember the course of things accurately." This stress on attestation is one of the devices James shares with Le Fanu:

> I'm particularly concerned with the development of witnessing in his narrative techniques, and the game with authority, the epistemology of reading; because it is simultaneously religious and secular. Le Fanu quite consciously contrived an overdetermined 'equilibrium of explanation' for the events in his narratives. . . . [T]he notion of testimony is framed as an antiquarian and anthropological necessity. . . . But the stress on "evidence" has a particular relationship to the cultural narrative of the Gothic . . . (Sage, *Le Fanu's Gothic* 6)

If the Gothic novel is seen by Sage as largely based on a Protestant reaction against what it perceived as an irrational and arbitrary set of mythologies promoted with unswerving ferocity by the Catholic church, attestation in the Protestant world becomes both a secular tool and a sacred one— secular in its separation of what is known by faith from what is proven by science, and sacred in distinguishing faiths based on doctrine handed down by the religious hierarchy from those based on the individual's access to written proofs and the testimony of credible eye-witnesses, i.e. Scripture. Le Fanu and James are both singularly adept at simultaneously inviting doubt in the outrageous events they describe and supplying evidence that makes the "loophole for a natural explanation" for these events "so narrow as not to be quite practicable" (James, "Introduction" 248), a method that undermines post-Reformation contempt for naïve faith in the supernatural by satisfying the intellect's demand for authentication. James further blurs the line between secular belief in attested fact and religious belief in a supernatural world by linking aspects of his prodigies to characters and quotations from the Bible.

The eleventh paragraph acts as a critical nexus in the tale; referring back to the tale's beginning by offering two new crisscrossing instances of looking outward and inward (which will be echoed and clarified toward the end of the story); revelation of even more odd behavior from Lord Saul, including wrathful indifference toward the welfare of his younger companion Frank, and yet another example of dumb-show. The paragraph also offers a good example of dramatic irony, with Dr. Ashton's frequent jesting remarks concerning his wife's pure black cockerel "making a suitable sacrifice to Aesculapius" being not only very close to the mark, as confirmed by the evidence of burnt feathers brought in by Lord Saul, but possibly also at least partially responsible for putting the idea in the boys' heads in the first place.

The chiasmic effect produced by superimposed views looking outward and inward in this paragraph begins with Dr. Ashton "looking out of an upper window" at the two boys playing . . . at a game he did not understand." He is separated from the boys by the glass of the window, the distance to the garden, and his inability to hear what they are saying, just as the reader is further separated from all of them by the remote time period established at the tale's beginning and this additional layer of flashback. While the doctor looks out through his window, Frank is looking "at something in the palm of his hand," something "glittering" (revealed to be a scrying glass later in the tale), and as he looks into this glass, the placement of Lord Saul's hand on his head causes Frank to instantly drop the object and clap "his hands to his eyes." Only Dr. Ashton's rap at the window keeps Lord Saul from abandoning his companion in a huddled condition on the grass, and with this rap at the window, Lord Saul looks up "as if in alarm." There may seem to be only two lines of sight here—Dr. Ashton looking out of the window and Frank looking into the glittering object—however, it is more than likely, supported by the explanation he was so ready to give concerning the way he and Frank had behaved in the garden that Lord Saul looked in to the window at Dr. Ashton observing him, just as it is tempting to believe that once Lord Saul placed his hand on Frank's head whatever was in the glass was conscious of his presence and able to look out at him; hence the appearance in the twelfth paragraph of creatures invisible to Mrs. Ashton which Frank incessantly begs her, "Keep them off! Keep them off!" Thus the X formed by one person looking out of the window, another person looking into the glass, some thing looking out of the glass, and another thing—the reputedly "possess'd" Lord Saul, smiling that same night at the feverish state into which he had put his companion—looking into the window.

With the thirteenth paragraph, James returns the reader to the time and place of the tale's opening, leading to another of the lengthy paragraphs in this story into which he has imbedded a tense dialogue, this time between Dr. Ashton and Lord Saul. Dr. Ashton's willingness to believe everything the young man tells him, and his ability to ignore or downplay troubling details such as Lord Saul's reference to second sight and his evident anger when asked to explain why he had laid his hand on Frank's head, has diminished only fractionally; because he cannot understand Lord Saul's motive in harming Frank, he bring himself to censure him in only the mildest and vaguest terms: "I am willing to believe you had no bad intention, as assuredly you could have no reason to bear the boy malice: but I cannot wholly free you from blame in the affair." There is a callousness and stupidity to the comments he makes when his wife enters to tell him Frank is dying— "Going? Frank? Is it possible? Already?"—which suggests, that, even though he has just told Lord Saul the seriousness of Frank's condition, he may have already begun to convince himself this unpleasantness too had never happened. It is all Saul can do to contain his mirth.

Despite spending time in the first two paragraphs of this tale describing Dr. Ashton, his dress, and his surroundings, James began paring his narrative of inessential detail in the interest of preventing unnecessary delays in the plot as soon as the exposition began in paragraph four, even going so far as to admit, "though I have made some attempt at indicating the doctor's costume, I will not enterprise that of his wife." Faced with the first of two grave tragedies punctuating the first portion of this narrative, James opts out of writing the kind of long, dramatic, sentimental deathbed scene traditional at this point, and admits to another act of compression in paragraph fifteen: "I have no inclination to imagine the last scene in detail." Sullivan's assessment of this aspect of James's art is characteristically lucid:

> Compared to the stateliness of Le Fanu's prose, James's seems spare and unadorned. Tense and controlled, his stories give the sense of a ruthless paring down of incidents and characters, a constant editing out of anything which might clutter up the supernatural experience or the antiquarian setting. . . . Assuming the reader knows the basics, James is ever-anxious to move ahead toward his own variations. (Sullivan 77)

As a result of this compression, the few statements James delivers from the dying, but now lucid Frank register with all the more power, cryptic as they may seem to the reader at this point in the story. In a few short sentences couched in simple language: he apologizes for his part in killing his aunt's black cockerel; states that he is now free of whatever had pursued him, though the effort has cost him his life; and in the warnings he relays to Lord Saul implies that the lord will never again find warmth and that whatever had just lost scent of the boy might recoil upon his older companion.

Two paragraphs follow, which have a peculiar relationship to each other and the rest of the story. The first, seemingly straightforward, deals with Dr. Ashton's thoughts following the death of his nephew, and the beginning of a vague suspicion that Frank's death and that of the black cockerel may have had something to do with witchcraft. Paradoxically, James opens the second of these paragraphs with the statement, "I rather guess these thoughts of his than find written authority for them," a very odd statement from a writer as careful about attestation in his fiction as James. The obvious reason for this admission of speculation in the absence of documentation is that since the thoughts of a man are in question during the prior paragraph, rather than his statements or actions, James feels free to sacrifice the perceived validity of what it contains in order to thereby prove the accuracy of every other portion of his narrative: if the writer is scrupulous enough to admit when he does not have the facts at his disposal, the reader is all the more likely to suspend disbelief during those portions when the source has been clearly identified. Another reason in addition to the first also presents itself: since Dr. Ashton has already proven reticent in recording events which could reflect badly on Lord Saul concerning the household's difficulties in securing and retaining chambermaids, as well as being reluctant to place any real blame on the young man when it is perfectly clear from the doctor's own account that Lord Saul's actions were somehow responsible for Frank's death, there is no reason to believe that Dr. Ashton entertained any of the thoughts recorded in paragraph sixteen nor that Dr. Ashton risked any of the benefits he associated with the man's presence in his home by telling Lord Saul any more than Frank's deathbed warnings and asking if he knew what they meant. The only scrap of genuine documentation provided in these two paragraphs is, "It is only said that Saul sat all evening in the study, and when he bid good night, which he did reluctantly, asked for the doctor's prayers," and knowledge of what Frank said before he died would have been enough to elicit this response.

That Lord Saul's doom was a foregone conclusion from the moment of Frank's death, James drives home through the manner in which he constructs the paragraph telling of his death. Instead of keeping the setting in Whitminster and leading up to the event, James immediately changes the scene to the Embassy at Lisbon where Lord Kildonan, Saul's father receives news of his son's death, and then shifts back again to Whitminster for the day of Frank's burial. This eighteenth paragraph is full of terse, telling details, sharp contrasts, and grim implications. Saul's "white and fixed" face contrasts with the "flapping black pall" of the coffin; one moment his visage is "as that of one dead" and the next "alive with a terrible expression of fear." James's use of the pathetic fallacy in describing the gale in terms of an angry beast—buffeting windows, howling over the upland, and roaring through the woodland—turns out, as implied by the condition of Saul's body when found (and confirmed in the second portion of the story) to be more than mere poeticism. James grants him no farewell, in fact no words at all, he denies him even the ability to cry for help: due to the ferocity of the storm "no voice of shouting or cry for help could possibly be heard."

A great many ghost story writers would have been content to conclude the story with the detached description of the Lord Viscount Saul's final resting place in the subsequent paragraph, a villain's violent comeuppance and the irony of his having to share a tomb with his commonplace victim deemed sufficient for most readers and virtually any marketplace; but for James the last nineteen paragraphs have only provided a solid and tantalizing background for the real ghost, the Thin Ghost who lends his name to the collection in which this story first appeared.

Like paragraphs five and thirteen, the twentieth paragraph marks a transition. Here time moves forward "over thirty years" while Dr. Ashton continues to live in his house—"I do not know how quietly, but without visible disturbance"—then an additional sixty years during which time his successor, a Mr. Hindes, left the house vacant in favor of a home he already owned; and another year or so into "1823 or 1824" while another man was found to fill the post and move into the house following the death of Mr. Hindes. James covers this gap with a characteristic mixture of precision and generality, as if the tale's editor had been working from records complete in some particulars, but vague in others.

Victor Sage has remarked that Le Fanu "has a habit of layering and back-dating his texts which sometimes gives them a double or triple sense of time, affecting their reader's point of view" (Sage, *Le Fanu's Gothic* 3), an effect one finds James employing with considerable ingenuity throughout this story. The staggered progression of roughly 93 years described in the prior paragraph, following the initial backward leap of 189 years from the story's publication date in 1919 to its opening in December 1730; the flashback to September of the same year; and the progression of the first portion of the narrative into January 1731 creates a complex, layered distancing effect, which serves a number of purposes. First of all, it invites the reader to view differences in response and narrative tone between the portion of the story set in the eighteenth century and that set in the nineteenth, let alone how each of these differs from what might be expected of a contemporary. Secondly, it sets up a tension between what the reader knows or is able to infer from events in this second portion of the narrative and what this new set of characters knows or is able to discover about their home's past and its repercussions into their own world. Buried within this game of dates is a third purpose, set up in this paragraph and delivered with the casualness of a jest in the story's final paragraph, because the tale's temporal layering does not end in 1824, but extends into the year the story was first published and beyond. Just as 93 years had passed between the tragedies of 1730 and the flare-up of supernatural activity in 1824, so 95 years pass between the time Dr. Oldys hides Saul's tainted effects and the year A *Thin Ghost and Others* first saw print. If the haunting was already at least a few years overdue for a recurrence in James's day, readers subsequent to that time must imagine that the "Jack-in-the-box awaiting some future occupant" contains a long overdue and very dangerous ghost indeed.

Returning to the paragraphs in sequence, by the time Dr. Oldys, his niece, and his servants have moved into the house and set it up to their satisfaction, 1823 has assuredly come and gone, moving the tale, and paragraph twenty-one, into "a certain morning in June" of 1824, an idyllically beautiful day of "very blue sky, and very white little clouds" without a trace of threat. This tranquil, even pretty introduction of the house's restoration and its new occupants marks the beginning of the story's crescendo:

> two ingredients most valuable in the concocting of a ghost story are, to me, the atmosphere and the nicely managed crescendo. . . . Let us then be introduced to the actors in a placid way; let us see them going about their ordinary business, undisturbed by forebodings, pleased with their surroundings; and into this calm environment let the ominous thing put out its head, unobtrusively at first, and then more insistently, until it holds the stage. (James, "Introduction" 248)[1]

"The ominous thing" has already started to "put out its head" in the next paragraph. James has already taught the reader in the first portion of this story to expect tension from these longer paragraphs containing imbedded dialogue. As a result, despite the amicability of this conversation between Dr. Oldys and his niece, Mary, and Mary's statement that "nothing could be more charming," the structure of the paragraph works to associate clues the reader already recognizes from the tale's first portion—such as the "round and perfectly smooth tablet . . . of what seemed clear glass" recently located in the rubbish heap—with the title of Scott's novel *The Talisman*, the lock on the linen closet, and the incursion of sawflies near Dr. Oldys's distant bedroom.

James is courteous enough in the next paragraph to playfully reference the author he is imitating after identifying a letter by Mary as his source for the initial part of the second narrative. Peter Penzoldt is not alone in finding

---

1. Cf. Penzoldt (193–98), who plots the crescendo in James's "The Diary of Mr. Poynter."

that "The exact language of the century in which he places his stories, or from which he 'quotes documents', gives his stories an air of authenticity which is missing from the work of most ghost-story writers who take their themes from the past" (Penzoldt 198). Unfortunately, even before Penzoldt had written his assessment of James, many authors had already incorporated this device into their arsenal of tricks as an easy-to-use shortcut to suspending their readership's disbelief, resulting in a spate of atrocious *olde Recordes* and *Meffages* lacking any of James's affection for their originals or even a trace of his finesse in employing them.

This affection and finesse are readily evident in the pastiche of Anna Seward's style, which follows in paragraph twenty-four, reinforcing the time and manners of the age in which the tale is set while portraying Mary as a gently witty young woman with as much sense in her as there is sensibility. But James has a ghost story to tell not a novel of manners, and breaks off his narrator with a short paragraph warning of "an abrupt break both in the writing and the style" before allowing Mary to resume.

Here follows a long paragraph describing what Mary saw when she looked into the glass her uncle had brought her. The three scenes she views in the mirror clarify and expand for the reader events, which had occurred in the first portion of the story, and link her nineteenth century world with the eighteenth century world of Lord Saul through dumb-show. There is no chiasmic effect as dramatic as that noted in paragraph eleven, but there is one balancing view by Mary out of her window to confirm that one of the places she saw in the glass was "clearly" her own garden. Furthermore, James dramatically and chillingly violates the silence of dumb-show when Mary "seem[s] to hear the echo of a cry of despair" as she watches dim canine shapes run down the figure the reader knows to be Saul, another reminder of the sight-then-sound construction of the tale's opening. The verb "seem" is a tricky word in James, which his readers soon learn to mistrust; because the writer's use of it tends to produce a falsely reassuring effect suggesting that things are less serious than they appear, when evidence soon proves that they are often worse.[2]

Hints of something unusual in the present having led to the leakage of uncanny sights and sounds from the past, the phenomena developing around the house at Whitminster now begin to threaten physical contact. Even though the first encounter occurs as early as paragraph twenty-seven, James delays relating details of this event until paragraph thirty, focusing instead

---

2. Penzoldt makes a similar observation during his brilliant analysis of how James's "descriptives" function in "The Ash-Tree" (181).

on the effects this experience has on its victim and the rest of the household. Dr. Oldys, the stolid man of "robust common sense" at the beginning of the paragraph contrasts sharply with the bellowing, trembling man found alone in a dark room beside his smashed candle a few hours later. Neither James nor his narrator, Mary Oldys, make any attempt to diminish the subjective impact this event has on the dream which follows; however, as the reader has learned from Parkins's dream in "'Oh, Whistle, and I'll Come to You, My Lad'" and others among James's oeuvre, dreams have a way of lending shape to threats the protagonist does not yet recognize, as if a person robbed of the use of the body during sleep were more receptive and vulnerable to the encroachment of the supernatural. Without knowledge of her uncle's tactile encounter with some thing sharing the room with a locked press and chest of drawers, Mary dreams of finding the locked-away linen in her own chest of drawers, then attempts to flee when a "feeble" groping hand emerges, gathers into a "rustling and bustling" behind the door she is using to shield herself, then quickly increasing in strength, plucks the door from her hand "with an irresistible force." Something associated with the locked closet is inimical and gathering strength.

Paragraphs twenty-eight and twenty-nine mark the end of one narrative source and the beginning of a new one, a "young spark" and prospective beau of Mary's with "some vestiges of sense," named Mr. Spearman. This fellow, a "copious" diarist, turns out to be both an asset and a bit of a hindrance to the remainder of the narrative. His ability to objectively record nearly everything he sees and hears with a minimum of filtering or subjective reflection is remarkable: here is a man who will neither willingly overlook anything nor allow his judgment to be clouded by preconceptions, if one excepts his infatuation with his future wife Mary. It is precisely his penchant for relaying every single word in a conversation that earns the reader's trust at the same time it risks trying his patience. If the earlier portions of this story resemble a compressed novel in reporting a plenitude of incident involving a multitude of characters over a great span of time with extreme concision, James's willingness to allow his characters in this second portion to step out of their roles as mere tools for propelling the plot and thus display their personalities regardless of the relevance the author had hitherto insisted upon maintaining, increases this novelistic feel to the tale. This represents a calculated risk on James's part, because just as the greater involvement with his characters' individuality intensifies the reader's concern over their welfare, it also threatens to destroy the balance between the mundane setting and steadily encroaching menace James has carefully built up to this time. Fortunately, this results in only a few prolix passages over the subsequent paragraphs, even if these do tend to stand out in an author as compact as James is wont to be, and the two longest paragraphs in the story, paragraphs thirty and forty-one are not among them.

Paragraph thirty, another of the long tense paragraphs in this tale containing imbedded dialogue and the initial entry supplied from Mr. Spearman's diary, reveals the advantages of James's decision to narrate the rest of his story in this manner. He captures Uncle Oldys's impatience and politeness with his interlocutor, as well as the terror, confusion, disgust, and embarrassment he felt during after his encounter with the unknown perfectly. Mr. Spearman must drag the story out of him, one probing question at a time, and the resultant slow buildup to the event which had left him bellowing and trembling in a dark room the previous night, from the first questions about the maximum size of sawflies, through the long trip from one end of the house to his distant bedroom, the extinguishing of his candle, the twitching of the book out of his hand, the "dry, light, rustling sound" that fills the room containing the locked press as soon as he enters it, the "sensation of long thin arms, or legs, or feelers, all about my face, and neck, and body," to the sight of an immense insect leg waving in the dim light cast past the curtain he has torn open has a marvelous cumulative power. Fortunately for Uncle Oldys, these insectile limbs had "very little strength in them," implying that, as "horrified and disgusted" as he may have been by his encounter, based on the groping menace of gathering strength haunting Mary's dream of the same night, matters could have been, and might still be, much worse.

The following paragraph is less successful, as James allows Mr. Spearman to relay every single step in the conversation between the two men before leading them to the room in question. The resultant succession of short questions and answers, I saids, he replieds, "come along," "go in," and the like is simply distracting so that it is with as much relief as concern that the reader follows the characters into the haunted room. The room itself, thanks to Mr. Spearman's detached descriptions is a gloomy affair, though "well-lighted," filled with hundreds of dead and dying sawflies, the "skeleton" of a bedstead, "a gaunt old press of dark wood," a similarly locked chest of drawers, and somewhere "a faint rustling sound." Dull, sensible man that he is, Mr. Spearman makes nothing of the rustling sound regardless of what he has just heard from his host, and moves straight to the question of unlocking the chest and press.

This leads to a comic interlude consisting of several short paragraphs—numbers thirty-two through thirty-seven—during which the garrulous housekeeper dilates upon the absence of "them keys" from the rest of those attached to the house, their suspected presence in a separate box she had taken the liberty of rattling, and her failure to recall precisely where she had placed this mysterious box "without Miss Mary comes to my room and helps me to my recollection." This interlude is rather like the knocking at the gate in *Macbeth* written in the style of Jane Austen, to whose Miss Bates Mr. Spearman pays tribute: it offers one more clue to deepen the mystery and in providing a momentary respite is intended to thereby cast the preceding tension into sharper relief and increases suspense.

Artifacts from the past—box, keys, and even an accompanying paper written by Dr. Ashton himself—arrive in paragraph thirty-eight. Reticent as always, Dr. Ashton identifies the keys as those belonging to "the Press and Box of Drawers" containing the "Effects" of the late Lord Saul, "only Child and Heire" to the presumably extinct "noble Family of Kildonan," Saul's father "having been, as is notorious, cast away at sea." But this is not the last of the mysteries contained within this paper, for among the legalities and signatures attendant upon the locking up of these effects is a veiled warning to anyone "not being of the Family of Kildonan" to leave them unseen and undisturbed "unless grave discomfort arise," for which warning Dr. Ashton and those adding their signatures to his paper have "sufficient and weighty reason." From this the reader surmises that Dr. Ashton may not have lived so quietly in his home after all, or at least not until 1753 when he consigned Lord Saul's belongings to two pieces of locked furniture in a disused room. Unless the canine shapes and other presences associated with Lord Saul before and after his death create such "grave discomfort" as to necessitate retrieving these effects for some desperate attempt at exorcism, it is best to let sleeping dogs lie, especially since Mary had already discerned in paragraph twenty-six that "dogs such as we have seen they assuredly were not."

Unlike many of those victimized by the supernatural in James's and other stories in the antiquarian tradition, Uncle Oldys had not pried into any hidden mystery before he was attacked: he had simply moved into a long-disused house that happened to be haunted. He also deviates from the template in his reluctance to dig any deeper into the mystery, after combining what he already knew of Lord Saul from his reading with what he now suspects from Dr. Ashton's paper and his experience of the previous night. Despite his curiosity and Mr. Spearman's eagerness to see what has been locked away, he has "some slight hesitation about using the key," holding onto them over the ensuing paragraphs while asking the housekeeper, "What's the story, I wonder? Do you know it, Mrs. Maple?"

This question launches the fortieth paragraph, the longest one in the story, a bravura performance from the hitherto flighty and somewhat irritating Mrs. Maple, consisting of an elaborate oral ghost story 1158 words long, which resorts and elaborates upon the tale's prior motifs. It is a superb illustration of James's kinship with Le Fanu: "Le Fanu's texts are acutely, but deceptively, aware of the act of narration itself, poised in a space between written and spoken language, which from the outset of his career employ their own poetics of interruption and alienation" (Sage, *Le Fanu's Gothic* 2). The starts, stops, and divagations that had been so distracting when she tried to remember the placement of the keys now add to the credibility of the yarn she tells, and with each shred of new detail she adds to what had already been laid before the reader, an ever darker, deadlier, and more pathetic story emerges. And within her narrative are even further layers, as she speaks for three generations of the Simpkins family whose knowledge of the village and the residence at Whitminster date back a hundred years. Saul, like his namesake who had bade the Witch of Endor raise the spirit of Samuel from the grave, wanders the graveyards with the things he brought over with him from Ireland, possibly gathering other souls to him as he goes. At such times, the Simpkinses dare not look out for fear that "them that was with him following through the grass at his hills" might look in; just as after Saul's death, they dare not open their windows despite their pity for the thin frozen spirit staring in at them lest they let him, and God knows what else in with him.

This knowledge is enough to satisfy Uncle Oldys, who despite even Mary's curiosity decides to have both locked pieces of furniture hauled to the garret and the keys hidden. Mary sends the last piece, the scrying crystal, along with them. Thus it is that the final paragraph finds the dangerous secret hidden, and seemingly dormant, yet still a threat to some future generation either too distant to be aware of the danger or too curious and careless to be wary of it. Any future Wraxalls or Dennistouns: take heed!

Works Cited

Aickman, Robert. "An Essay." In *First World Fantasy Awards*, ed. Gahan Wilson. Garden City, NY: Doubleday, 1977. 63–65.

James, M. R. "Introduction to *Ghosts and Marvels*." In *The Haunted Dolls' House and Other Ghost Stories*. Ed. S. T. Joshi. New York: Penguin, 2006.

———. "Preface to *A Thin Ghost and Others*." In *A Pleasing Terror*. Ashcroft, BC: Ash-Tree Press, 2001. 220.

———. "Some Remarks on Ghost Stories." In *The Haunted Dolls' House and Other Ghost Stories*. Ed. S. T. Joshi. New York: Penguin, 2006.

Joshi, S. T. *The Weird Tale*. Austin: University of Texas Press, 1990.

Le Fanu, Joseph Sheridan. *Mr Justice Harbottle and Others*. Ashcroft, BC: Ash-Tree Press, 2005.

Penzoldt, Peter. *The Supernatural in Fiction*. London: Peter Nevill, 1952.

Sage, Victor. *Horror Fiction in the Protestant Tradition*. New York: St. Martin's Press, 1988.

————. *Le Fanu's Gothic: The Rhetoric of Darkness*. Houndmills, BC: Palgrave Macmillan, 2004.

Sullivan, Jack. *Elegant Nightmares: The English Ghost Story from Le Fanu to Blackwood*. Athens: Ohio University Press, 1978.

Nightmares of Punch and Judy in Ruskin and M. R. James

Roger Craik

For the fifty-year-old John Ruskin, 1869 was marked by ill-health, fretfulness and nightmares. He began to note the latter in his journal, from which we learn that the night of Saturday, October 23rd was particularly troubled:

> Bad cold coming on. Sleep broken. Dreamed I was going up a lovely mountain-ravine and met a party of Germans, four very ugly women and their papa and mama—indefinite—and they were arranging themselves to picnic, as I thought, with their backs to the beautiful view. But when I looked, I saw they were settling themselves to see Punch, and wanted me out of the way lest I should get any of it gratis; and I was going on up the ravine contemptuously, when, Punch appearing on the stage, I looked back for a minute and was startled by his immediately knocking down his wife without dancing with her first, which new reading of the play made me stop to see how it went on; and then I saw it was an Italian Punch, modernized, and that there was no idea of humour in it, but all the interest was in a mad struggle of the wife for the stick, and in her being afterwards beaten slowly, crying out, and with a stuffed body, which seemed to bruise under the blows, so as to make the whole as horrible and nasty as possible. So I woke, and wondered much at the foolishness, coherence, uselessness, ludicrous and mean unpleasantness of it all. (Ruskin 2:684)

In 1919, nineteen years after Ruskin's death, M. R. James wrote his ghost story "The Story of a Disappearance and an Appearance" in which a man seeking his missing uncle meets a bagman who enthuses about a Punch and Judy show he has just seen. That very night the man has the following alarming dream:

> It began with what I can only describe as a pulling aside of curtains: and I found myself seated in a place—I don't know whether indoors or not. There were people—only a few—on either side of me, but I did not recognize them, or indeed think much about them. They never spoke, but, as far as I can re-

member, were all grave and pale-faced and looked fixedly before them. Facing me was a Punch and Judy show, perhaps rather larger than the ordinary ones, painted with black figures on a reddish-yellow ground. Behind it and on each side was only darkness, but in the front there was a sufficiency of light. I was "strung up" to a high degree of expectation and looked every moment to hear the pan-pipes and Roo-too-too-it. Instead of that there came suddenly an enormous—I can use no other word—an enormous single toll of a bell, I don't know from how far off—somewhere behind. The little curtain flew up and the drama began.

I believe someone once tried to rewrite Punch as a serious tragedy; but whoever he may have been, this performance would have suited him exactly. There was something Satanic about the hero. He varied his methods of attack: for some of his victims he laid in wait, and to see his horrible face—it was yellowish-white, I may remark—peering around the wings made me think of the Vampyre in Fuseli's foul sketch. To others he was polite and carneying. . . . But with all of them I came to dread the moment of death. The crack of the stick on their skulls, which in the ordinary way delights me, had here a crushing sound as if the bone was giving way, and the victims quivered and kicked as they lay. The baby—it sounds more ridiculous as I go on—the baby, I am sure, was alive. Punch wrung its neck, and if the choke or squeak which it gave were not real, I know nothing of reality.

The stage got perceptibly darker as each crime was consummated, and at least there was one murder which was done quite in the dark, so that I could see nothing of the victim, and took some time to effect. It was accompanied by hard breathing and horrid muffled sounds, and after it Punch came and sat on the footboards, and hung his head on one side, and sniggered in so deadly a fashion that I saw some of those beside me cover their faces, and I would have gladly done the same. (James, *Collected Ghost Stories* 449–50)

The drama continues with the appearance of a figure hooded with a whitish bag, who pursues Punch, catches him, and then thrusts his unmasked face into Punch's.

James's narrator remembers from the dream that the names over the front of the booth were Kidman and Gallop. Later, a real Punch and Judy show comes to the town, and with mixed feelings the narrator decides to watch it:

I was half delighted, half not—the latter because my unpleasant dream came back to me so vividly; but, anyhow, I determined to see it through, and I sent Eliza out with a crown-piece to the performers and a request that they would face my window if they could manage it.

The show was a smart new one; the names of the proprietors, I need hardly tell you, were Italian, Foresta and Calpigi. (*Collected Ghost Stories* 452)

From his vantage point, the speaker sees a terrified head rise into view and, behind it, the nightcapped head of a criminal about to be executed. The two figures break free, the nightcapped one being discovered shortly afterwards in a chalk pit, with his throat horribly mangled yet recognizable as the speaker's missing uncle. The names of the Punch and Judy proprietors turn out to be Kidman and Gallop.

Of course James might not have known of Ruskin's experience: the violence in Punch and Judy shows is distressing enough in itself to give rise to nightmares, and besides, it is a natural response of imaginative people to wonder what would happen if the show were real. On the other hand, there is more to link Ruskin and James's writing than their being involved with dreams of Punch and Judy. Both make mention of an Italian Punch (Ruskin in his dream and James when his narrator sees the Italian names on the real booth), and both envisage a Punch played seriously: for Ruskin it is "an Italian Punch, modernised" but one in which there is "no idea of humour," while James's narrator, writing to his brother with his nightmare fresh in his mind, recalls that "someone once tried to re-write Punch as a serious tragedy." The "seriousness" takes a particularly macabre form. From what I remember of Punch and Judy shows from my childhood, Punch delivers several short cracks to his opponents' heads, and they drop down dead, much to the relish of an audience enjoying the vigor of it all, and laughing and cheering at the spectacle of death dealt out without pain. By contrast, Ruskin and James portray the opposite—a series of ghastly murders distinguished by their slowness as the victims die by degrees, in a horribly lifelike real way. Ruskin's Judy is "beaten slowly, crying out, and with a stuffed body, which seemed to bruise under the blows"; while James's Punch's stick deals out blows which "had here a crushing sound as if the bone were giving way, and the victims quivered and kicked as they lay." Furthermore, there are only a few people present at each performance (six Germans in Ruskin and "only a few" in James); this makes both shows seem private and somehow sinister. The final similarity between the two accounts is that each involves payment in advance; the Germans want Ruskin out of the way so that he will not see any of the show without paying (they by implication having paid), while James's narrator, when he sees the real show, pays the performers to carry it out facing his hotel window.

If, as these many similarities suggest, M. R. James did know of Ruskin's dream, how could he have done so? Their two recorded meetings, if they can be called that, were when the schoolboy James heard Ruskin lecture at Eton: nothing is known of James's response to the first lecture, but Ruskin's second (on Amiens Cathedral, in 1880) had a decisive influence on the precocious eighteen-year-old. Over forty years later he distinctly recalled it: "For the first time I learned what might be read, and in what spirit, in the imagery of a great church: and what the thirteenth century had to say to the nineteenth. I say I then learned it first; yet I doubt if in so saying I do justice to my tutor, who, a faithful disciple of Ruskin (and long Master of his Guild), had at the very least prepared my mind to absorb that lesson" (James, *Eton and King's* 55). "My tutor" is Henry Luxmoore (1841–1926) who after Eton and Oxford returned to his old school and taught there until his death, while the "Guild" is the Guild of St. George, a society established in 1871 of men who pledged a tithe of their income to acquiring and developing land according to Ruskin's idea and ideals (Leon 458). Of all the Eton College schoolmasters influenced by Ruskin in the 1850s and 1860s, Luxmoore seems to have been the most committed; in his letters he asks, "Am I not Ruskinese all through?" (Luxmoore 141) and later acknowledges "some intercourse with John Ruskin" (Luxmoore 262). The two must have known each other well, for Ruskin's short-lived Guild of St. George had only 32 members and it can be assumed that Ruskin knew all of them personally. Not only that, but Ruskin was a frequent visitor to Eton in the 1860s and early 1870s (Browning 182).

In his turn, Luxmoore was deeply influential on M. R. James from the day the latter entered Eton in 1876 until his own death in 1926. From 1902 until 1917 he was present at the informal Christmas gatherings which James held in his rooms at King's College, Cambridge, and at which James would read aloud his latest ghost story: Luxmoore heard the first reading of "A Story of a Disappearance and an Appearance" there (Cox 143). If James did indeed know of Ruskin's dream it was almost certainly from his Eton tutor, Henry E. Luxmoore, that he heard it.

Works Cited

Browning, Oscar. *Memories of Sixty Years at Eton, Cambridge and Elsewhere.* London: John Lane, 1910.

Cox, Michael. *M. R. James: An Informal Portrait.* London: Oxford University Press, 1983.

James, M. R. *The Collected Ghost Stories of M. R. James.* London: Edward Arnold, 1931.

———. *Eton and King's.* London: Williams & Norgate, 1926.

Leon, Derrick. *Ruskin, the Great Victorian.* London: Routledge & Kegan Paul, 1949.

Luxmoore, H. E. *Letters of H. E. Luxmoore.* Ed. M. R. James. Cambridge: Cambridge University Press, 1929.

Ruskin, John. *Diaries.* Ed. Joan Evans and John Howard Whitehouse. Oxford: Clarendon Press, 1956–59. 3 vols.

An Elucidation (?) of the Plot of M. R. James's "Two Doctors"

Lance Arney

> The reading of many ghost stories has shown me that the greatest suc-
> cesses have been scored by the authors who can make us envisage a definite
> time and place, and give us plenty of clear-cut and matter-of-fact detail, but
> who, when the climax is reached, allow us to be just a little in the dark as to
> the working of their machinery.
>
> —M. R. James, "Some Remarks on Ghost Stories"

I. An Enigma

Indeed, it seems as though M. R. James had this very formula in mind when
he wrote "Two Doctors," for this nebulous story is sure to leave almost any
reader in the dark—and more than just a little in the dark. Even Jack
Sullivan bluntly remarked, "The ending of 'Two Doctors' makes almost no
sense" (89).[1] But James thought it proper that, for ghost stories, the setting
must be "distanced" from the reader.[2] Distanced "Two Doctors" is: the
primary narrator, finding extraneous papers cached in a ledger that he
purchased sometime around 1911, presents the reader with extracts—which
consist mainly of witnesses' recollections of isolated events occurring in
1718—from a group of papers once belonging to a lawyer. What is more, the
primary narrator never offers an explanation of his own, so the actual "story"

---

1. Sullivan also says that in order to understand the ending, we must compare
"Two Doctors" to the stories in *Ghost-Stories of an Antiquary* and other "Le
Fanuesque pursuit tales by James" (88). I hope to show by this essay, however,
that such a tedious comparison is quite unnecessary.

2. For James's theories on the writing of ghost stories see his Preface to *More
Ghost Stories of an Antiquary* (1911), his Introduction to *Ghosts and Marvels*, ed.
H. V. Collins (1924), and his articles "Some Remarks on Ghost Stories" (1929)
and "Ghosts—Treat Them Gently!" (1931), all reprinted in *Casting the Runes
and Other Ghost Stories*.

is never told. Thus it becomes the task of the reader to reconstruct the plot by piecing together the available clues harmoniously and chronologically into a coherent narrative. Whether or not the "distancing" methods James used in this essay were at all successful, we shall determine in the conclusion of this essay.

A matter that first needs our attention is the very nature of the story, as it produces several textual problems. The narrator—or, rather, editor—himself says at the beginning, "The *dossier* is not complete,"[3] meaning that all the documents pertaining to the case were not to be found in the ledger. Is it possible that the whole story never can be known or reconstructed from the material that *is* there? I do not think so, for if that were true, one wonders why James would even trouble himself with writing the story. We must assume that he is providing us with all the information we need to understand and reconstruct the story or an approximation of it. Even so, similar textual problems arise in association with Dr. Quinn's murderer, whom we must now expose.

II. Who Killed Dr. Quinn?

This will be a startling question to those who think the answer is obviously Dr. Abell, but, in reality, it is never stated explicitly in the story who the murderer of Dr. Quinn is, nor is it stated explicitly that he was murdered at all. Indeed, the physician who examines Dr. Quinn's body after his death cannot even medically explain how he died, hence his verdict "Death by the visitation of God." We must, therefore, justify the presumption that James wants us to think that Dr. Abell has killed Dr. Quinn.

Dr. Abell is not one of the witnesses—or at least, if he is, his statement is not with the other statements that the narrator has found inside the ledger. Dr. Abell not being a witness leads us almost immediately to believe that he is the one being accused of the murder. But the editor conceivably could be omitting accusations against other suspects; or perhaps there was a statement by Dr. Abell in the ledger, and for some unknown reason the editor does not quote from it or even make reference to it. But the fact that there may be more material relating to the case does not entail that this material contains any decisive evidence of any kind: it may have no relevance or bearing on the case, and this could be why the narrator does not quote or mention it—that is, if it exists. In any case, we must simply trust the editor to be choosing all the pertinent information he can.

There is, nevertheless, even a problem with our concession of reliability to

---

3. All citations of "Two Doctors" are taken from *The Collected Ghost Stories of M. R. James*, pp. 459–71.

the editor. Toward the end of the story he states, "Annexed to the other papers is one which I was at first inclined to suppose had made its way among them by mistake." If the editor misjudges one paper as being irrelevant, then there could very well be other papers in the bundle that the editor thinks have no relevance to the case but that actually do have relevance to the case.

But at most these are only minor textual problems and can all be swept aside by taking for granted that the material in the story is *all* the material that James wants us to work with. Or in other words, (almost) all the clues that are needed to solve the enigma can be found in the text itself.

Returning to the query of who the murderer is, we can now state confidently that by having the statements of Luke Jennett and Jonathan Pratt center so much around their relationship with Dr. Abell and his relationship with Dr. Quinn—to say nothing of the conclusive evidence found within these statements—, James is giving the story a tone that points to Dr. Abell as the killer. (One is also tempted to deduce this from the very title of the story, which seems to imply that something momentous has occurred between the two doctors, not the other characters in the story.)

As expected, the incriminating evidence found in the statements does validate our assumption that Dr. Abell is the murderer. He displays murderous tendencies toward his servant, Luke Jennett, at the beginning of the story. As it goes, Dr. Abell becomes angry after Jennett tells him both that he is going to quit his service and why he is going to quit:

> "I told him that, much against my will, I must look out for another place. He inquired what was my reason, in consideration I had been so long with him. . . .
>
> ". . . I told him, not seeing how I could keep it back, the matter of my former affidavit and of the bedstaff in the dispensing-room, and said that a house where such things happened was no place for me. At which he, looking very black upon me, said no more, but called me a fool, and said he would pay what was owing me in the morning . . ."

Dr. Abell then becomes even angrier when he discovers that Jennett did not sleep in his house on the night of his quitting: "'. . . that night I lodged with my sister's husband near Battle Bridge and came early next morning to my late master, who then made a great matter that I had not lain in his house and stopped a crown out of my wages owing.'" Dr. Abell apparently had plans to dispose of Jennett in his sleep for reasons we will discuss later. But this is not Dr. Abell's only premeditated plan of murder. The other instance adds to the condemning evidence and assures us more than anything else that it was Dr. Abell who killed Dr. Quinn. Consider the following excerpt from Jennett's statement concerning an incident that occurred *while* he was working for Dr. Quinn:

"I had never any communication with Dr. Abell after I came back to Islington, but one day when he passed me in the street and asked me whether I was not looking for another service, to which I answered I was very well suited where I was [i.e., with Dr. Quinn], but he said I was a tickleminded fellow and he doubted not he should soon hear I was on the world again, which indeed proved true."

Dr. Abell is subtly foreshadowing to Jennett that he is going to kill Dr. Quinn, although Jennett, of course, did not realize it at the time.

This is all the proof we really need in order to label Dr. Abell as the killer, as there is no evidence with which to accuse any of the other characters in the story. But why would he want to end the life of the benevolent Dr. Quinn?

III. The Motive: Vengeance

The reason Dr. Abell kills Dr. Quinn is simple enough: he thinks that Dr. Quinn is stealing his patients, and he wants revenge. Jonathan Pratt recalls a conversation that he had with Dr. Abell that reveals Dr. Abell's animosity toward Dr. Quinn: "'Damn Quinn,' says he; 'talk no more of him: he has embezzled four of my best patients this month; I believe it is that cursed man of his, Jennett, that used to be with me, his tongue is never still; it should be nailed to the pillory if he had his deserts.'" Our first question might be: Did some of his patients really leave him as he says? Pratt provides us with the answer: "'It could not be denied that some respectable families in the parish had given him the cold shoulder, and for no reason that they were willing to allege.'" Pratt also remarks about his conversation with Dr. Abell:

> "This, I may say, was the only time of his showing me that he had any grudge against either Dr. Quinn or Jennett, and as was my business, I did my best to persuade him he was mistaken in them. . . . The end was that he said he had not done so ill at Islington but that he could afford to live at ease elsewhere when he chose, and anyhow he bore Dr. Quinn no malice."

This admission that he "bore Dr. Quinn no malice" is only inevitable and does not contradict what we have said so far of Dr. Abell, if we realize who it is that he is talking to: Jonathan Pratt, the Rector of Islington. It is highly doubtful that he would openly discuss his intention of killing a man with the parish priest—or anyone, for that matter.

Dr. Abell may have been mistaken in accusing Dr. Quinn of having a part in the plot to steal his patients, for Dr. Quinn does not seem like the type of man that would involve himself in such devious schemes. Jennett tells us:

> "My master, Dr. Quinn, was a very just, honest man, and no maker of mischief. I am sure he never stirred a finger nor said a word by way of in-

ducement to a soul to make them leave going to Dr. Abell and come to him; nay, he would hardly be persuaded to attend them that came, until he was convinced that if he did not they would send into the town for a physician than do as they had hitherto done."

This view twice receives corroboration from Pratt: "'Dr. Q. [was] to my eye a plain, honest believer, not inquiring closely into points of belief, but squaring his practice to what lights he had'"; and later: "'Dr. Quinn, as I said, was a plain, honest creature, and a man to whom I would have gone—indeed I have before now gone to him—for advice on matters of business.'" That the Rector of Islington upholds Jennett's estimation of Dr. Quinn leads us to believe that he is in fact innocent, and therefore that Dr. Abell's vengeance has been misdirected.

But if Dr. Quinn is not persuading Dr. Abell's patients to come to him, then who is? The answer can be found in the passage I quoted earlier, wherein Pratt recounts a conversation he had had with Dr. Abell: "'"I [Dr. Abell] believe it is that cursed man of his, Jennett, that used to be with me, his tongue is never still; . . ."'" Dr. Abell thinks Jennett is spreading rumors that are damaging his reputation; and apparently he anticipated that this was going to happen, hence his (failed) attempt to murder Jennett that we discussed earlier. Jennett, however, denies defaming Dr. Abell's name twice in a single paragraph: "'I never told tales of my master, Dr. Abell, to anybody in the neighbourhood. . . . And when I came back to Islington and found Dr. Abell still there, . . . I was clear that it behoved me to use great discretion, for indeed I was afraid of the man, and it is certain I was no party to spreading any ill report of him.'" We must conclude that Jennett is lying here, and there is evidence to support this conclusion. Jennett's very comment that he did not slander Dr. Abell's name presupposes the fact that he was expecting to be charged with the allegation. And there is a certain nervousness in the tone of the paragraph in question—Jennett is so overzealous in trying to clear his own name that he succeeds rather in betraying his feigned honesty. Having a servant lie almost seems like something James would do anyway. In this story—more precisely, in Jennett's very statement—there is a typical James aside, which displays his low esteem of servants: "'I said if he would excuse me he would do me a great kindness, because (this appears to have been common form even in 1718) I was one that always liked to have everything pleasant about me.'"

The topic, it seems, of Jennett's malediction is the elusive bedstaff incident, which is a riddle in itself and which we shall later attempt to resolve. Jennett, when discussing his conversation with Dr. Abell as to why he is quitting, makes a single reference to an affidavit that he has drawn up, and evidently it is concerned with the bedstaff incident: "'Then,' says he, 'you must have some complaint to make, and if I could I would willingly set it right.' And at that I told him, not seeing how I could keep it back, the matter of my former affidavit and of the bedstaff in the dispensing-room, and said that a house where such things happened was no place for me.'" One is inclined to suppose, by Jennett's attitude toward it and by the fact that it caused him to leave Dr. Abell's house, that the bedstaff incident was not at all pleasant. The editor of the material is of no help at all in elucidating this whole matter; he merely tells us that the affidavit was not in the ledger:

> There is one very obscure part in this statement—namely, the reference to the former affidavit and the matter of the bedstaff. The former affidavit is not in the bundle of papers. It is to be feared that it was taken out to be read because of its special oddity, and not put back. Of what nature the story was may be guessed later, but as yet no clue has been put into our hands.

We shall return to this matter later; it may be linked with the method Dr. Abell uses to dispatch Dr. Quinn. But in any event, Jennett does admit that he has mentioned the bedstaff incident to others: "'When I was in another service I remember to have spoken to my fellow-servants about the matter of the bedstaff, but I am sure I never said either I or he [Dr. Abell] were the persons concerned, and it met with so little credit that I was affronted and thought best to keep it to myself.'" This is from the same paragraph wherein he denies spreading rumors about Dr. Abell, so notice how he adds, "I am sure I never said either I or he were the persons concerned."

There is even a slight chance that Jennett may be innocent, too. If the only people to whom he described the bedstaff incident were his fellow servants, then it is possible that they were the ones who told other people about it, leaving Jennett to be blamed only for accidental libel. This does not seem to be the case, however, as there is no evidence to support it. And it does not appear that James wants us to regard Jennett as being innocent anyway. Certainly, Dr. Abell does not know that Dr. Quinn is innocent—that is, Dr. Quinn is not supervising or instructing Jennett's defamatory endeavors—and it is only Dr. Quinn's misfortune that this is so.

IV. A Ghoulish Murder

With reference to the murder in "Two Doctors," Jack Sullivan stated that "one doctor uses an unexplained supernatural device to do in another" (88). James is extremely vague as to the details of the murder, and I am still not convinced that anything approaching coherence can be made of this aspect of the story, but I hope to demonstrate that this device Sullivan is referring to is not as unexplained as he thinks it is.

There are a few parts of the story that we have thus far left untouched and that therefore need to be examined in order to understand the very peculiar murder in this story. One such part is the long argument that Dr. Abell has with Pratt:

"Dr. A. was to me a source of perplexity . . . [and] interested himself in questions to which Providence, as I hold, designs no answer to be given us in this state: he would ask me, for example, what place I believed those beings now to hold in the scheme of creation which by some are thought neither to have stood fast when the rebel angels fell, nor to have joined with them to the full pitch of their transgression.

"As was suitable, my first answer to him was a question, What warrant he had for supposing any such beings to exist? for that there was none in Scripture I took it he was aware. It appeared—for as I am on the subject, the whole tale may be given—that he grounded himself on such passages as that of the satyr which Jerome tells us conversed with Antony; but thought too that some parts of Scripture might be cited in support. 'And besides,' said he, 'you know 'tis the universal belief among those that spend their days and nights abroad, and I would add that if your calling took you so continuously as it does me about the country lanes by night, you might not be so surprised as I see you to be by my suggestion.' 'You are then of John Milton's mind,' I said, 'and hold that

　　Millions of spiritual creatures walk the earth
　　Unseen, both when we wake and when we sleep.'

"'I do not know,' he said, 'why Milton should take upon himself to say "unseen"; though to be sure he was blind when he wrote that. But for the rest, why, yes, I think he was in the right.' 'Well,' I said, 'though not so often as you, I am not seldom called abroad pretty late; but I have no mind of meeting a satyr in our Islington lanes in all the years I have been here; and if you have had the better luck, I am sure the Royal Society would be glad to know of it.'

"I am reminded of these trifling expressions because Dr. A. took them so ill, stamping out of the room in a huff with some such word as that these high and dry parsons had no eyes but for a prayer-book or a pint of wine."

For all the suggestiveness of this passage, it really has no relevance to the rest of the story, save as an indication of Dr. Abell's intellectual preoccupations, suggesting that he is some sort of student of the occult. But, curiously, even though Dr. Abell's real interest lies in the dark arts, he nonetheless finds time to go to church, as Pratt informs us: "'It is not to be supposed . . . that a physician should be a regular attendant at morning and evening prayers, or at the Wednesday lectures, but within the measure of their [Drs. Abell and

Quinn] ability I would say that both these persons fulfilled their obligations as loyal members of the Church of England.'" Dr. Abell's act of attending the church sermons is more than likely a social pretense, used to conceal his real beliefs from the community so that they will not suspect him of being a member of an opposing religious order—as we shall soon see he is. Thus it should come as no astonishment that, as we are told by Jennett, Dr. Abell eventually ceases to pose as a righteous man: "'I came back to Islington and found Dr. Abell still there, who I was told had left the parish.'"

Pratt relates another conversation in his statement in which, by referring to their other strange talk quoted above, he unintentionally tricks Dr. Abell into revealing his horrible secret to him:

> "There was an evening when he came in, at first seeming gay and in good spirits, but afterwards as he sat and smoked by the fire falling into a musing way; out of which to rouse him I said pleasantly that I supposed he had had no meetings of late with his odd friends. A question which did effectually rouse him, for he looked most wildly, and as if scared, upon me, and said, '*You* were never there? I did not see you. Who brought you?' And then in a more collected tone, 'What was this about a meeting? I believe I must have been in a doze.' To which I answered that I was thinking of fauns and centaurs in the dark lane, and not of a witches' Sabbath; but it seemed he took it differently.
>
> "'Well,' said he, 'I can plead guilty to neither; but I find you very much more of a sceptic than becomes your cloth. If you care to know about the dark lane you might do worse than ask my housekeeper that lived at the other end of it when she was a child.' 'Yes,' said I, 'and the old women in the almshouse and the children in the kennel.'"

It appears as though Dr. Abell is in an unholy cult of some kind; and whether it be pagan or satanic, we are left to guess (probably the latter); Dr. Abell says neither, but this is after he has regained his senses. The hint about his housekeeper "living in the dark lane" may lead us to suppose that she is the one who introduced Dr. Abell to the mystic arts. He may have done more than just profane Christianity, though, as we shall see in a moment.

The reason we have gone to such lengths discussing Dr. Abell's occult leanings is that they might have several connections with other circum-stances relating to Dr. Quinn's murder. One such connection is with a spe-cial ability that Dr. Abell seems to have. Consider what is implied in the following excerpt from Pratt's statement:

> "'A convenient thing enough,' said Dr. Abell to me, 'if by some arrangement a man could get the power of communicating motion and energy to inanimate objects.' 'As if the axe should move itself against him that lifts it;

something of that kind?' 'Well, I don't know that that was in my mind so much; but if you could summon such a volume from your shelf or even order it to open at the right page.'

"He was sitting by the fire—it was a cold evening—and stretched out his hand that way, and just then the fire-irons, or at least the poker, fell over towards him with a great clatter, and I did not hear what else he said."

Does Dr. Abell have the power of psychokinesis, the ability to move objects with his mind? Apparently so; he accidentally demonstrated his faculties to Pratt, who of course is unaware of what actually has happened. But if he is not psychokinetic, and the poker fell of its own accord, one wonders why James would include this passage in the story. And yet, if he is psychokinetic, then why does he muse over acquiring the ability? Maybe the rest of the passage can provide us with some illumination:

"But I told him that I could not easily conceive of an arrangement, as he called it, of such a kind that would not include as one of its conditions a heavier payment than any Christian would care to make; to which he assented. 'But,' he said, 'I have no doubt these bargains can be made very tempting, very persuasive. Still, you would not favour them, eh, Doctor? No, I suppose not.'"

This "arrangement" seems to involve some sort of sacrifice, one which Pratt, the Rector of Islington, has—not surprisingly—no preference or approval for. What it is exactly, we shall try to ascertain in a moment; presently we are concerned with whether or not Dr. Abell is psychokinetic at the time of this conversation. Perhaps our decision might be influenced by an earlier event: the dubious bedstaff incident. What happened that so frightened Jennett into leaving Dr. Abell's service? Initially I had thought that Jennett saw Dr. Abell, who was totally unaware of his presence, use his psychokinetic powers to make the bedstaff tidy his bed, thus giving to Jennett the appearance that the bedstaff was moving by itself.[4] But Jennett

---

4. James was apparently fascinated by the thought of inanimate objects being able to move by themselves. He wrote in "Stories I Have Tried to Write" what seems to be the essence of "Two Doctors": "In parenthesis, many common objects may be made the vehicles of retribution, and where retribution is not called for, of malice. Be careful how you handle the packet you pick up in the carriage-drive, particularly if it contains nail-parings and hair. Do not, in any case, bring it into your house. It may not be alone . . ." (*Collected Ghost Stories* 646). And he would later write a whole story on the subject, "The Malice of Inanimate Objects" (1933). But these are by no means the only stories to make use of the concept: "'Oh, Whistle, and I'll Come to You, My Lad,'" in which a linen sheet

says, "the bedstaff *in the dispensing-room.*" So what must have happened is this: Dr. Abell, wanting a new article of bedding (a pillowcase, for example), commands the bedstaff to fetch it for him; then Jennett, who is meanwhile doing his laundry duties in the dispensing-room (putting away clean sheets, for example), suddenly sees the bedstaff come floating in on thin air and is scared out of his wits. And he must have seen the bedstaff with its cargo float back into Dr. Abell's hands, hence his later remark about the bedstaff incident, "'I am sure I never said either I or he [Dr. Abell] were the persons concerned.'" If this or something similar to it is actually what happened, then Dr. Abell obviously has psychokinesis during his strange chat with Pratt, for it takes place long after Jennett has stopped working for Dr. Abell. Why, then, does Dr. Abell pretend that he is not psychokinetic? One reason might be that he does not want to be ridiculed by Pratt, who throughout the story gives the reader the impression of being a pitifully dense person who disbelieves anything which is a little removed from the normal or which is not printed in the Bible. From another perspective, the tone of the passage suggests that Dr. Abell is suffering from a guilty conscience and wants Pratt's sympathy. Or is he just having second thoughts about what he did to obtain his supernatural power? Any one of these reasons could be true; the last one, incidentally, focuses our attention on our next inquiry: What *did* Dr. Abell do to become psychokinetic? During the conversation, he refers to an "arrangement" that must be made; Pratt then tells him that "'one of its conditions [must be] a heavier payment than any Christian would care to make,'" and Dr. Abell agrees with him. Did Dr. Abell sell his soul to the devil, then, in exchange for psychokinesis?[5] This is evidently what the arrangement was; more verification can be found in Dr. Abell's reflection, "I have no doubt these bargains can be made very tempting, very persuasive"— human beings have long designated the devil as the symbol of temptation. So, then, Dr. Abell has made the ultimate sacrifice in order to be psychokinetic; we will soon see that this special faculty plays a very important role in his murder scheme, the subject of our next investigation.

Trying to unfold how Dr. Abell accomplished the murder is a stressful and problematic job. We shall begin by citing a curious passage in Jennett's statement that seems to disclose a portion of Dr. Abell's murderous plan:

"I believe it may be proved that Dr. Abell came into my master's house more than once. We had a new chambermaid out of Hertfordshire, and she

floats around, and "Count Magnus," in which the padlocks of a sarcophagus unlock themselves and drop to the floor, are other well-known examples.
5. This was suggested to me by S. T. Joshi, to whom I am most grateful.

asked me who was the gentleman that was looking after the master, that is
Dr. Quinn, when he was out, and seemed so disappointed that he was out.
She said whoever he was he knew the way of the house well, running at once
into the study and then into the dispensing-room, and last into the bed-
chamber. I made her tell me what he was like, and what she said was suitable
enough to Dr. Abell; but besides she told me she saw the same man at
church, and someone told her that was the Doctor."

What was Dr. Abell doing in Dr. Quinn's house? Was he surveying the
rooms, trying to select the best location in which to kill Dr. Quinn? No, he
already "'[knows] the way of the house well.'" The chambermaid says that
Dr. Abell at last went into Dr. Quinn's bedroom; immediately after relating
the above passage, Jennett says: "'It was just after this that my master began
to have his bad nights, and complained to me and other persons, and in
particular what discomfort he suffered from his pillow and bedclothes.'" So
Dr. Abell must have done something to Dr. Quinn's bedclothes. As to the
"bad nights," we will simply note for now that Dr. Quinn would wake up
from a terrifying nightmare "'fighting for his breath.'" Later we will analyze
the dream that he has; we are at present simply concerned with what
occasions it. When Dr. Abell went into Dr. Quinn's bedchamber, did he
place on Dr. Quinn's bedclothes some sort of magical spell that produced
the nightmares? Dr. Quinn wakes up fighting for his breath—was this spell
supposed to kill him? Does he prove to be too strong-willed for the spell to
be fully effective? Or was this spell merely intended to make Dr. Quinn's
bedclothes uncomfortable, thus, as part of Dr. Abell's plan, compelling him
to buy a whole new set? This, as Jennett informs us, Dr. Quinn does:

> "He said he must buy some [bedclothes] to suit him, and should do his
> own marketing. And accordingly brought home a parcel which he said was of
> the right quality, but where he bought it we had then no knowledge, only
> they were marked in thread with a coronet and a bird. The women said they
> were of a sort not commonly met with and very fine, and my master said they
> were the comfortablest he ever used, and he slept now both soft and deep.
> Also the feather pillows were the best sorted and his head would sink into
> them as if they were a cloud: which I have myself remarked several times
> when I came to wake him of a morning, his face being almost hid by the pil-
> low closing over it."

These new bedclothes—where did Dr. Quinn get them? Or more precisely,
where did the dealer from whom he bought them originally get them? The
very last paragraph of the story, which is the editor's paraphrasing of what we
are inclined to believe is a newspaper clipping, can help us answer this
question:

It relates to the rifling of a mausoleum in Middlesex which stood in a park (now broken up), the property of a noble family which I will not name. The outrage was not that of an ordinary resurrection man. The object, it seemed likely, was theft. The account is blunt and terrible. I shall not quote it. A dealer in the North of London suffered heavy penalties as a receiver of stolen goods in connexion with the affair.

There is one telltale clue that gives it all away: the mausoleum was owned by a noble family. If we remember that Jennett said Dr. Quinn's new bedclothes "'were marked in thread with a coronet and a bird,'" and if we are aware that the coronet sewn into them is a small crown used to denote nobility, we should be able to deduce that these new bedclothes are actually the burial sheets that were once wrapped about a corpse resting inside the mausoleum in question. In other words, Dr. Quinn was for a time sleeping under blankets that once embraced a dead man (or woman). This is one of the few things in the whole story that can be known for certain, for many other details confirm it. The editor says that something was stolen from the mausoleum and that "the outrage was not that of an ordinary resurrection man," which means that bodies were not the objects taken; and he likewise refers to "stolen *goods*." Jennett says the women servants said that "'they [the bedclothes] were of a sort not commonly met with and very fine,'" and there are parallels in Dr. Quinn's dream that we shall enumerate shortly. First we must inquire, assuming that Dr. Abell intended for Dr. Quinn to buy the mausoleum bedclothes, how does Dr. Quinn obtain the right ones? There must be many shops in the area that sell bedclothes, and even if Dr. Quinn went to the right shop, how would the dealer know to sell *him* the mausoleum bedclothes? And how did the dealer manage to get them in the first place? The editor says that "A dealer in the North of London suffered heavy penalties as a receiver of stolen goods in connexion with the affair." This must be the same dealer from whom Dr. Quinn bought the stolen bedclothes. Perhaps this dealer is a member of the secret cult that Dr. Abell is in. This would explain how the dealer obtained the mausoleum bedclothes—another member of the cult might have stolen them for him or for Dr. Abell. And as for Dr. Quinn buying the right ones, this would simply be a matter of Dr. Abell telling the dealer to sell the mausoleum bedclothes to Dr. Quinn and no one else, for Dr. Abell would be expecting him to be looking for new bedclothes because of the spell he put on the old ones. How Dr. Quinn just happened to go to the correct store—well, this seems to be due to a little contriving on the part of James.

We shall now analyze Dr. Quinn's nightmare and its relation to other aspects of the story. Pratt goes to some lengths reiterating what Dr. Quinn told him about the dream:

"He was . . . every now and again, and particularly of late, not exempt from troublesome fancies. There was certainly a time when he was so much harassed by his dreams that he could not keep them to himself, but would tell them to his acquaintances and among them to me. I was at supper at his house, and he was not inclined to let me leave him at my usual time. 'If you go,' he said, 'there will be nothing for it but I must go to bed and dream of the chrysalis.' 'You might be worse off,' said I. 'I do not think it,' he said, and he shook himself like a man who is displeased with the complexion of his thoughts. 'I only meant,' said I, 'that a chrysalis is an innocent thing.' 'This one is not,' he said, 'and I do not care to think of it.'

"However, sooner than lose my company he was fain to tell me (for I pressed him) that this was a dream which had come to him several times of late, and even more than once in a night. It was to this effect, that he seemed to himself to wake under an extreme compulsion to rise and go out of doors. So he would dress himself and go down to his garden door. By the door there stood a spade which he must take, and go out into the garden, and at a particular place in the shrubbery, somewhat clear, and upon which the moon shone (for there was always in his dream a full moon), he would feel himself forced to dig. And after some time the spade would uncover something light-coloured, which he would perceive to be a stuff, linen or woollen, and this he must clear with his hands. It was always the same: of the size of a man and shaped like the chrysalis of a moth, with the folds showing a promise of an opening at one end.

"He could not describe how gladly he would have left all at this stage and run to the house, but he must not escape so easily. So with many groans, and knowing only too well what to expect, he parted these folds of stuff, or, as it sometimes seemed to be, membrane, and disclosed a head covered with a smooth pink skin, which breaking as the creature stirred, showed him his own face in a state of death. The telling of this so much disturbed him that I was forced out of mere compassion to sit with him the greater part of the night and talk with him upon indifferent subjects. He said that upon every recurrence of this dream he woke and found himself, as it were, fighting for his breath."

There are certain similarities between events in this dream and events yet to occur in the waking world. Just as Dr. Quinn digs up his own grave in his dream, so does he dig his own grave—figuratively—by buying the mausoleum bedclothes, for they eventually take his life. What looks to him like a chrysalis in his dream is described by him as being "'light-coloured'" and materially "'linen or woollen'"—a description that could very well suit the mausoleum bedclothes, which are wrapped very tightly around him when he is found dead, just as the chrysalis is wrapped around him in his dream.

He digs up this chrysalis as if it were in a grave, and the new bedclothes that he is soon going to buy are from a grave (or, more precisely, a mausoleum). Dr. Quinn seeing "'his own face in a state of death'" is a foreshadowing that he is going to die (soon), as is the fact that he finds himself buried as if in a grave (people were sometimes buried without being placed in a coffin during this period). And the fact that he wakes up from this dream fighting for his breath adumbrates his manner of death: suffocation.

We are now left to wonder: What was the cause of the dream? We speculated earlier that perhaps the dream was a result of the uncomfortable-bedclothes spell that Dr. Abell cast on the bedclothes, but surely he did not intend for Dr. Quinn to have dreams that would divulge all the details of his murder plan before he had a chance to enact it. Is the dream a sort of pre-monition, then, or a 'message sent from Heaven' warning Dr. Quinn of fatal events to come? We may never know (I am inclined to believe that James inserted the dream—rather clumsily—merely as a sort of tool to assist the reader in resolving the plot), for there is one persistent event that seems to refute any theory we make as to the origin of the dream, and it is Dr. Quinn waking up fighting for his breath. What induces him to do this? If the dream is a heavenly message of some sort notifying him that he is going to be killed, it is highly doubtful if it would in the process force him almost to choke to death. But as said before, if the dream is caused by Dr. Abell's spell, then why would he be giving way his method of murder to the murdered-to-be? Perhaps the dream is merely a side-effect of the spell, provoked inadvertently by the uncomfortable bedclothes. Perhaps James does not even know.

Finally we can discuss the death itself. Pratt has all the details on this:

> "On the 16th I was called up out of my bed soon after it was light—that is about five—with a message that Dr. Quinn was dead or dying. Making my way to his house I found there was no doubt which was the truth. All the persons in the house except the one that let me in were already in his chamber and standing about his bed, but none touching him. He was stretched in the midst of the bed, on his back, without any disorder, and indeed had the appearance of one ready laid out for burial. His hands, I think, were even crossed on his breast. The only thing not usual was that nothing was to be seen of his face, the two ends of the pillow or bolster appearing to be closed quite over it. These I immediately pulled apart, at the same time rebuking those present, and especially the man, for not at once coming to the assistance of his master. He, however, only looked at me and shook his head, having evidently no more hope than myself that there was anything but a corpse before us.
>
> "Indeed it was plain to anyone possessed of the least experience that he was not only dead, but had died of suffocation. Nor could it be conceived

that his death was accidentally caused by the mere folding of the pillow over his face. How should he not, feeling the oppression, have lifted his hands to put it away? whereas not a fold of the sheet which was closely gathered about him, as I now observed, was disordered. The next thing was to procure a physician. I had bethought me of this on leaving my house, and sent on the messenger who had come to me to Dr. Abell; but I now heard that he was away from home, and the nearest surgeon was got, who, however, could tell no more, at least without opening the body, than we already knew.

"As to any person entering the room with evil purpose (which was the next point to be cleared), it was visible that the bolts of the door were burst from their stanchions, and the stanchions broken away from the door-post by main force; and there was a sufficient body of witness, the smith among them, to testify that this had been done but a few minutes before I came. The chamber being, moreover, at the top of the house, the window was neither easy of access nor did it show any sign of an exit made that way, either by marks upon the sill or footprints below upon soft mould."

Pratt says that "'it [could not] be conceived that his death was accidentally caused by the mere folding of the pillow over his face'" and then asks, "'How should he not, feeling the oppression, have lifted his hands to put it away?'" The answer to his question is to be found in his own words immediately following it: "'not a fold of the sheet which was closely gathered about him . . . was disordered.'" It appears that Dr. Abell not only 'communicated motion' to the pillow—that is why it envelops Dr. Quinn's head—, but also to the sheets, so that they would wrap tightly around Dr. Quinn's body to prevent him from pushing the pillow off his face. As for someone entering the room with an evil purpose and no apparent signs of escape, it seems as though Dr. Abell did not even have to go near Dr. Quinn's house to kill him; he merely used his psychokinetic powers to communicate motion to the mausoleum bedclothes—before Dr. Quinn bought them, of course—so that they would automatically envelop and smother him whenever he lay down to sleep. But why did Dr. Abell need Dr. Quinn to sleep in bedclothes from a mausoleum? Why would regular bedclothes not work? Maybe the cult has discovered mystical properties in burial shrouds . . .

In any event, Dr. Abell's object was to make the death look as natural as possible, and, judging from the editor's statement at the beginning of the story—"The man who would have been the defendant or prisoner seems never to have appeared"—and from the lack of any observations of unnatural conditions in the surgeon's report—"it has nothing but remarks upon the healthy state of the larger organs and the coagulation of blood in various parts of the body"—he apparently succeeded.

V. Conclusion

Now that our task of reconstructing the plot has ended, what do we behold before us? There is nothing especially noteworthy in this story—except, perhaps, the rather novel murder device. "Two Doctors" simply amounts to another version of the vengeance motif—a theme that James was very fond of using—, although this instance seems to involve the use of an ironic wordplay with a Biblical allusion: acute readers probably have noticed the phonetic similarity between the names *Abel* and *Abell* and between the names *Cain* and *Quinn*. And we without a doubt find in this story a good, honest man being killed by an evil, jealous man. James, however, in a sort of lighthearted playfulness, reverses the names with the personalities: instead of the traditional Biblical fable of Cain killing Abel, we have Abel (Dr. Abell) killing Cain (Dr. Quinn). Drs. Quinn and Abell are not brothers, of course, in the sense that they have the same parents; but they are brothers in the sense that they are both involved in the same profession, a meaning of the term that Pratt even uses in the story, saying to Dr. Abell, ""I would send to your brother Quinn for a bolus to clear your brain."" All this wordplay is amusing and gives the mind something else to think about if it has grown weary of trying to figure out the rest of the story; it reminds me, incidentally, of what S. T. Joshi keenly noted with respect to James's fictional career: "It is as if writing a ghost story . . . [became] an intellectual game for James" (139). Precisely: instead of appearing in a book of ghost stories, it might be more categorically appropriate for "Two Doctors" to appear in a book of puzzles or riddles.

We might now consider whether or not "Two Doctors" was distanced successfully. In his introduction to *Ghosts and Marvels* (1924), James wrote: "For the ghost story a slight haze of distance is desirable. 'Thirty years ago,' 'Not long before the war,' are very proper openings. If a really remote date be chosen, there is more than one way of bringing the reader in contact with it. The finding of documents about it can be made plausible . . ." (*Casting the Runes* 339). James employs these very methods in "Two Doctors"—in the first paragraph we find, "Now it was a practice of mine before the war . . ." and the narrator does find old documents—but still too much of the plot remains in almost impenetrable obscurity. There is even one wrinkle in the plot that James never ironed out—perhaps he did not even notice it. Jennett says that when he came back to Islington to work for Dr. Quinn, he heard that Dr. Abell had left the parish; and yet we find Dr. Abell talking to Pratt, the Rector of Islington, about Jennett working for Dr. Quinn. Yes, Jennett might have heard a false rumor, but contradictions in plot such as this are not likely to leave a favorable impression on the reader. In fact, I know not how the story itself could leave a favorable impression on any reader, rather one of bewilderment and anger. James once said, in reference to the ghost story "genre": "These stories are meant to please and amuse us. If they do so, well; but, if not, let us relegate them to the top shelf and say no more about it" (*Casting the Runes* 352). His stories are just as susceptible to this criterion as any others, and I predict that "Two Doctors" is going to collect a considerable amount of dust.

Works Cited

James, M. R. *Casting the Runes and Other Ghost Stories.* Ed. Michael Cox. London: Oxford University Press, 1987.

————. *The Collected Ghost Stories of M. R. James.* London: Edward Arnold, 1931.

Joshi, S. T. *The Weird Tale.* Athens: University of Texas Press, 1990.

Sullivan, Jack. *Elegant Nightmares: The English Ghost Story from Le Fanu to Blackwood.* Athens: Ohio University Press, 1978.

Landmarks and Shrieking Ghosts

Jacqueline Simpson

Number eight of the "Twelve Medieval Ghost-Stories," whose Latin texts M. R. James published in the *English Historical Review* in 1922, begins as follows (p. 419, my translation):

> Concerning a certain ghost which followed William of Bradford and yelled "Hoo, hoo, hoo" three times on three occasions. It happened on the fourth night, towards the middle of the night, that he had been to a new place from the village of Ampleforth, and while he was on the homeward road he heard a terrible voice shouting out far behind him, as if among the hills, and shortly afterwards it shouted again in the same way, but closer, and a third time it yelled at the cross-roads ahead of him.

To this MRJ appends a footnote: "For three nights William of Bradford had heard the cries. On the fourth night he met the ghost. And I suspect he must have been imprudent enough to answer the cries, for there are many tales, Danish and other, of persons who answer the shrieking ghost with impertinent words, and the next moment they hear it close to their ear."

We know from his comments at the start of "Twelve Medieval Ghost-Stories" that MRJ owned several volumes of the local legends from Jutland which the indefatigable Evald Tang Kristensen collected and published, among which he would indeed have found a good many "shrieking ghosts." It is particularly significant that this motif almost invariably occurs in association with another: the ghost whose "walking" is a punishment for dishonest appropriation of land. The most common version, found throughout Scandinavia and especially popular in Denmark, tells of a farmer (or a land-surveyor bribed by a farmer) who secretly shifted the stones which marked the boundary between one man's land and the next, and whose ghost wanders across the fields by night, wailing or shouting. In Denmark, the theme is regularly associated with a large-scale redistribution of peasant land holdings imposed in the 1820s, which aroused much suspicion and bitterness.

In these stories, answering the ghost's shouts is assumed to be very risky, but can turn out well after all. Here is a translation (by Dr. Reimund Kvideland) of a version Kristensen printed in 1897 in *Danske Sagn*, Vol. 5, p.423:

> There was a man who walked again on Bundegard's field in Krejbjaerg because he had moved a boundary stone. People could hear him shout in the night: "Where should I put it? Where should I put it?"
>
> One evening there were some young people gathered outside of town and they heard him too. One of them, a brash young man, shouted back: "You devil! Put it where you found it!"
>
> And after that, no one ever saw him again.

Similar stories appear in the volumes MRJ is known to have owned, e.g. *Jyske Folkesagn* (1876), pp. 148–51, and *Sagn og Overtro fra Jylland* (1883), pp. 115–18. In a second *Sagn og Overtro fra Jylland* (1886) is one story (p. 199) where somebody who hears a ghost screaming intermittently foolishly calls out "Shout again now, man!"—and it shouts right close beside him.

English readers will probably see such stories as funny, and in some cases this may well have been the Danish storyteller's intention too; in others, the text is too brief for any "tone" to come across. But there undoubtedly was fear too; here is part of a text published by Kristensen in 1934, which is a woman's direct personal memory, and in which the vital importance of silence when in the presence of the supernatural is stressed (*Danske Sagn: Ny Raekke*, Vol. 5, p. 310, my translation):

> There's a big fiery light that passes across the field at Jedsted. It comes up from the meadows and glides along the fields, and pauses at each boundary stone. It is a land-surveyor whose spirit walks, and anybody who comes across him loses his way. I've seen it many times when I was a child . . .
>
> [One night, going home after dark with her father, the child sees the light.]
>
> "Now here comes the big fire," says I.
>
> "Hold your tongue," says my father.
>
> [They lose their way and wander for a while.]
>
> "There it stands, father," says I.
>
> "Oh, for God's sake hold your tongue," says he, all anxious. Of course, I was only a child. Well, we did get home in the end.

English local legends do not, as far as I know, include the idea of a ghost whose sin consisted of shifting a boundary marker; certainly it is not a regular theme, as it is in Scandinavia. So I think it very probable that the inspiration for MRJ's "A Neighbour's Landmark" was Danish. As with "The Rose Garden" (whose sources I discussed in *Ghosts & Scholars* No. 22), he thoroughly transposed it to an English setting, heightened the horror by changing a mere shout to an ear-shattering shriek, and found an antiquarian explanation in the old law records he relished so much. A fine example of his skill in covering his tracks!

Addendum

Rosemary Pardoe

In her article "Landmarks and Shrieking Ghosts" [*Ghosts & Scholars* No. 25], Jacqueline Simpson proposed Danish folklore, specifically as recounted in the writings of E. T. Kristensen, as the source for the theme of M. R. James's 1924 story "A Neighbour's Landmark." The Commination Service (on Ash Wednesday) in the *Book of Common Prayer* warns: "Cursed be he that removeth his neighbour's landmark." The ghost who haunts because, like Lady Ivie in the story, it has ignored this warning and moved a landmark, appears in Kristensen's works. MRJ is known to have read several of these and mentions them, for instance, in his notes on the "Twelve Medieval Ghost-Stories." Jacqueline Simpson comments that "English local legends do not, as far as I know, include the idea of a ghost whose sin consisted of shifting a boundary marker, certainly it is not a regular theme, as it is in Scandinavia."

Similarly, in her seminal paper on "'The Rules of Folklore' in the Ghost Stories of M. R. James," she describes "a characteristically Danish motif, the so-called 'boundary ghost' whose sin is to have wrongfully acquired a neighbour's land, either by literally shifting a boundary stone, or by a false oath, and whose doom is to walk round it forever." "[L]and-theft," she adds, "is not a usual theme in English ghost legends, whereas it is common in Danish collections, including the ones which James owned" (Simpson 13).

I'm sure that Jacqueline Simpson is correct in identifying Kristensen as the main source for the haunted landmark idea, but there is a non-Scandinavian example which is rather closer to (MRJ's) home: in *The Folk-Lore of Hereford-shire* by Ella Mary Leather (1876–1928). First published in 1912 (and often re-printed), this is described in the *Oxford Dictionary of English Folklore* as "one of our best books based on personal fieldwork" (210–11). While I can't prove definitely that MRJ read Mrs. Leather's work, I think it probable that he did. He may well have encountered it during his very frequent visits to the McBryde family in Herefordshire (from 1906 almost up until his death). It is, at any rate, possible to prove MRJ read *about* the volume, a year before creating "A Neighbour's Landmark," and this could have whetted his appetite in the event that he did not already know about it. The folklorist, Edwin Sidney Hartland, who wrote the introduction to *The Folk-Lore of Herefordshire,* also provided extensive input into MRJ's translation of Walter Map's *De Nugis Curialium,* published in 1923. Hartland produced an introduction and vast, in-depth footnotes on the folkloric aspects of the latter (whilst noting that "in spite of his too modest preference to leave this work to others, Dr. James has helped very materially in putting before the reader the facts about the folk-tales so abundantly given by Map" [Map vii–viii]). On at least one occasion he cites Mrs. Leather's book, annotating Map's story about a Welsh vampire, with reference to her description of attempts to lay a wandering Herefordshire ghost by turning its corpse face down (Map 111).

Here is what Mrs. Leather writes on the subject of landmark ghosts and their inability to rest until their sin is remedied—or, as Mrs. Emma Frost says in "A Neighbour's Landmark," "before someone take and put it right again":

Old Taylor's Ghost.

"Nonagenarian" tells the story of another Hereford ghost, who could not rest because he had moved a landmark. I have heard several similar stories, including one of a man who "wasted away like" until he died, through remorse, and afterwards could not rest until the landmark was replaced in its original position. The Nonagenarian's version is as follows:— There was old Taylor's ghost, that used to walk about at the White Cross. He couldn't rest, because he had moved a landmark. He used to ride upon a little pony, and sometimes he would be seen sitting on a stile. I have never seen old Taylor myself, but have heard many say they had seen him. At last his ghost was laid. . . . One stormy night a fellow whose name I have forgotten, walked into the bar of the Nag's Head, and said he had seen old Taylor, and had promised to meet him in the Morning Pits that night at twelve. Of course nobody believed him, and as the night wore on the others jeered him, and said "I would not go on such a night as this." He said he would not; but as the hour drew near he was obliged to go. Something forced him to run, so that he reached the Morning Pits as the clock struck twelve. There the old man was waiting.

"Follow me," said he; the other followed him into some strange place, which they seemed to reach in a very short time. In the place were two immense stones. "Take up these stones," said Taylor. "I can't," said Denis (he was nicknamed "Denis the Liar"). "You can," said Taylor, "try." He tried, and tilted them easily.

"Now come with me," said Taylor, "and place them where I shall show you." He carried them, and put them down with ease. "Now," said the other, "I caution you never tell anybody what you see here this night." He promised. "And now," said he, "lie down on your face, and as you value your life, don't attempt to look either way, until you hear music, and then get away as fast as you can." He lay a long time without hearing what he earnestly desired, but at last the welcome sound was heard. . . . He was a very different man after that, though he soon died from the effects of his fright. (Leather 32)[1]

---

1. Mrs. Leather gives the *Hereford Times*, 15 April 1876, as the origin of the "Nonagenarian" account.

Works Cited

Leather, Ella Mary. *The Folk-Lore of Herefordshire: Collected from Oral and Printed Sources*. Hereford: Jakeman & Carver, 1912; facsimile edition Yorkshire: S. R. Publishers 1970.

Map, Walter. *De Nugis Curialium*. Translated by M. R. James. London: Honourable Society of Cymmrodorion, 1923.

Simpson, Jacqueline. "'The Rules of Folklore' in the Ghost Stories of M. R. James." *Folklore* 108 (1997): 9–18.

Simpson, Jacqueline, and Steve Roud. *Oxford Dictionary of English Folklore*. Oxford: Oxford University Press, 2000; paperback edition, 2003.

Bibliography

A. Primary

Casting the Runes and Other Ghost Stories. Ed. Michael Cox. London: Oxford University Press, 1987.

Collected Ghost Stories. London: Edward Arnold, 1931.

Count Magnus and Other Ghost Stories. Ed. S. T. Joshi. New York: Penguin, 2005.

Eton and King's: Recollections, Mostly Trivial, 1875–1925. London: Williams & Norgate, 1926. Ashcroft, BC: Ash-Tree Press, 2005.

The Five Jars. London: Edward Arnold, 1922.

Ghost-Stories of an Antiquary. London: Edward Arnold, 1904.

The Ghost Stories of M. R. James. Ed. Michael Cox. London: Oxford University Press, 1986.

The Haunted Dolls' House and Other Ghost Stories. Ed. S. T. Joshi. New York: Penguin, 2006.

Letters to a Friend. London: Edward Arnold, 1956.

M. R. James: The Book of the Supernatural. Ed. Peter Haining. Sliugh, UK: Foulsham, 1979. New York: Stein & Day, 1982 (as *M. R. James: The Book of Ghost Stories*).

More Ghost Stories of an Antiquary. London: Edward Arnold, 1911.

A Pleasing Terror: The Complete Supernatural Writings of M. R. James. Ed. Barbara and Christopher Roden. Ashcroft, BC: Ash-Tree Press, 2001.

A Thin Ghost and Others. London: Edward Arnold, 1919.

Two Ghost Stories: A Centenary. Ed. Barbara and Christopher Roden. London: Ghost Story Press, 1993.

A Warning to the Curious. London: Edward Arnold, 1925.

B. Secondary

i. Bibliographies

Pardoe, Rosemary. *A Bibliography of the Writings of M. R. James.* Chester, UK: Haunted Library, 2007.

Pfaff, Richard William. "Bibliography of the Scholarly Writings of M. R. James." In Pfaff's *Montague Rhodes James.* London: Scolar Press, 1980, pp. 427–38.

Rogers, Nicholas. "A Bibliography of the Published Works of Montague Rhodes James." In *The Legacy of M. R. James,* ed. Lynda Dennison. Donington, UK: Shaun Tyas, 2001, pp. 239–67.

Scholfield, A. F. "List of Writings." In S. G. Lubbock, *A Memoir of Montague Rhodes James.* Cambridge: Cambridge University Press, 1939, pp. 47–87.

ii. Biographies and Memoirs

Cox, Michael. *M. R. James: An Informal Portrait.* London: Oxford University Press, 1983.

Lubbock, S. G. *A Memoir of Montague Rhodes James.* Cambridge: Cambridge University Press, 1939). Rpt. in *A Pleasing Terror,* xxvii–xlix.

Pfaff, Richard William. *Montague Rhodes James.* London: Scolar Press, 1980.

iii. Critical Studies

Ackroyd, Peter. "Ghosts." In Ackroyd's *Albion: The Origins of the English Imagination.* London: Chatto & Windus, 2002, pp. 375–79.

Briggs, Julia. "No Mere Antiquary: M. R. James." In Briggs's *Night Visitors: The Rise and Fall of the English Ghost Story.* London: Faber & Faber, 1977, pp. 124–41.

Buchanan, Carl Jay. "Notes on the Structure and Ubiquity of Mr. Humphreys' Maze." *Ghosts & Scholars M. R. James Newsletter* No. 1 (March 2002): 6–11.

Carraciolo, Peter L. "Wyndham Lewis, M. R. James and Intertextuality." [3 parts] *Wyndham Lewis Annual* 6 (1999): 21–28; 7 (2000): 43–54; 8 (2001): 9–29.

John Crook, "The Weighty and the Trivial: M. R. James and St. Bertrand de Comminges." *Country Life* No. 4549 (25 October 1984): 1248–49.

Dennison, Lynda, ed. *The Legacy of M. R. James.* Donington, UK: Shaun Tyas, 2001.

Doig, James. "The Antiquarian Background of M. R. James's Ghost Stories." *Ghosts & Scholars M. R. James Newsletter* No. 8 (September 2005): 6–11.

Fielding, Penny. "Reading Rooms: M. R. James and the Library of Modernity." *Modern Fiction Studies* 46 (Fall 2000): 749–71.

Grant, Helen. "'He Was Laughing in the Church': A Visit to St. Bertrand de Comminges." *Ghosts & Scholars M. R. James Newsletter* No. 7 (March 2005): 15–23.

————. "'The Shadow of the Occupant of Number 13': A Visit to Viborg." *Ghosts & Scholars M. R. James Newsletter* No. 11 (March 2007): 5–10.

Grant, Helen. "The Treasure of Steinfeld Abbey: A Visit to the Scene of 'The Treasure of Abbot Thomas.'" *Ghosts & Scholars M. R. James Newsletter* No. 5 (February 2004): 4–8.

Harrington, Ralph. "Storyteller Haunted by Christian Conscience." *Tablet* (30 December 2006): 15–16.

Hendershot, Cyndy. "The Return of the Repressed in M. R. James's 'Martin's Close.'" *University of Mississippi Studies in English* NS 11–12 (1993–95): 134–37.

Holland-Toll, Linda J. "From Haunted Gardens to Lurking Wendigos: Liminal and Wild Places in M. R. James and Algernon Blackwood." *Studies in Weird Fiction* No. 25 (Summer 2001): 12–17.

Holmes, Richard. "Of Ghosts and King's." *Times* (London) (23 November 1974): 7, 12. Rpt. as "M. R. James and Others" in Holmes's *Sidetracks: Explorations of a Romantic Biographer*. London: HarperCollins, 2000, pp. 161–71.

Howard, John. "Old England, New England: M. R. James, Mary Wilkins Freeman and Sarah Orne Jewett." *Wormwood* No. 6 (Spring 2006): 13–23.

Hughes, Martin. "Murder of the Cathedral: A Story by M. R. James." *Durham University Journal* 87, No. 1 (January 1995): 73–98.

Joshi, S. T. "M. R. James" The Limitations of the Ghost Story." In Joshi's *The Weird Tale*. Austin: University of Texas Press, 1990.

McCorristine, Shane. "Academia, Avocation and Lucidity in the Supernatural Fiction of M. R. James." *Limina* 13 (2007): 54–65.

Michalski, Robert. "The Malice of Inanimate Objects: Exchange in M. R. James's Ghost Stories." *Extrapolation* 37 (Spring 1996): 46–62.

Newman, Simon. "The Value of Art and Inanimate Objects in the Ghost Stories of M. R. James." *Ghosts & Scholars M. R. James Newsletter* No. 7 (March 2005): 23–30.

Oldknow, Antony. "Concerns for Women in 'The Tractate Middoth' by M. R. James." *Readerly/Writerly Texts* 9 (Spring/Summer 2001 & Fall/Winter 2001): 147–57.

Oliver, Reggie. "The Scholar and the Story-Teller: Two Aspects of M. R. James in *Eton and King's.*" *All Hallows* No. 41 (February 2006): 31–36.

Pardoe, Rosemary. "'I Seen It Wive at Me out of the Winder': The Window as Threshold in M. R. James's Stories." *Ghosts & Scholars M. R. James Newsletter* No. 4 (August 2003): 11–15.

———. "'I've Seen It': 'A School Story' and the House in Berkeley Square." *Ghosts & Scholars* No. 29 (1999): 41–43.

———. "The Manuscript of 'A Warning to the Curious.'" *Ghosts & Scholars* No. 32 (2001): 47–49.

———. "'The Old Man on the Hill': Beelzebub in 'An Evening's Entertainment.'" *Ghosts & Scholars M. R. James Newsletter* No. 7 (March 2005): 30–33.

Pardoe, Rosemary, and Darroll Pardoe. "The Herefordshire of 'A View from a Hill.'" *Ghosts & Scholars M. R. James Newsletter* No. 6 (September 2004): 4–9.

Pardoe, Rosemary, and Jane Nicholls. "'The Black Pilgrimage.'" *Ghosts & Scholars* No. 26 (1998): 48–54. Rpt. in *A Pleasing Terror*, 601–8.

———. "James Wilson's Secret." *Ghosts & Scholars* No. 24 (1997): 45–48. Rpt. in *A Pleasing Terror*, 596–600.

Penzoldt, Peter. "Dr. M. R. James (1862–1936)." In Penzoldt's *The Supernatural in Fiction*. London: Peter Nevill, 1952, pp. 191–202.

Pincombe, Mike. "Class War in 'Casting the Runes.'" *Ghosts & Scholars M. R. James Newsletter* No. 9 (March 2006): 4–8.

Pincombe, Mike. "'No Thoroughfare': The Problem of Paxton in 'A Warning to the Curious.'" *Ghosts and Scholars* No. 32 (2001): 42–46.

Rath, Tina. "M. R. James and the Vampires." *Ghosts & Scholars M. R. James Newsletter* No. 10 (September 2006): 20–25.

Russell, Samuel D. "Irony and Horror: The Art of M. R. James." *Haunted* No. 2 (December 1964): 43–52; No. 3 (June 1968): 96–106. Rpt. in *A Pleasing Terror*, 609–30.

Schweitzer, Darrell. "M. R. James and H. P. Lovecraft: The Ghostly and the Cosmic." *Studies in Weird Fiction* No. 15 (Summer 1994): 12–16. Rpt. in Schweitzer's *Windows of the Imagination*. San Bernadino, CA: Borgo Press, 1998.

Simpson, Jacqueline. "Ghosts in Medieval Yorkshire." *Ghosts & Scholars* No. 27 (1998): 40–44. Rpt. in *A Pleasing Terror*, 631–37.

————. "Repentant Soul or Walking Corpse? Debatable Apparitions in Medieval England." *Folklore* 114 (March 2003): 389–402.

Smith, Andrew. "M. R. James's Gothic Revival." *Diegesis* No. 7 (Summer 2004): 16–22.

Smith, Clark Ashton. "The Weird Works of M. R. James." *Fantasy Fan* (February 1934). Rpt. in Smith's *Planets and Dimensions*. Baltimore: Mirage Press, 1973, pp. 30–32.

Sullivan, Jack. "The Antiquarian Ghost Story: Montague Rhodes James." In Sullivan's *Elegant Nightmares: The English Ghost Story from Le Fanu to Blackwood*. Athens: Ohio University Press, 1978, pp. 69–90.

Thompson, Terry W. "'I Shall Most Likely Be out on the Links': Golf as Metaphor in the Ghost Stories of M. R. James." *Papers on Language and Literature* 40 (Fall 2004): 339–52.

Wagenknecht, Edward. *Seven Masters of Supernatural Fiction*. Westport, CT: Greenwood Press, 1991, pp. 49–67.

Ward, Richard. "In Search of the Dread Ancestor: M. R. James's 'Count Magnus' and Lovecraft's *The Case of Charles Dexter Ward*." *Studies in Weird Fiction* No. 36 (Spring 1997): 14–17.

Warren, Austin. "The Marvels of M. R. James, Antiquary." In Warren's *Connections*. Ann Arbor: University of Michigan Press, 1970.

Winall, Steve. "A Warning to the (Urban) Curious: Folklore and Historic Preservation in the Ghost Stories of M. R. James." *Ghosts & Scholars M. R. James Newsletter* No. 8 (September 2005): 15–22.

iv. Miscellany

Campbell, Ramsey, ed. *Meddling with Ghosts: Stories in the Tradition of M. R. James*. London: British Library, 2001.

Dalby, Richard, and Rosemary Pardoe, ed. *Ghosts and Scholars: Ghost Stories in the Tradition of M. R. James*. Wellingborough, UK: Crucible, 1987.

Acknowledgments

The editors and publisher are grateful to the following parties for permission to reprint the following previously published essays in this volume (those articles for which permission is not indicated are believed to be in the public domain):

Stephen Gaselee, "Montague Rhodes James: 1862–1936," *Proceedings of the British Academy* 22 (1936): 418–33. Reprinted by permission of Mrs. Stephana R. I. Babbage representing the Estate of Stephen Gaselee.

Shane Leslie, "Montague Rhodes James," *Quarterly Review* 304 (January 1966): 45–56. Reprinted by permission of Sir Norman Ide Leslie representing the Estate of Sir Shane Leslie.

Norman Scarfe, "The Strangeness Present: M. R. James's Suffolk," *Country Life* No. 4655 (6 November 1986): 1416–19. Reprinted by permission of the author.

Michael Cox, "M. R. James and Livermere," in *M. R. James at Livermere: A Celebration* (Rosemary Pardoe, 1998), pp. 4–7. Reprinted by permission of the author.

H. P. Lovecraft, "Supernatural Horror in Literature," *Recluse* (1927): 23–59 (esp. 56–59).

Mary Butts, "The Art of Montagu [sic] James," *London Mercury* 29 (February 1934): 306–17.

L. J. Lloyd, "The Ghost Stories of Montague Rhodes James," *Book Handbook* 4 (1947): 237–53.

Simon MacCulloch, "The Toad in the Study: M. R. James, H. P. Lovecraft and Forbidden Knowledge," *Ghosts & Scholars* No. 20 (1995): 38–43; No. 21 (1996): 37–42; No. 22 (1996): 40–46; No. 23 (1997): 54–60. Rpt. in *Studies in Weird Fiction* No. 20 (Winter 1997): 2–12; No. 21 (Summer 1997): 17–28. Reprinted by permission of the author.

Michael A. Mason, "On Not Letting Them Lie: Moral Significance in the Ghost Stories of M. R. James," *Studies in Short Fiction* 19 (1982): 253–60.

Ron Weighell, "Dark Devotions: M. R. James and the Magical Tradition," *Ghosts & Scholars* No. 6 (1984): 20–30. Revised for this appearance. Reprinted by permission of the author.

David G. Rowlands, "M. R. James's Women," *Ghosts & Scholars* No. 15 (1993): 32–34. Reprinted by permission of the author.

Jacqueline Simpson, "'The Rules of Folklore' in the Ghost Stories of M. R. James," *Folklore* 108 (1997): 9–18. Reprinted by permission of *Folklore* and the author.

Brian Cowlishaw, "'A Warning to the Curious': Victorian Science and the Awful Unconscious in M. R. James's Ghost Stories," *Viuctorian Newsletter* No. 94 (Fall 1998): 36–42. Reprinted by permission of the author.

Steve Duffy, "'They've Got Him! In the Trees!' M. R. James and Sylvan Dread," *Ghosts & Scholars* No. 29 (1999): 46–50.

Mike Pincombe, "Homosexual Panic and the English Ghost Story: M. R. James and Others," *Ghosts & Scholars M. R. James Newsletter* No. 2 (September 2002): 5–13. Reprinted by permission of the author.

John Alfred Taylor, "'If I'm Not Careful': Innocents and Not-So-Innocents in the Stories of M. R. James." Original to this volume. Printed by permission of the author.

Steven J. Mariconda, "'As Time Goes On I See a Shadow Coming': M. R. James's Grammar of Terror." Original to this volume. Printed by permission of the author.

Scott Connors, "'What Is This That I Have Done?' The Scapegoat Figure in the Stories of M. R. James." Original to this volume. Printed by permission of the author.

Helen Grant, "The Nature of trhe Beast: The Demonology of 'Canon Alberic's Scrap-book,'" *Ghosts & Scholars M. R. James Newsletter* No. 6 (September 2004): 17–24. Reprinted by permission of the author.

C. E. Ward, "A Haunting Presence," in *Formidable Visitants*, ed. Roger Johnson (Chelmsford, UK: Pyewacket Press, 1999), pp. 27–30. Reprinted by permission of the author.

Rosemary Pardoe, "'A Wonderful Book': George MacDonald and 'The Ash-Tree,'" *Ghosts & Scholars M. R. James Newsletter* No. 3 (January 2003): 18–21. Reprinted by permission of the author.

Rosemary Pardoe, "Who Was Count Magnus? Notes towards an Identification," *Ghosts & Scholars* No. 33 (2001): 50–53. Reprinted by permission of the author.

Nicholas Connell, "A Haunting Vision: M. R. James and the Ashridge Stained Glass," *Hertfordshire's Past* 49 (Autumn 2000): 2–7. Reprinted by permission of the author.

Martin Hughes, "A Maze of Secrets in a Story by M. R. James," *Durham University Journal* 85, No. 1 (January 1993): 81–93. Reprinted by permission of the author.

Jim Rockhill, "Thin Ghosts: Notes toward a Jamesian Rhetoric." Original to this volume. Printed by permission of the author.

Roger Craik, "Nightmares of Punch and Judy in Ruskin and M. R. James," *Fantasy Commentator* No. 49 (Fall 1996): 12–14. Reprinted by permission of the author.

Lance Arney, "An Elucidation (?) of the Plot of M. R. James's 'Two Doctors,'" *Studies in Weird Fiction* No. 8 (Fall 1990): 26–35. Reprinted by permission of the author.

Jacqueline Simpson, "Landmarks and Shrieking Ghosts," *Ghosts & Scholars* No. 25 (1997): 42–44. Reprinted by permission of the author.

Index

Ecclesiasticus 228–29
Edwards, Jonathan 219
Elegant Nightmares (Sullivan) 279
English Historical Review 119, 316
English Hours (James) 38
"Episode of Cathedral History, An"
 40, 52, 56, 74, 108, 116, 121–22,
 157–58, 170, 174, 199, 281
Epistle of Titus 34
Eton and King's 15, 21, 28, 29, 42–43,
 44, 242
Eton College 7, 15, 20, 23–24, 28, 29,
 30–31, 36, 42–43, 71n3, 145, 254,
 298
Eton College Chronicle 16, 24
Eton Rambler 145
"Evening's Entertainment, An" 106,
 141, 145–46, 178, 221
"Experiment, The" 142n1

Fabricius, J. A. 26, 68
"Fall of the House of Usher, The"
 (Poe) 95
"Fenstanton Witch, The" 94
Fitzwilliam Museum (Cambridge) 7,
 15, 16, 21, 22
Five Jars, The 28, 50, 54, 60, 65, 243–
 44
Flaubert, Gustave 33
Fleming, Peter 9
Fletcher, Walter 22, 25–26
Folk-Lore of Herefordshire, The
 (Leather) 318
Ford, Lionel 186
Fourth Ezra 16
Freud, Sigmund 163, 171–73, 175,
 204
Frye, Northrop 216–17, 218, 221, 223
Fuller, J. F. Q. 130

Gaselee, Stephen 10
Ghost-Stories of an Antiquary 8, 28, 50,
 54, 66, 142, 217, 239, 255, 299n1
"Ghost Stories of Montague Rhodes
 James, The" (Lloyd) 11
"Ghost Story Competition, The" 95
"Ghosts—Treat Them Gently!" 207,
 299n2

Ghosts and Marvels (Collins) 70n2,
 116, 204, 207, 299n2, 314
Ghosts & Scholars 11, 241
Gissing, George 35
Golden Bough, The (Frazer) 143, 179,
 222
Golden Legend 143
Golding, William 240
Gospel and Revelation of Peter, The 16,
 33–34
Gospel to the Hebrews 34
Grahame, Kenneth 177
Grant, Helen 12
Granta 30
Green Man, The (Amis) 119
"Green Tea" (Le Fanu) 35
Grey, Edward 15
Grimmelshausen, Hans Jakob
 Christoffel von 236
Guardian 134
Guerber, H. A. 127
"Guy, The" (Campbell) 83

Halifax, Lord 36
Hallam, Arthur Henry 115
Hamlet (Shakespeare) 69, 187n3
Hardy, Thomas 128
Hare, Augustus 31
Harrison, Jane 143
Hartland, Edwin Sidney 143, 318
"Haunted Dolls' House, The" 84,
 103, 170, 200, 222–23
"Haunter of the Dark, The" (Love-
 craft) 95–97, 98
Hawthorne, Nathaniel 181–82
"'He Cometh and He Passeth By'"
 (Wakefield) 130
Headlam, Walter 25, 27
Henry VI (King of England) 42
Hereford Times 319n1
Hermes Trismegistus 149n6
Herodotus 233
Hichens, Robert 202
Hitchcock, Alfred 180
Hogarth, D. G. 16
Hone, William 35
Hopkins, R. Thurston 190n5
Horman, William 20